HANDBOOK OF SOVIET
SOCIAL SCIENCE DATA

ELLEN MICKIEWICZ

THE FREE PRESS   NEW YORK

COLLIER-MACMILLAN PUBLISHERS   LONDON

The Free Press
A Division of Macmillan Publishing Co., Inc.

Collier-Macmillan Canada Ltd., Toronto, Ontario

Library of Congress Catalog Card Number: 72–86510

printing number
1   2   3   4   5   6   7   8   9   10

for Denis

CONTENTS

LIST OF TABLES, vii

ACKNOWLEDGMENTS, xvi

ABBREVIATIONS OF SOURCES FREQUENTLY CITED, xv

USSR TERRITORIAL CHANGES, xvi

SOVIET TERRITORIAL-ADMINISTRATIVE LEVELS, xvii

CONTRIBUTORS, xix

FOREWORD
**TOWARD THE STUDY OF POLITICAL AND SOCIAL INDICATORS
ACROSS DIFFERENT SOCIAL SYSTEMS** KARL W. DEUTSCH   xxi

INTRODUCTION ELLEN MICKIEWICZ   1
    Uses and Strategies in Data Analysis of the Soviet Union: Cleavages in
    Industrialized Society

CHAPTER I
DEMOGRAPHY WARREN W. EASON
    Introduction, 49
    Tables, 51

CHAPTER II
AGRICULTURE ROY D. LAIRD
    Introduction, 65
    Tables, 68

CHAPTER III
PRODUCTION STANLEY H. COHN
    Introduction, 91
    Tables, 93

CHAPTER IV
HEALTH   Mark G. Field
Introduction, 101
Tables, 102

CHAPTER V
HOUSING   Henry W. Morton
Introduction, 119
Tables, 122

CHAPTER VI
EDUCATION   A. Jonathan Pool and Jeremy Azrael
                 B. Jaan Pennar, Ivan I. Bakalo, and George Z. F. Bereday
Introduction, 137
Tables, 139

CHAPTER VII
ELITE RECRUITMENT AND MOBILIZATION   Ellen Mickiewicz
Introduction, 159
Tables, 161

CHAPTER VIII
COMMUNICATIONS   Gayle D. Hollander
Introduction, 175
Tables, 177

CHAPTER IX
INTERNATIONAL INTERACTIONS   Roger Kanet
Introduction, 197
Tables, 199

LIST OF TABLES

I. DEMOGRAPHY

1. Total Population, 51
2. Birth and Death Rates per 1,000 Population and Percentage Rates of Natural Increase, 51
3. The Population by Sex and Five-year Age Groups, 52
4. Population by Urban and Rural Areas, 54
5. The Population and Labor Force by Sex and Broad Age Groups, 54
6. The Labor Force and Civilian Employment, by Major Occupational Categories, 55
7. Number of Wage and Salary Workers by Sex and by Major Branches of the National Economy, 56
8. Average Number of Days and Hours Worked in Industry by Wage and Salary Workers, 58
9. Population by Nationalities, 58
10. Population of Republics, by Major Nationalities, 59
11. Average Number of Members per Family, by Nationality and Urban and Rural Residence, 160
12. Population By Republics, 160

II. AGRICULTURE

1. Number of Farms, 68
2. Agricultural Machinery, 68
3. Sown Area, 69
4. Gross Yield, 69
5. Productivity, 70
5a. Productivity per 100,000 Population, 70
6. Number of Livestock, 71
7. Cows, 71
8. Livestock Production, 72
9. Averages per Farm: Kolkhozy Only, 72
10. Number of Livestock: Kolkhozy Only, 73
11. Cows: Kolkhozy Only, 73

12. Livestock Production: Kolkhozy Only, 73
13. Averages per Farm: Sovkhozy Only, 74
14. Number of Livestock: Sovkhozy Only, 74
15. Cows: Sovkhozy Only, 74
16. Livestock Production: Sovkhozy and Other State Enterprises Only, 75
17. Specialists with Higher or Secondary Training, 75
18. Workers and Employees in the Kolkhozy and Sovkhozy, 75
19. Private Production, 76
19a. Livestock Production per Capita, 76
20. Sown Area, 77
21. Sown Area (continued) and Tractors, 78
22. Gross Yield and Mineral Fertilizer, 79
23. Number of Livestock, 80
24. Livestock Production, by Republics, 81
25. Kolkhozy Only, 82
26. Sovkhozy Only, 83

III. PRODUCTION

1. Gross National Product, 93
2. Gross National Product per Capita, 93
3. Growth of GNP: Aggregate and per Capita, 93
4. Percentage and Value of GNP Originating in Agriculture, 94
5. Private Consumption: Per Capita Value and Percentage of GNP, 94
6. Fixed Capital Investment: Value and Percentage of GNP, 94
7. Defense: Value and Percentage of GNP, 94
8. Electric Power Production per Capita, 95
8a. Regional Distribution of Electric Power Production, 95
9. Fuel Production per Capita, 96
10. Steel Output per Capita, 96
11. Motor Vehicle Production, 96
12. Cement Production per Capita, 97
13. Cotton Cloth Production per Capita, 97
14. Meat Production per Capita, 97
15. Incomes by Economic Sector, 98
16. Incomes by Branches of Industry, 98

IV. HEALTH

1. Average Life Expectancy at Birth, by Sex, Urban and Rural Area, 102
2. Mortality, Age-specific, 102
3. Mortality by Sex and Age, 103
4. Mortality, Age-specific and Average Life Expectancy, Both Sexes, 103
4a. Mortality, Age-specific and Average Life Expectancy, Males, 104
4b. Mortality, Age-specific and Average Life Expectancy, Females, 105
5. Infectious Diseases, 106
6. Physicians, Including Stomatologists and Dentists, Excluding the Military, 107
7. Physicians, Excluding the Military, by Republics, 108
8. Physicians, Excluding the Military, by basic Specialty, 109
9. Semi-professional Health Personnel, Excluding the Military, by Specialty, 110
10. Professional and Semi-professional Health Personnel, Excluding the Military, 110

11. Total Reported and Projected Annual Average Employment, Non-agricultural Sectors, 111
12. Hospital Institutions, Excluding Military Hospitals, by Type and Number of Beds, 112
13. Hospital Beds, Excluding Military Hospitals, by Republics, 112
14. Hospital Beds, by Specialty, 114
15. Hospital Beds for Pregnant Women and Infants, 115
16. Women's Consultation Clinics, Children's Consultation Clinics, and Polyclinics, by Republics, 115
17. List of Higher Medical Educational Institutions, 116

V. HOUSING

1. Urban Housing: State and Private Share, 122
2. Aggregate and per Capita Urban Housing, 122
3. Aggregate and per Capita Housing, by Republics, 123
4. Aggregate and per Capita Housing Fund for Fifteen Largest Cities, 124
5. Urban Housing Fund owned by State and Private Sectors, by Republics, 125
6. Housing Built by State Including Cooperatives; Collective Farms, Collective Farmers, and Rural Intelligentsia; and Privately, 127
7. Percentage of Housing Built by State Including Cooperatives; Collective Farms, Collective Farmers, and Rural Intelligentsia; and Privately, 127
8. Percentage of Housing Built by State Including Cooperatives; Collective Farms, Collective Farmers, and Rural Intelligentsia; and Privately, by Republics, 128
9. Percentage of Housing Space Built by Urban and Rural Areas in the USSR, 129
10. Average Square Meters of Housing Space per Housing Unit Built by Republics, 130
11. Housing Space per Capita Built by Republics, 130
12. Percentage of Housing Units and Square Meters of Housing Space Built by Republics, 131
13. Increase in Urban Housing, 132
14. Cooperative Housing Built as Percentage of Total Housing Built and per Capita by Republic, 132
15. Per Capita Investment in Housing Construction by Republics, 133
16. Percentage of Total Housing Construction Budget Allocated to Republics, 134.
17. Housing Units Built per 1,000 People in the USSR, 134

VI. EDUCATION A.

A.1. Literacy: Percentage of Population Aged 9–49, 139
A.2. Kindergartens and Combined Nursery School–Kindergartens, 140
A.3. Children Enrolled in Kindergartens and Combined Nursery School–Kindergartens, 140
A.3a. Children Enrolled in Kindergartens and Combined Nursery School–Kindergartens, per 1,000 population, 141
A.4. Persons with Secondary Education, 142
A.4a. Persons with Secondary Education per 1,000 Population, 143
A.5. Primary and General Secondary Schools, 143
A.6. Pupils Enrolled in Primary and General Secondary Schools of All Types, 144

A.6a. Pupils Enrolled in Primary and General Secondary Schools, of all Types per 1,000 Population, 145

A.6b. Primary and Secondary Pupils as Percentage of Population Aged 5–19, 145

A.7. Vocational Secondary Schools, 146

A.8. Number of Students Enrolled in Vocational Secondary Schools, 146

A.9. Institutions of Higher Education, 147

A.10. Number of Students Enrolled in Institutions of Higher Education, 148

A.10a. Number of Students Enrolled in Institutions of Higher Education per 100,000 Population, 148

A.11. Students Enrolled in Institutions of Higher Education by Branch, 149

A.12. Females as Percentage of Students Enrolled in Institutions of Higher Education, 149

A.13. Evening, Extension, and Correspondence Students as Percentage of Students Enrolled in Institutions of Higher Education, 149

A.14. Graduates of Higher Education, 150

A.14a. Graduates of Higher Education per 1,000 Population, 151

A.15. Student-Teacher Ratio in Primary and General Secondary Schools of All Types; Graduates of Higher Education as Percentage of Teachers in Regular Primary and General Secondary Schools, 152

VI. EDUCATION B.

B.1. Percentage of Population and Percentage of Students in Institutions of Higher Education by Republic, 152

B.2. National Composition of Students in Institutions of Higher Education, 153

B.3. National Composition of the Population of Union Republics Compared with the National Composition of Post-graduate Students, 153

B.4. National Composition of Scientific Workers by Republic, 1960, 154

B.5. National Composition of Scientific Workers in Selected Years, 154

B.6. Percentage of Doctors and Candidates of Science among Research Workers and Faculty, 155

B.7. Expenditures for Education and Culture from USSR Budget and Union Republican Budgets, 155

B.8. Expenditures for Institutions of Higher Education, 156

VII. ELITE RECRUITMENT AND MOBILIZATION

1. CPSU Membership, 161

2. CPSU Membership: Republics, 161

3. CPSU Congresses, 163

4. CPSU Membership: Ethnic Representation, 163

5. CPSU Membership: Age, 164

6. CPSU Membership: Sex, 164

7. CPSU Membership: Level of Education, 165

8. CPSU Membership: Number of Years in Party, 165

9. CPSU Membership: Social Position, 165

10. CPSU Membership: Occupation—Agricultural and Nonagricultural, 165

11. CPSU Membership: Occupation—Production and Services, 166
12. CPSU Membership: Candidates Taken into Party, 166
13. CPSU: Education of Secretaries of Republic, Oblast, and
    Krai Organizations, 167
14. CPSU: Education of Secretaries of Okrug, City and District
    Organizations, 167
15. CPSU: Education of Secretaries of Primary Party Organizations, 167
16. CPSU Graduates of Party Instruction Schools, 168
17. Distribution of Propaganda Personnel, 168
18. Evening Universities of Marxism–Leninism, 168
19. CPSU: Primary Party Organizations, 169
20. Komsomol Membership, 169
21. Trade Union Membership, 170
22. Voting, 170
23. Annual Number of Lectures Given by "Znanie" Society and
    Estimated Audience, 171
24. Average Annual Letters Received by Newspapers, 171
25. Average Annual Letters to Newspapers, 172
26. Participation as Percentage of Relevant Age Group and
    Rate of Increase, 173

VIII. COMMUNICATIONS

A. TRANSPORTATION

A.1. Total Length of Railroad Tracks, 177
A.2. Total Length of Roads, 177
A.3. Passenger Kilometers by Type of Transportation, 178
A.4. Urban Transport Facilities and Annual Number of Passengers, 178

B. MASS MEDIA AND MAIL FLOW

B.1. Offices of Communication, 179
B.2. Domestic Mail Flow, 179
B.2a. Domestic Mail Flow per Capita, 180
B.3. Telephones, 180
B.3a. Telephones per 1,000 Population, 181
B.4. Film Projectors and Movie Attendance, 181
B.5. Production of Films, 182
B.6. Television Broadcasting Network, 182
B.7. Growth of Radio and Television Receiving Network, 183
B.7a. Radio and Television Sets per 1,000 Population, 183
B.8. Book Publishing: Total and by Republic, 184
B.8a. Book Publishing per 1,000 Population, 185
B.9. Books and Pamphlets by Subject Matter, 186
B.10a. and b. Book Publishing by Content, 187
B.11. Publication of Textbooks, 188
B.12. Newspaper Publication, 188
B.12a. Newspaper and Magazine Circulation per 1,000 Population, 189
B.13. Newspaper Publication by Language Category, 190
B.14. Newspaper Publication by Subject Matter, 190
B.15. Magazine Publication, 191

C. FOREIGN CONTACTS

C.1. Foreign Cultural Contacts: "Representatives of Science, Education,
    and Culture" to and from USSR, 191

C.2. Foreign Cultural Contacts: Athletes, Journalists, and Scientists to and from USSR, 192
C.3. Tourism, 192
C.4. Attendance at U.S. and USSR Exhibits, 193

D. PUBLIC AGENCIES

D.1. Mass Libraries and Books in Them, 193
D.2. Clubs and Houses of Culture, 194

IX. INTERNATIONAL INTERACTIONS

A. TRADE

A.1. Tsarist Russian Trade, 199
A.2. Soviet Trade, 199
A.3. Soviet Trade: Selected Trading Partners, 200
A.4. Major Trading Partners of the Soviet Union, 201
A.5. Percentage of Soviet Trade with Socialist Countries, 202
A.6. Major Commodities in Soviet Trade, 203
A.7. Number of Soviet Trading Partners, 203
A.8. Per Capita Value of Soviet Trade, 204
A.9. Growth of Soviet Trade, 204

B. ECONOMIC ASSISTANCE OF COMMUNIST COUNTRIES TO DEVELOPING NATIONS

B.1. Communist Economic Credits and Grants Extended to Less Developed Countries, 205
B.2. Communist Military Aid Extensions, 206
B.3. Communist Economic Technicians in Less Developed Countries, 207
B.4. Communist Economic Technicians in Less Developed Countries, 207
B.5. Academic Students Studying in Communist Countries, 207
B.6. Technical Trainees from Developing Countries Training in Communist Countries, 208

C. COUNCIL ON MUTUAL ECONOMIC ASSISTANCE

C.1. Basic Data on CMEA Countries, 208
C.2. Relative per Capita Outputs in CMEA Countries, 209
C.3. Growth of Industrial Output of CMEA Countries, 209
C.4. Growth of Industrial Output of CMEA Countries, 209
C.5. Industrial Output in CMEA, 210
C.6. Output of Power and Various Raw Materials in CMEA Countries, 210
C.7. Selected CMEA Indicators, 210
C.8. Trade of CMEA Countries, 211
C.9. Per Capita Trade of CMEA Countries and Trade as a Percentage of National Income, 213
C.10. Intra-CMEA Trade, 214
C.11. Direction of CMEA Exports, 214
C.12. CMEA Foreign Trade by Region, 214
C.13. Fuel and Raw Material Imports from USSR, 215
C.14. Engineering Goods and Raw Materials in CMEA Trade, 215
C.15. USSR Credits Promised to Eastern Europe, 216

C.16. Annual Foreign Aid Deliveries (Drawdowns) to
   CMEA Countries from the Soviet Union, 216
C.17. Inter-CMEA Loans, 217
C.18. CMEA Organization, 217
C.19. Bilaterial Treaties and Agreements between the Soviet Union
   and Other CMEA Countries, 217
C.20. Treaties with CMEA Countries as a Percentage of
   All Soviet Treaties, 218
C.21. Warsaw Pact, Armed Forces, 218
C.22. Warsaw Pact Military Expenditures, 219

D. WORLD COMMUNIST PARTY MEMBERSHIP

D.1. Membership of Communist Parties, 219
D.2. Rank of Major Communist Parties, 221
D.3. Communist Party Membership by Region, 222

ACKNOWLEDGMENTS

I am most appreciative of the invaluable assistance provided by several people during the many months of the preparation of this book. I am particularly grateful to Professor Karl Deutsch of Harvard University; Professor Edward Azar of the University of North Carolina; and Professors Bo Anderson, and J. Allan Beegle of Michigan State University: Their perceptive and stimulating suggestions greatly enriched the conceptual framework of the book. I am also most grateful for the comments of my colleague Professor Timothy Hennessey. Elizabeth Andrus provided a consistently high level of research and organizational assistance throughout the period of time in which this book was being prepared; her impeccable research skills, her mastery of the sources, and her ability to direct the work of others made her a most valuable assistant. Additional research was done by James Seroka. Mike Mueller and Larry Walter, of the Computer Institute for Social Science Research at Michigan State University, were very helpful in the cluster analysis in the introductory essay. Mrs. Thomas Cooley performed with enormous skill the task of preparing all the tables for photographic duplication, and the secretaries of the Political Science Department at Michigan State University typed the other sections of the book. I thank the Russian and East European Studies Program and the International Programs Center of Michigan State University for their support of the research involved in the comparison of Soviet republics in the introductory chapter. For the use of the excellent facilities of the Computer Institute for Social Service Research, I should like to thank the director, Professor Charles F. Wrigley.

Tables 12, 14, 16, and 17 in the Introduction appeared in *Public Opinion Quarterly,* Winter 1972–73, and are used with their permission.

B. S. E. Ezhegodnik	S. E. Vavilov, ed., *Bolshaya Sovetskaya Entsiklopedia, Ezhegodnik,* Moscow, for the appropriate years.
Pechat SSSR	*Pechat SSSR v . . . godu,* Moscow, for the appropriate years.
Pechat SSSR za 40 L	*Pechat SSSR za 40 Let, 1917–1957,* Moscow (1957).
Pechat SSSR za 50 L	*Pechat SSSR za 50 Let,* ed. P. Chuikov, Moscow (1968).
N.K.	*Narodnoe Khozyaistvo v . . . ,* Moscow, for the appropriate years.
SS za 50 L.	*Strana Sovetov za 50 Let,* Moscow (1968).
The USSR Economy	*The USSR Economy, A Statistical Abstract,* London, Lawrence and Wishart (1957).
Cultural Progress in the USSR	*Cultural Progress in the USSR (Statistical Returns),* Moscow (1958).
Trud	*Trud v SSSR,* Moscow (1968)
Prom	*Promyshlennost SSSR,* Moscow (1964).
Selsk	*Selskoe Khozyaistvo SSSR: Statistichesky Sbornik,* Moscow (1960).
SS-SSSR	*Sotsialisticheskoe Stroitelstvo SSSR: Statistichesky Ezhegodnik, Moscow* (1934).
Vneshnyaya torgovlya	*Vneshnyaya torgovlya Soyuza SSR za . . . ,* Moscow, for the appropriate years.
KPSS	*KPSS: Naglyadnoe posobie po partynomu stroitelstvu,* Moscow (1969).

	Area (Millions of Square Kilometers)
Russia in 1913	22.3
USSR within the boundaries prior to September 17, 1939	21.7
USSR within the 1940 boundaries:	
Including areas ceded to Poland by the Treaty of 1945	22.2
Excluding areas ceded to Poland by the Treaty of 1945	22.1
USSR within the present boundaries	22.4

Note: Russian territory of 1913 and USSR territory in subsequent years includes the following areas first surveyed during the period 1947–1951: water surface area of closed bays (Obskaya Bay, Tazovskaya Bay, Chaunskaya Bay, and several others), an additional land area reclaimed as a result of a decrease in the size of the Caspian Sea (shallowing) and as the result of more precise area measurements carried out in 1956 for the purpose of producing new cartographic materials.

SOURCE: Narodnoe Khozyaistvo SSSR: Statistichesky Sbornik, Moscow, 1956, p. 20.

SOVIET TERRITORIAL—ADMINISTRATIVE LEVELS

All-Union	Federal, Central
Republic	One of the 15 constituent national divisions
Oblast	Province
*Krai**	Territory
Autonomous Republic*	
okrug	National region
gorod	City
raion	District

* According to Jerry Hough, these territorial units are similar to the oblasts, "the only difference in terminology being associated with the desire to give recognition to various nationality groups." *The Soviet Prefects,* Cambridge, Harvard University Press (1969), p. 9.

CONTRIBUTORS

JEREMY R. AZRAEL is Professor of Political Science and Chairman of the Committee on Slavic Area Studies at the University of Chicago. His research is concerned with comparative politics with special reference to the Soviet Union and Eastern Europe. He is the author of *Managerial Power and Soviet Politics* (1966) and the forthcoming *Education and Development in the USSR.*

IVAN I. BAKALO is an economist who taught in the Soviet Union before the Second World War. He is a member of the Institute for the Study of the USSR and was formerly Deputy Director of this Institute in Munich. He has published works on agriculture and education, including a number of articles on education in *The Ukraine: A Concise Encyclopedia* (1969–1970).

GEORGE Z. F. BEREDAY is Professor of Comparative Education at Teachers College, Columbia University and Associate of the Russian Institute at that institution. He has taught courses on Soviet education at Columbia, Tokyo University, and the University of Hawaii. He serves on the advisory board of the magazine *Soviet Education* and is co-editor of *The Changing Soviet School* (1960) and *The Politics of Soviet Education* (1960).

STANLEY H. COHN is Professor of Economics at the State University of New York at Binghamton. His research is focused on Soviet economic development and performance. His publications include: *Economic Development in the Soviet Union* (1970), "Soviet Growth Retardation" in *New Directions in the Soviet Economy* (1966), and "Perspectives on Soviet Economic Growth and Productive Efficiency," in *Michigan Business Review* (1963).

WARREN W. EASON is Professor of Economics at the Ohio State University. His research is concerned with human resources in Soviet economic development, and he is currently engaged in research on the processes of demographic development in imperial Russia and the Soviet Union. He has contributed to *The Transformation of Russian Society: Aspects of Social Change Since 1861,* edited by Cyril E. Black (1960), *Economic Trends in the Soviet Union,* edited by Abram Bergson and Simon S. Kuznets (1963), and *Population: The Vital Revolution,* edited by Ronald Freedman (1964).

MARK G. FIELD is Professor of Sociology at Boston University, Associate of the Russian Research Center of Harvard University, and Assistant Sociologist in the Department of Psychiatry at Massachusetts General Hospital. His research speciality is the sociology of medicine with special emphasis on the Soviet health system and comparative health systems. He is the author of *Doctor and Patient in Soviet Russia* (1957) and *Soviet Socialized Medicine* (1967), and co-author of *Social Approaches to Mental Patient Care* (1964).

GAYLE DURHAM HOLLANDER is Assistant Professor of Political Science at Hampshire College. Her research interests are Soviet public opinion, mass communications, propaganda and agitation; and the status of women in the Soviet Union and Eastern Europe. She is the author of *Soviet Political Indoctrination: Mass Communications and Propaganda in the Post-Stalin Period* (1972) and various monographs on Soviet propaganda and mass communications published by the Center for International Studies at the Massachusetts Institute of Technology and articles and book reviews on the same subject in *Public Opinion Quarterly*.

ROGER E. KANET is Associate Professor of Political Science and Slavic and Soviet Area Studies and Associate Chairman of the Department of Political Science at the University of Kansas. His research is concerned with Soviet foreign policy, and he is the author of *The Behavioral Revolution and Communist Studies* (1971); "Soviet Economic Policy in Sub-Saharan Africa," in *Canadian Slavic Studies I* (1967); and "The Recent Soviet Reassessment of Developments in the Third World," in *The Russian Review*, XXVII (1968).

ROY D. LAIRD is Professor of Political Science and Slavic and Soviet Area Studies at the University of Kansas. He is a member of the Staff of the Slavic and Soviet Area Center and editor of the University of Kansas Slavic Series. His research interests include Soviet politics, agriculture, and ideology. He is the author of *The Soviet Paradigm: An Experiment in Creating a Monohierarchical Polity* (1970), co-author of *Soviet Communism and Agrarian Revolution* (1970), and co-editor of *Soviet Agriculture: The Permanent Crisis* (1965).

ELLEN MICKIEWICZ is Associate Professor of Political Science at Michigan State University. Her research is concerned with propaganda and ideology in the Soviet Union and comparative studies in social and political development. She is the author of *Soviet Political Schools* (1967) and "The Modernization of Party Propaganda in the USSR," in the *Slavic Review*, XXX (1971); and co-author of "American Views of Soviet-American Exchanges of Persons," in *Communication in International Politics,* edited by Richard L. Merritt (1972).

HENRY W. MORTON is Professor of Political Science at Queens College of the City University of New York. His research centers on Soviet and comparative politics, and he is the author of *The Soviet Union and Eastern Europe* (1971) and *Soviet Sport: Mirror of Soviet Society* (1963). He is co-author and co-editor of *Soviet Policy-Making* (1967).

JAAN PENNAR is Senior Fellow at the Research Institute on Communist Affairs at Columbia University. He has also served as Counselor for the Institute for the Study of the USSR in New York. His research is concerned with Soviet education, Soviet nationalities, and Soviet approaches to the Middle East. He is co-editor of *The Politics of Soviet Education* (1960).

JONATHAN POOL is Assistant Professor of Political Science at the State University of New York at Stony Brook and Associated Scholar of the Program on Soviet Nationality Problems at Columbia University. His research interests include political linguistics and the politics of Soviet Central Asia. He is the author of "National Development and Language Diversity," in *Advances in the Sociology of Language,* edited by Joshua A. Fishman (1971); and co-author of forthcoming *Poliscide* and of the forthcoming *Modern Democracies: A Comparative and Behavioral Analysis*.

TOWARD THE STUDY OF POLITICAL AND SOCIAL INDICATORS ACROSS DIFFERENT SOCIAL SYSTEMS

BY KARL W. DEUTSCH, HARVARD UNIVERSITY

THE IDEA of using quantitative data as indicators of the structure, performance, and development of a political system is old. Germs of its practice can be seen in the tax records of empires and irrigation bureaucracies such as those of ancient Egypt and Mesopotamia and in the tax and voting classifications embodied in the constitutions of some of the city states of ancient Greece and Italy. Seeds of its theory can be found in Plato's *Republic* and in Plato's and Aristotle's concern with the size and proportions of the state and its components.

In more modern times, Sir James Petty in 1672 called his collection of statistics "political arithmetick," although it has since become the custom to regard the kind of data he collected as mainly economical. In the eighteenth century, the study of taxation, public revenues, and economic activity was often treated as a single field of interest for statesmen and their advisers; it was included among what was then called the "science of government," or the *Staatswissenschaften,* the "sciences of the state," and the collection, tabulation, and analyses of quantitative data relevant to matters of state gave the emerging new science the name "statistics."

THE INTERPLAY OF THEORY AND DATA

In the nineteenth century, major thinkers studied time series and cross-sectional distributions of data, often extrapolating or projecting them to challenging inferences and conclusions, which were not always borne out by later experience. Karl Marx, Vilfredo Pareto, Max Weber, Werner Sombart,

Otto Bauer, Rudolf Hilferding, V. I. Lenin, John Maynard Keynes, Simon Kuznets, and others all used at times quantitative data and quantitative reasoning without which they could not have done much of their work. Far from being merely a pedantic concern of men with small and grubby minds, quantitative data and quantitative inferences were an essential part of the work of some of the boldest and most important thinkers in the political and social sciences.

Out of the political experiences of the 1920's and 1930's came two new ideas for the future "data movement" in political and social science. Otto Neurath in Vienna developed a municipal "Museum of Society and Economy" which attempted to show in colorful statistical exhibits, often combining maps and "isotype" (or "pictograph") statistics, the structure of past and contemporary social and political systems and some of their components. In 1929, a large and impressive atlas, containing much of this material, was published at Leipzig, and the Museum in Vienna attracted many visitors. In 1933 and 1934, the Nazi dictatorship in Germany and the Dollfuss dictatorship in Austria cut short these developments.

In the same decade, however, the quantitative approach to politics developed strongly in the United States, particularly through the work of the "Chicago school" of political science and such scholars as Harold D. Lasswell, Harold Gosnell, and Quincy Wright. Published in 1936, Lasswell's slim book *Politics: Who Gets What, When, How* set a new standard in the broad application of quantitative reasoning and data, in combination with other methods of analysis, to the general study of political systems. In the 1950's, Lasswell then developed his idea of a "Museum of the Future." Such an institution not only was to show the structure and development of various governments, societies, and other political and social institutions in their past and present aspects, but it was to show extrapolations and projections of past trends into the future. In particular, it was to show possible alternative long-run futures in the light of projections of possible alternative trends and decisions in the present or in the future just ahead. If Neurath's Museum had been closed, Lasswell's proposed museum never opened. Yet both contributed to a trend in political and social science that is still growing.

SOME RECENT WORK IN THE QUANTITATIVE DATA FIELD

In 1961, work began at Yale University by Harold D. Lasswell and myself, and soon by a larger group which included Bruce M. Russett, Hayward R. Alker, Richard L. Merritt, and several others. Still somewhat later, Ellen Propper Mickiewicz, Michael Hudson, Charles Taylor, Michitoshi Takabatake, and others joined in various aspects of this work. Limited financial support was provided in the early stages by the Carnegie Corporation and by Yale University, and support on a larger scale through a succession of grants by the National Science Foundation. Books stemming from this work included Bruce M. Russett *et al., World Handbook of Political and Social Indicators* (1964); Richard L. Merritt and Stein Rokkan, eds., *Comparing Nations* (1966); Charles L. Taylor, ed., *Aggregate Data Analysis* (1968); and Charles L. Taylor and Michael Hudson, eds., *Second World Handbook of Political and Social Indicators*, Yale University Press, New Haven, 1972.

Parallel but independent efforts in the analysis of aggregative data were carried forward at several other institutions under the leadership of Arthur S. Banks and Robert Textor, Donald V. McGranahan, Harold Guetzkow, Rudolf Rummel, and others, while voting studies and survey research had been developed most strongly by Paul F. Lazarsfeld and Herbert Hyman at Columbia University and by Angus Campbell, Philip Converse, Warren Miller, and Donald Stokes at the University of Michigan.

As work on quantitative data has developed, so have methods of analysis which now often can extract far more information and meaning from an array of raw data than would be apparent on the surface. In comparisons across nations, or across relatively few states, provinces, or districts within a nation— such as 50 states in the United States, 15 Union Republics in the USSR, or 97 French Departments—we can now work with the entire universe of cases for which data are available, for large numbers of subdivisions such as counties, municipalities, or wards; we can take samples and check in what respects they are or are not representative of the total. Expectable error margins can be estimated and indicated for whole series of data as well as for particular countries or districts. We can use ratio scales and rank order scales, and by the consistent use of rank ordering of states along each variable we can get a new picture of the international system or of the variety among territorial units within a nation. The computing of ratios between different types of data, such as the ratio of public expenditures to GNP, or foreign trade to GNP, or domestic to foreign mail, we can gain insight into the relative growth or decline of the public or private, or else the international or national, sectors of attention, activity, and potential political interests and pressures. Distribution profiles, Lorentz curves, and Gini indices can throw more light on inequalities of income or power, their extent, and the rate and direction of their change. Generally, from many series of comparable data collected for more than one point in time, rates of change can be computed and projected, and past or prospective inconsistencies or cross-overs among different trends noted. Indices of correlation and of determination between pairs of variables can be found, the best straight-line and simple curvilinear regression lines computed, and the strength, significance, and elasticity of the relationship noted. For any one variable, all other variables can be printed out by the computer in the rank order of the strength of their positive or negative coefficient or correlation, and this rank order used as an additional test for those political or social hypotheses which would lead us to expect a particular rank ordering of correlations which now may be confirmed or not.

Proceeding beyond pair correlations among variables, we may look for triads and thus for discriminating variables which may help us separate spurious correlations from genuine ones. We may then go on to multivariate analysis, multiple regression methods, and factor analysis in order to tease further information from our data.

All these methods are well known, and these things have been done, at least to some extent, and for some groups of data. But they have not been done to any large degree in the field of Soviet studies, mainly because the data were not, or were not readily, available, and partly because few area specialists in the Soviet field have had enough familiarity even with these well-known quantitative methods to apply them themselves, or even to cooperate effectively with methods specialists who could have been added to their team.

Beyond this, new methods are being developed or else imported into the field of political studies from other areas of inquiry. Causal modelling is still being developed; still more work is needed on systems of simultaneous equations that could represent arrays of feedback effects with possible asymmetrical couplings in a political system (so that a strong effect from component i to j would be followed by a weaker but still relevant effect from j to i, and this again to a strong but somewhat modified effect from i to j, etc.). Random walk models for conflict processes under conditions of uncertainty are needed; applications of waiting line theory to problems of overloaded channels of communication, of political patronage and preferment, of welfare state services, or of resource allocation, still need development. Something similar is true of game theory and the further development of relevant theoretical models and experimental data in this field. And all these advances will be needed in order to make our efforts at computer simulation of political and social processes at the levels of the nation-state and of international politics less primitive and inefficient than they now still are. These thoughts, too, apply to the field of Soviet studies. Here, too, the essential first step is the ready availability of relevant data, carefully gathered and critically evaluated for expectable margins of error; and this crucial step has now been taken by Dr. Mickiewicz and her associates.

Ellen Mickiewicz began to work at Yale on quantitative political and social indicators for the Soviet Union. Her *Handbook of Soviet Social Science Data,* however, goes very far beyond these primitive beginnings. It's fully hers, both in conception and in execution. Both as editor and contributor, Dr. Mickiewicz, together with her fellow contributors, has given us a fundamentally important work of a kind and quality that have not been available before in the field of Soviet studies.

Dr. Mickiewicz's book represents a major step toward the possibility of true comparative political and social analysis—analysis in which the social system itself can be treated as a variable in comparing nations in addition to the customary variables of region, occupation, ethnicity, per capita income, rural-urban balance, and the like. Just how do the United States, the Soviet Union and, say France and Italy compare in regard to interregional differences, rural education, or women's jobs, earnings, and free time? Dr. Mickiewicz comments on some Soviet data concerning these matters, but now she has made it possible for more detailed comparative studies to be made which may confirm or modify her current perspective.

For other comparisons we may need more data. Since the USSR records the ethnic background—*natsionalnost*—of each citizen among his permanent personal characteristics, it should be possible to obtain rates of fertility and of natural population increase for the different nationalities. How different are these rates? Are the differences growing, declining, or unchanged? Are there discrepancies between the expectable number of, say, Ukrainians from past census data and known birth and death rates and the actual number of Ukrainians at a later census? To what extent can these discrepancies be accounted for by internal migrations—e.g., from the Ukraine to new industrial or agricultural projects east of the Urals—and by the assimilation of the migrants to the Great Russian language and culture in their new locations? To what extent do such calculations suggest a rate of assimiliation of, say, Ukrainians to Russians (a) outside the Ukraine Republic, and (b) within the Ukraine; and (c) a rate of assimilation of Russians to Ukrainians within the Ukraine? Data presumably existing within the Soviet Union would thus make possible a better knowledge of the extent and speed of the processes of ethnic, linguistic, and cultural assimilation within the USSR and would permit comparisons with similar processes of assimilation in other countries. (If the Soviet data should remain unavailable, a computer simulation might start by assuming either (a) uniform birth and death rates for all major ethnic groups in the USSR, or (b) birth and death rates varying only by such cross-ethnic factors as age, occupation, education, and urban-rural residence, and hence calculable for each major nationality from its known composition in terms of these particular factors. After these initial assumptions about natural increase, the model would compute the putative assimilation rate, or the range of such rates, which these demographic assumptions would produce. Some iterative procedure might then be devised to compute successive further approximations and to improve their mutual fit until the best—or most plausible—estimates of the rates of demographic change, internal migration, and ethnic assimilation have been found within the constraints of those data that are known.

In other cases, we may have to wait until the relevant data are released by the Soviet authorities. We know that the criminal homicide rate in the United States is about six times that in Britain, but I think we do not know how the USSR compares in this respect with either of these two countries. Similarly, comparative data would be desirable on intranational and international contacts such as foreign and domestic travel and mail, and on social problems, such as suicide, robbery, burglary, divorce, alcoholism, and prostitution. All these refer to problems which are to some extent common to industrializing or highly industrialized countries, and it would be important to know to what extent the different national cultures and political and social systems are coping with them.

Governments and their officials may be understandably reluctant to reveal some of these data. Any information a government gives to outsiders could be used by someone as a basis for criticism or attack on it. The temptation to reveal nothing, and thus avoid possible embarrassment, is even stronger if the prevailing national belief system asserts that there are no serious social problems or malfunctions left in the country, since the excellence of the nation's institutions—such as the United States' wealth and freedom, or the Soviet Union's socialism and social justice—already has reduced these evils to insignificance. (At most, foreign agitators, immigrants, or, in the USSR, remnants of "former classes" might be held responsible for any surviving crimes or other troubles.)

But a government that does not publish quantitative data on a political or social problem of this kind denies the information to its own people and indeed to a large portion of its officials and political leaders. The top leaders cannot pay attention to all problems, and the lower echelons cannot get very much genuine information if secrecy is not to be endangered. Moreover, what the government thinks it knows in these matters remains shielded from correction through criticism and discussion. The effective thought of the community cannot be brought to bear on problems that are not adequately reported to the population.

Adequate data and a vigorous political and social science, with the possibility of critical verification and self-correction, are essential elements for the effective self-direction of a society and its political system. In recent years we have learned something of this rather painfully in the United States. Pervasive secrecy begets drift, unnoticed by decision-makers. Manipulative communications, untrue or only partly true, eventually return as popular beliefs and become decision premises in the minds of many of the nation's leaders, making errors more likely. But the vast powers of modern industrial technology have increased the cost of errors in their application, in military clashes, in the impact on the natural environment of water, soil, and air, and in the effects of chemical and pharmacological technology on the lives of people. With the rise of costs of errors, and of delays in self-correction and in discovering solutions, these costs of error and delay eventually may come to outweigh by far the costs of a temporary setback in the contest for international prestige, or of political or ideological embarrassment in domestic politics. If so, the rational case for secrecy will eventually weaken in most of the world's highly developed countries, including eventually perhaps both the Soviet Union and the United States.

The greatest discoveries of political and social science, and the greatest benefits from their application, are not in the past but in the future. They must be approached step by step, using at each step all the relevant knowledge we can get. Ellen Mickiewicz and her associates are helping us to take one long step in this direction. They are providing us with a crucial beginning for the long journey toward a better understanding of Soviet society and politics, and of our own.

USES AND STRATEGIES IN DATA ANALYSIS OF THE SOVIET UNION: CLEAVAGES IN INDUSTRIALIZED SOCIETY

ELLEN MICKIEWICZ

IT HAS BECOME POSSIBLE, really for the first time, for the Western scholar to use Soviet data in research and to be assured that, generally speaking, the supply will be ample enough to indicate trends. Since the death of Stalin there has been a much greater amount of data released to the public, both Soviet and non-Soviet, and it has been of a much higher quality. Discontinuities in data are less frequent and extrapolation is facilitated. Increasingly, statistical gathering techniques and methods of analysis have become more and more advanced. Until recently, the tremendous dislocations caused by the social and political upheaval instituted by Stalin's regime and the impact of the Second World War disrupted and undermined the tasks of data collection and analysis. Although the present supply of data is vastly superior to that of the past, political criteria still influence the objective quality of data in five important ways.

First, and most simply, for categories that are politically sensitive in the opinion of the regime, data are not released to the public, Soviet or non-Soviet. This is a practice generally observable throughout the world's political systems; what is important is the scope and extent of what is politically permissible. In his introduction to "International Interactions," for example, Roger Kanet indicates some of the areas in which data are unavailable, probably because the areas are considered to be politically sensitive. Criteria of sensitivity may change, as do regimes, so that future data collections of this type may be enlarged or contracted.

Second, changes from one reported period to the next may involve shifting criteria for what has been included in the data or such a vague description of the criteria that it is difficult to determine the exact base to which the data refer. The user of Soviet data must be alert to such changes of base, and, with careful attention to the definitions in use, many problems can be avoided. The too vaguely defined data category also presents a difficulty for the scholar, as

Gayle Hollander observes in her discussion of the definition of books and periodicals in the introduction to Chapter VIII, "Communications."

Third, changes over time may be given only in percentage differences, with no provision of the base from which the change has been calculated. In my introduction to "Elite Recruitment and Mobilization," for example, I note that although we have a great deal of information on percentage changes in level of education and other attributes of the top Communist Party professional bureaucracy, we really do not know how many of them there are, and we have to use various kinds of estimates for this important category of Soviet elite.

Fourth, it is sometimes particularly difficult to make cross-national comparisons which include the Soviet Union and use Soviet data because Soviet statisticians use definitions that differ significantly from the definitions widely in use among other nations of the world. This presents a serious problem of comparability, and some operations must be executed to bring the Soviet data in line with commonly adopted practices. For example, Stanley Cohn observes in his introduction to "Production" that Soviet data on national income and production must be recalculated to fit the definitions which are becoming standard for the rest of the world. Another example is the way in which housing space is figured: Henry Morton shows in his introduction to "Housing" how Soviet definitions differ from Western ones, and Roger Kanet discusses in his introduction some problems associated with international rates of exchange. Although standardization of units of measurement and definitions of data categories at the international level might be most desirable (and the United Nations has greatly aided this kind of development), nations do differ, presenting a problem not unique to Soviet sources.

The fifth way in which use of Soviet data may be limited by political criteria is a problem more peculiar to the Soviet Union. The Soviet plan for economic development, although in large part centrally formulated, is subsequently broken down into regional or local plans. Overseeing and aiding fulfillment of the plan are two of the major duties of the Communist Party, and economic production has profound political implications. Failure to fulfill the requirements of the plan has, in the past, entailed rather severe sanctions, and although the recent tentative reforms have attempted to mitigate the dysfunctions of the tensions and constraints surrounding plan fulfillment, nonfulfillment still carries with it the risk of opprobrium and possible career termination. Thus, there is a tremendous pressure for the subnational units to falsify the results of their planned production to indicate, at the very least, successful fulfillment. This tendency to distort local performance presents a very serious problem for Soviet planners, for they must work with this distorted material, and the entire process of planning suffers from its consequences. Khrushchev's violent outbursts in Soviet Central Asia, upon his discovering such typical local distortion, attest to the difficulties that the Soviet planners themselves must experience in dealing with the consequences of political pressures.

One imperative emerges from the combined efforts of the contributors to this handbook: Be aware of the limitations of Soviet data, but take advantage of their increasing variety and amount. Seldom do the Soviet sources print outright and deliberate falsification of data.

One of the main purposes of this handbook is to aid scholars in making cross-national comparisons that include the Soviet Union. For this reason, wherever they would be useful, we selected data for dicennial years, since such data are often provided at the international level. Often, however, data were not available for these years, and in each such case the nearest available year was substituted. Certain other years were added because of their importance for the development of the Soviet Union. Thus, 1926, the year of a census, appears for certain categories; 1928, the beginning of the first Five-Year Plan, is used for certain other data. The pre-Soviet year of 1913 was chosen as having the best data available for the prerevolutionary context. This handbook is mainly oriented toward modern, post-Stalin data which, as noted above, are both more abundant and more reliable than earlier data. The data here focus on the more recent problems of development, social, political, and economic; therefore, the bulk of the information relates to the decades beginning with the 1950's. Earlier data have been included to provide contextual information and points of reference for purposes of comparison and to facilitate the analysis of trends.

There is at present no other source which makes such a wealth of data available in English to the Western scholar. The task of making cross-national comparisons of problems of development and modernization, for example, lies at the center of much current scholarly research, and yet the Soviet Union is rarely a component part of the theories elaborated. United Nations sources, although they present much valuable information, cannot provide the scholar with enough data to bring the Soviet Union into a sufficiently comparative framework. On the other hand, looking into Soviet publications requires collection from many scattered sources and experience with Soviet statistical problems and definitions, not to mention the intricacies of the language. Certain kinds of data, especially survey research and public opinion polling, are particularly valuable in studying problems of social stratification, ethnic identification, propensities toward integration and perceptions of authority, norms of behavior, dissatisfaction, life goals, and other aspects of culture and socialization. In general, Western cross-national studies involving surveys of this type are prevented from including the Soviet Union,[1] but, as shown in the next section of this chapter, Soviet scholars are increasingly using these techniques, and some information is available with which to illuminate the quantitative data presented here. Perhaps in the future, collections of Soviet data will be able to include systematized data of this type. Until then, this handbook provides in a single source the widest variety of data about the Soviet Union currently available in the social sciences and should enable the Western scholar to enrich significantly his research.[2]

This handbook serves still another purpose. It is a detailed guide to the Soviet sources most useful in research on the USSR in some of the major divisions of the social sciences. The notes to each section indicate the sources used by the author and constitute a useful form of bibliographic training for the student. Facility in using these sources should greatly aid the scholars who focus on the functioning of the Soviet system.

Two considerations determine the choice of variables for which data are provided in this volume: First, what are the questions being asked by Western scholars in the cross-disciplinary and cross-national fields of development and modernization? The transition from rural to city life and from an agricultural to an industrial economy are central to these investigations, as is the process by which small units—whether of ethnic, religious, cultural, economic, geographic, or political homogeneity—become part of a larger identification and structure. We have tried to include data which help to illuminate these processes, which are by no means necessarily inevitable or parallel over time or across cultures. In fact, the Soviet system may present a variant which would be extremely helpful in categorizing the basic patterns. Second: What is the availability of data? Certain questions, such as those about suicide rates or prison populations, for example, simply cannot be answered at present, and we have been bound by the Soviet regime on what data should be released in what forms to the public domain. It is hoped that, as scholars use this handbook, additional variables will be proposed and less useful ones may, perhaps, be deleted. Our task is the building of a systematic data base, and we hope that we have helped to advance that process.

Looking through the handbook will, it is hoped, lead the reader to inquiry along interesting lines and suggest further directions that research might take. For example, in several sections of the book there are data given for urban as opposed to rural residence. Taken together, they form a picture of several dimensions of rural life as compared with urban. That picture, which is presented in the following section, led to the following conclusion: The urban/rural gap actually seemed to be widening or narrowing with respect to certain of the variables. These facts suggest that certain theoretical concepts might be relevant here. The theoretical investigations of political development, modernization, and the cleavages that emerge during these processes seem to apply to the Soviet case as to other political systems. We shall regard as evidence of a potential for cleavage the reappearance of the same relative position across a series of dimensions. The urban/rural gap represents one area in which these theoretical considerations amplify and illuminate the data, and this is discussed in the next section.

Similarly, the data provide interesting breakdowns for males and females. If one compares the standing of women for these variables and then compares that to the proportion of women in the population, given in Chapter I, "Demography," some interesting paths open up for the researcher. As will be discussed in the next section of this chapter, in terms of education, women are represented both at the secondary and higher level roughly as they are in the population—a position of equality matched nowhere else in the world. However, on other variables, a different, less favorable representation is typical. Here again, one is led by the data to inquire into other ways in which the status of women could be investigated. In the next section, we add to the data information on mobility, occupational preference, political participation, and style and quality of life.

Finally, in every section but the one on international interactions, data are available for the union republic level. Here one might investigate the importance of interregional differences in Soviet society, for the subnational data allow the researcher to compare behavior over time along economic, cultural, and political dimensions. The possibility further opened up for analysis of regions in the USSR. Do the republics behave similarly or differently for different variables? Are some favored and others deprived? Are groups of republics emerging that could be important for a consideration of the integration of the country as a whole? These are the kinds of questions which the data suggest, and we have chosen the statistical technique of cluster analysis to test these hypotheses.

URBAN/RURAL CLEAVAGES

The Soviet Union has accomplished the most rapid movement of population from the countryside to the city. As Warren Eason notes: "The proportion of the labor force in agricultural occupations declined to below 50 percent in the course of three decades in the Soviet Union, but took four decades for Sweden, five for the United States, six for Japan, and ten for France."[3]

At present 43.7 percent of the Soviet population is rural. This compares with the communist countries of Eastern Europe as follows: Rumania's rural inhabitants made up 59.9 percent of the population in 1968; Hungary, 55.4 percent in 1969; Czechoslovakia, 52.4 percent in 1961; Bulgaria, 49 percent in 1968; Poland, 48.7 percent in 1969. An exception is East Germany, with 28.3 percent rural in 1959. In this range, too, are some of the Soviet Union's neighbors: Finland, with 50 percent rural in 1969; Norway, with 57.2 percent rural in 1968; and Denmark, with 53.7 percent rural in 1966. Sweden differs markedly with 22.6 percent rural in 1965.[4]

Data from this collection show some very interesting trends that might significantly affect the potential for an urban/rural cleavage in the Soviet Union.[5] We have comparative urban/rural data for population proportion; rural housing space built as a percentage of total housing space built; differences between rural and urban telephones per 1,000; numbers of rural offices of communications; and rural movie attendance as a percentage of total movie attendance. Figure 1 shows these data interpreted as rates of change. The unbroken black line represents the average annual decrease in the rural population as a percentage of the total population. If we compare the slopes of the rates of change of all of these factors in Figure 1, we discover that in many ways life in the country is becoming qualitatively inferior to that in the cities at a rate that is faster than that at which the population is leaving for the cities, thus suggesting that the Soviet pattern of development favors the city,

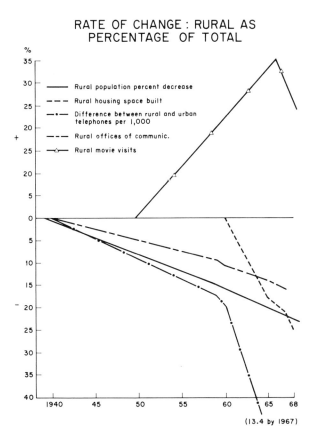

RATE OF CHANGE : RURAL AS
PERCENTAGE OF TOTAL

in contrast to that of China, which favors the countryside. An urban/rural gap could be conceived of as an absolute difference, expressed, for example, in rubles. Or it could be pictured as a relative relationship, expressed in terms of a percentage difference. For our study, the absolute difference between city and countryside will be of less importance than the position of the country-side relative to that of the city and the trends that might indicate either a convergence or a widening gap. In order to investigate this potential for cleavage we shall bring into our investigation additional evidence taken from Soviet studies of rural communities mainly around Novosibirsk, where the most sophisticated sociological research is carried out. We shall examine the following dimensions of cleavage: educational attainment, educational aspira-tions, occupational preferences, leisure time, and mobilization.

OPPORTUNITY FOR EDUCATION

In the modern world, education and occupation are the key determinants of social position. In fact, insofar as an increasingly complex economic and political system demands experts with specialized training and skills, educa-tion becomes the basic underlying factor in the allocation of occupations and, therefore, of social status.[6] Are the rural resident's chances for getting an adequate education relatively slimmer than those of the urban resident? If we find that they are, then we may expect that the rural person will be, practically speaking, disqualified from occupational advancement to a considerable de-gree. As the table providing data on level of education attained shows, in 1939, although the rural population represented 67.1 percent of the entire population, 33.2 percent of the entire number of persons with secondary education were rural. By 1959, the rural population had diminished to 52.1 percent of the population, and 37.3 percent of the persons with secondary education were rural.[7] Thus, whereas in 1939 about five out of every ten rural residents had a chance to complete high school, by 1959 the rural resi-dent's chances for secondary education had advanced to about seven in ten. Secondary school enrollment figures for 1965 show an essentially similar relationship.[8] Rural chances for higher education also improved, but, as might be expected, not as dramatically as those for secondary education. The policy is clearly to press for improvement beginning with the lower grades first. In 1939, 18 percent of those with higher education were rural; by 1959, the percentage was 16.1 percent. In terms of rural chances for completion of higher education, about one out of four could reach it by 1939, and one out of three by 1959.

It is interesting to compare rural/urban differences of another highly de-veloped industrial society, the United States. Do the same problems occur, and might they relate to processes of development? First, it is important to note a difference of definition as to what constitutes rural or urban. For the Soviet Union, as Henry Morton points out in his introduction to Chapter V, the definition of urban tends to be fairly elastic. By the criteria of the 1959 census, the term urban is applied to an officially designated town or city (varying in size, depending on republic, from 5,000 to 12,000) or settlement of an urban type, with from 1,000 to 3,000 inhabitants. In the 1926 and 1939 censuses, this urban settlement had to have no fewer than 500 in-habitants, and more than half of the labor force had to be engaged in nonagricultural pursuits. The United States Bureau of the Census uses two different definitions: In some cases, distinctions are drawn between metropolitan and nonmetropolitan, and, in some cases, between farm and nonfarm. We shall use the farm/nonfarm definition in which the farm population is defined as "all persons living in rural territory on places of 10 or more acres if as much as $50 worth of agricultural products were sold from the place in the reporting year. It also includes those living on places of under 10 acres if as much as $250 worth of agricultural products were sold from the place in the reporting year."[9] In 1960 the farm population represented only 8.7 percent of the total American population, and in 1970 that figure had been reduced to 4.8 percent. The Soviet definition of rural population is not directly comparable to the definition used by the U.S. Census Bureau for the farm population. We might compare the Soviet rural population with the American nonmetropolitan population: 43.7 percent (for the Soviet Union) to 35.1 percent (for the United States) in 1970. However, this comparison is not apropriate, since the definition of nonmetropolitan involves proximity to a city of 50,000 or more inhabitants; thus, "nonmetropolitan" would probably be more urbanized than Soviet "rural." Another type of comparison would involve, for the Soviet Union, agricultural labor as a percentage of the civilian labor force: This figure was 33.1 percent for 1968. The American equivalent, farmers and farm laborers as a percentage of the civilian labor force, was 3.5 percent in 1968.

In 1970, in the United States, about 40 percent of the farm population over age 25 had completed high school, as compared with 55.2 percent of the total population.[10] Thus, American farm residents had slightly more unequal chances to complete high school than did urban residents, and they were somewhat less than half as likely to have completed higher education. More obvious evidence of a gap in educational attainment for the United States comes from a white/black comparison. In 1970, blacks represented about 11 percent of the American population; and in the age group of 25 and over, they represented 6.3 percent of all those with high school education, and 3.9 percent of all those with higher education. This means that six out of ten blacks are likely to have completed secondary education by 1970, and only one out of three is likely to have completed higher education.[11] Comparisons between the Soviet Union and the United States should, of course, bear in mind the large numerical difference between the rural sectors of these countries. In spite of this difference, however, it does seem that both the United States and the Soviet Union have more or less established rural/urban parity for secondary education, although not, as yet, for higher education.

The educational attainment of the rural resident may well relate to the prior question of motivation and aspiration. It is generally true, at least for the Soviet Union and the United States, that the lower the social position, the more limited the aspiration for advancement.[12] Work done by innovating Soviet sociologists in Novosibirsk province in the Russian Republic tends to support this finding. A recent study by Ivanova of seven towns in Novosibirsk province tried to assess the kinds of desires parents have for their children's educational futures. She found that only 11 percent of the families interviewed felt that their children should limit their education to the required eight years. The picture changed strikingly in regard to higher education: Among the various kinds of workers including farmers, only 14 percent desired higher education for their children, but the figure for the rural intelligentsia (those with higher education) was fully 100 percent. However, this was obviously a particularly sensitive survey to conduct, and 40 to 42 percent of those questioned refused to answer.[13] Another study shows that there might well be a relationship between the low aspirations of peasant families and their children's leaving school. In a survey conducted among all the graduates of secondary schools in Novosibirsk province in 1963 to 1965, the noted sociologist Shubkin found that 69 percent of the graduates of city schools go on to higher education, although only 49 percent of the rural graduates do so. He concluded that motivation for continuing education was closely associated with place of residence—urban or rural.[14] A related study polled those who had little education and preferred not to continue in school. This study, which was conducted in several towns of the Russian Republic, found that about half of those who left school, most of them women, cited family reasons or too many obligations to be able to go to school. About a third simply felt no stimulus to continue their education.[15]

The problem of lower motivation and lack of stimulus for further education is one that seriously affects farm youth in the United States as well. In 1963, the National Committee for Children and Youth sponsored a conference on "Problems of Rural Youth in a Changing Environment." The results of the papers presented supported the findings of previous, less complete studies: American farm children lag well behind urban children in their educational aspirations.[16] Also supported was Rogoff's study which found that high school students from rural communities (defined as under 2,500) were much less likely to have plans for college than were those who attended school in larger communities.[17] One of the papers presented at the conference reported a statewide study of Wisconsin high school seniors. The table below shows the urban/rural differences:[18]

Plan on Further Education		*Plan on College Education*
From farms	37%	21%
From villages	44%	28%
From cities	50%	37.4%

The conclusion emerged that "clearly rural life seems to be associated with limited educational perspectives."[19] Further findings suggested that "rural boys expect to enter blue-collar occupations (including farming) to a much greater extent than urban boys, whose choices are predominantly in the white-collar group," and that "the proportion of farm boys aspiring to the professional occupations is considerably lower than for village boys (24 percent and 34 percent, respectively), and both are markedly lower than for urban boys (48 percent)."[20]

In the Soviet Union as in the United States, it is obvious that the rural pupil's inferior economic conditions significantly affect his motivation to continue his schooling. Shubkin, in his study of Novosibirsk high school graduating classes, explored the relationship between life plans of the students and the father's occupation. Table 1 summarizes his findings. If one divides these results by urban/rural residence, it can be seen that the rural children, those from families of both the rural intelligentsia and the agricultural workers, have a much higher percentage of those wishing to work or to work and study simultaneously, and the urban residents have far fewer in these categories. A related study conducted in Ufa in 1965 showed that the rural student must, to a much greater degree than his urban counterpart, acquire supplementary funds to continue studying. Some 47 percent of the students

Table 1. FATHER'S OCCUPATION AND CHILDREN'S ASPIRATIONS

	Percentage of children desiring to		
	Work	Work and Study	Study
Urban Intelligentsia	2	5	93
Rural Intelligentsia	11	13	76
Workers in Industry and Construction	11	6	83
Agricultural Personnel	10	14	76
Personnel in Service Occupations	9	15	76

Source: V. N. Shubkin, in Kolichestvennye metody v sotsiologii, Moscow, 1966. Cited in Shlyapentokh, p. 118.

from peasant background had to get additional money by working while studying; only 38 percent of those from urban workers' families and 22 percent of those from urban employees' families had to manage this additional obligation.[21] The rural student coming into the urban setting for his schooling cannot, obviously, rely on the assistance of his family, as can his urban counterpart.

In the Wisconsin study cited earlier, it was found that 50 percent of the students whose families ranked in the top one-third economically and socially were planning on a college education, and only 21 percent from families in the bottom two-thirds had such plans. Further, about 20 percent of the farm students come from the families which ranked high economically and socially, and 29 percent of the village and 38 percent of the urban students came from this rank. The study concludes that "we may infer that the lower socioeconomic status of the farm village students may help to account for their lower educational aspirations."[22] "Variables related to the socioeconomic and educational level of the student's family are among the most powerful determinants of educational and occupational perspectives. Each is significantly related to college plans and on every one of them the rural students rank well below urban students in the Wisconsin study."[23]

As in the Soviet Union, not only is the economic status of the rural family apt to be lower than that of the urban, but the whole educational climate is apt to be inferior. The rural child will be likely to have parents whose educational attainment is inferior to that of urban counterparts; it will be more difficult for the rural child to discuss his educational plans with and receive encouragement for them from his family. In the school, too, rural children have a peer group environment in which fewer plan to go to college. And, in fact, in most rural areas educational facilities are inferior to those in urban areas. In the Soviet Union, too, we find that about 40 percent of the peasant children begin their education in rural schools where educational facilities are distinctly inferior to their urban counterparts. Teachers, according to a recent Soviet study, have fewer qualifications in rural areas than in urban ones. In the large Russian Republic, as the following table shows, teachers with higher education were rather more characteristic of urban schools than of rural ones. And, in three-quarters of the urban school system, the directors had higher education; in only one-third of the rural schools were there such directors. The author also spoke of shortages of textbooks and technical equipment.[24]

It is estimated that roughly 30 percent of the peasant children in the Soviet Union terminate their education before the eighth or seventh grades.[25] This is well below the degree of educational opportunity offered the urban worker's

Table 2. Percentage of Teachers with Higher Education in the Russian Republic, by Grade, 1964–1965

	1-4 Grades	5-8 Grades	8-11 Grades
Rural	1.4	38.8	81.3
Urban	5.9	73.9	93.6

Source: N. M. Chasovnikova, "Selskoe Uchitelstvo i evo rol v likvidatsii razlichy mezhdu gorodom i derevnei," Sotsialno-politicheskoe, kulturnoe razvitie sotsialisticheskovo obshchestva, Moscow, 1969, p. 179.

or urban employee's child. As a recent Western study observed, two-thirds of the high school graduates from families of the urban intelligentsia enter institutions of higher education, only one-third from families of urban workers, and one-tenth from rural families.[26] In Novosibirsk's prestigious technological institutes, rural students comprised 18 percent of the entrants between 1963 and 1966; urban students made up 57 percent. In Novosibirsk university, rural entrants made up only 5 percent of the total entering during those years.[27] But in that same province, between 1964 and 1966, 49.3 percent of the rural boys and 55.8 percent of the rural girls were continuing some form of schooling after the eighth grade. For urban boys and girls the figure for 1966 is 62 percent.[28]

Bringing up one's minorities or one's disadvantaged is always a problem for any society. One solution to the problem of parity of educational attainment might involve a system of lowered entrance standards for certain elements of the population or favorable quotas. In the Soviet Union, rural residents do enjoy a certain preference in agricultural and pedagogical institutes, but it is not expected that the class composition of the institutions of higher learning will be substantially changed.[29] In 1961, in fact, "only one-third of the students admitted to higher agricultural institutions were of peasant origin."[30] Another solution would involve expansion to meet the needs of those competing for places; this would involve roughly a 20 percent expansion for Soviet institutions of higher education. According to the president of the Soviet Educational and Scientific Workers Union, however, universal higher education will not be a national goal, since only positions available in the national economy should govern college admission.[31]

The resultant squeeze between competitors and places has been called, in Shubkin's words, "a tragedy." He sees as a result that young people fill up faculties where there are places after the "prestige" places have already been taken. Thus, students take on specialized study when they have no motivation for the field itself. In some cases, when youths cannot enter an institution of higher learning at all, they do nothing for a year until they can once again compete for a place. According to Shubkin, the number of these idlers reaches "tens of thousands."[32] What happens to those in the former group, who go into any field of study where they can find an opening, can be seen in a survey conducted recently among 3,000 young engineers at 37 Leningrad factories of the machine-building, chemicals, food, and other light industries. The survey found that only 40 percent of the respondents had an interest in the specialty for which they entered the higher educational institution. Further, about 50 percent admitted that they entered "this or that educational institution not by reason of the anticipated vocation, but only from the desire to receive any kind of higher education."[33]

The question of motivation is clearly an important one, for those students with low motivation who fill up the places in the agricultural institutes often leave the rural areas as soon as possible. There is obvious concern among rural sociologists in the Soviet Union about this problem, and one of the most interesting studies in this regard came from the sociology section of Tartu State University in Estonia. Students conducted an extensive survey among the students and recent graduates of the Estonian Agricultural Academy to determine what motivated their choice of profession and what factors governed their decisions to remain in or leave the rural environment. It should be remembered, however, that Estonia is the republic which had the smallest rural population, 31.2 percent, in 1967.[34] In the survey, a total of 712 students and graduates were interviewed, and one of the principal findings concerning motivation was that, among males, unquestionably the strongest motive was a combination of two aims: to receive some kind of higher education and, by going into agriculture, to reduce the amount of time required in military service.[35]

OCCUPATIONAL PREFERENCES

An impression of the social mobility opportunities for rural families depends on which occupations are considered desirable or undesirable. Notions of upward social mobility are not necessarily congruent cross-nationally, since different political systems may have different judgments concerning desirability or undesirability. In both the United States and the Soviet Union, however, there is evidence that agricultural jobs are ranked relatively low. In an American study, when major occupational groups were broken down into eleven groups, farmers and farm managers ranked eighth and farm laborers and foremen ranked ninth. Below them were only private-household workers and laborers, excluding farm and mine laborers.[36] The Soviet sociologist Shubkin, in his study of graduating classes in high schools of Novosibirsk province, asked his subjects to rank and award grades to occupations, with the more attractive ones receiving the higher grades. Table 3 gives the result of this survey. Note that agriculture and service are definitely the least attractive of the occupations; science is more than twice as attractive. The anomalous position of biology probably reflects the high risk of maintaining political orthodoxy and the memory of Lysenko's thoroughly politicized rule of that science.

Table 3. OCCUPATIONAL PREFERENCES OF HIGH SCHOOL STUDENTS

Occupations Requiring Higher Qualifications	Grade	Occupations Requiring Average or Minimal Qualifications	Grade
Physics	7.69	Transport and Communications	5.28
Mathematics	7.50	Industry	4.26
Medicine	7.32	Construction	4.07
Chemistry	7.23	Agriculture	3.75
Geology	6.84	Service (salesman, etc.)	2.63
History	6.17		
Philosophy	6.05		
Economics	5.52		
Biology	4.66		

Source: V. N. Shubkin, cited in Shlyapentokh, p. 122.

From further research, it turns out that in fact agricultural occupations are heavily, in some cases predominantly, recruited from the rural population itself. Thus, those jobs ranked by today's youth as least attractive are virtually reserved for rural youth. The medical profession, higher in prestige, draws more from workers' families. The sociologist Mamaeva found the following backgrounds for rural professionals: [37]

| | Percentage of Total | | |
	Rural Teachers	Rural Doctors	Agricultural Specialists
From workers' families	30	40	3
From peasants' families	54	36	90

Conversely, it seems, from studies done by Novosibirsk sociologists, that aspirations tend to reflect the actual distribution of occupations. One example of this kind of "rural perpetuation syndrome" can be found in research conducted from 1963 to 1966 in Novosibirsk province. [38] Girls and boys were asked to rank the profession of teacher according to its attractiveness to them among other occupations. The results are given below:

	Rank	Description
Rural girls	2– 4th places	Very attractive
Urban girls	20–24th places	Adequately attractive
Rural boys	32–38th places	Unattractive
Urban boys	37–39th places	Unattractive

The results of this survey correspond to the actual composition of that profession. In the academic year of 1964–1965, 69 percent of the school teachers in the Soviet Union were women, and they formed 87 percent of the teachers in primary schools. It is important that although the profession of teacher may be highly rated in certain cultures, in the Soviet Union it is unattractive to and underpopulated by males, and in rural areas it is recruited largely from among females of rural background.

It is even more revealing of the limited aspirations of rural youth that the standard of living of rural school teachers, the profession considered extremely desirable by rural girls, is far below that of their urban counterparts. In spite of the striking relative deprivation of the rural school teacher, the peasant girl considers that profession the most desirable she can attain. Research conducted in 1966 compared urban with rural teachers according to the presence or absence of three types of material welfare: (1) income for a single individual in a family exceeding 51 rubles; (2) living space for a single individual exceeding 9 square meters; and (3) the presence of communal amenities. Table 4 shows vividly the relative deprivation of the rural school teachers.

The same tendency for rural boys to aspire to low-status occupations is observable in the United States. Of the rural boys in the Wisconsin study, 21 percent aspired to higher prestige occupations, whereas the figure was 37 percent for urban boys. [39]

In fact, it has been observed in the United States that the "rural perpetua-

Table 4. Rural/Urban Standards of Living for Teachers
(Novosibirsk Oblast)

		Urban	Rural
		Percentage of Total Number of Teachers	
Group I	(have all 3 types of material welfare)	15	3
Group II	(have any 2 of the 3 types of material welfare)	42	19
Group III	(have only 1 type of material welfare)	30	28
Group IV	(have none of the 3 types of material welfare)	10	45

Source: L. Borisova, cited in Shlyapentokh, p. 136.

tion syndrome" is characteristic of the rural population. At the national conference on rural youth cited earlier, in studies of Iowa, Michigan, and Wisconsin, it was observed that 40 percent of the high school senior farm boys wanted or expected to farm, even though only about 1 out of every 16 farm boys could expect to become actually established as a farm operator.[40] Further, in spite of obvious sacrifices in income and prestige, farm boys hesitated to leave the countryside: "Many farm boys say they are willing to become farmers even when it would mean a considerable financial loss as compared to taking a nonfarm job. Some of the nonmonetary values preferred more often by those who plan to farm are: out-of-doors work, physical activity, work with machines and tools, work in the local community, and contact with people and a relative dislike for change."[41] Parallel to these findings is the research of Tartu State University, in which it was found that of those who were students of or recent graduates from the Estonian Agricultural Academy, the most important reasons for choosing agriculture were the desire to live in the countryside, the variety of the work, the specialty, and the possibility of engaging in gardening, hunting, and fishing. Of all the respondents, 75 percent thought wages were important but certainly not decisive, and 23 percent thought wages played no noticeable role.[42]

What may be observable here, both for the American and the Soviet rural populations, is the likelihood that those with initiative, potential, and adventurousness are those who tend to leave the countryside, thus leaving behind the ones who are more cautious and less innovative. In the American study of farm youth cited earlier, this hypothesis was confirmed:

> The Michigan study, conducted in a good agricultural county in the midst of an industrial economy, showed, among other things, that farm boys tended to be lower in measured intelligence, more tied to relatives and to the local area, and lower in faith in their own ability to influence events than were nonfarm boys.
>
> The same investigation also showed that farm boys who do not plan to farm are more adventurous, more independent, have more control over their behavior, and have greater character stability than those who plan to farm.[43]

In the Estonian study, it was found that the most important factors in choosing the profession of agronomist stemmed from problems of family and place of residence.[44] As in the American studies, it is obvious that upward mobility for the rural youth means loss of the psychic rewards associated with family and native locale, for migration to the city results in the loss of those supportive elements. When questioned about what made rural life unpleasant, the Estonian respondents placed in the first six places the following factors: poor quality of labor force, absence of summer vacation, low level of mechanization in farm work, long working day, lack of transportation facilities, and poor living quarters.[45] In spite of these factors, the more conservative will, undoubtedly, choose to remain in the countryside.

Perhaps it could be argued that the rural resident, although he is relatively isolated, is fully compensated by exposure to bucolic tranquility and escape from the strains of urban life. Certainly some of the evidence given above might suggest this. In fact, the picture is far from tranquil for the Soviet peasant, at least. A very interesting study of leisure time revealed great differences between the urban and rural populations. The average urban male worker has about 4.9 hours per day of leisure time. The male collective farmer has only 2.25 hours a day of leisure time, less than half as much as his urban counterpart. Soviet sources attribute this large difference to the hours of intensive labor that the farmers put in on their private plots. Even if this is the case, it is nonetheless true that the proceeds of the private plot are considered by the peasant not as a luxury, but rather as a vital form of subsistence.[46] His wages are considerably lower than those of the urban industrial worker; as of 1965, the collective farmer received only 44 percent of an urban industrial worker's annual wages.[47] By 1967, that proportion had increased to 48.1 percent.[48] Although it is considerably less, some disparity of income does exist in the United States for farm families. In 1970, the median income of farm families was about 72 percent of the national mean income; the income for black families and families of other minority races was about 70 percent of the national mean. In 1970, the median income for all families was $9,867; for farm residents it was $6,773; and for blacks and those of other minority races, it was $6,516.[49] Thus the farm median income is approximately 69 percent of the national median income.

URBAN/RURAL DIFFERENCES IN MOBILIZATION

Another source of potential urban/rural cleavage is the very different pattern of mobilization. Participation of the rural inhabitant is well below that of the urban inhabitant for several indicators of the impact of mobilization. As a result, relative to the urban population, the rural population is rather isolated. Soviet sources maintain that newspaper circulation, for example, is available to the rural inhabitant at an unprecedented scale. In 1955, approximately 38 million newspapers and journals were distributed to the countryside; by 1966, that figure had more than doubled, reaching 77 million newspapers and journals.[50] Readership studies, however, indicate that the rural inhabitant is considerably behind his urban counterpart as an audience for newspapers and the mass media. Thus, comparisons between urban and rural circulation reveal that in 1967 less than a third of the national magazine and journal circulation figure (23.8 million out of a total 82.3 million) came from the countryside. Further, in the cities of Leningrad and Moscow, 1,500 magazines and newspapers were purchased for every 1,000 persons in 1967; for the rural areas the figure was 820 per 1,000 persons.[51] A Soviet study of sources of information about foreign news showed that the collective farmers represented the occupational group most infrequently using radio or television.[52] One additional measure of isolation might be the degree to which urban Soviet citizens are unaware of the quality of life and the demands and the dilemmas of the Soviet countryside. A very impressive readership study of the national newspaper, *Izvestia,* revealed that "the reader of *Izvestia* . . . is very poorly informed about the life of the rural population: The percentage refusing to answer the question 'Does the newspaper illuminate sufficiently the life of the collective farm and state farm workers?' reached forty-six."[53] Thus, almost half of the entire sample interviewed had nothing to say on this direct question. Still another indicator of the relative isolation of the peasants is their participation in the *rabselkor* organization. Rabselkor is the volunteer contributor to newspapers, and the government sponsors a vigorous program to elicit public contribution to newspapers. In a study conducted by the Sverdlov oblast Party committee, it was found that only about one-fifth of the volunteer reporter corps was made up of workers and collective farmers; fully 63 percent were engineering-technical personnel.[54]

Perhaps the most important agencies for eliciting mass participation are the Young Communist League, or Komsomol, and the Trade Unions. Table 5 shows the degree to which the rural community is underrepresented in these agencies. Compare the percentage of membership to the percentage of the population, given in Eason's Table 4, and the shortcomings of the national campaign for mass participation become clear.[55] A recent study by a Soviet sociologist in speaking about certain of the mass media and their impact on the population, announced that "More than half of the population does not watch television and does not go to the theater, one-tenth practically doesn't read newspapers, one-fourth [practically doesn't read] magazines, one-fifth [practically doesn't read] books, one-sixth does not listen to radio and does not go to the movies. . . ."[56]

Table 5. URBAN/RURAL DIFFERENCES IN MASS ORGANIZATIONS, 1967

	Komsomol Members		Trade Union Members	
	Number (in millions)	Percentage	Number (in millions)	Percentage
Rural	8	34	15	17
Urban	15	66	71	83

Source: N. Vasilev, "Vedushchaya sila kollektiva," Selskaya partynaya organizatsia, Moscow (1970), p. 13.

One important variable seems to be level of education. In 1959, persons with higher education constituted 4.3 percent of the population over twenty. Yet, they formed 39 percent of the readers of *Pravda,* 47 percent of the readers of *Izvestia,* 73 percent of the readers of *Literary Gazette,* and 25 percent of the readers of *Trud,* the trade union newspaper.[57] Here, too the rural population would rank below the urban population in readership.

PERSPECTIVES AND SOLUTIONS

In a curious way, both American and Soviet studies of the urban/rural gap point to similar policy recommendations. One noted Soviet sociologist warned that the rural world will fall further and further behind unless four courses of action are taken immediately: First, measures must be taken to improve rural schools; second, there must be special schools which can reveal gifted children and thus guarantee them a higher education; third, special preparatory sections must be created at the institutions of higher education; and fourth, effective methods must be found for testing and distinguishing abilities of young people at the same stages of development.[58] American sociologists, too, identify the youth as a crucial element in the closing of the urban/rural gap, and the study of rural youth cited earlier concludes:

> From all of the evidence it seems quite apparent that the rural students, particularly the farm students, are less academically oriented, somewhat less able, and considerably less convinced of the value of higher education than urban students. Consequently they have taken fewer of the steps which are necessary for college entrance, such as following of the college preparatory curriculum, giving consideration to colleges, and applying for scholarships, than the urban students.[59]

The authors recommend improving rural schools, instituting special programs informing rural youth and their parents about educational and occupational opportunities, identifying talent as early as possible, and providing financial assistance.[60] The recommendations are strikingly similar; only the scale and scope of the solutions must differ markedly to moderate for the Soviet Union, a relatively inferior quality of life affecting over 40 percent of the population.

MALE/FEMALE CLEAVAGE

Another area in which we might assess the relative position of two groups in industrialized society is that of male/female differences. We shall be interested to see if women reappear in a relatively inferior position across a number of relevant variables, and if a potential for cleavage might be found. As noted earlier, the importance of education as an underlying determinant of social class cannot be overemphasized. Table 6 compares the relation between females as a percentage of the population and as a percentage of the enrollment in institutions of higher education. The gap between these two percentages is smallest in Finland, followed by Bulgaria, Hungary, Rumania, the USSR, and the United States. The performance of the socialist countries of Eastern Europe, considering their overall level of economic development, appears, on this variable, at least, to be superior to that of the older systems of Western Europe. Further, women as a percentage of students in higher technical educational establishments make the Soviet Union by far the world leader, with 30.8 percent; whereas Czechoslovakia has 17.2 percent; Poland, 15.9 percent; and the German Democratic Republic, 8.6 percent. The United States has 0.8 percent; U.K., 0.9 percent; Italy, 6.2 percent; Finland, 7.6 percent; Sweden, 4.9 percent; and Denmark, 3.9 percent.[61]

One would expect educational preparation to be closely linked with choice of occupation, as it generally seems to be in the modern world. Women form a large part of the Soviet labor force; they make up 48 percent, with only 18 percent of the able-bodied age group of women neither studying nor working.[62] Soviet women made up 73 percent of all doctors in the Soviet Union in 1966, and 70 percent of all teachers in primary, incomplete secondary, and

Table 6. FEMALES AS A PERCENTAGE OF POPULATION AND OF ENROLLMENT IN HIGHER EDUCATION, 1965

	USSR	US[a]	UK	SWEDEN	NORWAY	DENMARK
Percentage of Population	54.1[c]	51.1	51.3[b]	50	50.2	50.4
Percentage of Enrollment in Higher Educational Institutions	44.4	40.6	39	36[c]	24	36

	FINLAND	ITALY	BULGARIA	CZECHOSLOVAKIA	GDR	HUNGARY
Percentage of Population	51.7[d]	51.0	50.0[b]	51.2[e]	54.2[b]	51.7[b]
Percentage of Enrollment in Higher Educational Institutions	49	36	46[c]	38[c]	35	44[c]

	POLAND	RUMANIA	YUGOSLAVIA
Percentage of Population	51.5[d]	51.0	51.3[f]
Percentage of Enrollment in Higher Educational Institutions	39[c]	42[c]	37[c]

Notes:
a 1970
b 1966
c 1967
d 1964
e 1961
f 1960

Sources: United Nations Statistical Yearbook for 1969, Louvain, 1970, pp. 268-272.
United Nations Demographic Yearbook, for appropriate years.
Nadezhda Tatarinova, Women in the USSR, Moscow, [n.d.], p. 17.

secondary schools in that year.[63] In the United States, 36.7 percent of the labor force is made up of women,[64] and of young women, aged 20 to 24, 57 percent were in the labor force in 1969, and 34 percent were keeping house as their major activity.[65]

There has been considerable investigation, among Soviet specialists, of the 18 percent of the female population that can be classified as housewives. It is customary to exhort that sector to enter the labor force and turn over child-rearing duties to state agencies. However, a recent Soviet study has sought to found these discussions on a scientific basis. The study observed, first, that the percentage of the female population engaged solely in household activities was falling. Thus, in 1960, it was 80 percent of the 1955 figure; in 1965, it was 53 percent of the figure for 1960.[66] Level of education also seemed to play an important role: Among those women engaged exclusively in household activities, the number of those with only primary education or unfinished high school education was higher than the average for Soviet urban residents; the number with higher education among the housewives was lower than the Soviet urban average.[67] Although some women were not in the labor force because of illness or invalidism, the majority of housewives did not work because of their child-rearing duties.[68] The study concludes with the recommendation that this category of women should not be drawn into the labor force because they are at present more effective child rearers than is the state. It would, claimed the study, be "economically irrational" for the state to spend the necessary amounts of money for the construction of preschool facilities and to provide them with the requisite number of service personnel, for this expenditure would far outweigh any contribution that the housewife-mothers could make to the labor force.[69]

But two cautionary notes should be sounded before the relative position of women in terms of occupational status is assessed. First, the occupations in which women form the majority may not represent occupations of prestige or desirability. For example, there is some evidence to suggest that teaching ranks low in the evaluation of Soviet youth.[70] Second, within the category of occupation, do women tend to be excluded from positions of power and managerial authority, and are they overrepresented at junior, subordinate levels? Table 7 shows how women are represented among all specialists with higher education. Table 8, however, shows the level at which scientific personnel are employed by the degree they hold. "Candidate of Science" is roughly equal to the American Ph.D.; "Doctor of Sciences" is a degree conferred after considerable contribution to the profession, and it has no American equivalent. As can be seen, women are underrepresented at the higher levels and overrepresented at the lower levels of scientific personnel. Statistics show that in the United States, women received 13.1 percent of the doctoral degrees granted in 1968; this represents about a 1 percent a year increase from 1966.[71] Table 9 shows the distribution of women with Ph.D.'s according to academic rank. Here, too, women are concentrated at the lower levels. In fact, there has, in the United States, been a decline since 1940 in the proportion of women among college and university faculties. In 1940, they were 28 percent; in 1930, 27 percent; and in 1920, 26 percent. The figure for 1965 to 1966 is shown on Table 9: 18.4 percent.[72]

In the Soviet Union, women form a significant portion of the agricultural

Table 7. WOMEN EMPLOYED IN SKILLED AND HIGHLY SKILLED JOBS IN THE SOVIET UNION, 1965 (Percentage)

	Percentage of Women among Specialists with a Higher Education
Engineers	30
Agronomists, livestock breeders, and veterinary personnel	39
Economists and statisticians, planners	60
Physicians and other medical personnel	73
Teachers, librarians and other workers in culture and education	67

Source: Nadezhda Tatarinova, Women in the USSR, Moscow, [n.d.], p. 50.

Table 8. SCIENTIFIC WORKERS IN THE USSR, YEAR-END, 1967

	Total Number (Thousands)	Number of Women (Thousands)	Women as Percentage of Total
Number of scientific workers	796.6	294.9	38.3
Including those with the academic degree of:			
Doctor of Sciences	18.3	2.2	12.0
Candidate of Sciences	169.3	45.4	26.8
From the total number of scientific workers those with the academic titles of:			
Academician, corresponding member, professor	14.7	1.3	8.8
Reader	56.9	11.6	20.2
Senior scientific worker	32.4	9.0	27.8
Junior scientific worker and assistant	46.3	22.9	49.5

Sources: Data for total figures from: SSSR v tsifrakh, 1967, Moscow, 1968, p. 130. Data for numbers of women from: Women in the Soviet Union: Statistical Returns, Moscow, 1970, p. 44.

Table 9. WOMEN PROFESSORS WITH PH.D.'S, BY RANK, 1965–1966, IN THE
UNITED STATES

	Women As Percentage Of Total
Professors	8.7
Associate Professors	15.1
Assistant Professors	19.4
Instructors	32.5
Total	18.4

Source: U.S. Department of Labor, Women's Bureau, 1969 Handbook on
Women Workers, Women's Bureau Bulletin 294, U.S.G.P.O., Washington,
D.C., 1969.

labor force. Norton Dodge notes that 57 percent of all collective farmers, 41 percent of all workers and employees on state farms, and 91 percent of all workers in private plot agriculture are women.[73] As seen in Table 7, women make up 39 percent of the agronomists, livestock breeders, and veterinary personnel with higher education. Their representation is lower with regard to the post of collective farm chairman. Of all collective farm chairmen, only about 1.7 percent are women.[74]

In both countries, we see incongruity between educational attainment and occupational rank. In spite of a background of higher education roughly equal to men's, women do seem to be excluded generally from positions of authority. On the basis of current information, it is difficult to assess social mobility trends in the USSR. One sociologist in the Novosibirsk area has observed, however, that evening and correspondence schools provide a good means for social mobility and that women make up only 20 percent of the students. In another Novosibirsk study, Arutiunyan found that in the least desirable occupational category (low-qualification physical work), a total of 25 percent of the workers were upwardly mobile; the mobility figure for women in this category, however, was only 5 percent.[75]

Are political channels open to women so that they may exercise civic authority and implement their aspirations? The political situation is obviously unfavorable to women. From 1926 through 1968, female membership in the Communist Party of the Soviet Union has grown at an average of 0.2 percent annually, and only 21.2 percent of the party is female. Further, the leadership of the mass "representative" organizations is reserved largely for men. There are no women in the position of first secretary in any republic Komsomol organization. There are no female first or second secretaries in the entire Estonian and Latvian republics, or in Tomsk, Kursk, Pskov, Orlov, or a host of other important organizations. In Ivanovo oblast, women make up 65 percent of the membership, but they occupy only 7 first secretaryships out of a total of 24; thus for that oblast the number of women in authority is roughly 30 percent lower than the number of women members.[76] In the trade unions, women occupy only 10 percent of the chairmanships of republic, oblast, and krai councils.[77]

Although women make up 33.7 percent of the deputies to the Supreme Soviets of the Union Republics and 28 percent of the deputies to the Supreme Soviet of the USSR elected in 1966,[78] they are generally absent from positions of managerial or directing power. A recent Soviet study of the executive committee of a soviet in a district in Leningrad examined the distribution of women according to level of function. Table 10 gives the results. At the national level there is only one female minister, the Minister of Culture, a

Table 10. EXECUTIVE COMMITTEE OF A LENINGRAD DISTRICT SOVIET

Groups	Women As Percentage Of Total
I Chairman, his deputies, and Secretary of the executive committee	
1962	24.9
1964	24.9
1966	24.9
II Directors and deputy directors of divisions, directors of sectors	
1962	63.1
1964	59.1
1966	40.0
III Specialists (instructors, inspectors, and others)	
1962	87.2
1964	82.2
1966	92.9
IV Clerical personnel	
1962	100.0
1964	100.0
1966	100.0

Source: V. G. Lebin and M. N. Perfilev, Kadry apparata upravlenia v USSR, Leningrad, 1970, p. 176.

typically female post. At the union-republic level, there is a total of 27 female ministers, probably less than 10 percent of the ministerial positions at that level.

Again, it is interesting to see if comparisons can be made with the United States. Only two women have filled a post in the cabinet since 1920.[79] In 1971, women made up 2.4 percent of the United States Congress, with 2.8 percent of the House of Representatives and 1 percent of the Senate. The percentage of women equalled that of blacks in each of the houses.[80] The percentage of women delegates to the 1952 Republican Convention ranged from 7.4 percent of the delegates from the South, to 16.5 percent of the delegates from the West, and the women as a percentage of the total number of delegates was 10.5. Women participated to a somewhat greater extent in the Democratic Convention of that year, representing 12.5 percent of the total. Again, the highest percentage of women was found among the delegates from the West, 21.6 percent, and the lowest from the Northeast, 7.8 percent, and the South, 10.3 percent.[81] In the U.S. Civil Service women are heavily concentrated in the lower ranks and underrepresented at the higher levels. At grades 01, 02, and 03, women form 69.4, 76.4, and 79.1 percent of the respective totals. At grades 16, 17, 18, and above 18, they make up 1.8, 1.5, 0.6, and 2.6 percent of the respective totals.[82] It is obvious from the data given above that in the United States a considerable distance must be traveled for women to achieve parity of political power. That they, as well as their Soviet counterparts, might not aspire to equal participation should not obscure the fact that a very real difference between men and women occurs along this dimension.

In the Soviet Union, the quality of life for women as a group marks them as distinct from men. The working Soviet woman must, on the average, spend 4.1 hours daily on household tasks, which is, after all, further work, while the working man spends only 1.4 hours daily on household tasks—about a third of the time a woman devotes to such work. The introduction of household appliances on a large scale might rectify the situation to some extent, but a study done in Pskov found that such mechanized assistance was available to only 3.4 percent of all of the families in that city, although the figure for

Moscow reached 20 percent. Thus, a truly massive investment in consumer durables would be necessary to equalize work patterns within a generation. As of now, however, women have only three hours of free time per day, while men have almost five.[83]

Some notion of the quality of life for Soviet women can be gleaned from the well known and very impressive work on family life done by Kharchev. He studied 1,000 divorce suits initiated in Leningrad in 1962. Kharchev gave the following reasons which women cited in initiating a divorce: drunkenness, 29%; crudity and cruelty, 27%; infidelity, 15%; and loss of feeling for husband, 12%. Much milder are the reasons given by men for initiating a divorce: incompatibility, 31%; loss of feeling for wife, 25%; infidelity, 16%; and love for another woman, 12%.[84]

Comparing the proportion of divorces to marriages for the Soviet Union and the United States, in 1960, divorces equalled 25.8 percent of the marriages for that year;[85] in the Soviet Union, as in the United States, there is considerable regional variation, with Latvia just under the American average, at 24.5 percent, closely followed by Estonia. The Russian Republic divorces average 16.8 percent of the marriages. Very low in divorces are the republics of the Caucasus and Central Asia, with the lowest rate in Tadzhikistan—3.8 percent of the marriages. The Soviet data are figured on an average of the years 1961 to 1965.[86]

Readership of newspapers and magazines is another area in which women rank below men. From a recent Soviet study that surveyed the reading habits of 2,308 workers and employees in the plants of the chemical industry in Leningrad in 1964 and 1965, it was observed that women are not as consistently readers of newspapers as are men. The findings are shown below:[87]

	Regular Readers	*Not Regular Readers*	*No Reading at All*	*Total*
Men	85.5%	11.3%	3.2%	100%
Women	61.0%	36.0%	3.0%	100%

No exactly comparable study has been done of American female workers, but American readership surveys do show that women in 1970 formed a large percentage of the total number of readers of national news magazines, with 43.4 percent of the readers of *Time*; 35.6 percent of the readers of *Newsweek*; 34.5 percent of the readers of *U.S. News and World Report*. They accounted for 47.9 percent of the readers of *Life*, and 45.1 percent of the readers of *Harper's* and *Atlantic*. Women were a much smaller proportion of the readers of business magazines, with 26.1 percent of the readers of *Fortune* and 23.1 percent of the readers of the *Wall Street Journal*. The high proportion of women mass media consumers was observed in a recent study of the "Division of Political Labor between Mothers and Fathers," in which it was noted that for the American couples studied, mass media behavior, as opposed to some of the other indices of politicization, provided the highest similarity between the spouses. In fact, what was characteristic was that there was considerable movement across the different types of political behavior assessed, so that a "wife who is distinctly inferior to her husband on matters of political knowledge may move to a status of equality with respect to media usage. Similarly, a husband who lags behind his wife on school affairs may be her equal in electoral endeavors."[88]

Whether this American pattern holds true for the Soviet Union cannot be determined until a parallel study is available. Certainly, for both systems, impressive gains have been made by women in attaining university education. The rapidity of these gains seems especially marked in the socialist countries, as shown in Table 6. However, significant disparities still exist both in the United States and in the Soviet Union in the degree to which women exercise professional and political power. In most of the variables touching on this dimension, women fail to achieve representation as they are represented in the population.

PUBLIC OPINION PROBES OF POTENTIAL CLEAVAGE

Perhaps the most important method of probing attitudinal cleavages among the population is the survey of public opinion. As noted earlier, Soviet sociologists are conducting interesting and valuable polls. However, one particularly important area of concern seems, most recently, to relate to attitudes towards the mass media, particularly in terms of salience and satisfaction with official news policies. According to the most innovative and creative sociologists in the Soviet Union, the year 1964, when the Brezhnev-Kosygin regime was installed, marked a turning point in elite recognition of the importance of public opinion. In the words of one prominent Soviet sociologist: "Our society after the 23rd Party congress, after the October Plenum of the Central Committee (1964), went a long way on the path toward liberation from subjectivism, voluntarism, bureaucratism—conditions hostile to the analysis of public opinion. And when individual sociologists consider the question about the importance of the study of public opinion as settled, they have in mind precisely these circumstances."[89] In their opinion, at least, the commitment of the new leadership is firm, even if it is not yet known how carefully circumscribed it will be. The sociologists cite another factor in the recent recognition of the importance of the study of mass attitudes; in 1964 the regime abolished limits on subscriptions to newspapers and journals, and circulation rapidly increased. For the first time, editorial staffs were forced to consider the ramifications of competing for readership.[90] Hence, it is in this area that many of the most important discussions of public opinion emerge.

Thus we begin to see the texture of Soviet public opinion as it emerges from the elite's own efforts to plumb the attitudes of its citizenry.[91] These efforts clearly involve, too, a differentiated approach to the various social strata of the country, with specialized probes conducted within the body of the Communist Party. I relate these projects to a new emphasis among the elite of the Party on optimality criteria for judging the efficacy of Party activity. In important new studies Party sociologists apply cost-benefit analysis to the arena of Party functions and thus begin to redefine the actual role of the Party itself. I have isolated concrete examples of political change resulting from public opinion research. One of the most significant of these is the emergence of the public opinion sociologist as "representative" of the configurations of the attitudes he studies and as the articulator of opinions calling for alteration of Party functions.

First, we will look at the impressive national newspaper surveys carried out between 1966 and 1969. There are gaps in the completeness with which they are reported, but they do provide significant insights into media attitudes. Although, for Americans, the 1969 Roper study reported that 59 percent of the population reported that they received most of their news from television, there is some contradictory evidence. A recent study based on a national probability sample found for *national* news programs, 20 percent of the sample could be classified as regular news viewers, and 80 percent as irregular or nonnews viewers. A W. R. Simmons poll in 1969 reported that 78 percent of the population reads the newspaper on an average weekday as opposed to 25 percent watching the evening *national* news. However, if *local* television newscasts are included, then, according to the Bogart Study (1968), television viewing increases to 60 percent watching newscasts on an average day, while newspaper reading was 78 percent.[92] Thus, although we have no directly comparable data for Soviet viewing habits, we may say as we will see below that, like Americans, Soviet citizens are highly likely to turn to the newspaper among the mass media, but that unlike Americans, they tend to provide a smaller audience for television viewing in general, and a much smaller proportion of that audience for programs providing directly political information.

For the Soviet Union, the preeminence of the newspaper as the mass medium most frequently used has not changed relative to radio and television, although the last two are continuing to expand. Newspapers are especially important as the primary source for political information. An important recent study of Leningrad television viewers found that for 70 percent of the sample, attention to that medium was relatively "depoliticized," that is, that they watched programs primarily for reasons of relaxation and entertainment.[93] Further, newspapers outrank other printed sources as principal providers of political information. In 1966 and 1967 Soviet sociologists carried out a pilot study, polling 500 foreign youths—between 50 and 100 for each of the following countries: German Democratic Republic, Czechoslovakia, Poland, United States, and France, during summer vacations at camps in the Soviet Union run by the youth tourist organization, Sputnik. The group's ages were from 19 to 25; females composed 60 percent of the group. The youths from the socialist countries are described as students from various higher educational institutions, "young engineering-technical intelligentsia," and personnel of youth organizations. The Americans were college and graduate students who were majoring in "social-economic specializations," Russian language, and history. The French were also described as students of higher technical institutions and "young technical intelligentsia." The results for foreign youths are compared to a study of Russian press patterns carried out in Leningrad in 1964 to 1965.[94] Table 11 presents the results of the survey. Although generalizations would be difficult to make concerning larger populations, the populations interviewed are hardly random or representative in the foreign cases; nonetheless, the very high attention to newspapers on the part of Soviet, American, and French youths stands in marked contrast to low attention in Czechoslovakia and Poland. Further, considering the high educational level and ambitious career expectations of the sample, the very low attention to printed sources on the part of the Poles and Czechoslovaks is extremely interesting. In every country except Czechoslovakia, the newspaper is the chief source of political information.

Table 11. Orientation of Youth to Information Differentiated by Type of Press (Percentage of Total Number Interviewed from Each Country)

Type of Press	USSR	East Germany	Czechoslovakia	Poland	USA	France
			Country			
Politics						
newspapers	100	70	37.2	45	98	100
magazines	41	14	67.2	30	93.5	32.5
books	25	4	43.1	20	84	45
Economics						
newspapers	67.7	70	65.6	40	86	63.6
magazines	37.5	30	70.6	40	84.1	54
books	12.5	4	29.4	30	67	63
Science						
newspapers	18.7	62	37.2	15	78	50
magazines	87.5	57	67.2	45	88.5	68
books	81.2	41	43	55	61	63
Culture, Art						
newspapers	62.5	45	58.7	20	73	50
magazines	81.2	14	67.3	35	86.3	59
books	68.7	30	26	40	84.1	54

Source: G. I. Khmara, "Pechat v sisteme massovykh kommunikatsy," Problemy Sotsiologii Pechati, Vol. 1, Novosibirsk, 1969, p. 199.

IMPACT OF PRESS

In terms of the impact of the mass media, Inkeles and Bauer offered some interesting conclusions, which may be substantially illuminated by massive Soviet surveys that have been carried out within the last six years. Although Inkeles and Bauer point to the limitations of their sample, they suggest "the propaganda system also succeeded somewhat in inculcating a series of standard images of the outstanding features of Soviet society—to wit, that it was 'democratic,' 'progressive,' 'classless,' 'without conflict," and so on. These images were apparently maintained by people in the face of evident contradiction provided by their own life experience."[95]

We cannot test these hypotheses in the same way that Inkeles and Bauer did; we do not have, and will not have, such an unusual opportunity to examine in depth the attitudes of thousands of Soviet citizens. But we do have, increasingly, major examples of Soviet investigations, which are conducted with professional integrity. They are, in general, less sophisticated methodologically than are American studies, but they do suggest ways in which the Inkeles-Bauer data may relate to current attitudes and perceptions.

THE SURVEYS

As noted above, 1964, and the ouster of Khrushchev, marked a turning point in the Soviet effort to investigate public opinion. All the national readership surveys date from that Party plenum. In 1966, the massive *Izvestia* survey was begun; 177,000 questionaires were given to readers, of which about 15 percent were returned. All major occupations were tapped, with about 150 to 200 questionnaires devoted to each of 100 major occupations in the country. About 8,000 interviews in the home were also conducted, and, in addition to covering all major occupations, communities of different sizes were investigated. Assisting in the survey were 269 newspaper correspondents, both professional and volunteer, and 517 "activists," professional Party and soviet personnel, students, faculty, communications, and postal personnel.[96] The total cost of the survey is put at about 57,000 rubles ($62,700 at the official rate of exchange).[97] There was also a survey of *Pravda* readers, which involved 4,000 interviews and 5,000 mailed questionnaires.[98] The *Trud* survey, 1967, used a total of 6,000 questionnaires,[99] and most recently and most carefully prepared is the *Literary Gazette* survey, 1967–1968, which cost more than 30,000 rubles. Chosen for investigation were 30 regions in the USSR, representing varying levels of density of subscription, from 2.8 per 10,000 (in Khorez oblast in Azerbaidzhan) to 98.2 per 10,000 (in Moscow). Demographic questionnaires were sent to about every fourth subscriber in these areas, totalling 80,000 for the country as a whole; a similar quantity of opinion questionnaires was also sent. These documents were supplemented by 3,000 interviews. The recipients of the questionnaire formed about 13 percent of the total number of subscribers to the newspapers.[100]

The most interesting and most ambitious material that has been reported by the sociologists conducting these surveys concerns the readership for *Izvestia* and *Literary Gazette*. There are, of course, faults with these and others of the sociological surveys currently being conducted in the Soviet Union. As David Lane remarks, "Much of the empirical research (both Western and state socialist) is deficient in that results of surveys are often given only in percentage form, the sampling is not truly representative of the population described, the questions put are ambiguous and the categories used by the researchers in analysing data are inadequately defined."[101] However, there is no question that they are among the most interesting glimpses of public opinion to come out of Soviet society since the Second World War. It is important that the Soviet scholars found, initially, considerable difficulty in eliciting attitudes of disagreement with editorial policy. The "no response" category was very high for the question: "Can you remember cases in the past when you did not agree with the evaluation of the newspaper of certain facts or events?" However, in the final questionnaires the question was reformulated to imply that disagreement was natural and expected. The final question read thus: "Probably, you don't agree sometimes with the evaluation of the newspaper about certain facts or events. In regard to what problems does this most often happen?"[102] Although we cannot know the degree to which this change of wording removes the particular constraints prevalent in Soviet society, it does indicate that the researchers are fully aware of those constraints and attempt to mitigate the consequences for their research.[103] The broad picture that emerges from these newspaper studies is that there is some dissatisfaction and selective reading. In the *Literary Gazette* study, hereinafter referred to as *L.G.*, it was found that 38 percent of the materials in the newspaper were fully read and 30 percent were selectively read. Generally 21 percent of the materials always satisfied the reader, and 34 percent frequently satisfied the reader.[104] In the *L.G.* survey, the sociologists strongly suggested that the criterion for evaluating the work of the editorial board of the newspaper should be based not only on the number reading the newspaper "but by the interrelationship between those actually interested in the topic [reading it fully] and those satisfied with it."[105] Table 12 shows the topics of the newspaper rank-ordered according to salience (types of articles most frequently read fully) and satisfaction by topic of the newspaper. We have used Kendall's *tau* for the rank-order correlation coefficient. We see that there is in fact a strong relationship between salience and satisfaction and a rather weak negative relationship (or, at least, certainly not a positive one),

Table 12. LG Survey: Rank Order of Salience and Satisfaction

A. Articles Read Fully	B. Articles Usually Satisfying Reader	C. Articles Frequently Dissatisfying for Reader
1. Feuilletons and humor	1. Feuilletons and humor	1. Poetry
2. Articles on moral issues	2. Articles on moral issues	2. Reviews of Soviet literature
3. Prose publications	3. Articles on international life	3. Articles on Soviet literature
4. Articles on Soviet art	4. Articles on science	4. Prose
5. Articles on sociology	5. Articles on sociology	5. Articles on Soviet art
6. Articles on international life	6. Articles on Soviet art	6. Articles on foreign art
7. Articles on science	7. Articles on economic questions	7. Reviews of foreign literature
8. Articles on questions of foreign art	8. Prose publications	8. Articles on moral issues
9. Poetry	9. Articles on foreign art	9. Feuilletons and humor
10. Articles on economic questions	10. Reviews of foreign literature	10. Articles on international life
11. Articles on Soviet literature	11. Poetry publications	11. Articles on sociology
12. Reviews of foreign literature	12. Reviews of Soviet literature	12. Articles on economics
13. Reviews of Soviet literature	13. Articles on Soviet literature	13. Articles on science

Rank Order correlation coefficient
   t for A and B = .641
   t for A and C = -.179

Source: "'Literaturnaya Gazeta' i ee chitatel," Problemy Sotsiologii Pechati, Novosibirsk, 1970, pp. 124-125.

between salience and dissatisfaction, thus indicating, perhaps, a pattern of selectivity based on gratification. A similar study, based on the *Trud* survey, compared reader preferences by topic with editorial preferences, the latter based on content analysis of four months of the newspaper during 1967. Table 13 gives the results. Only two of the topics which are given prime attention by editorial policy reappear among the reader preferences: sports and work of the trade union organs. When the *Trud* readers were asked in what areas they wished to gain more information, the greatest intensity of interest among all readers, regardless of level of education, concerned international issues.[106]

What emerges from the broad comparison of reader preferences and editorial policy is a differentiated and complex picture in which attitudes of readers, at least in terms of the questions asked, and editorial policy are often incongruent. This picture of reader attitudes may be further refined by examining the effects of education, age, and occupation. Some, although by no

Table 13. Subject-matter Preferences: Trud

Editorial Preferences*	Readership Preferences
1. Official information from TASS	1. Feuilletons
2. Sports	2. Life, morals, teaching
3. Entertaining information	3. Legal questions
4. Problems of industry	4. Sports
5. Foreign information from TASS	5. Critical materials
6. Advanced collectives	6. Events in capitalist countries
7. Literature and art	7. Science and Technology
8. Editorials	8. Medical themes
9. Propaganda materials	9. Work of trade union organs
10. Work of trade union organs	10. Advance workers in industry, socialist competition

*Measured by content analysis covering four months in 1967.

Source: V. Z. Kogan and Iu. I. Skvortsov, "Stroki, temy, zhanry," Problemy Sotsiologii Pechati, Novosibirsk, 1970, p. 56.

means complete, information about readership patterns can be gleaned from the surveys.

In the *L.G.* survey, it was found that the percentage of readers reading articles fully and being satisfied with those articles was roughly equal across all levels of education. However, the greatest percentage of disagreement with editorial points of view is found among those with higher education. With increasing levels of education, there is a decline in the percentage of those reading articles on literature and art in their entirety as well as a decline in the percentage of those satisfied with the articles. However, with increasing levels of education, there is an increase in attention to and satisfaction with articles on science, sociology, and economics. Although all educational groups are equally interested in articles about international affairs, the percentage of readers satisfied with those articles declines with rising levels of education.[107] When asked what "discussion themes" most interested them, readers with one to six grades of education gave "crime and legal proceedings" unqualified first place, in contrast with eighth place for those with graduate education and seventh place for those with higher education. Discussion themes devoted to ecology interested the least educated far less than any other group.[108] In two recent American surveys, however, two factors were distinguished which affect recognition of environmental pollution as a serious problem. In a survey in Illinois, when respondents were asked to identify the most important problems in the United States, without cues, only 13 percent mentioned either pollution or population as having prime importance. When asked directly whether they considered pollution a problem, over 90 percent responded affirmatively with no difference between rural and urban residence.[109] The other factor of some importance related to recognition of environmental pollution as a general national problem or an immediate and local one; in Durham, North Carolina, 74 percent of the sample found the problem serious at the national level, but only 13 percent saw it as serious in their immediate surroundings.[110] In the Soviet surveys reported here, we know neither whether cues were given nor whether respondents viewed the problem as a local or national one.

In the study of *Trud* (which, of the four national newspapers investigated here, most appeals to a broad educational spectrum), it was found that, in general, the reader with higher education favored articles concerning the humanities—art, literature, and history—and the "reader-worker" tended to choose technology.[111] This suggests that the declining numbers of the more educated reading literature articles in *L.G.* reflects not lack of interest but rather dissatisfaction. One final point, which bears on this discussion but is drawn from a survey in Leningrad, is the finding by Shkaratan that with the increase in professional qualifications goes a decline in interest in political literature, although there is an increasing interest in books and home libraries.[112]

Briefly, I conclude that the more highly educated reader is harder to please, more critical, more interested in theoretical problems of science and the humanities, and decreasingly interested in political literature. And, as I discuss below, the more highly educated are also much more critical of newspaper and television materials pertaining to news and national and international political issues.

Age differences also bear on differing attitudes toward the national press. Youths below the age of 24 showed much less interest than did other groups in sections of *L.G.* dealing with moral issues, economics, and sociology; in fact, all the nonliterary sections interested the young less than other age groups. They were, therefore, much more interested in the literature and art sections. However, this was also the age group that disagreed most with the editorial viewpoint offered in these sections. People over 55, for all topics, represented a percentage of disagreement roughly two times lower than that for the average reader. Those in the age group from 31 to 40 were most likely to disagree with the editors concerning material about Soviet literature, international life, and economics.[113] In addition, youths up to age 24 were roughly half as likely to be interested in discussion materials concerning conservation and ecology as their elders between 31 and 55, a pattern unlike that found in the United States.[114]

In terms of occupational differentiation of attitude, very little is given in the Soviet studies, but what is available is interesting. The "discussion materials," the liveliest, most topical portions of *L.G.*, are found most salient by scholars in the humanities, personnel of the Communist Party, and natural scientists; they are least salient for engineers, technicians, workers, employees, teachers, and students. Further, two categories of the dissatisfied are given: One, of general dissatisfaction, includes writers, people in the arts, and journalists. The second category represents those who are dissatisfied with the practical ineffectiveness of the discussion materials, and here are found employees in the government bureaucracy, people in the arts, natural scientists, teachers of natural science, journalists, and professional personnel in the sphere of culture.[115] The dissatisfaction, especially because of lack of efficacy, is, thus, particularly marked among some members of the elite who are perhaps most vitally involved in the functioning of the political system and who certainly occupy positions of high prestige.

This highly differentiated and complex pattern of reader attitudes suggests that there are several dimensions involved in assessing the press's success in inculcating officially approved images. Further, it may not be true, at least at present, that official characterizations of life in Soviet society are generally accepted in spite of contradictions experienced by the respondent in his own life. Alekseev compared both the newspaper surveys discussed above and the Leningrad study of television viewers[116] and found that, at first glance, it seemed that increase in level of education was associated with increase in the evaluation of news and current events material as unsatisfactory. However, it was also true that those with the least education, up to the fourth grade, experienced the greatest dissatisfaction. The group with education of from five to nine grades were least likely to be dissatisfied with these communications. What operates here, according to Alekseev, is the interaction of two variables. In the case of the least educated, the dissonance created by confronting the official picture of life and living under obviously differing conditions stimulates reactions of criticism and dissatisfaction. The other variable, low level of education, would, however, tend to stimulate attitudes of agreement with the official view, but it is of less weight than the dissonance experienced by the respondent. In the case of those with higher education, education is the variable which stimulates a critical attitude, and the superiority of material conditions would diminish the dissatisfaction. At the level of those with intermediate education, both variables balance, which accounts for the relatively low degree of critical evaluation of the media. This is an interaction that Rosenberg calls a conditional relationship, one in which the relation may be strong under one condition and weak under another. In the case above, with low standard of living, the effect of low level of education, which should diminish criticism, is reduced; with a high level of education, a high living standard, which should diminish critical attitudes, is reduced. At the secondary level of education, if we were not aware of the conditional relationship, we might have a spurious noncorrelation in which the "contingent associations cancel one another, producing a total relationship between the original two variables which is low or completely absent."[117] This cancellation of effects at the level of secondary education produces the relatively flat portion of a U-shaped curve in which the least educated and the most highly educated exhibit similar attitudes. I suggest that it is this relationship that underlies Bauer's and Inkeles's impression that the intelligentsia sounded more like the worker than anyone else.[118]

THE PARTY AS SPONSOR OF SOCIOLOGICAL RESEARCH: CHANGING COMPOSITION AND PERSPECTIVES

How far off are the experts in their assumptions about the masses? In order to demonstrate the utility of their research, the Novosibirsk sociologists asked a group of experts to predict the results of the *Izvestia* survey.

Table 14. Expert Prediction of Responses to Questions from Izvestia Survey

Groups of Experts	Can you remember instances when you did not agree with the newspaper?			With what detail do you read articles? (Editorial)		
	Yes	No	Don't Remember	Entirely	Partly	Don't Read
1. Sociologists and economists	34%	34%	32%	16%	36%	48%
2. Journalists						
a) Most prominent	5%	85%	10%	25%	55%	20%
b) Less prominent	30%	30%	40%	15%	25%	60%
3. Representatives of the precise and natural sciences	49%	29%	22%	39%	38%	23%
4. Survey Results	11%	25.5%	54.3%	30%	53.3%	9.4%

Source: V. T. Davydchenkov, "Organizatsia sotsiologicheskovo obsledovania i vnedrenie poluchennykh rezultatov v tsentralnoi gazete," Voprosy Sotsiologii Pechati, Novosibirsk, 1970, p. 165.

Although all these experts presumably are members of the Party, the group called "prominent journalists" would be closest to professional Party members, occupying places high in the official communications apparatus. Their prediction of very low disagreement with editorial communications was, of course, the most faulty of the predictions. The scholars, on the other hand, all overestimated the degree to which the respondents disagreed. All the experts considerably underestimated the degree to which respondents fell into the "don't remember" category. If this may be taken as a "no opinion" answer, it may be an indicator of alienation, of failure to identify or agree with the appropriate group or norms,[119] and it is interesting that the professional communications specialist of prominent rank is least able to predict this outcome.

When Inkeles and Bauer made their study, they found that Party members were significantly more exposed to the mass media than the rest of the population.[120] We add to this finding that, since the circulation of at least the major newspapers is drawn disproportionately from the educated and Party members are more highly educated than the masses, the relationship probably still holds true. Table 15 compares the levels of education attained for the USSR

Table 15. LEVEL OF EDUCATION ATTAINED (Percentage)

	1947			1957			1967		
	Primary	Secondary	Higher	Primary	Secondary	Higher	Primary	Secondary	Hi
Population USSR[a]	---	14.7[b]	1.2	---	19.5	3.8	---	28.2	
Communist Party	---	24.2	7.5	---	26.2	11.6	---	34.1	1
Party Apparat									
Secretaries of Republic and Territorial Party Organizations	19.1	39.6	41.3	0.8	12.4	86.8	---	2.4	9
Secretaries of City and District Party Organizations	46.7	40.6	12.7	2.3	58.1	39.6	---	8.9	9
Secretaries of Primary Party Organizations	41.0	50.2	8.8	48.5	39.0	12.5	20.1	49.8	3

[a]Data are for 1939, 1959, and 1967
[b]Includes "incomplete secondary education"

Sources: Ellen Mickiewicz, "Elite Recruitment and Mobilization," Handbook of Soviet Social Science Data, ed. Ellen Mickiewicz, N.Y., Free Press, 1973. Ellen Mickiewicz, "The Modernization of Party Propaganda in The USSR," Slavic Review XXX (June 1971) p. 275. Soviet Union 50 Years, Moscow, 1969 p. 282.

as a whole, Communist Party members, and professional members of the *apparat*. This last group is rapidly becoming far more highly educated than the average for the population or for the Party rank and file. Does the finding, noted earlier, that critical attitudes increase with increase in education hold true for Party members, who were among the survey respondents but were not reported separately?

That the Party has begun to pay attention to surveys of nonelite as well as elite attitudes is well known. The mass surveys reported above were made with the concurrence of the Academy of Sciences and the major newspapers and certainly required direct Party approval. But, beyond that, there is considerable activity within the Party itself to carry out its own surveys. This activity is tied to the search for new indicators of Party efficacy. There is evidence of a rejection of the single criterion of efficacy which was employed consistently in the past—increase in production. Instead, a "complex of indicators" is sought, in part objective and economically oriented, such as percentage of norm fulfilled, percentage of those performing high quality work, percentage of rationalizers (innovators in efficiency production), and conditions of labor discipline. Some are called subjective indicators. Of these, two are related to alienation and the work process: motives governing people in their work and feelings of satisfaction or dissatisfaction. Further subjective indicators will be plumbed to discover the sources of creative work: feelings of civic duty, consciousness of ego, and desire for affluence. The whole range of subjective indicators—ideals, goals, life plans, values, moods—is given as appropriate for research carried out by the Party itself to increase the effectiveness of its role. Effectiveness is, itself, a concept that the Party hopes to define in a different way. Not only are there differences between effective and ineffective but also between degrees of effectiveness; what is sought is a solution of optimality, which assures that tasks are carried out in the shortest possible time with the least expenditure of labor, materials, and financial resources.[121] In the search for optimal efficacy, the Party seems to be redefining its role, seeking an arena of activity with specific functions. The following are the most innovative examples of Party-sponsored sociological research and projected policies to be reported publicly, although with limited circulation. There is a clear notion of the boundaries of legitimate Party functions and an effort toward conformity with cost-benefit analysis. In all five cases discussed below, the limits of Party activity are clearly defined:[122]

1. Religious norms: In 1964–1965 a survey was conducted among 2,914 persons in the city of Gorky who had had their children baptized. Prior to the survey, the Party had acted upon the assumption that unskilled and uneducated workers formed the large majority of this group. Research indicated that skilled workers made up 66 percent of the group and that the average monthly salary of the group did not differ from those who did not baptize their children; the majority had good living conditions—their own house or individual apartment or rooms. Sixty percent were under thirty years of age. The prime motivation for baptism, according to the survey, was the desire to avoid conflict with grandparents who, because of the crowded housing conditions and the necessity of having both young parents work, were vital for child care and would not perform that function were the child not baptized. Further, the day care centers in the city had room for only 18.3 percent of the preschool children. The role of the Party in this case, then, becomes one of increasing welfare and housing facilities—a specific allocation of resources for the particular norm it desires fulfilled.

2. Aesthetic norms: In 1967, 2,077 high school students were surveyed to determine their patterns of music consumption. It was found that the great majority were simply consumers of light or popular music; they rarely performed themselves and did not favor the types of music officially determined as aesthetically superior. The Party judged that the family had abandoned its role in socialization of aesthetics to the peer group and that it was imperative that the process be reversed. Beyond this recognition of a trend not inconsistent with that found in the United States,[123] no concrete measures were recommended.

3. Work discipline: From 1965 to 1967, a survey conducted among workers in Gorky factories (numbers and methods unspecified) established differing evaluations of the methods of dealing with disruptions of the work process by leading communist workers and by violators of work discipline and varying actual measures taken by the management. Table 16 gives the results. In this

Table 16. METHODS OF DISCIPLINE PREFERRED BY WORKERS AND TAKEN BY MANAGEMENT

Measures For Dealing With Violators of Labor Discipline	Advance Workers of Communist Labor N = 1070	All Violators of Labor Discipline N = 1930	Measures Taken by Management: Percentage N = 1930
1. Discussion at meetings of the collective	69.2	58.2	43.1
2. Discussion in comrades' courts	46.9	25.7	19.1
3. Loss of bonus	38.5	20.0	40.0
4. Criticism in the press	35.9	10.5	No data
5. Talk by director with violator	31.2	28.0	Average of 2 talks with each
6. Transfer to lower salaried work	29.9	6.3	5.1
7. Shift of vacation	25.4	4.5	1.0
8. Postponement in the assignment of living quarters	24.8	8.3	0.8
9. Loss of trip to sanitorium, resort	20.6	3.4	3.1
10. Disciplinary penalty	19.0	11.4	64.9
11. Other measures (postponement in awarding rank, conviction for petty hooliganism, etc.)	1.4	6.3	12.4

Source: V. A. Smirnov, *Sotsiologicheskie issledovania v praktike partynnoi raboty*, Volga-Vyatka, 1969, p. 42.

case, Party recommendations should, according to the author, concentrate more on peer group pressure (through discussions and appearances before comrades' courts), a rather inexpensive measure, and less on punitive measures, which are rather expensive in their alienating effect.

4. Transience of labor force: In the research described above, it was found that 43.4 percent of the violators of work discipline had worked at the particular factory for less than three years, even though they were skilled workers and generally were married. Obviously, work infractions then became closely tied to the disaffection of workers who go from job to job. In Party sponsored research conducted in both Leningrad and Gorky, similar results obtained. The main reason why workers left their jobs was not dissatisfaction with wages, but rather dissatisfaction with the conditions of work and the administration of the enterprise or factory. In this case, Party recommendations applied entirely to alleviation of deficient plant conditions and operated directly upon management personnel.

5. Adjustment to labor reforms: In July 1968 the Party set a special plenum in the city of Gorky to discuss the newly imposed five-day work week. In preparation for the discussion, a survey was conducted among 2,068 workers. It was found that 46 percent often were forced to forfeit their day off because of "storming" and other semi-illegal practices associated with last-minute rushing at the end of the plan period to fulfill norms.[124] Further, 40 percent were dissatisfied with the plant's food provision, 34 percent with the urban transport system, and 27 percent with the schedule of medical facilities. Again, Party activity was to be directed entirely toward managerial personnel.

In none of these cases is there the assurance that Party guidelines or recommendations will be carried out. Like any other political situation, there are a multiplicity of interests, and influence is neither monolithic nor uni-directional. However, in all the cases, the Party has targeted with precision the group it wishes to influence and has delineated the costs and boundaries of its activities. It may be that the costs are too high or the norms are of too low priority (one suspects that this is the case with the socialization of aesthetics study) for Party goals to be met.

POLITICAL CHANGE FROM SOCIOLOGICAL RESEARCH

The chain of events that followed the massive *Izvestia* survey discussed above presents political consequences of considerable importance.[125] First, it is evident that a direct channel was open between the research sociologists in Novosibirsk and the editorial staff of *Izvestia* in Moscow. The Novosibirsk scholars went to Moscow and were able to present their results to the top political communications hierarchy of the newspaper, presided over by Tolkunov, the chief editor. Working commissions were established to study the results of the survey, representing every department of the newspaper. Theses, or recommendations, emerged from the working committees, and these were presented, once again, to the chief editor and his staff. The theses were many, and I have isolated the most important in terms of the present analysis; they deal, as did so many of the Party concerns noted above, with alienation of the worker and urban welfare and living standards. For example, the theses recommended that space in *Izvestia* be devoted to questions of public opinion at the place of work: How does it differ from policies and decisions taken by the factory management or public organizations? How can worker attitudes be transmitted to the management and actually result in changes in the conditions of factory labor? Attention should also be devoted to the ethics of leadership; the relation of the leader, or director, to his subordinate; and the whole area of interpersonal relations in the factory. Further, the theses recommend that newspaper space be set aside for questions concerning the participation of urban dwellers in the economic and political decisions affecting their lives. For example, it was asserted that public opinion should be tapped to guide local governments in their location of stores, cinemas, markets, sports fields, and pharmacies. Local soviets, the organs of government, are advised to make use of all local resources, foremost among them public opinion, in the planning of urban transport systems and shopping complexes. In its allocation of finances for urban housing, the local soviet is strongly advised to base its agenda on the wishes of the urban populace. "Housing is for the individual, and not the individual for housing. . . . Concerning the centralization of the way of life: Should the state take upon itself concern for the satisfying of all tastes and individual habits of people?"[126]

There followed a period of three months during which the newspaper staff studied the theses. At the end of 1967 new columns were introduced in *Izvestia*. Seven were devoted to international questions, presumably to tap the interest in international affairs revealed by the survey; and seven were devoted to local matters, including the organization of work conditions, use of leisure time, and health and shopping notes. The sociologists conclude that some direct results emerged from their work, and most significant, perhaps, is that "the editorial board began to seek the help of sociologists." And, indeed, in February 1968, the editors of *Izvestia* requested that the sociologists carry out a survey investigating the "migration" of readers and the flow of subscriptions. As in the previous surveys, the sociologists intend to append to their results a list of recommendations for policy alternatives.

While we cannot make judgments about the degree, if any, of influence of the "representatives" of public opinion on political leaders, we can nonetheless observe that this does seem to be the role in which the sociologists see themselves. Although they do not fail, in their writings, to support the guiding role of the communications experts, all their practical suggestions and the preponderant weight of their research are directed toward portraying public opinion, demonstrating the incongruity between that picture and official assumptions and policies, and, finally, recommending ways in which the political elites must alter their behavior. The suggested alterations may be thought modest; they involve, for the most part, problems of local administration and factory management. The implications however, are wide-ranging; they suggest a significantly increased and officially sanctioned role for participation in decision making.

Within the operations of the Party itself, again, at least, at the local level, some similar kind of activity seems to be going on. In 1968 and 1969, the city Party committee of Gorky directed all primary Party organizations to plan their agendas for their meetings by asking Party members: "What questions do you consider now to be the most important for you as a communist and for all of your Party organizations, and what should be first in order of discussion at meetings?"[127] The committee polled 4,724 communists, representing about 5 percent of the Party members of the city. Almost 20 percent had been in the Party for three years or less, similar to the 17 percent for the city organization as a whole. Most of the preferences concerned labor problems. The last two places in the rank order of preferences were occupied by "tasks of communists in keeping public order" (only 30.2 percent) and "communists' work at the place or residence" (only 17 percent—this represents a relatively low interest in the campaign, introduced with the reduction of the work week, to shift the main burden of agitation to the place of residence).[128]

While evidence of this type cannot be conclusive, it is extremely interesting in terms of the concerns noted above, among mass media sociologists, for wider participation in decision making. At this level, among sociologists studying Party work, the evidence may be less decisive, but it is also more sensitive and directly relevant politically. As we observed earlier, in the discussion of the methods used for the newspaper surveys, the sociologists recognize that under present conditions, it may be extremely difficult to elicit opinions critical of economic, social, or political conditions. Thus, one of the main policy stands taken by the sociologists concerns widening the officially sanctioned arena of criticism. In one study, the sociologists note that the "life" and "viability" of a newspaper are represented by the amount of critical material it carries. As a result of the content analysis of *Trud,* it was found that this type of material formed one forty-third of total newspaper space.[129] Letters to the editor have always been encouraged by all Soviet regimes as providing feedback essential to the functioning of the system. In an analysis of critical letters to *Izvestia,* Davydchenkov found that in 1967 there were 18,019 such letters. About 4,000 of them gave the age and education of their authors. The results are given in Table 17. The researcher concludes that the editorial staff of *Izvestia* is prevented from obtaining opinions which would be valuable because of the severe underrepresentation of "scientists, [and] people in the free professions [the arts]," and, we might add, of readers under forty, the age group most likely to disagree with the editorial point of view. Further, the editors will be unable, the sociologists assert, to form an "objective understanding," and the ties between the editors and the readership must bear a one-sided character.[130] Thus, it is concluded, official perspectives can never be accurate, and without the kind of public opinion research discussed above, Party effectiveness will not be optimal. The search for Party efficacy goes on within the Party itself, as well, and as the level of education among that elite rises, so, too, emerge more refined and critical attitudes—attitudes that may support a redefinition of role, more pragmatic, more concretely defined, and more widely based on empirical research.

Table 17. AUTHORS OF CRITICAL LETTERS TO IZVESTIA

Age	%	Education	%
15 - 19	0.5	1 - 3 Grades	3
20 - 24	2	4 - 6 Grades	5
25 - 30	5	7 - 9 Grades	15
31 - 40	4.5	10 - 11 Grades	15
41 - 55	14	Specialized Secondary	16.5
56 - 65	32	Incomplete higher	45.5
66 and over	44	Complete higher	----

Source: V. T. Davydchenkov, "Organizatsia sotsiologicheskovo obsledovania i vnedrenie poluchennykh rezultatov v tsentralnoi gazete," <u>Voprosy Sotsiologii Pechati</u>, Novosibirsk, 1970, p. 152.

CLEAVAGES AND CLUSTERS AMONG SOVIET REPUBLICS

The Soviet Union, as a multinational state, is divided into 15 union republics, each of which theoretically represents the dominant nationality, although there are over 120 different ethnic groups in the country. The study of the ethnic minorities in the Soviet Union is a difficult task and requires highly specialized skills. A great deal has been written about the problems and prospects of ethnic identity, and an excellent procedure for discovering the propensity for change has been worked out by John Armstrong.[131] He presents three main categories of indicators followed by examples of the appropriate type of data; many of these can be found in this handbook. The first category comprises "indicators of the extent of social mobilization (change from traditional to modernized ways of life) of the ethnic groups," for example: degree of urbanization; level of education, especially of technical or scientific higher education; relative education of women; geographical mobility; and access to media of communication. The second group of indicators relates to the "specific objectives and tactics of Soviet policy." Here, one would look at proportion of schools providing instruction in the non-Russian languages and students enrolled in them, enrollment in the Communist Party, publication in the national languages, and employment of members of the ethnic groups in official posts. The third group of indicators examines "the degree of Russification achieved," and the two best indices, although difficult to find, might be the extent to which non-Russians regard Russian as their principal language of discourse and rates of intermarriage.

Ethnic minorities are not coterminous with the union republics. In many cases, members of the dominant nationality of a republic may live outside its bounds. For example, 45 percent of the Armenians live in other parts of the Soviet Union, where they supply many of the entrepreneurial skills.[132] On the other hand, all republics include many minority elements, some of them immigrants. For example, Russians constitute 20 percent of the Estonian republic, 27 percent of the Latvian republic, and 9 percent of the Lithuanian republic.[133] The forced resettlements of populations during the Second World War increased the population of the five republics of Central Asia by 38.1 percent.[134] The study of ethnic identity, then, must necessarily transcend the territorial-administrative division of the 15 republics.

The problem proposed for research here, however, is a very different, though related, one. We propose to examine the union republics over time in order to determine whether or not there are groups or clusters of them, whether or not they behave generally alike over time, or whether there is a commonness about certain of them that distinguish them from the rest. This is the problem of cleavages and clusters, or regions, rather than one of nationalism and ethnic distinctiveness. Considerable work in this area has been done by economists, who study the transfer of resources and relative efficiency among the republics. Our research will be broadened to include variables along several dimensions, cultural, political, and social as well, in order to form an idea of the homogeneity and heterogeneity of the group over time. Research of this type has been conducted in the field of international relations, which uses factor analysis and other types of statistical operations to determine the characteristics of various groups of nations and the ways in which they might be considered as regions of the world.[135]

The research reported in the following pages is the result of a pilot study, a first step in the broader research project that will relate the behavior of the Soviet republics to the prospects and preconditions for integration. This project will also investigate political regime, policy directives, and inter-regional variation. The pilot study described here examined the behavior of the republics with respect to rates of change over time for the period of time given in the relevant tables. We wished to determine whether or not stable groups or clusters of republics could be detected, which might indicate what problems are posed for integration and for the success of Soviet policies which project a *sblizhenie*, a coming together, or integration, of its constituent elements.

The first step in this research involved selecting some 23 variables from this handbook, which contains information about the differences among republics. They are (by chapter and table numbers):

I-12.	Population
II-21.	Sown area and Tractors
II-24.	Livestock production: Meat, Milk, and Eggs
III-8a.	Regional distribution of electric power production
IV-7.	Physicians
IV-13.	Hospital beds
V-3.	Urban housing space (aggregate and per capita)
V-10.	Average square meters of housing space per housing unit built
V-11.	Total urban housing space built
V-15.	Capital investment in housing construction
VI-A.3.	Children enrolled in kindergartens and combined nursery school–kindergartens
VI-A.6.	Pupils enrolled in primary and general secondary schools of all types
VI-A.8.	Number of students enrolled in vocational secondary schools
VI-A.10.	Number of students enrolled in institutions of higher education
VII-2.	Communist Party membership
VII-20.	Komsomol membership
VII-21.	Trade union membership
VIII-B.8.	Books published

Each of these variables was coded on a per capita basis and the total amount of information resulted in about 3,800 data units. It was hoped that this selection of variables would provide information along several dimensions, with much attention given to education—a process which, as noted earlier, underlies so many of the facets of development and modernization and to housing, on which depends so many aspects of urbanization. Only the international dimension has been omitted, since, although the Ukraine and Belorussia are in theory empowered to conduct international relations via a seat in the United Nations, no meaningful republic behavior can be isolated.

A preliminary step in our analysis involved testing for the possibly unchanging position of relative advantage of the republics. The Kendall's *tau* rank order correlation coefficient gives "a measure of the degree of association or correlation between the two sets of ranks."[136] What was suggested by these tests was a fairly stable pattern of rank ordering which tends to persist over time. As might be expected from a consideration of the pattern of development of the Soviet republics, European Russia, with the exception of Moldavia, consistently ranks ahead of Asian Russia with the exception of Kazakhstan, where the plan for rapid development thrusts it ahead of its regional neighbors. Within the Baltic region, Estonia nearly always leads in the rank-order, whereas Lithuania very often places several ranks below both Estonia and Latvia, reflecting a clear difference in the level of economic and political development, as well as a cultural and religious difference. Similarly, where cleavages occur in the Caucasus region, it is between Georgia and Armenia on the one hand and Azerbaidzhan on the other, again reflecting a clear cultural, economic, and historical divergence, with Aberbaidzhan ranking below its Caucasian neighbors and tending to decline over time. The Russian Republic is consistently placed in the forefront of the rank-order, generally closely associated with Estonia, Latvia, Georgia, or Armenia.

In summary, it appears that criteria of economic development and cultural similarity serve to distinguish a republic's rank, and this implies a continued disadvantage for the republics of Central Asia, with the exception of Kazakhstan. In general, then, Turkmenia, Tadzhikistan, Kirgizia, Uzbekistan, and, for some variables, Azerbaidzhan are rarely found among the first six or seven ranks. This similarity of low placement is particularly marked in the mobilization variables, Komsomol, trade union, and Communist Party membership, where these republics—without Azerbaidzhan, but together with Moldavia, the least developed of the republics of European Russia—consistently fill the last places. Also implied is a continuing advantage for the Baltic and Russian republics, as they occupy the first ranks over time.

However, rank-order analysis gives only a very rough picture of the trends over time, and in order to develop a more complex analysis of republic behavior, computer graphs were generated which plotted change over time in each variable for all republics. A second set of graphs showed change over time in each republic for the whole set of variables. This second set of graphs would help us to identify whether the different components of development, political, industrial, welfare, etc., were moving together, or whether some aspects of development tended to advance or decline much more rapidly than did others. The first set of graphs would, of course, indicate whether some republics, or groups of them, developed or declined excessively with respect to the others. The initial finding from these graphs was that rarely did the curves intersect; rather, there seemed to be a general pattern of parallel movement over time.

A correlation analysis was then made which took each of the above variables and compared all the republics over time. Another correlation analysis took each of the republics and compared all the variables over time.[137] This was followed by two sets of cluster analyses, one with each republic for all variables and one with each variable for all republics. The cluster analysis uses as input the correlation matrices produced by the program described above. The basic assumptions are that the correlations over time are actually measures of the interassociation of the various republics or variables over time and that by considering the total correlation matrix, republics or variables can be grouped into "clusters" having a large amount of internal homogeneity and distinctiveness from other groups. Thus, the within-cluster similarities will be kept high, and the between-cluster similarities will be kept low. Groupings with the *l*argest *a*verage *w*ithin-cluster *s*imilarity (l.a.w.s.) are accepted. The output shows a large number of clusters evaluated in terms of the average correlation similarity and lists them hierarchically in terms of this similarity.[138] In no cases were clusters accepted for which the average correlation similarity fell below .800, so that differences among the republics in the cluster, for the given variable, tended to be quite low.

The major finding of this statistical operation showed a remarkable absence of clusters meeting these criteria for almost all the variables. The exceptions were: average square meters of housing space per housing unit built; total urban housing space built; capital investment in housing construction; Komsomol membership; books published; and certain of the agricultural variables, which seem directly related to specific central economic decisions, such as the virgin lands program. For all the other variables, clusters in which all but one of the actors, or republics, were grouped, had a correlation similarity of above .950, and in most of the clusters which contained all the actors, the correlation similarity was well above .900. What emerged, therefore, was the similarity of behavior over time of all the union republics: There was scant evidence for the hypotheses that certain of the republics were growing or declining at rates far different from certain others or that with changes of regime there were vast changes of priority of republic growth. It may well be, however, that our data were too sparse and incomplete to show such a relation; perhaps, with an expanded data base, more subtle distinctions and patterns can be observed. But with the present data base, the similarities, not the differences, in republic behavior are emphasized. Cluster analysis also reveals that almost all the variables cluster with a correlation similarity of .940 for each republic. Thus, the variables seem to interrelate insofar as they increase or decrease at the same rate for all the republics.

In terms of our hypothesis, there would seem to be a good case for optimism concerning prospects for integration. However, this cluster analysis does not investigate an important dimension. Perhaps, as the rank-order similarities would suggest, although all the republics are growing or declining similarly, some are consistently out in front, and others always place last. Thus it may be the case that the relative advantage remains unchanged over time and that little is being done to assist the less developed to leap ahead. Assistance to the less developed, after all, involves not equal treatment, but grossly unequal treatment, so that the disadvantages of backwardness can be overcome.[139] In the language of the economist, a great deal of time and investment are necessary in order to bring up the least developed to the level of the more developed. "The gap between the two levels decreases from the beginning only if the absolute increment in the comparatively higher level is absolutely smaller than the absolute increment of the comparatively lower level, and this happens at the point in time when the gap between the two levels is a maximum."[140] Usually, however, these conditions are not met, and the process of economic development is a slow one:

> The comparative regional endowment with natural and other "fixed" resources, geographic location and distances from and to markets, the historically given levels of economic development and the given structure of industries, as well as the sociocultural and political conservatism on the part of the local population and leadership may all combine to hinder, if not completely prevent, the equalization and convergence of the levels of development in the short run. Time is indeed needed to develop natural resources, to expand and specialize local industries and the regional export-import relations, and to break through conservative traditions.[141]

In economic terms, therefore, a policy of unequal treatment over time is necessary for any change in the relative advantage of any of the republics. Such a persistent pattern of unequal treatment does not seem to be the regime's policy, judging by the results of the cluster analysis.[142]

Returning now to the cluster analysis, it will be useful to explore the situations in which clusters of republics do appear or in which there is not the overall parallel movement characteristic of most of the variables. One such case is the variable providing information on the number of books published each year in the republics. Most social science research operates on the hypothesis that book publication, literacy, and urbanization all vary together and that book publication should therefore have a high degree of correlation with urbanization. Our cluster analysis shows, first of all, that there is no cluster with a correlation similarity of .900 or better. Rather, there seems to be no stable pattern, with the number of books rising and falling in different ways for each republic. Estonia and the Russian Republic cluster with a correlation similarity of .830, Latvia and Lithuania with .869, and Georgia and Lithuania with .878. Estonia, Latvia, and the RSFSR are the most urbanized republics, but they do not cluster together; Lithuania, far less developed, clusters with Latvia. It appears that there is no central communications policy, as far as book publication is concerned, which projects a growth and expansion of facilities as urbanization is achieved. If there were, we would find clusters roughly approximating the levels of urbanization of the republics. Instead, we find a patternless picture of dips and rises. Although, as we stated earlier, our data are far from complete, they do suggest the absence of a centrally formulated communications policy that is coordinated with development objectives and that survives from one leadership period to the next.

Cluster analysis of three of the housing variables yields more stable groups of republics. For total urban housing space per capita built, two distinct sets are visible: One, set A, shows that Azerbaidzhan, Georgia, Kazakhstan, Moldavia, RSFSR, Turkmenia, and the Ukraine, cluster with a correlation similarity of .887. The other, set B, with a correlation similarity of .820, is composed of Belorussia Latvia, Kirgizia, Tadzhikistan, and Uzbekistan. Clearly anomalous republics are Armenia, with an unstable overall rise, Lithuania, with an overall sharp rise, and Estonia, with a sharp decline followed by a sharp rise. The next variable, capital investment in housing construction per capita, shows, if one uses more refined criteria for the acceptance of clusters, a similar cluster breakdown, as well as a similar pattern of growth and decline. For this variable, set A, at .950 correlation similarity, consists of Moldavia, RSFSR, and the Ukraine; set B, at a .940 correlation similarity, contains Belorussia, Kirgizia, Latvia, Tadzhikistan, Estonia, and Lithuania. For set A the pattern as on the previous variable, is one of a rise and a dip of virtually equal proportions; for set B, the pattern is one of slight upward rise, as on the previous variable, although Estonia and Lithuania exhibit more rapid increase in housing space built than in investment—an indication, possibly, of a greater relative efficiency. Once again, Armenia is anomalous, with a slow rise tapering off into a decline, a pattern at variance with the amount of housing space built. In a certain sense, the variable describing average square meters of housing space per housing unit built per capita may be taken as a measure of the quality of housing. Here we see a cluster that spans sets A and B and consists of Azerbaidzhan, Belorussia, Kirgizia, Moldavia, RSFSR, Tadzhikistan, Turkmenia, and the Ukraine. No other cluster of more than two republics emerges above the .800 level. What is interesting about the cluster noted above is that even though it embraces rather different patterns of housing construction and investment, it represents a rather constant and unchanging quality. Or, to put it somewhat differently, the housing space per housing unit is neither improving nor declining, regardless of the number of housing units built or the amount of investment put into housing construction. In this instance, the measure of quality bears little relation to that of quantity.

The final variable for which we shall look at clusters is that for Komsomol members per capita. Here, the basic set is made up of Belorussia, Estonia, Latvia, Lithuania, Moldavia, Turkmenia, and the Ukraine; the correlation similarity is .938. The pattern of membership reveals a fairly steep rise followed by a clear decline. By incorporating four additional republics into this cluster, Georgia, Kirgizia, RSFSR, and Uzbekistan, the correlation similarity is reduced to .854, but the pattern is essentially similar, with a slightly less rapid rise, followed by a slightly less rapid decline. Only Armenia and Azerbaidzhan, with a correlation similarity of .889, form a cluster exhibiting two overall periods of decline separated by a slight upswing. Overall, we see a basic pattern into which 11 of the 15 republics fit, but, unlike the pattern of data for the other two mobilization variables, 4 republics—Armenia, Azerbaidzhan, Kazakhstan, and Tadzhikistan, all of which fail to exhibit the prominent rise in membership per capita of the other republics—are not part of the dominant cluster. Insofar as the Komsomol is playing an increasingly important role as the recruiter of Communist Party members and the socializer of the masses of Soviet youth, these membership data could be a very important indicator of the degree of future recruitment of Party members in these republics. This would be of particular import for Armenia, where urbanization, education, and other criteria of development are very advanced, and for Kazakhstan, where the wealth of natural resources and the ambitious development plan project an important economic and political role for the future.

Our cluster analysis and rank order analysis indicate, on the whole, that over time the union republics are changing in a similar manner, but this covariance itself tends to eliminate the possibility for an equalization of opportunity and development, as the old patterns are perpetuated and roughly the same ranking persists. Any plan for long-range equality would have to institute radically dissimilar treatment, which would involve the favoring of the less advanced at the expense of the more advanced. What is crucial to the future is whether the relatively equal treatment over time, a factor promoting integration, is a more powerful determinant of psychological perceptions than the unchanging position in the rank-ordering of republics, a factor which might well breed perceptions of frustration and apathy.

MOBILIZATION AND CHANGE

What is the significance of the cleavages or potential for cleavage discussed here? Every society has many potential cleavages, and very often a society is strengthened by the contributions of its dissimilar components. The crucial factor against which potential cleavages must be seen is the scope and rapidity of change which is attempted by the central leadership. It is this factor of change, and the divisions which it exacerbates, which makes the attempt at social mobilization so important a policy. As Seymour Martin Lipset has written:

> As a general hypothesis, I suggest that the greater the changes in the structure of the society or organization that a governing group is attempting to

introduce, the more likely the leadership is to desire and even require a high level of participation by its citizens or members. The radical changes that accompany social revolution . . . put severe strains on group loyalties and create the potential for strong membership hostility toward the leadership. A high level of controlled and manipulated rank-and-file parti ipation is perhaps the only effective way, given the leadership's purposes, of draining off or redirecting the discontent which violent or sudden changes in traditional patterns and relationships engender.[143]

It might appear that effective, large-scale mobilization was decisively accomplished by Stalin's regime. But mobilization is not a process that is achieved for all time. Rather, there is evidence to suggest that mobilization must be a continuous process and that, as development proceeds and the old, ascriptive criteria of loyalty and commitment disappear, the sources of political support become fluid and have to be won over to each policy for change. Eisenstadt argues that difficulties are compounded for the Soviet-type regime because political passivity cannot be taken for granted, "because such passivity may become in these systems a potential focus for the crystallization of the potential political power of the citizens."[144]

But there may be levels above which the effort toward mass mobilization assumes a dysfunctional aspect. At the very least, as the Soviets recognize, mass participation may conflict with normal work activities and may lower production rates. In a Central Committee resolution of December 1963, for example, industrial and agricultural directors were criticized for "taking from their jobs workers, collective farmers, and employees for the purpose of fulfilling public duties and taking part in all kinds of mass measures—meetings, discussions, gatherings, seminars, performance of artistic activities, sports, competitions—which lowers work discipline and leads to losses of production."[145] Much more important, however, is the finding among Western students of constitutional democracies that very high levels of participation may stimulate and deepen political differences and thus put a strain on the political system, and that low- to moderate-level participation tends to mute differences and create an operating consensus. It is precisely that "moderate participation levels are helpful in maintaining a balance between consensus and cleavage in society. High participation levels would actually be detrimental to society if they tended to politicize a large percentage of social relationships."[146] It is highly likely that one can see in the current dissent in the Soviet Union evidence that the campaign for mass mobilization has stimulated political awareness in a nonconsensual way.[147]

Ultimately, maintenance of the balance between consensus and cleavage is the task of the Communist Party, the agency officially charged with the role of integration. As can be seen in Chapter VII, its professional personnel are much more highly educated than the average for the population, and recent Western studies describe recruitment policies that provide for an increasingly important role for specialists in technology and economics. It will be their function to recognize and channel the sources of cleavage through a program of modernization and social mobilization and to manage the conflicts and expectations that arise from the effects of enforced participation in the context of rapid change. As shown above, study of Soviet data reveals that the sources of cleavage do exist, that the present system of mobilization has wide gaps, and that much significant change will have to come about for an equalization in the levels of development of the union republics. The central leadership can depend on high rates of literacy, impressive educational attainments among the general population, and a record of rapid industrialization. In fact, the similarity of technological and political problems of industrialized society suggests that ideological solutions have limited usefulness and that the very continuity of the data presented here might indicate a certain limitation to a regime's power. How the continuous challenges are met and what consequences will follow will be read, in part, in future collections of Soviet data.

NOTES

1. An important exception is the work with Soviet and American schoolchildren conducted by Urie Bronfenbrenner and described in several articles and his recent book: *Two Worlds of Childhood: U.S. and U.S.S.R.,* New York, Russell Sage Foundation, 1970.

2. The United States Government has, at various times, published specialized data collections for study of the Soviet Union, particularly by the Joint Economic Committee of Congress and the Bureau of the Census. These and other excellent sources which deal with defined areas of Soviet society may be found in the listings of the Slavic Bibliographic and Documentation Center in Washington, D.C.

3. Warren W. Eason, "Population Changes," in *Prospects for Soviet Society,* ed. Allen Kassof, New York, Praeger, 1968, p. 233.

4. *United Nations Demographic Yearbook,* New York: 1969, p. 145; 1967, pp. 184, 194; 1960, p. 387.

5. Soviet sources refer to the peasant as a distinct social class, but this refers only to the "less advanced" type of economic organization that the collective farm represents. Actually, of course, the rural community consists of other types of agricultural and other workers as well as the collective farmer.

6. For discussions of the influence on occupation and education on social status, see: Ralf Dahrendorf, *Class and Class Conflict in Industrial Society,* Stanford, Stanford University Press, 1959, p. 59 ff; Alex Inkeles, "Social Stratification in the Modernization of Russia," *Social Change in Soviet Russia,* Cambridge, Harvard University Press, 1968. See also: *Toward a Social Report,* United States Department of Health, Education, and Welfare, Washington, D.C. For the most extensive survey of Soviet defectors, see the classic *The Soviet Citizen,* by Alex Inkeles and Raymond A. Bauer, Cambridge, Harvard University Press, 1961.

7. New census data for these categories will be available within the next five years.

8. *Migratsia selskovo naselenia,* ed. T. I. Zaslavsky, Moscow, 1970, p. 248.

9. U.S. Bureau of the Census, *Current Population Reports,* Series P-27, no. 42, "Farm Population," U.S. Government Printing Office, Washington, D.C., 1971, p. 3.

10. U.S. Bureau of the Census, *Current Population Reports,* Series P-20, no. 207, "Educational Attainment: March 1970," U.S. Government Printing Office, Washington, D.C., 1970, p. 3.

11. *Ibid.*

12. See Inkeles and Bauer, cited above, and *Toward a Social Report,* cited above.

13. R. Ivanova, *Sotsialnye problemy trudovykh resursov sela,* Novosibirsk, 1968, cited in V. Shlyapentokh, *Sotsiologia dlya vsekh,* Moscow, 1970, p. 120.

14. V. Shubkin, *Kolichestvennye metody v sotsiologii,* Moscow, 1966, cited in Shlyapentokh, p. 119.

15. L. Lyashenko and T. Mochilskaya, in *Sotsialnye problemy trudovykh resursov sela,* cited by Shlyapentokh, p. 119.

16. See Lee G. Burchinal, "Differences in Educational and Occupational Aspirations of Farm, Small-town, and City Boys," *Rural Sociology,* June

1961, **26**, 107–121; and Russell Middleton and Charles M. Grigg, "Rural–Urban Differences in Aspirations," *Rural Sociology,* December 1959, **24**, 247–254.

17. Natalie Rogoff, "Local Social Structures and Educational Selection," in A. E. Halsey, Jean Flood, and C. Arnold Anderson, *Education, Economy, and Society,* New York, Free Press, 1961, pp. 241–251.

18. William H. Sewell and Archibald O. Haller, "Educational and Occupational Perspectives of Farm and Rural Youth," in *Rural Youth in Crisis: Facts, Myths, and Social Change,* ed. Lee G. Burchinal, U.S. Department of Health, Education, and Welfare, U.S. Government Printing Office, Washington, D.C. [n.d.], pp. 150, 151.
    Rural is defined as farm and village (under 2,500).
    Urban is defined as small city (2,500–25,000); medium city (25,000–100,000; and large city (100,000 or more).

19. *Ibid.,* p. 151.

20. *Ibid.,* p. 152.

21. N. Aitov, in *Sotsialnye problemy trudovykh resursov sela,* cited by Shlyapentokh, *op. cit.*

22. Sewell and Haller, *op. cit.,* pp. 158–159.

23. *Ibid.,* p. 161.

24. N. M. Chasovnikova, "Selskoe uchitelstvo i evo rol v likvidatsii razlichy mezhdu gorodom i derevnei," *Sotsialno-politicheskoe i kulturnoe razvitie sotsialisticheskovo obshchestva,* Moscow, 1969, pp. 179–180.

25. Jeremy Azrael, "Bringing Up the Soviet Man: Dilemmas and Progress," *Problems of Communism,* May/June 1968, p. 26.

26. Alexander Vucinich, "The Peasants as a Social Class," *The Soviet Rural Community,* ed. James R. Millar, Urbana, University of Illinois Press, 1971, p. 313.

27. *Migratsia selskovo naselenia, op. cit.,* p. 248.

28. *Ibid.,* p. 243.

29. Azrael, *op. cit.*

30. Norton T. Dodge, "Recruitment and Quality of the Soviet Agricultural Labor Force," *The Soviet Rural Community,* Urbana, University of Illinois Press, 1971, p. 201.

31. Tamara Yanushkovskaya, in a communication to the author, March 5, 1971.

32. Shubkin, *op. cit.,* pp. 123–124.

33. A. E. Golomshtok, "O roli shkoly v professionalnoi orientatsii uchashchikhsya," *Shkola i vybor professii,* Moscow, 1969, p. 6.

34. L. S. Chizhova, "Sostoyanie trudovykh resursov i problemy zanyatosti," *Demograficheskie problemy zanyatosti,* ed. P. P. Litvyakov, Moscow, 1969, p. 143.

35. K. R. Soolep, "Vybor professii agronoma i genezis professionalnovo interesa," *Toid Sotsioloogia Alalt/Trudy po sotsiologii,* Tartu, 1968, p. 21.

36. Albert J. Reiss, Jr., *Occupations and Social Status,* New York, Free Press, 1961, p. 155.

37. K. Mamaeva, in *Opyt sotsiologicheskovo izuchenia sela v SSSR,* Moscow, 1968, cited in Shlyapentokh, *op. cit.,* p. 116.

38. L. Borisova, in *Sotsialnye problemy trudovykh resursov sela,* cited in Shlyapentokh, *op. cit.,* p. 123.

39. Sewell and Haller, *op. cit.,* p. 153.

40. *Ibid.,* p. 164.

41. *Ibid.,* 165.

42. Soolep, *op. cit.,* pp. 24–25.

43. Sewell and Haller, *op. cit.,* p. 165.

44. Soolep, *op. cit.,* p. 22.

45. *Ibid.,* p. 26.

46. B. Grushin, *Svobodnoe vremya,* Moscow, 1967, p. 46.

47. Arcadius Kahan, "Agriculture," *Prospects for Soviet Society,* ed. Allen Kassof, New York, Praeger, 1968, p. 289.

48. David W. Bronson and Constance B. Krueger, "The Revolution in Soviet Farm Household Income, 1953–1967," *The Soviet Rural Community,* ed.

James R. Millar, Urbana, University of Illinois Press, 1971, p. 229. This wage does not include the proceeds from private plots.

49. U.S. Bureau of the Census, *Current Population Reports,* Series P-60, no. 80, "Income in 1970 of Families and Persons in the United States," U.S. Government Printing Office, Washington, D.C., 1971, p. 18.

50. R. A. Ivanova, "Gazety i chitateli," *Pechat i stroitelstvo kommunizma,* ed. A. L. Mishuris, Moscow, 1969, p. 200.

51. Mark W. Hopkins, *Mass Media in the Soviet Union,* New York, Pegasus, 1970, p. 336.

52. *Ibid.,* p. 335.

53. B. E. Shlyapentokh, "Nekotorye metodologicheskie i metodicheskie problemy sotsiologii pechati," *Problemy sotsiologii pechati,* ed. G. N. Paderin, Novosibirsk, 1969, p. 179.

54. S. V. Karavashkova, "Novy etap v razvitii rabselkorovskovo dvizhenia," *Pechat i stroitelstvo kommunizma,* ed. A. L. Mishuris, Moscow, 1969, p. 234.

55. Legally, collective farmers are not workers and cannot thus be represented by trade unions.

56. Shlyapentokh, *Sotsiologia dlya vsekh, op. cit.,* p. 162.

57. *Ibid.,* p. 169.

58. *Ibid.,* p. 121.

59. Sewell and Haller, *op. cit.,* p. 160.

60. *Ibid.,* pp. 167–168.

61. *Women in the Soviet Union,* Moscow, 1970, p. 47. Data are, depending on country, for 1962–1966.

62. Mark G. Field, "Workers (and Mothers): Soviet Women Today," in *The Role and Status of Women in the Soviet Union,* ed. Donald R. Brown, New York, Teachers College Press, Columbia University, p. 14.

63. *Women in the Soviet Union,* pp. 42–43.

64. *Handbook of Labor Statistics, 1971,* U.S. Department of Labor, Washington, D.C., 1971, Table 1, p. 25.

65. U.S. Bureau of the Census, *Current Population Reports,* Series P-23, no. 34, "Characteristics of American Youth, 1970," U.S. Government Printing Office, Washington, D.C., 1971, p. 3.

66. I. V. Vdovenko and V. P. Korchagin, "Zanyatost v domashnem khozyaistve kak istochnik rabochei sily," *Demograficheskie problemy zanyatosti,* ed. P. P. Litvyakov, Moscow, 1969, p. 197.

67. *Ibid.,* p. 201.

68. *Ibid.,* pp. 203–204.

69. *Ibid.,* p. 204.

70. L. Borisova, *op. cit.*

71. U.S. Department of Health, Education, and Welfare, "Earned Degrees Conferred: 1968–1969," Washington, D.C., U.S. Government Printing Office, 1971, p. 3.

72. U.S. Department of Labor, *1969 Handbook on Women Workers,* Women's Bureau Bulletin 294, Washington, D.C., U.S. Government Printing Office, 1969, p. 98.

73. Norton T. Dodge, *op. cit.,* p. 181.

74. *Women in the Soviet Union, op. cit.,* p. 11.

75. Yu. V. Arutiunyan, "Opyt sotsiologicheskovo izuchenia sela," cited in Shlyapentokh, *op. cit.,* p. 117.

76. *Pervichnaya partynaya organizatsia,* Moscow, 1970, p. 723.

77. Bohdan Harasymiw, "*Nomenklatura:* The Soviet Communist Party's Leadership Recruitment System," *Canadian Journal of Political Science,* vol. II, no. 4 (December 1969), 511.

78. *Women in the Soviet Union, op. cit.,* p. 33.

79. *World Almanac and Book of Facts, 1971,* Newspaper Enterprise Association, Inc., New York, 1971, pp. 737–739.

80. U.S. Bureau of the Census, *Statistical Abstract of the United States, 1968* (89th edition), Washington, D.C., 1968, p. 355.

81. Paul T. David, R. Goodman, and R. Bain, *The Politics of National Party Conventions,* Brookings Institution, Washington, D. C., 1960, pp. 515–516.

82. U.S. Civil Service Commission, Bureau of Management Services, *Study of Employment of Women in the Federal Government: 1969*, U.S. Government Printing Office, Washington, D.C., 1970, p. 19.

83. *Ob osnovnykh itogakh izuchenia byudzheta vremeni zhitelei g. Pskova*, cited in Shlyapentokh, *op. cit.*, p. 147.

84. A. Kharchev, in *Sotsialnye issledovania*, Moscow, 1965, cited in Shlyapentokh, *op. cit.*, p. 147.

85. U.S. Bureau of the Census, *Statistical Abstract of the United States, 1968* (89th edition), Washington, D.C., 1968, p. 62.

86. V. G. Kostakov, "Demograficheskaya kharakteristika trudosposobnovo naselenia," *Demograficheskie problemy zanyatosti*, Moscow, 1969, p. 61.

87. G. I. Khmara, "Pechat v sisteme massovykh kommunikatsy," *Problemy sotsiologii pechati*, Novosibirsk, Vol. 1, 1969, p. 197.

88. M. Kent Jennings and Richard G. Niemi, "The Division of Political Labor between Mothers and Fathers," *American Political Science Review*, LXV (March 1971), p. 75. Readership data are from W. R. Simmons and Associates, "Simmons 1970 Magazine Audience Study," *Advertising Age*, March 23, 1970, p. 106.

89. V. E. Shlyapentokh, "Nekotorye metodologicheskie i metodicheskie problemy sotsiologii pechati," *Problemy Sotsiologii Pechati*, vol. 1, Novosibirsk, 1969, p. 109.

90. V. T. Davydchenko, "Organizatsia sotsiologicheskovo obsledovania i vnedrenie poluchennykh resultatov v tsentralnoi gazete," *Problemy Sotsiologii Pechati*, vol. 2, Novosibirsk, 1970, p. 155.

91. The classic studies of Soviet public opinion were conducted by Inkeles and Bauer: *The Soviet Citizen*, Harvard University Press, 1959. This is the most complete picture of prewar attitudes of Soviet citizens. They were able to discuss differences in attention and gratification with respect to official and nonofficial information sources.

92. John P. Robinson, "The Audience for National TV News Programs," *Public Opinion Quarterly*, XXXV:3 (Fall 1971), pp. 404–405.

93. A. N. Alekseev, "Opyt sopostavitelnovo analiza rezultatov raznykh issledovany massovoi kommunikatsii," *Problemy Sotsiologii Pechati*, vol. 2, Novosibirsk, 1970, p. 183.

94. G. I. Khmara, "Pechat v sisteme massovykh kommunikatsy," *Problemy Sotsiologii Pechati*, vol. 1, Novosibirsk, pp. 198–200.

95. Inkeles and Bauer, *op. cit.*, p. 178.

96. Davydchenkov, " 'Izvestia' izuchaut chitatelya," *Zhurnalist*, no. 2, 1968, p. 23.

97. V. E. Shlyapentokh, "Nekotorye metodologicheskie i metodicheskie . . .", *op. cit.*, p. 110.

98. *Ibid.*, p. 129.

99. V. A. Kolmogorov, "Obrabotka sotsiologicheskoi informatsii na EVM," *Problemy Sotsiologii Pechati*, vol. 1, Novosibirsk, 1969, p. 272.

100. " 'Literaturnaya Gazeta' i ee chitatel," *Problemy Sotsiologii Pechati*, vol. 2, Novosibirsk, 1970, pp. 92–117.

101. David Lane, *The End of Inequality? Stratification under State Socialism*, Middlesex, Penguin, 1971, p. 12.

102. V. E. Shlyapentokh, "Nekotorye metodologicheskie i metodicheskie . . .," *op. cit.*, p. 174.

103. Nor can we make judgments cross-nationally about the inferences to be drawn from a "don't know" or "no opinion" answer. Andrzej Sicinski suggests some of the pitfalls in underestimating the importance of varying styles of response in France, Norway, and Poland, in " 'Don't Know' Answers in Cross-national Surveys," *Public Opinion Quarterly*, XXXIV:1 (Spring 1970), pp. 126–129.

104. " 'Literaturnaya Gazeta' i ee chitatel," *op. cit.*, p. 130.

105. *Ibid.*, p. 125.

106. Shlyapentokh, "K Voprosu ob izuchenii esteticheskikh vkusov chitatelya gazety," *Problemy Sotsiologii Pechati*, vol. 2, Novosibirsk, 1970, p. 60.

107. " 'Literaturnaya Gazeta' i ee chitatel," *op. cit.*, pp. 127–129.

108. *Ibid.*, p. 134.

109. Rita James Simon, "Public Attitudes toward Population and Pollution," *Public Opinion Quarterly,* XXXV:1 (Spring 1971), pp. 93–99.

110. Arvin W. Murch, "Public Concern for Environmental Pollution," *Public Opinion Quarterly,* XXXV:1 (Spring 1971), pp. 99–101.

111. Shlyapentokh, "K Voprosu ob izuchenii . . . ," *op. cit.,* pp. 62–63.

112. Khmara, pp. 209–210.

113. " 'Literaturnaya Gazeta' i ee chitatel," *op. cit.,* pp. 127–129.

114. *Ibid.,* p. 132.

115. *Ibid.,* pp. 135–138.

116. Alekseev, *op. cit.* The survey of Leningrad television viewers referred to here was conducted in 1967 among 1916 residents of that city. The sample was constructed to represent the characteristics of the city as a whole, in terms of occupation, education, sex, and age groups. The findings are reported by Boris Firsov, "Srednovo zritelya net," *Zhurnalist,* no. 12, 1967, pp. 42–45.

117. Morris Rosenberg, *The Logic of Survey Analysis,* New York, Basic Books, 1968, p. 118. I am indebted to Ada W. Finifter for bringing this source to my attention.

118. Inkeles and Bauer, *op. cit.,* p. 181.

119. Robert E. Lane and David O. Sears, *Public Opinion,* Englewood Cliffs, Prentice-Hall, 1964, p. 40.

120. Inkeles and Bauer, *op. cit.,* p. 168.

121. V. A. Smirnov, *Sotsiologicheskie issledovania v praktike partynoi raboty,* Volga-Vyatka, 1969, pp. 28–38.

122. The following is based on *Ibid.,* pp. 24–74.

123. Comparisons of peer group socialization versus parental socialization between the Soviet Union and the United States can be found in Urie Bronfenbrenner, *Two Worlds of Childhood: U.S. and U.S.S.R.,* New York, Russell Sage Foundation, 1970.

124. Such informal labor practices are described by Joseph Berliner, *Factory and Manager in the USSR,* Cambridge, Harvard University Press, 1957.

125. Davydchenkov, *op. cit.,* pp. 168–177.

126. *Ibid.,* p. 173.

127. Smirnov, *op. cit.,* p. 68.

128. *Ibid.,* pp. 68–69.

129. V. Z. Kogan and Iu. I. Skvortsov, "Stroki, temy, zhanry," *Problemy Sotsiologii Pechati,* vol. 2, Novosibirsk, 1970, p. 56.

130. Davydchenkov, *op. cit.,* p. 152.

131. John A. Armstrong, "The Ethnic Scene in the Soviet Union: The View of the Dictatorship," *Ethnic Minorities in the Soviet Union,* ed. Erich Goldhagen, New York, Praeger, 1968, p. 6.

132. *Ibid.,* p. 12.

133. *Ibid.,* p. 43. In 1959, Russians made up 43 percent of Kazakhstan and Kazakhs made up only 29 percent. Lowell R. Tillett, "Nationalism and History," *Problems of Communism,* September/October 1967, p. 37.

134. Garip Sultan, "Demographic and Cultural Trends among Turkic Peoples of the Soviet Union," *Ethnic Minorities in the Soviet Union, op. cit.,* p. 255.

135. See especially *World Handbook of Political and Social Indicators,* Bruce M. Russett, Hayward R. Alker, Jr., Karl W. Deutsch, and Harold D. Lasswell, New Haven, Yale University Press, 1964; and *Quantitative International Politics,* ed. J. David Singer, New York, Free Press, 1968.

136. The comparisons were dyadic, and the program used calculated the Pearson product-moment correlation adjusted for missing data. The program, run on the CDC 6500 computer at Michigan State University, was developed by David Kline of the Computer Institute for Social Science Research of Michigan State, and was entitled "Incomplete Data Correlation Program."

137. The program used for this process is the "Hierarchical Clustering Based on a Criterion of *L*argest *A*verage *W*ithin-Cluster *S*imilarity," by Leighton A. Price, as modified for use on the CDC 6500 by James E. Hylen, both of the Computer Institute for Social Science Research of Michigan State University.

138. Soviet Central Asia, with a much higher birth rate than that of the rest of the Soviet Union, may in fact require favored treatment simply to maintain parity of change.
139. Vsevolod Holubnychy, "Some Economic Aspects of Relations among the Soviet Republics," *Ethnic Minorities in the Soviet Union, op. cit.,* p. 66.
140. *Ibid.,* p. 65.
141. Holubnychy argues that, excluding the Baltic republics and Moldavia, the RSFSR, with respect to certain economic indices, is developing more rapidly than other republics.
142. Sidney Siegel, *Nonparametric Statistics,* New York, McGraw-Hill, 1956, p. 214.
143. *Political Man,* New York, Anchor Books, 1963, p. 184.
144. S. N. Eisenstadt, "Initial Institutional Patterns of Political Modernization," *Political Modernization,* ed. Claude E. Welch, Jr., Belmont, Calif., Wadsworth, 1967, p. 295.
145. *Pervichnaya partynaya organizatsia,* Moscow, 1970, p. 385.
146. Lester W. Milbrath, *Political Participation,* Chicago, Rand McNally, 1965, p. 153.
147. See, for example, the legalistic mode of expression and analysis adopted by many of the young Soviet dissidents as they claim their "constitutional rights." In a recent study, Ada Finifter observes that the alienation produced by feelings of normlessness (feelings that "the norms or rules intended to govern political relations have broken down and that departures from prescribed behavior are common") may in fact derive from "*allegiance* to a set of ideals to which the community formally adheres, but which are commonly violated." "Dimensions of Political Alienation," *American Political Science Review,* LXIV (June 1970), pp. 390–391 and p. 407. Italics are in the original.

DEMOGRAPHY

WARREN W. EASON

MOST OF THE DATA on population that appear in this book are taken directly
from official statistics published in Soviet sources; the remainder are estimates
based on the published statistics. Soviet population data of the type and detail
presented here, at least for recent decades, are considered to be reasonably
accurate and reliable. Data for the earlier decades of the Soviet period, however, are less reliable, if only because the methods and operations of the
Central Statistical Administration (TsSU) had not yet become firmly established; but the main difficulty of these years concerns the 1930's and 1940's,
for which relatively little aggregate data on the population, though gathered
by TsSU, were ever published. At least for the 1930's, fortunately, general
population trends may be indicated with reference to the selected years for
which some data are available.

Soviet interest in population statistics and demographic questions has always been high, in keeping with a tradition which began in the eighteenth
century and was already well developed by the end of the nineteenth century.
During the first decade of Soviet power (1917 to 1927), no fewer than four
population censuses were taken, although not all were completed, and the
collection of vital statistics, previously confined to the provinces of European
Russia, was expanded to include the whole of the USSR. The volume and
variety of statistics on employment and other aspects of labor also greatly
increased. By the beginning of rapid industrialization (1928), in other words,
a sound basis had been established for gathering (and analyzing) statistics on
the population and labor force, and most of these data, moreover, were published.

During the 1930's, the publication of statistics in virtually all fields was
drastically curtailed. But even in these years, three censuses of population were
planned, two were carried out, and the results of one (1939) were partially
released; the system of gathering statistics on the labor force, from production
enterprises, state and collective farms, and administrative and other institutions, was expanded and refined; and the collection and processing of vital

statistics, which had suffered during the difficulties of the early 1930's, particularly in the countryside, returned more or less to normal. Wartime conditions, of course, made it impossible to carry out a census, but institutional data continued to be assembled and selected studies of the population were also made.

Since the mid-1950's, the quality and—most dramatically—the quantity of population data being published have greatly improved, culminating in the all-Union census of 1959, which was published in 16 volumes, and the succeeding census of 1970, from which preliminary data are reproduced in this handbook. Beyond the data themselves, furthermore, there is a genuine "renaissance" of the science of demography taking place within the academic and government-research community, reestablishing, one might say, the tradition in population studies which began more than 200 years ago.

The following comments by specific types of population data presented here are offered as a further guide to the reader:

1. Data on the *total, urban and rural population* (Tables 1 and 4) are from the censuses of 1926, 1939, 1959 and 1970, and, for other years, are the official estimates prepared on a continuing basis by TsSU. These noncensus estimates are drawn up for intercensal years through the use of vital statistics and data on migration as well as from population records maintained by the local branches of government. Intercensal estimates are typically revised with the advent of yet another census, and the data here reproduced are the latest figures available.

2. *Birth and death rates* and the resulting rate of natural increase of the population (Table 2) are the official Soviet figures. Those for 1928 and 1930 are considered to suffer from a certain degree of underreporting of births and deaths at the primary source, but postwar data are reasonably complete.

3. Data on the *population by age and sex* (Table 3), by *nationalities* (Table 9), by *republics* (Tables 10 and 12) and by *size of family* (Table 11) are taken directly as reported from the respective censuses. Data on the *labor force by age and sex* (Table 5) are also from the censuses, except that an estimated adjustment was required for 1959 to provide consistent data by age groups.

4. Data on *wage and salary workers* (Table 7) and on *days and hours worked* (Table 8) are the official statistics taken from various statistical handbooks published by TsSU.

5. Data on the *labor force and civilian employment* (Table 6) are estimates developed in the secondary (non-Soviet) sources listed in the notes. Although these estimates draw extensively on data from Soviet sources, they represent attempts to develop consistent measures over time of the indicated categories which are not, in all cases, reported as such in Soviet sources. The reader is referred to the secondary sources for detailed explanation of method.

Table 1. Total Population, USSR: Census Data, 1926, 1939, 1959, and 1970; Soviet Estimates, 1913, 1928–1931, 1940–1941, 1950–1951, and 1958–1971 (In Thousands)

1913	139,313[a]	1958	204,925
	159,153[b]	1959 Census	208,827
		1960	212,400
1926 Census	147,028[c]	1961	216,300
		1962	220,000
1928	150,500[d]	1963	223,500
1929	154,300	1964	226,700
1930	157,700	1965	229,600
1931	160,600	1966	232,200
		1967	234,800
1939 Census	170,557	1968	237,200
		1969	239,500
1940	194,077[e]	1970 Census	241,748
1941	196,659	1971	243,900
1950	178,547		
1951	181,603		

Notes:

[a] Territory of U.S.S.R. before September, 1939.

[b] Present territory of U.S.S.R.

[c] Census dates are: December 17, 1926, January 17, 1939, January 15, 1959, and January 15, 1970.

[d] Non-census data are January 1, except 1913, which is "average for year."

[e] Data from 1940 are for present territory of U.S.S.R.

Table 2. Birth and Death Rates per 1,000 Population and Percentage Rates of Natural Increase, USSR

Year	Birth Rates	Death Rates	Percent of Increase
1913	47.0[a]	30.2	1.68
	45.5[b]	29.1	1.64
1928	44.3	23.3	2.10
1930	39.2	20.4	1.88
1940	31.2[c]	18.0	1.32
1950	26.7	9.7	1.70
1958	25.3	7.2	1.81
1959	25.0	7.6	1.74
1960	24.9	7.1	1.78
1961	23.8	7.2	1.66
1962	22.4	7.5	1.49
1963	21.1	7.2	1.39
1964	19.5	6.9	1.26
1965	18.4	7.3	1.11
1966	18.2	7.3	1.09
1967	17.3	7.6	0.97
1968	17.2	7.7	0.95
1969	17.0	8.1	0.89

Notes:

[a] Territory of U.S.S.R. before September, 1939.

[b] Present territory of U.S.S.R.

[c] Data from 1940 are for present territory of U.S.S.R.

Table 3. THE POPULATION BY SEX AND FIVE-YEAR AGE GROUPS, USSR: CENSUS DATA, 1926, 1939, AND 1959; ESTIMATE, 1941 (In Thousands)

Age	Both Sexes	Males	Females	Percentage Distribution Both Sexes	Males	Females	Males per Hundred Females
			A. Census of 1926				
0-4	22,322	11,237	11,085	15.2	15.8	14.6	101.3
5-9	15,270	7,650	7,620	10.4	10.8	10.0	100.3
10-14	17,090	8,643	8,447	11.6	12.2	11.1	102.3
15-19	16,993	8,142	8,851	11.6	11.5	11.6	92.0
20-24	13,827	6,720	7,107	9.4	9.5	9.4	94.6
25-29	12,049	5,497	6,552	8.2	7.7	8.6	83.9
30-34	9,073	4.302	4,771	6.2	6.1	6.3	90.2
35-39	8,461	3,999	4,462	5.8	5.6	5.9	89.6
40-44	6,962	3,397	3,565	4.7	4.8	4.7	95.3
45-49	5,913	2,896	3,017	4.0	4.1	4.0	96.0
50-54	5,046	2,346	2,700	3.4	3.3	3.5	86.9
55-59	4,209	1,889	2,320	2.9	2.6	3.0	81.4
60-64	3,839	1,711	2,128	2.6	2.4	2.8	80.4
65-69	2,567	1,159	1,408	1.7	1.6	1.9	82.3
70 and over	3,407	1,455	1,952	2.3	2.0	2.6	74.5
TOTAL	147,028	71,043	75,985	100.0	100.0	100.0	93.5
0-9	37,592	18,887	18,705	25.6	26.6	24.6	101.0
10-14	17,090	8,643	8,447	11.6	12.2	11.1	102.3
15 and over	92,346	43,513	48,833	62.8	61.2	64.3	89.1
0-14	54,682	27,530	27,152	37.2	38.8	35.7	101.4
15-49	73,278	34,953	38,325	49.9	49.3	50.5	91.2
50 and over	19,068	8,560	10,508	12.9	11.9	13.8	81.5
0-15	58,326	29,340	28,986	39.7	41.3	38.1	101.2
16-59	78,889	37,378	41,511	53.7	52.7	54.6	90.0
60 and over	9,813	4,325	5,488	6.6	6.0	7.3	78.8
0-15	58,326	29,340	28,986	39.7	41.3	38.1	101.2
16-54	76,569	....	39,191	52.1	...	51.6	95.4
16-59		37,378			52.7		
55 and over	12,133	....	7,808	8.2	...	10.3	55.4
60 and over		4,325	....		6.0	...	
			B. Census of 1939				
0-4	21,255	10,752	10,503	12.5	13.2	11.8	102.4
5-9	18,469	9,245	9,224	10.8	11.3	10.4	100.2
10-14	21,735	10,833	10,902	12.7	13.3	12.3	99.4
15-19	15,203	7,505	7,698	8.9	9.2	8.7	97.5
20-24	14,415	7,193	7,222	8.4	8.8	8.1	99.6
25-29	16,499	8,051	8,448	9.7	9.9	9.5	95.3
30-34	13,759	6,653	7,106	8.1	8.1	8.0	93.6
35-39	11,770	5,508	6,262	6.9	6.7	7.0	88.0
40-44	8,526	3,909	4,617	5.0	4.8	5.2	84.7
45-49	6,812	3,117	3,695	4.0	3.8	4.2	84.4
50-54	5,974	2,544	3,430	3.5	3.1	3.8	74.2
55-59	4,951	2,115	2,836	2.9	2.6	3.2	74.6
60-64	4,039	1,639	2,400	2.4	2.0	2.7	68.3
65-69	3,096	1,209	1,887	1.8	1.5	2.1	64.1
70 and over	4,054	1,422	2,632	2.4	1.7	3.0	54.0
TOTAL	170,557	81,695	88,862	100.0	100.0	100.0	91.9
0-9	39,724	19,997	19,727	23.3	24.5	22.2	101.4
10-14	21,735	10,833	10,902	12.7	13.3	12.3	99.4
15 and over	109,098	50,865	58,233	64.0	62.2	65.5	87.3
0-14	61,459	30,830	30,629	36.0	37.8	34.5	100.7
15-49	86,984	41,936	45,048	51.0	51.3	50.7	93.1
50 and over	22,114	8,929	13,185	13.0	10.9	14.8	67.7
0-15	65,336	32,756	32,580	38.3	40.1	36.7	100.5
16-59	94,032	44,669	49,363	55.1	54.7	55.5	90.5
60 and over	11,189	4,270	6,919	6.6	5.2	7.8	61.7
0-15	65,336	32,756	32,580	38.3	40.1	36.7	100.5
16-54	91,196	....	46,527	53.5	...	52.4	96.0
16-59		44,669	....		54.7	...	
55 and over	14,025	....	9,755	8.2	...	10.9	43.8
60 and over		4,270	....		5.2	...	

Table 3. THE POPULATION BY SEX AND FIVE-YEAR AGE GROUPS, USSR: CENSUS DATA, 1926, 1939, AND 1959; ESTIMATE, 1941 (Continued)

Age	Both Sexes	Males	Females	Percentage Distribution Both Sexes	Males	Females	Males per Hundred Females
			C. January 1, 1941, Including Annexed Territories				
0-4	24,398	12,336	12,062	12.4	13.0	11.9	102.2
5-9	20,936	10,523	10,413	10.7	11.1	10.2	101.1
10-14	22,619	11,300	11,319	11.5	12.0	11.1	99.8
15-19	19,718	9,795	9,923	10.1	10.4	9.7	98.7
20-24	16,044	7,967	8,077	8.2	8.4	7.9	98.6
25-29	17,264	8,483	8,781	8.8	9.0	8.6	96.6
30-34	16,490	8,013	8,477	8.4	8.5	8.3	94.5
35-39	13,685	6,499	7,186	7.0	6.9	7.1	90.4
40-44	10,616	4,906	5,710	5.4	5.2	5.6	85.9
45-49	8,289	3,784	4,505	4.2	4.0	4.4	84.0
50-54	6,859	3,011	3,848	3.5	3.2	3.8	78.2
55-59	5,941	2,535	3,406	3.0	2.7	3.3	74.4
60-64	4,929	2,046	2,883	2.5	2.2	2.8	70.9
65-69	3,816	1,520	2,296	1.9	1.6	2.3	66.2
70 and over	4,746	1,735	3,011	2.4	1.8	3.0	57.6
TOTAL	196,350	94,453	101,897	100.0	100.0	100.0	92.7
0-14	67,953	34,159	33,794	34.6	36.1	33.2	101.1
15-49	102,106	49,447	52,659	52.1	52.4	51.6	93.9
50 and over	26,291	10,847	15,444	13.3	11.5	15.2	70.2
0-15	73,101	36,716	36,385	37.2	38.9	35.7	100.9
16-54	106,352	....	53,916	54.2	...	52.9	97.3
16-59		52,436	....		55.5	...	
55 and over	16,897	....	11,596	8.6	...	11.4	45.7
60 and over		5,301	....		5.6	...	
			D. Census of 1959				
0-4	24,326	12,417	11,909	11.6	13.2	10.4	104.3
5-9	22,036	11,191	10,845	10.6	11.9	9.4	103.2
10-14	15,311	7,771	7,540	7.3	8.2	6.6	103.1
15-19	16,498	8,296	8,202	7.9	8.8	7.1	101.1
20-24	20,343	10,056	10,287	9.7	10.7	9.0	97.8
25-29	18,191	8,917	9,274	8.7	9.5	8.1	96.2
30-34	19,001	8,612	10,389	9.1	9.2	9.1	82.9
35-39	11,592	4,529	7,063	5.6	4.8	6.1	64.1
40-44	10,409	3,999	6,410	5.0	4.2	5.6	62.4
45-49	12,264	4,706	7,558	5.9	5.0	6.6	62.3
50-54	10,447	4,010	6,437	5.0	4.3	5.6	62.3
55-59	8,700	2,906	5,794	4.2	3.1	5.0	50.2
60-64	6,697	2,349	4,348	3.2	2.5	3.8	54.0
65-69	5,041	1,751	3,290	2.4	1.9	2.9	53.2
70 and over	7,971	2,540	5,431	3.8	2.7	4.7	46.8
TOTAL	208,827	94,050	114,777	100.0	100.0	100.0	81.9
0-9	46,362	23,608	22,754	22.2	25.1	19.8	103.8
10-14	15,311	7,771	7,540	7.3	8.2	6.6	103.1
15 and over	147,154	62,671	84,483	70.5	66.7	73.6	74.2
0-14	61,673	31,379	30,294	29.5	33.3	26.4	103.6
15-49	109,298	49,115	59,183	51.9	52.2	51.6	83.0
50 and over	38,856	13,556	25,300	18.6	14.5	22.0	53.6
0-15	63,496	32,300	31,196	30.4	34.3	27.2	103.5
16-59	125,622	55,110	70,512	60.2	58.6	61.4	78.2
60 and over	19,709	6,640	13,069	9.4	7.1	11.4	50.8
0-15	63,496	32,300	31,196	30.4	34.3	27.2	103.5
16-54	119,828	....	64,718	57.4	...	56.4	85.2
16-59		55,110	....		58.6	...	
55 and over	25,503	....	18,863	12.2	...	16.4	35.2
60 and over		6,640	....		7.1	...	

Table 4. POPULATION BY URBAN AND RURAL AREAS, USSR (In Thousands)

		Population		Percent	
	Total	Urban	Rural	Urban	Rural
1913	139,313[a]	24,820	114,493	17.8	82.2
	159,153[b]	28,452	130,701	17.9	82.1
1926 Census	147,028[c]	26,314	120,714	17.9	82.1
1928	150,500[d]	27,600	122,900	18.3	81.7
1929	154,300	29,200	125,100	18.9	81.1
1930	157,700	30,900	126,800	19.6	80.4
1931	160,600	32,000	128,600	19.9	80.1
1939 Census	170,557	56,125	114,432	32.9	67.1
1940	194,077[e]	63,112	130,965	32.5	67.5
1941	196,659	64,908	131,751	33.0	67.0
1950	178,547	69,414	109,133	38.9	61.2
1951	181,603	73,005	108,598	40.2	59.8
1958	204,925	95,576	109,349	46.6	53.4
1959 Census	208,827	99,978	108,849	47.9	52.1
1960	212,400	103,600	108,800	48.8	51.2
1961	216,300	107,900	108,400	49.9	50.1
1962	220,000	111,200	108,800	50.6	49.4
1963	223,500	114,400	109,100	51.2	48.8
1964	226,700	117,700	109,000	51.9	48.1
1965	229,600	120,700	108,900	52.6	47.4
1966	232,200	123,700	108,500	53.3	46.7
1967	234,800	126,900	107,900	54.0	46.0
1968	237,200	129,800	107,400	54.7	45.3
1969	239,500	132,900	106,600	55.5	44.5
1970 Census	241,748	136,003	105,745	56.3	43.7

Notes:

See Table 1.

Table 5. THE POPULATION AND LABOR FORCE BY SEX AND BROAD AGE GROUPS, USSR (In Thousands)

		1926			1959		
		Popula-tion	Labor Force	Per-cent	Popula-tion	Labor Force	Per-cent
MALES	0-9	18,887	...	...	23,600	...	...
	10-15	10,451	6,479	62.0	8,600	600	7.0
	16-59	37,335	36,310	97.3	55,200	48,600	88.0
	60 and over	4,370	3,425	78.4	6,600	3,200	48.5
	10 and over	52,156	46,214	86.7	70,400	52,400	74.4
	TOTAL	71,043	46,214	65.1	94,000	52,400	55.7
FEMALES	0-9	18,705	...	...	22,800	...	...
	10-15	10,280	5,858	57.0	8,500	500	5.9
	16-54	39,160	30,208	77.1	64,600	49,100	76.0
	55 and over	7,840	3,942	50.3	18,900	7,000	37.0
	10 and over	57,280	40,008	69.8	92,000	56,600	61.5
	TOTAL	75,985	40,008	52.7	114,800	56,600	49.3
BOTH SEXES	0-9	37,592	...	...	46,400	...	...
	10-15	20,731	12,337	59.5	17,100	1,100	6.4
	16-54(59)	76,495	66,518	87.0	119,800	97,700	81.6
	55(60) and over	12,210	7,367	60.3	25,500	10,200	40.0
	10 and over	109,436	86,222	78.8	162,400	109,000	67.1
	TOTAL	147,028	86,222	58.6	208,800	109,000	52.2
FEMALES percent of BOTH SEXES in the LABOR FORCE			46.4			51.9	

Table 6. THE LABOR FORCE AND CIVILIAN EMPLOYMENT, USSR, BY MAJOR OCCUPATIONAL CATEGORIES (In Thousands)

	1928	1940	1950	1958	1959	1960	1961
				Labor Force			
Civilian Labor Force							
Nonagricultural	16,200	39,800	42,500	55,700	58,000	60,800	63,800
Agricultural	69,300	58,000	49,900	49,500	47,600	44,600	43,000
State	400	2,500	4,400	6,200	6,400	7,800	8,500
Collective Farm	1,500	44,700	35,700	32,900	31,700	28,900	26,800
Private	67,400	10,800	9,800	10,400	9,500	8,000	7,700
Total	85,500	97,800	92,400	105,300	105,600	105,300	106,800
Armed Forces	600	3,000	4,600	3,800	3,600	3,300	3,000
TOTAL LABOR FORCE	86,100	100,800	97,000	109,100	109,200	108,600	109,800
				Civilian Employment			
Nonagricultural Employment							
Industry	...	12,700	15,300	21,000	21,700	22,600	23,800
Other	...	19,100	21,700	29,200	30,800	32,600	34,500
Total	13,300	31,800	37,000	50,200	52,500	55,200	58,300
Agricultural Employment							
State	400	3,000	3,400	5,300	5,400	6,800	7,600
Collective Farm	...	28,000	27,600	25,400	24,500	22,300	20,700
Private	...	14,800	11,900	12,600	11,500	10,900	11,300
Attached	...	...	200	500	500	500	500
Total	38,100	48,000	43,100	43,800	41,900	40,500	40,000
TOTAL CIVILIAN EMPLOYMENT	50,700	79,800	80,100	94,000	94,400	95,700	98,300

	1962	1963	1964	1965	1966	1967	1968
				Labor Force			
Civilian Labor Force							
Nonagricultural	66,000	68,100	70,400	73,700	76,300	79,000	81,700
Agricultural	42,700	42,500	42,300	43,100	41,700	42,400	40,800
State	8,700	8,900	9,300	9,700	9,900	9,800	9,900
Collective Farm	25,900	25,100	24,800	24,500	24,100	23,800	23,400
Private	8,100	8,500	8,100	8,900	7,800	8,800	7,500
Total	108,800	110,600	112,700	116,800	118,100	121,400	122,500
Armed Forces	3,800	3,600	3,300	3,200	3,200	3,200	3,200
TOTAL LABOR FORCE	112,600	114,200	116,000	119,900	121,200	124,600	125,800
				Civilian Employment			
Nonagricultural Employment							
Industry	24,700	25,400	26,300	27,400	28,500	29,400	30,400
Other	35,900	37,200	38,600	40,800	42,300	44,000	45,800
Total	60,500	62,600	64,900	68,200	70,800	73,400	76,200
Agricultural Employment							
State	7,800	7,900	8,400	8,700	8,900	8,800	8,900
Collective Farm	20,000	19,400	19,200	18,900	18,600	18,400	18,100
Private	11,300	10,900	10,900	12,000	12,700	11,900	11,600
Attached	400	400	400	500	500	500	500
Total	39,500	38,600	38,900	40,100	40,700	39,600	39,100
TOTAL CIVILIAN EMPLOYMENT	100,000	101,200	103,800	108,300	111,500	113,100	115,300

Notes:

Labor Force: comprises the number of persons according to their "usual occupation," regardless of the amount of time actually worked.

Employment: the annual average, full-time equivalent number of persons actually working.

Table 7. THE NUMBER OF WAGE AND SALARY WORKERS, USSR, BY SEX AND BY MAJOR BRANCHES OF THE NATIONAL ECONOMY (In Thousands)

	Both Sexes	Males	Females	Percent Females	Both Sexes	Males	Females	Percent Females
	National Economy				Industry[e]			
1913	11,400[b]	...	...	...	...	...	...	...
	12,900[c]	...	...	...	...	...	...	...
1928	11,444	8,649	2,795	24.4[d]	4,339	3,198	1,141	26.3
1940	33,926	20,736	13,190	38.9	13,079	8,142	4,937	37.7
1950	40,420	21,240	19,180	47.5	15,317	8,312	7,005	45.7
1958	56,005	30,055	25,950	46.3	...	...	...	45.0
1959	57,900	30,630	27,170	46.9				
1960	62,032	33,782	29,250	47.2	22,600	12,400	10,200	45.0
1961	65,861	34,431	31,430	47.7	23,475	12,794	10,681	45.5
1962	68,300	35,470	32,830	48.1	24,300	13,100	11,200	46.0
1963	70,526	36,451	34,075	48.3	25,100	13,800	11,300	45.0
1964	73,258	37,553	35,705	48.7	29,900	14,000	11,900	46.0
1965	76,914	39,234	37,680	49.0	27,400	14,800	12,600	46.0
1966	79,709	40,209	39,500	49.6	28,500	15,100	13,400	47.0
1967	82,274	41,214	41,060	49.9	29,400	15,600	13,800	47.0
1968	85,100	42,420	42,680	50.2	30,400	16,100	14,300	47.0
1969	87,922	43,512	44,410	50.5	31,200	16,200	15,000	48.0
	Construction[d]				Agriculture[d]			
1928	749	702	47	6.3	1,660	1,267	393	23.7
1940	1,620	1,240	380	23.4	2,703	1,896	807	29.9
1950	2,603	1,741	862	33.1	3,437	2,001	1,436	41.8
1958	...	...	...	31.0	...	...	...	...
1959	...	...	...	...	...	...	...	...
1960	5,143	3,642	1,501	29.2	6,800	3,900	2,900	43.0
1961	5,270	3,726	1,544	29.3	7,800	4,500	3,300	42.0
1962	5,200	3,700	1,500	29.0	8,200	4,800	3,400	42.0
1963	5,200	3,700	1,500	29.0	8,339	...	...	...
1964	5,400	3,800	1,600	29.0	8,552	...	...	...
1965	5,700	4,000	1,700	29.0	8,704	...	...	...
1966	5,900	4,200	1,700	28.0	8,900	5,000	3,900	44.0
1967	6,100	4,400	1,700	28.0	8,800	5,000	3,800	44.0
1968	6,300	4,600	1,700	27.0	8,900	5,100	3,800	43.0
1969	6,700	4,900	1,800	27.0	9,100	5,200	3,900	43.0
	Transportation				Communications			
1928	1,302	1,217	85	6.5	95	69	26	27.4
1940	3,525	2,775	750	21.3	484	251	233	48.1
1950	4,117	2,946	1,171	28.4	542	224	318	58.7
1958	...	...	...	26.0	...	...	...	63.0
1959	...	...	...	...	...	...	...	...
1960	6,279	4,778	1,501	23.9	738	262	476	64.4
1961	6,518	4,888	1,630	25.0	790	283	508	64.2
1962	6,700	5,000	1,700	25.0	800	300	500	64.0
1963	6,800	5,100	1,700	25.0	900	300	600	64.0
1964	7,100	5,400	1,700	24.0	900	300	600	65.0
1965	7,300	5,600	1,700	24.0	1,000	300	700	65.0
1966	7,364	5,603	1,761	23.9	1,073	366	707	65.9
1967	7,500	5,700	1,800	24.0	1,100	400	700	66.0
1968	7,600	5,800	1,800	24.0	1,200	400	800	66.0
1969	7,800	5,900	1,900	24.0	1,300	500	800	67.0
	Trade				Housing			
1928	606	489	117	19.3	158	...	...	...
1940	3,351	1,860	1,491	44.5	1,500	800	700	43.0
1950	3,360	1,442	1,918	57.1	1,400	700	700	54.0
1958	...	...	...	64.0	...	...	...	...
1959	...	...	...	...	...	...	...	...
1960	4,675	1,577	3,098	66.3	1,900	900	1,000	53.0
1961	5,010	1,478	3,532	70.5	2,030	...	...	...
1962	5,300	1,600	3,700	71.0	2,096	...	...	...
1963	5,500	1,500	4,000	73.0	2,182	...	...	...
1964	5,800	1,700	4,100	71.0	2,282	...	...	...
1965	6,000	1,700	4,300	72.0	2,400	1,100	1,300	53.0
1966	6,261	1,664	4,597	73.4	2,500	1,100	1,400	53.0
1967	6,600	1,700	4,900	74.0	2,700	1,300	1,400	51.0
1968	7,000	1,800	5,200	75.0	2,800	1,400	1,400	51.0
1969	7,300	1,800	5,500	75.0	2,900	1,400	1,500	51.0

Table 7. THE NUMBER OF WAGE AND SALARY WORKERS, USSR, BY SEX AND BY MAJOR BRANCHES OF THE NATIONAL ECONOMY (Continued)

	Both Sexes	Males	Females	Percent Females	Both Sexes	Males	Females	Percent Females
	Public Health				Education			
1928	399	147	252	63.2	725	326	399	55.0
1940	1,512	366	1,146	75.8	2,678	1,095	1,583	59.1
1950	2,051	318	1,733	84.5	3,315	1,040	2,275	68.6
1958	...	...	...	85.0	...	...	...	69.0
1959	...	...	...	...	...	...	...	...
1960	3,461	510	2,951	85.3	4,803	1,448	3,355	69.9
1961	3,677	526	3,151	85.7	5,200	1,600	3,600	70.0
1962	3,800	500	3,300	96.0	5,500	1,600	3,900	70.0
1963	3,900	500	3,400	86.0	5,800	1,700	4,100	70.0
1964	4,100	600	3,500	86.0	6,200	1,800	4,400	71.0
1965	4,300	600	3,700	86.0	6,600	1,900	4,700	71.0
1966	4,427	650	3,777	85.3	6,895	1,953	4,942	71.7
1967	4,500	700	3,800	85.0	7,200	2,000	5,200	72.0
1968	4,700	700	4,000	85.0	7,500	2,100	5,400	72.0
1969	4,900	700	4,200	85.0	7,800	2,200	5,600	72.0
	Science and Scientific Services				Credit and Insurance Agencies			
1928	82	49	33	40.2	95	59	36	37.9
1940	362	208	154	42.5	267	158	109	40.8
1950	714	408	306	42.9	264	112	152	57.6
1958	...	...	...	42.0	...	...	...	66.0
1959	...	...	...	...	...	...	...	...
1960	1,763	1,029	734	41.6	265	84	181	68.3
1961	2,011	1,157	854	42.5	300	100	200	68.0
1962	2,200	1,200	1,000	44.0	300	100	200	69.0
1963	2,400	1,400	1,000	44.0	300	100	200	70.0
1964	2,500	1,400	1,100	44.0	300	100	200	72.0
1965	2,600	1,400	1,200	44.0	300	100	200	72.0
1966	2,741	1,517	1,224	44.7	313	82	231	73.8
1967	2,900	1,600	1,300	45.0	300	100	200	75.0
1968	3,000	1,600	1,400	46.0	400	100	300	76.0
1969	3,100	1,600	1,500	47.0	400	100	300	77.0
	State Apparatus and Socialized Organizations				Others			
1928	1,010	820	190	18.8	224	148	76	33.9
1940	1,837	1,212	625	34.0	992	17	975	98.3
1950	1,831	1,038	793	43.3	1,498	287	1,211	80.8
1958	...	...	...	49.0	...	...	...	...
1959	...	...	...	...	...	...	...	...
1960	1,245	615	630	50.6	2,326	511	1,815	78.0
1961	1,300	600	700	51.0	2,505	...	...	...
1962	1,300	600	700	52.0	2,625	...	...	...
1963	1,300	600	700	53.0	2,771	...	...	...
1964	1,400	700	700	54.0	2,954	...	...	...
1965	1,500	700	800	55.0	3,163	...	...	...
1966	1,546	679	867	56.1	3,322	748	2,574	77.5
1967	1,600	700	900	58.1	3,491	...	...	...
1968	1,700	700	1,000	58.0	3,537	...	...	...
1969	1,800	700	1,100	60.0	3,622	...	...	...

Notes:

[a] Data by sectors do not necessarily add to the numbers in the national economy, due to rounding.

[b] Territory of U.S.S.R. before September, 1939.

[c] Present territory of U.S.S.R.

[d] Percentages to nearest tenth are derived; others are reported.

[e] Data for industry and agriculture for 1960, and for industry, construction and agriculture for 1965-1969, inclusive, are somewhat inconsistent with corresponding data for other years, because TsSU revised its method of classifying certain wage and salary workers in construction activities in these three sectors, as reported in the first three sources listed.

Table 8. AVERAGE NUMBER OF DAYS AND HOURS WORKED IN INDUSTRY BY WAGE AND SALARY WORKERS, USSR

	1913	1928	1940	1950	1955	1958	1959	1960
Average number of days worked per year per wage earner	...	263.0	269.8	276.3	273.3	268.0	266.5	266.9
Average scheduled number of man-hours worked per day per adult wage earner	9.90	7.81	8.00	8.00	8.00	7.70	7.56	6.94
Average scheduled number of hours worked per week per adult wage and salary worker	58.5	...	...	...	47.8	...	...	...

	1961	1962	1963	1964	1965	1966	1967	1968	1969
Average number of days worked per year per wage earner	264.2	263.4	264.5	266.5	266.4	263.1	249.6	234.0	232.6
Average scheduled number of man-hours worked per day per adult wage earner	6.93	6.93	6.93	...	6.93	...	...	...	...
Average scheduled number of hours worked per week per adult wage and salary worker	...	...	...	...	...	40.6	40.6	40.7	40.7

Table 9. POPULATION BY NATIONALITIES, USSR (In Thousands)

Nationality[a]	1926 Population	Percentage[b]	1939 Population	Percentage	1959 Population	Percentage	1970 Population	Perce
Russian	77,791	52.9	99,019	58.1	114,114	54.6	129,015	53
Ukrainian	31,191	21.2	28,070	16.5	37,253	17.8	40,753	16
Belorussian	4,738	3.2	5,267	3.1	7,913	3.8	9,052	3
Uzbek	3,954	2.7	4,844	2.8	6,015	2.9	(9,195)	(3
Tatar	3,477	2.3	4,300	2.5	4,968	2.4	5,931	2
Kazakh	(3,968)[c]	(2.7)[c]	3,098	1.8	3,622	1.7	5,299	2
Azerbaidzhan	1,706	1.2	2,274	1.4	2,940	1.4	4,380	1
Armenian	1,567	1.1	2,151	1.3	2,787	1.3	3,559	1
Georgian	(1,821)	(1.2)[d]	(2,248)	(1.3)	2,692	1.3	3,245	1
Lithuanian	(42)	...	(32)	...	2,326	1.1	2,665	1
Jewish	(2,672)	(1.9)	(3,020)	(1.8)	2,268	1.1	2,151	0
Moldavian	278	0.2	260	0.2	2,214	1.0	(2,698)	(1
Latvian	154	0.1	126	...	1,400	0.7	1,430	0
Tadzhik	(980)	(0.7)	(1,228)	(0.7)	1,397	0.7	(2,136)	(0
Turkmen	(763)	(0.5)	(811)	(0.5)	1,002	0.5	(1,525)	(0
Estonian	(155)	(0.1)	(142)	...	989	0.5	1,007	0
Kirgiz	(762)	(0.5)	(884)	(0.5)	969	0.5	1,452	(0
Subtotal	136,019	92.5	157,774	92.5	194,869	93.3	225,493	93
Other	11,009	7.5	12,693	7.5	13,958	6.7	16,227	6
TOTAL	147,028	100.0	170,467	100.0	208,827	100.0	241,720	100

Notes:

[a] Listed in rank order of the data for 1959.

[b] Nationalities are listed which correspond to the Union Republics or which comprise 1.0 percent or more of the total population in 1959.

[c] Data in parentheses are out of rank order for the respective year.

[d] Less than one-tenth of one percent.

Table 10. POPULATION OF REPUBLICS, BY MAJOR NATIONALITIES, USSR, CENSUS OF 1970 (In Thousands)

	Population	Percent		Population	Percent
U.S.S.R.			**Uzbek S.S.R.**		
Russian	129,015	53.4	Uzbek	7,734	64.7
Ukrainian	40,753	16.9	Russian	1,496	12.5
Uzbek	9,195	3.8	Tatar	578	4.8
Belorussian	9,052	3.7	Kazakh	549	4.6
Tatar	5,931	2.5	Tadzhik	457	3.8
Kazakh	5,299	2.2	Karakalpakh	230	1.9
Azerbaidzhan	4,380	1.8	Korean	151	1.3
Armenian	3,559	1.5	Ukrainian	115	1.0
Georgian	3,245	1.3	Subtotal	11,310	94.6
Moldavian	2,698	1.1	Other	650	5.4
Lithuanian	2,665	1.1	TOTAL	11,960	100.0
Subtotal	215,792	89.3			
Other	25,928	10.7	**Kazakh S.S.R.**		
TOTAL	241,720	100.0	Russian	5,500	42.8
			Kazakh	4,161	32.4
R.S.R.S.R.			Ukrainian	930	7.2
Russian	107,748	82.8	Tatar	284	2.2
Tatar	4,758	3.7	Uzbek	208	1.6
Ukrainian	3,346	2.6	Belorussian	198	1.5
Chuvash	1,637	1.3	Subtotal	11,281	87.7
Subtotal	117,489	90.4	Other	1,568	12.3
Other	12,590	9.6	TOTAL	12,849	100.0
TOTAL	130,079	100.0			
			Georgian S.S.R.		
Ukrainian S.S.R.			Georgian	3,131	66.8
Ukrainian	35,284	74.9	Armenian	452	9.7
Russian	9,126	19.4	Russian	397	8.5
Jewish	777	1.6	Azerbaidzhan	218	4.6
Subtotal	45,187	95.9	Ossetin	150	3.2
Other	1,939	4.1	Greek	89	1.9
TOTAL	47,126	100.0	Abkhaz	79	1.7
			Jewish	55	1.2
Belorussian S.S.R.			Ukrainian	50	1.1
Belorussian	7,290	81.0	Subtotal	4,621	98.7
Russian	938	10.4	Other	65	1.3
Polish	383	4.3	TOTAL	4,686	100.0
Ukrainian	191	2.1			
Jewish	148	1.6	**Azerbaidzhan S.S.R.**		
Subtotal	8,950	99.4	Azerbaidzhan	3,777	73.8
Other	52	0.6	Russian	510	10.0
TOTAL	9,002	100.0	Armenian	484	9.4
			Lezginy	137	2.7
			Subtotal	4,908	95.9
			Other	209	4.1
			TOTAL	5,117	100.0
Lithuanian S.S.R.			**Tadzhik S.S.R.**		
Lithuanian	2,507	80.1	Tadzhik	1,630	56.2
Russian	268	8.6	Uzbek	666	23.0
Polish	240	7.7	Russian	344	11.9
Belorussian	45	1.5	Tatar	71	2.4
Subtotal	3,060	97.9	Kirgiz	35	1.2
Other	68	2.1	Ukrainian	32	1.1
TOTAL	3,128	100.0	Subtotal	2,778	95.8
			Other	122	4.2
Moldavian S.S.R.			TOTAL	2,900	100.0
Moldavian	2,304	64.6			
Ukrainian	507	14.2	**Armenian S.S.R.**		
Russian	414	11.6	Armenian	2,208	88.6
Gagauz	125	3.5	Azerbaidzhan	148	5.9
Jewish	98	2.7	Russian	66	2.7
Bulgarian	74	2.1	Kurds	37	1.5
Subtotal	3,522	98.7	Subtotal	2,459	98.7
Other	47	1.3	Other	33	1.3
TOTAL	3,569	100.0	TOTAL	2,492	100.0
Latvian S.S.R.			**Turkmen S.S.R.**		
Latvian	1,342	56.8	Turkmen	1,417	65.6
Russian	705	29.8	Russian	313	14.5
Belorussian	95	4.0	Uzbek	179	8.3
Polish	63	2.7	Kazakh	69	3.2
Ukrainian	53	2.3	Tatar	36	1.7
Lithuanian	41	1.7	Ukrainian	35	1.6
Jewish	37	1.6	Armenian	23	1.1
Subtotal	2,336	98.9	Subtotal	2,072	96.0
Other	28	1.1	Other	87	4.0
TOTAL	2,364	100.0	TOTAL	2,159	100.0
Kirgiz S.S.R.			**Estonian S.S.R.**		
Kirgiz	1,285	43.8	Estonian	925	68.2
Russian	856	29.2	Russian	335	24.7
Uzbek	333	11.3	Ukrainian	28	2.1
Ukrainian	120	4.1	Finnish	19	1.4
Tatar	69	2.4	Belorussian	19	1.4
Subtotal	2,663	90.8	Subtotal	1,326	97.8
Other	270	9.2	Other	30	2.2
TOTAL	2,933	100.0	TOTAL	1,356	100.0

Table 11. AVERAGE NUMBER OF MEMBERS PER FAMILY, BY NATIONALITY AND URBAN AND RURAL RESIDENCE, USSR, CENSUS OF 1959

Nationality	Average Number of Members per Family		
	Total	Urban	Rural
Ranked by Population (Table 10)			
Russian	3.6	3.5	3.7
Ukrainian	3.5	3.3	3.6
Belorussian	3.7	3.4	3.7
Uzbek	5.0	4.9	5.0
Kazakh	4.6	4.7	4.5
Azerbaidzhan	4.8	4.6	4.9
Armenian	4.7	4.4	5.0
Georgian	4.0	4.8	4.1
Lithuanian	3.6	3.4	3.6
Moldavian	3.9	3.6	4.0
Latvian	3.1	3.0	3.2
Tadzhik	5.2	5.1	5.2
Turkmen	5.0	4.7	5.1
Estonian	3.0	3.1	3.0
Kirgiz	4.5	4.3	4.6
Ranked by Family Size (Total Population)			
Tadzhik	5.2	5.1	5.2
Uzbek	5.0	4.9	5.0
Turkmen	5.0	4.7	5.1
Azerbaidzhan	4.8	4.6	4.9
Armenian	4.7	4.4	5.0
Kazakh	4.6	4.7	4.5
Kirgiz	4.5	4.3	4.6
Georgian	4.0	3.8	4.1
Moldavian	3.9	3.6	4.0
Belorussian	3.7	3.4	3.7
Russian	3.6	3.5	3.7
Lithuanian	3.6	3.4	3.6
Ukrainian	3.5	3.3	3.6
Latvian	3.1	3.0	3.2
Estonian	3.0	3.1	3.0

Table 12. POPULATION BY REPUBLICS, USSR (In Thousands)

	1940	1950	1955	1956	1957	1958	1959 Census	1960	1961
RSFSR	110,098	101,438	110,537	112,266	114,017	115,665	117,534	118,922	120,546
Ukrainian SSR	41,340	36,588	39,271	39,742	40,422	41,179	41,869	42,466	43,089
Belorussian SSR	9,046	7,709	7,757	7,850	7,910	7,962	8,055	8,143	8,224
Uzbek SSR	6,645	6,264	7,275	7,450	7,701	7,978	8,262	8,524	8,828
Kazakh SSR	6,054	6,522	7,596	8,174	8,457	8,748	9,154	9,678	10,207
Georgian SSR	3,612	3,494	3,803	3,876	3,924	3,975	4,044	4,129	4,197
Azerbaidzhan SSR	3,274	2,859	3,277	3,375	3,484	3,595	3,698	3,817	3,970
Lithuanian SSR	2,925	2,573	2,613	2,644	2,667	2,665	2,711	2,761	2,804
Moldavian SSR	2,468	2,290	2,602	2,652	2,722	2,806	2,885	2,969	3,039
Latvian SSR	1,886	1,944	2,010	2,020	2,059	2,079	2,093	2,113	2,142
Kirghiz SSR	1,528	1,716	1,885	1,920	1,961	1,994	2,066	2,137	2,221
Tadzhik SSR	1,525	1,509	1,757	1,808	1,869	1,932	1,980	2,033	2,097
Armenian SSR	1,320	1,347	1,535	1,592	1,639	1,702	1,763	1,823	1,892
Turkmen SSR	1,302	1,197	1,340	1,371	1,408	1,460	1,516	1,565	1,624
Estonian SSR	1,054	1,097	1,157	1,162	1,174	1,185	1,185	1,197	1,209
USSR	194,077	178,547	194,415	197,902	201,414	204,925	208,827	212,289	216,101

	1962	1963	1964	1965	1966	1967	1968	1969	1970 Census
RSFSR	122,084	123,436	124,700	125,768	126,555	127,312	127,911	128,526	130,090
Ukrainian SSR	43,529	44,052	44,646	45,100	45,516	45,966	46,381	46,752	47,136
Belorussian SSR	8,317	8,413	8,455	8,533	8,633	8,744	8,820	8,897	9,033
Uzbek SSR	9,160	9,489	9,818	10,130	10,569	10,896	11,266	11,669	11,963
Kazakh SSR	10,751	11,266	11,511	11,853	12,124	12,413	12,678	12,877	12,850
Georgian SSR	4,270	4,340	4,415	4,483	4,547	4,611	4,659	4,710	4,688
Azerbaidzhan SSR	4,116	4,231	4,382	4,518	4,664	4,802	4,917	5,042	5,111
Lithuanian SSR	2,853	2,878	2,908	2,949	2,986	3,026	3,064	3,103	3,129
Moldavian SSR	3,106	3,172	3,242	3,303	3,368	3,425	3,484	3,531	3,572
Latvian SSR	2,170	2,186	2,217	2,241	2,262	2,285	2,298	2,323	2,365
Kirghiz SSR	2,317	2,377	2,492	2,659	2,651	2,749	2,836	2,926	2,933
Tadzhik SSR	2,183	2,263	2,346	2,482	2,573	2,654	2,736	2,823	2,900
Armenian SSR	1,957	2,007	2,069	2,134	2,193	2,253	2,306	2,363	2,493
Turkmen SSR	1,682	1,742	1,803	1,862	1,913	1,966	2,029	2,085	2,158
Estonian SSR	1,235	1,244	1,259	1,273	1,285	1,294	1,304	1,316	1,357
USSR	219,730	223,096	226,253	229,198	231,839	234,396	236,689	238,943	241,748

CHAPTER I TABLE SOURCE NOTES

TABLE 1

1913, 1926, 1939: *Vestnik statistiki,*
1963, no. 11, pp. 92–95.
1951, 1958–1959: *Vestnik statistiki,*
1964, no. 4, pp. 86–87.
1941: *Vestnik statistiki,* 1969, no. 4,
p. 95.
1928: *Statistichesky spravochnik za
1928,* p. 20.
1929: *N.K. SSSR: statistichesky
spravochnik 1932,* p. xxiii.
1930–1931: M. Avdienko, "Sdvigi v
strukture proletariata v pervoi
pyatiletke," *Planovoe khozyaistvo,*
1932, no. 6–7, p. 145.
1940: *N.K. 1964,* pp. 9–11.
1960–1970: *N.K. 1969,* pp. 7, 9. Data
for the intercensal years, 1960 to
1969, from this source are revised
by the Central Statistical Administration, compared to earlier published figures for consistency with
the results of the 1970 census.
The revision serves to increase
the respective figures by amounts
ranging (to the nearest 100,000)
from 100,000 for 1960 to 500,000
for 1969, or by about one- or
two-tenths of one percent. Per
capita data appearing elsewhere
in this book were drawn from
earlier Soviet sources and were
therefore calculated by the Central Statistical Administration on
the basis of the official population estimates made prior to the
1970 census.
1971: *Trud,* February 4, 1971, p. 2.

TABLE 2

1913–1928, 1940–1969: *N.K. 1969,*
p. 31. Data for 1963, 1964, and
1967 from this source are revised
by the Central Statistical Administration, compared to earlier published rates, to account for population totals revised on the basis
of the 1970 census (see notes to
Table 1). Rates for other intercensal years, 1961–1968, to the
decimal place reported, are un-
affected by the revision of the
population totals.
1930: B. Ya. Smulevich, *Burzhuaznye
teorii narodonaselenia v svete
Marksistsko-leninskoi kritiki,*
Moscow (1936), pp. 146, 1150.

TABLE 3

Census of 1926: *Vsesoyuznaya perepis
naselenia 1926,* vol. XVII, Moscow (1930).
Census of 1939: Estimated from official
data from the census, as reported
in *Vestnik statistiki,* 1956, no. 6,
pp. 89–90, and *Itogi vsevoyuznoi
perepisi naselenia 1959 goda,*
USSR Summary Volume, Mos-
cow (1962), p. 49.
Census of 1959: *Ibid.,* pp. 49–51.
January 1, 1941, including annexed
territories: estimated from the
reported data from the 1939 census, above, from which the Soviet
estimates for the population of
the annexed territories by age and
sex may be derived. Natural increase of the population from the
date of the 1939 census to January 1, 1941, is from reported
vital statistics.

TABLE 4

1913, 1959: *Vestnik statistiki,* 1963,
no. 11, pp. 92–95.
1926, 1941, 1961, 1966–1969: *Vestnik
statistiki,* 1969, no. 4, p. 95.
1950–1951, 1958, 1960, 1962–1964:
Vestnik statistiki, 1964, no. 4,
pp. 86–87.
1940: *N.K. 1964,* pp. 9–11.
1960–1970 census: *N.K. 1969,* pp. 7,
13. Data for intercensal years,
1960–1969, from this source were
revised by the Central Statistical
Administration, compared to
earlier published figures, for consistency with the results of the
1970 census. The effect of the
revision on the total population
figures is explained in the notes
to Table 1. The revision serves to
decrease the respective figures for
the urban population by amounts
ranging (to the nearest 100,000)
from 200,000 for 1960 to
1,300,000 for 1969, or by from
0.2 to almost one percent. The
revision serves to increase the
corresponding figures for the rural
population by amounts ranging
from 300,000 for 1960 to
1,800,000 for 1969, or by from
0.3 to 1.7 percent. In other
words, the urban population increased less rapidly and the rural

population decreased less rapidly than had been (officially) estimated during the 1960's.

Total, 1928–1931: See Table 1.

Urban, 1928: *Statistichesky spravochnik za 1928*, Moscow (1929), p. 20.

Urban, 1929: *Sotsialisticheskoe stroitelstvo SSSR, 1935*, Moscow (1935), p. 539.

Urban, 1930–1931: Avdienko, cited in Table 1, p. 145.

Rural, 1928–1931: Total minus urban.

All percentages are calculated from the corresponding absolute data.

TABLE 5

1926: *Vsesoyuznaya perepis naselenia 1926*, vol. XXXIV, Moscow (1930).

1959: Estimated from official data from the census as reported in *Itogi vsesoyuznoi perepisi naselenia 1959*, USSR, Summary Volume, Moscow (1962), pp. 98–99 and 117–121.

TABLE 6

1928, 1940: Labor Force, from data in Warren W. Eason, *Soviet Manpower*, unpublished Ph.D. dissertation on deposit with the Columbia University Library (1959), p. 360.

1928: Employment: Estimated from data on the labor force, according to method for 1926 set forth in Warren W. Eason, "Labor Force," Abram Bergson and Simon Kuznets, eds., *Economic Trends in the Soviet Union*, Cambridge, Harvard University Press, 1963, p. 47.

1940, Employment: From data in Murray S. Weitzman and Andrew Elias, *The Magnitude and Distribution of Civilian Employment in the U.S.S.R.: 1928–1959*, International Population Reports, Series P-95, no. 58, April, 1961 (U.S. Department of Commerce, Bureau of the Census), p. 57.

1950–1968: Labor force and employment: Murray Feshbach, *Estimates and Projections of the Labor Force and Civilian Employment in the U.S.S.R.: 1950–1980* (U.S. Department of Commerce, Bureau of the Census, Foreign Demographic Analysis Division, February, 1970), p. 3.

TABLE 7

Compiled from data on the number of both sexes, the number of females, and percent females from the following sources:

N.K. 1969, pp. 530–531, 536.

N.K. 1968, pp. 548–549, 552.

Trud, Moscow (1968), pp. 22, 24–25, 73, 75–76.

N.K. 1967, p. 654.

N.K. 1965, p. 564.

N.K. 1964, p. 552.

N.K. 1963, p. 480.

N.K. 1962, p. 459.

Zhenshchiny i deti v SSSR, Moscow (1963), pp. 102–103.

TABLE 8

1913 and 1956: Man-hours per day, *N.K. 1956*, p. 593.

1913, 1955, 1966: Hours per week, *SS za 50 L.*, pp. 222–223.

1928–1963: Man-hours per day and days per year, from Soviet sources, in U.S. Congress, Joint Economic Committee, *Current Economic Indicators for the USSR*, U.S. Government Printing Office (1965), pp. 80–81.

1964: *N.K. 1964*, p. 139.

1965–1967: Days per year, *N.K. 1967*, p. 209.

1967: Hours per week, *Trud*, Moscow (1968), p. 239.

1968: Hours per week, *N.K. 1967*, p. 664.

1968–1969: Days per year, *N.K. 1969*, p. 167.

1969: Hours per week, *N.K. 1969*, p. 541.

TABLE 9

1926 and 1939: From the respective census results, as set forth in F. Lorimer, *The Population of the Soviet Union: History and Prospects*, Geneva: League of Nations (1946), pp. 138–139.

1959: *Itogi Vsesoyuznoi perepisi naselenia 1959*: USSR Summary Volume, Moscow (1962), p. 184.

1970: *Trud*, April 17, 1971, p. 3.

TABLE 10

Trud, April 17, 1971, p. 3.

TABLE 11

*Itogi vsesoyuznoi perepisi naselenia
1959:* USSR Summary Volume,
Moscow (1962), p. 252.

TABLE 12

1940, 1966, 1969: *N.K. 1968,* p. 9.
1950, 1955–1958: *Vestnik statistiki,*
1964, no. 4, pp. 86–87.
1959–1970: *Vestnik statistiki,* 1971,
no. 2, pp. 85–86.
Data for intercensal years 1960–1969
from this source were revised by
the Central Statistical Administration, compared to earlier published figures, for consistency with
the results of the 1970 census.

AGRICULTURE

ROY D. LAIRD

THE OFFICIAL Soviet agricultural statistics that are published are of enormous value in any attempt to understand the nature and progress of the Soviet agricultural system. During the Stalin years, very little by way of statistical data was systematically published. Since 1956, however, most years have seen the publication of the annual statistical handbooks (the *Narodnoe khozyaistvo* . . . , or *Peoples Economy* . . . , series) which, however lacking in many areas, are an enormous improvement. Thus, each year some one-fifth or one-sixth of the annual volumes are devoted to the presentation of tables reporting on levels of achievement in various agricultural activities (e.g., the 1967 volume has 1,008 pages of which some 175 are devoted to agriculture).

Unfortunately, there are many deliberate gaps in the data (e.g., the tables that follow provide a measure of the income per household for the kolkhoz peasants, but no similar systematic measure for sovkhoz workers is published, although the latter are on the state payroll). Moreover, Western specialists often disagree with the bases used for producing the data. The most serious problem in this regard is related to grain statistics. Although the Stalinist practice of reporting grain yields on the basis of "biological" estimates (i.e., estimates made in the field prior to harvesting) has been abandoned, Western students of Soviet agriculture are nearly unanimous in agreeing that the so-called "barn yields" that are reported by the Soviet statisticians are inflated in that consistently they overestimate by some 10 to 15 percent the actual grain available for animal feed and human consumption. For example, the official Soviet claim is that total grain harvest in 1967 amounted to 147.9 million metric tons. However, after adjusting for such factors as "excess moisture and foreign matter," the foreign agricultural analysts in the U.S. Department of Agriculture estimate that actual 1967 output was only some 124.9 million metric tons. Similarly, many specialists disagree with the Soviet practice of reporting meat in terms of carcass weight, thus including fat and offal, but the problem here may not be as serious.

Still other vexing problems with Soviet agricultural statistics stem from such practices as reporting changes in terms of percentage differences as related to earlier years (after a base year for which hard data are not available) or shifting the criteria used for reporting data—e.g., as shown in the tables, for many years under Khrushchev total grain figures included the ripe grain equivalent of green corn cut in the milky wax stage for silage.

Falsification of data probably is another major problem, although not in the sense that many assume—i.e., deliberately presenting erroneous data to mislead Western analysts. This view should have been laid to rest during the Second World War when secret Soviet economic data fell into outside hands and tallied with official statistics published previously. After all, the USSR's is a complex economy that must depend upon a widespread internal communication (thus knowledge that could not be kept secret) of various statistical measures. This, however, does not mean that unofficial, and illegal, falsification cannot greatly distort official published statistics. Thus, for example, a major widespread scandal occurred when large areas of the USSR were discovered to have distorted milk output statistics. Since output success is measured largely by the fulfillment of state plan, numerous farms unable to deliver the required amount of butter to the state were discovered to have purchased butter outside, to be sold to the state as an ostensible part of their production in order to assure the paper meeting of production plan.

The tables that follow have been drawn from the statistical handbook. Basic criteria used in their selection have been their importance as a measure of change and their comparability over a wide enough span of years to reflect patterns of change. As implied, isolated data of interest are published from time to time, but in isolation they are relatively valueless in measuring the course of Soviet affairs.

Beyond the material presented here, the reader is particularly urged to consult two valuable publications of the U.S. Department of Agriculture Economic Research Service, available from the United States Government Printing Service:

1. An annual publication, *The Europe and Soviet Union Agricultural Situation.*

2. A volume of 99 tables entitled *Agricultural Statistics of Eastern Europe and the Soviet Union, 1950–66,* February 1969.

Although the latter volume parallels much of what is presented here, for the 1950 to 1966 period, it also includes additional material such as vegetable and wool production figures and investment inputs which have not been included here because of problems of interpretation and/or space. The title of the USDA annual series will vary somewhat from year to year; thus the 1969 publication's title is *The Agricultural Situation in Communist Areas: Eastern Europe, the Soviet Union, and Mainland China.* . . . The following Table of Conversion Equivalents is copied from the back page of that publication.

TABLE OF CONVERSION EQUIVALENTS

Pounds per bushel

Wheat and potatoes	60
Rye and corn	56
Barley	45
Oats	32

One kilogram	equals	2.2046 pounds
One centner or metric quintal	"	220.46 pounds
One metric ton	"	10. centners or 2204.6 pounds
One hectare	"	2.471 acres
One acre	"	0.4 hectare
One kilometer	"	0.6 mile

Metric tons to bushels

One metric ton	*Bushels*
Wheat and potatoes	36.743
Rye and corn	39.368
Barley	43.929
Oats	69.894

Bushels to metric tons

One bushel	*Metric tons*
Wheat and potatoes	.02722
Rye and corn	.02840
Barley	.02177
Oats	.01452

To convert centners per hectare to bushels per acre, multiply by:

Wheat and potatoes	1.487
Rye and corn	1.593
Barley	1.8587
Oats	2.788

To convert bushels per acre to centners (metric quintals), per hectare multiply by:

Wheat and potatoes	0.6725
Rye and corn	0.6277
Barley	0.5380
Oats	0.3587

One metric ton of seed cotton = 1.562 bales of 480 pounds.
One metric ton of ginned cotton = 4.593 bales of 480 pounds.

Table 1. NUMBER OF FARMS, TOTAL USSR

Year	Collective Farms (Kolkhozy) Thousands	State Farms (Sovkhozy) Thousands	Agricultural (Kolkhozy) Thousands
1918	1.6	...	...
1926	17.9	...	...
1927	14.8	...	...
1928	33.3	1.4	33.3
1930	85.9	2.8	...
1940	236.9	4.2	235.5
1950	123.7	5.0	121.4
1955	87.5	5.1	85.6
1956	84.8	5.1	83.0
1957	78.2	6.0	76.5
1958	69.1	6.0	67.7
1959	54.6	6.5	53.4
1960	44.9	7.4	44.0
1961	41.3	8.3	40.5
1962	40.5	8.6	39.7
1963	39.5	9.2	38.8
1964	38.3	10.1	37.6
1965	36.9	11.7	36.3
1966	37.1	12.2	36.5
1967	36.8	12.8	36.2
1968	36.2	13.4	35.6

Note:

    First column includes fishing kolkhozes for 1928-29, 1940-1968. 1918-27 data does not state whether fishing kolkhozes are included. Third column excludes fishing kolkhozes.

Table 2. AGRICULTURAL MACHINERY, TOTAL USSR

Year	Tractors (15 hp)[a]	Grain Combines[a]	Mineral Fertilizer[b] (Million Tons)
1913	...	...	0.2 (0.1)[c]
1928	18	...	0.2 (0.1)[c]
1932	148	...	(0.9)[c]
1940	684	182	3.2 (3.0)[c]
1950	933	211	5.4 (5.5)[c]
1955	1,439	338	8.6
1956	1,542	375	9.4
1957	1,635	482	10.4
1958	1,744	501	10.6
1959	1,899	494	11.1
1960	1,985	497	11.4
1961	2,171	498	12.1
1962	2,399	519	13.6
1963	2,612	517	15.9
1964	2,821	513	21.9
1965	3,032	520	27.1
1966	3,233	531	30.5
1967	3,485	553	33.7
1968	3,776	581	36.3 / 46.0[d]

Notes:

    [a]At end of year.

    [b]Total ingredients "delivered" to the rural areas.

    [c]Total ingredients "produced."

    [d]1970.

Table 3.   SOWN AREA,[a] TOTAL USSR (In Million Hectares)

Year	All Crops	All Grains	Fodder Crops	Corn[b]	Sugar Beets[c]	Flax	Winter Wheat	Spring Wheat	Rye	Potatoes
1913[d]	118.2	104.6	3.3	2.1	0.6	1.2	8.3	24.8	25.8	4.2
1920	97.2	87.0	...	1.7	0.2	0.9	6.7	21.0	23.5	3.7
1926	110.3	93.7	...	3.0	0.5	1.6	9.0	20.4	28.5	5.2
1927	112.4	94.7	...	2.7	0.6	1.6	10.7	20.6	27.3	5.5
1928	113.0	92.17	3.87	4.5	0.8	1.7	6.2	21.6	24.6	5.7
1930	127.2	101.8	...	3.7	1.0	2.3	...	...	...	5.7
1940	150.41	110.57	18.07	3.7	1.2	2.1	...	...	...	7.7
1950	146.30	102.87	20.74	4.8	1.3	1.9	...	...	...	8.5
1955	185.85	126.40	35.72	9.1/17.9	1.8	1.5	18.3	42.2	19.1	9.1
1956	194.7	128.3	41.7	9.3	2.0	1.9	12.9	49.1	...	9.2
1957	193.7	124.6	45.4	5.8/18.3	2.1	1.7	18.5	50.5	...	9.8
1958	195.6	125.2	46.5	4.4/19.7	2.5	1.6	18.2	48.4	18.0	9.5
1959	196.3	119.7	52.6	8.7/22.4	2.8	1.6	17.4	45.6	...	9.5
1960	203.0	115.6	57.0	5.1/28.2	3.0	1.6	12.1	48.3	16.3	9.1
1961	204.6	128.3	52.0	7.2/25.7	3.1	1.6	17.3	45.7	...	8.9
1962	216.0	128.7	55.2	7.0/37.1	3.2	1.7	18.1	49.3	16.9	8.7
1963	218.5	130.0	...	7.0	3.7	1.5	16.4	48.3	15.0	8.5
1964	212.8	133.3	53.5	5.1	4.1	1.6	19.0	48.9	16.8	8.5
1965	209.1	128.0	55.2	3.2	3.9	1.6	19.8	50.4	16.0	8.6
1966	206.8	124.8	56.6	3.2	3.8	1.4	19.8	50.2	13.6	8.4
1967	206.9	122.2	59.6	3.5	3.8	1.4	19.7	47.3	12.4	8.3
1968	207.0	121.5	60.7	3.4	3.6	1.3	19.0	48.2	12.2	8.3

Notes:

[a]Posevnye ploshchad.

[b]Left column is ripe corn; right column includes corn for grain, silage and green feed. Single column indicates ripe corn.

[c]Industrial.

[d]Present boundaries.

Table 4.   GROSS YIELD,[a] TOTAL USSR (Barn Yield, in Million Tons)

Year	All Grains	Corn[c]	Sugar Beets[d]	Wheat	Rye	Flax	Potatoes
1913[b]	86.0	2.1	11.3	26.3	22.7	.40	31.9
1918	49.5	...	...	...	...	...	...
1928		3.2			...		
1928–1932	73.6		9.8	21.7	...	.43	45.9
1940	95.6	5.17	18.8	31.8	21.1	.35	76.1
1950	81.2	6.64	20.8	31.1	18.0	.26	88.6
1955	103.7	11.6/14.7	31.0	47.3	16.5	.38	71.8
1956	127.6	9.9/12.5	32.4	67.4	14.1	.52	96.0
1957	105.0	4.6/ 7.0	39.6	58.1	14.5	.44	87.8
1958	141.2	10.2/16.7	54.3	76.6	15.7	.44	86.5
1959	119.5	5.7/12.0	43.9	69.1	16.9	.36	86.6
1960	125.5	9.8/18.7	57.7	64.3	16.4	.43	84.4
1961	130.8	17.1/24.3	50.9	66.5	...	.40	84.3
1962	140.2	15.5/23.5	47.4	70.8	17.0	.43	69.7
1963	107.5	11.1	44.0	49.7	11.9	.38	71.8
1964	152.1	13.9	81.2	74.4	13.6	.35	93.6
1965	121.1	8.03	72.3	59.7	16.2	.48	88.7
1966	171.2	8.42	74.0	100.5	13.1	.46	87.9
1967	147.9	9.16	87.1	77.4	13.0	.49	95.5
1968	169.5	8.8	94.3	93.4	14.1	.40	102.2
1970	186.9[e]	...	78.3	...	...	...	96.6

Notes:

[a]Western specialists argue that Soviet grain yields continue to be grossly overstated; thus such specialists consistently reduce Soviet grain figures by some 10-15%.

[b]Present boundaries.

[c]Left column is ripe; right column is both ripe and milk-wax stage. Single column indicates ripe corn.

[d]Industrial.

[e]Calculated from average annual yield 1966-70 and the known 1966-69 data.

←——→Averages for years indicated.

Table 5. Productivity,[a] Total USSR (In Centners/Hectare)

Year	Grain	Corn[c]	Sugar Beets[d]	Winter Wheat	Spring Wheat	Flax	Potatoes	Winter R
1913[b]	8.2	9.4	168	10.0	7.3	3.2	76	8.0
1926	...	11.5	...	...	...	...	..	8.3
1927	...	11.3	118.4	...	...	...	..	8.8
1928		7.2	156.5					7.8
	7.5			8.6	6.1	2.3	78	
1930		7.6	95					8.4
1932								8.4
1940	8.6	13.8/13.9	146	10.1	6.6	...	99	9.1
1950	7.9	13.8	159	9.1	7.6	1.3	104	7.6
1955	8.4	18.9/10.5	176	13.5	5.3	2.6	79	8.6
1956	10.0	15.2/10.0	162	11.6	10.7	2.7	104	7.7
1957	8.4	14.2/ 9.4	188	14.7	6.1	2.6	90	8.0
1958	11.3	23.3/17.4	218	16.2	9.7	2.7	91	8.8
1959	10.4	16.0/12.4	159	15.2	9.4	2.3	91	9.9
1960	10.9	19.3/14.5	191	15.1	9.5	2.6	92	10.1
1961	10.7	23.9/12.0	164	16.9	8.2	2.5	95	...
1962	10.9	22.1/11.2	152	16.8	8.2	2.5	80	10.1
1963	8.3	15.9	120	12.9	5.9	2.6	84	7.9
1964	11.4	27.0	199	13.8	9.9	2.2	110	8.1
1965	9.5	25.2	188	16.1	5.5	3.3	103	10.1
1966	13.7	26.0	195	20.4	12.0	3.3	105	9.7
1967	12.1	26.2	230	17.8	8.9	3.5	115	10.5
1968	14.0	26.2	266	18.3	12.2	3.0	123	11.5

Notes:

[a] See Note to Table 4.

[b] Present boundaries.

[c] Left column is ripe corn; right column is cut in milk-wax stage; recalculated to ripe grain. Single column indicates ripe corn.

[d] Industrial.

←——→ Averages for years indicated.

Table 5a. Productivity per 100,000 Population (In Centners/Hectare)

Year	Grain	Corn[a]	Sugar Beets[b]	Winter Wheat	Spring Wheat	Flax	Potatoes	Winter Rye
1950	.004	.008	.089	.005	.004	.001	.058	.004
1955	.004	.010/.005	.091	.007	.003	.001	.041	.004
1956	.005	.008/.005	.082	.006	.005	.001	.053	.004
1957	.004	.007/.005	.093	.007	.003	.001	.045	.004
1958	.006	.011/.008	.106	.008	.005	.001	.044	.004
1959	.005	.008/.006	.076	.007	.005	.001	.044	.005
1960	.005	.009/.007	.090	.007	.004	.001	.043	.005
1961	.005	.011/.006	.077	.008	.004	.001	.044	...
1962	.005	.010/.005	.069	.008	.004	.001	.036	.005
1963	.004	.007	.054	.006	.003	.001	.038	.004
1964	.005	.012	.088	.006	.006	.001	.049	.004
1965	.004	.011	.082	.007	.002	.001	.045	.004
1966	.006	.011	.084	.009	.005	.001	.045	.004
1967	.005	.011	.098	.008	.004	.001	.049	.004
1968	.006	.011	.112	.008	.005	.001	.052	.005

Notes:

[a] Left column is ripe corn; right column is cut in milk-wax stage; recalculated to ripe grain. Single column indicates ripe corn.

[b] Industrial.

Table 6. Number of Livestock, Total USSR (In Million Head)

Year	Cattle	Swine	Sheep & Goats
1918	50.8	19.3	86.7
1928	60.1	22.0	107.0
1930	50.6	14.2	93.3
1940	47.8	22.5	76.7
1950	58.1	22.2	93.6
1955	56.7	30.9	113.0
1956	58.8	34.0	116.2
1957	61.4	40.8	119.6
1958	66.8	44.3	130.1
1959	70.8	48.7	139.2
1960	74.2	53.4	144.0
1961	75.8	58.7	140.3
1962	82.1	66.7	142.5
1963	87.0	70.0	146.4
1964	85.4	40.9	139.5
1965	87.2	52.8	130.7
1966	93.4	59.6	135.3
1967	97.1	58.0	141.0
1968	97.2	50.9	144.0
1969	95.7	49.0	146.1
1971	99.1	67.2	143.2

Table 7. Cows, Total USSR

Year	Number (Million Head)	Milk/Cow[a] (Kilograms)
1913[b]	...	982
1918	25.3	...
1926	27.8	...
1927	28.5	...
1928	29.3	...
1930	28.5	...
1940	22.8	1,124
1950	24.6	1,137
1955	26.4	1,422
1956	27.7	1,693
1957	29.0	1,930
1958	31.4	1,974
1959	33.3	2,067
1960	33.9	1,938
1961	34.8	1,847
1962	36.3	1,747
1963	38.0	1,584
1964	38.3	1,684
1965	38.8	1,987
1966	40.1	2,021
1967	41.2	2,128
1968	41.6	2,232
1970	41.2	2,302
1971	41.0	...

Notes:

[a] In the Kolkhozy and Sovkhozy.

[b] Boundaries not indicated.

Table 8. Livestock Production, Total USSR (In Million Tons)

Year	Meat (Carcass Weight)	Milk	Eggs (Billions)
1913*	5.0	29.4	11.9
1928	4.9	31.0	10.8
1930	4.3	27.0	8.0
1940	4.7	33.6	12.2
1950	4.9	35.3	11.7
1955	6.3	43.0	18.5
1956	6.6	49.1	19.5
1957	7.4	54.7	22.3
1958	7.7	58.8	23.1
1959	8.9	62.0	20.1
1960	8.7	61.7	27.4
1961	8.7	62.6	29.3
1962	9.5	63.9	30.1
1963	10.2	61.2	28.5
1964	8.3	63.3	26.7
1965	10.0	72.6	29.1
1966	10.7	76.0	31.7
1967	11.5	79.9	33.9
1968	11.6	82.1	35.5
1969	11.6	81.5	37.2
1970	12.3	82.9	40.4

Note:
 *Present boundaries.

Table 9. Averages per Farm: Kolkhozy Only

Year	Households	Collective Sown Area (Hectares)	Income (Rubles) Per Household	Agricultural Land (1,000 Hectares)	Tractors/Farm (15 H.P.)
1928	13	41	...	.096	..
1930	70	443	...	...	..
1940	81	492	1,107	1.4	..
1950	165	967	1,685	3.0	..
1955	229	1,699	3,821	4.4	..
1956	238	1,800	4,763	4.5	..
1957	245	1,696	5,053	4.1	..
1958	276	1,881	7,015	4.5	14
1959	343	2,316	7,417	5.5	..
1960	383	2,745	782	6.4	..
1961	399	2,665	830	6.2	
1962	404	2,837	940	6.2	..
1963	411	2,896	996	6.1	31*
1964	418	2,881	1,127	6.0	35
1965	421	2,861	...	6.1	38
1966	417	...	...	6.0	41
1967	418	2,814	...	6.0	45
1968	420	2,837	...	6.1	50

Note:
 *Computed from data.

Table 10. NUMBER OF LIVESTOCK: KOLKHOZY ONLY (In Thousand Head)

Year	Cattle	Swine	Sheep & Goats
1929	0.4	0.1	0.7
1941	20.1	8.2	41.9
1951	28.1	12.3	68.3
1955	27.8	13.6	77.9
1956	26.9	12.8	72.7
1957	27.9	16.2	74.8
1958	29.2	20.0	71.3
1959	32.1	23.2	75.1
1960	36.9	26.8	77.9
1961	36.3	27.4	72.4
1962	36.8	30.1	68.0
1963	38.6	31.9	67.5
1964	37.3	16.0	61.4
1965	37.1	22.3	54.0
1966	38.3	24.6	54.6
1957	39.8	24.8	56.1
1968	40.2	22.1	56.4
1969	39.9	21.6	56.4

Table 11. COWS: KOLKHOZY ONLY

Year	Number (Million Head)	Milk/Cow (Kilograms)
1929	0.2	...
1940	...	1,017
1941	5.7	...
1950	...	1,027
1951	7.0	...
1955	8.7	1,315
1956	10.0	1,611
1957	10.8	1,858
1958	10.7	1,937
1959	11.5	2,004
1960	12.8	1,854
1961	12.8	1,762
1962	12.8	1,684
1963	13.6	1,504
1964	13.8	1,583
1965	13.7	1,906
1966	13.7	1,949
1967	14.0	2,042
1968	14.2	...
1969	14.2	...

Table 12. LIVESTOCK PRODUCTION: KOLKHOZY ONLY (In Million Tons)

Year	Meat	Milk	Eggs (Billions)
1940	0.9	5.6	0.5
1950	1.1	3.6	0.4
1955	2.2	13.6	1.7
1958	2.5	21.3	2.1
1959	3.1	23.7	2.7
1960	3.2	22.5	2.9
1961	2.7	21.6	3.1
1962	2.9	21.7	3.4
1963	3.1	20.3	3.2
1964	2.5	21.2	2.8
1965	3.0	25.3	3.8
1966	3.2	26.1	4.1
1967	3.6	27.6	4.5
1968	3.8	29.3	4.9

Table 13. AVERAGES PER FARM: SOVKHOZY ONLY

Year	Number of Workers	Sown Area (1,000 Hectares)	Agricultural Land (1,000 Hectares)	Tractors/Farm (15 H.P.)
1940	285	2.8	12.2	24
1950	303	2.6	12.9	26
1955	384	5.0	17.4*	...
1956	399	6.2	15.9	61
1957	510	8.4	24.3	82
1958	605	8.7	24.9	90
1959	610	8.3	23.5	92
1960	745	9.0	26.2	103
1961	794	9.7	28.3	113
1962	825	10.1	28.3	124
1963	775	9.8	28.2	124
1964	721	8.6	27.2	121
1965	663	7.6	24.6	114
1966	651	7.3	23.7	114
1967	617	6.9	22.8	115
1968	...	6.7	21.9	116

Note:

*Zemelnaya ploshchad.

Table 14. NUMBER OF LIVESTOCK: SOVKHOZY* ONLY (In Million Head)

Year	Cattle	Swine	Sheep & Goats
1941	2.5	1.9	5.9
1951	2.8	2.5	7.6
1956	3.3	3.3	10.3
1957	3.8	5.3	10.8
1958	7.1	7.4	23.5
1959	8.2	8.1	26.4
1960	10.5	9.8	29.3
1961	14.4	12.7	31.6
1962	19.1	15.6	38.7
1963	20.9	16.8	41.2
1964	21.6	7.6	44.8
1965	22.2	11.5	44.2
1966	24.5	12.5	46.4
1967	25.3	12.8	49.5
1968	25.8	11.7	51.6
1969	25.8	11.6	53.1

Note:

*Excluding other state enterprises.

Table 15. COWS: SOVKHOZY* ONLY

Year	Number (Million Head)	Milk/Cow (Kilograms)
1940	...	1,803
1941	0.9	...
1950	...	2,256
1951	0.8	...
1956	1.3	...
1957	1.4	...
1958	2.5	2,258
1959	2.8	...
1960	3.6	2,185
1961	5.1	2,030
1962	6.6	1,873
1963	7.5	1,734
1964	7.9	1,870
1965	8.3	2,121
1966	9.1	2,134
1967	9.4	2,262
1968	9.6	2,319
1969	9.6	...

Note:

*Excluding other state enterprises.

Table 16. Livestock Production: Sovkhozy and Other State Enterprises Only (In Million Tons)

Year	Meat	Milk	Eggs (Billions)
1940	0.4	1.9	0.2
1950	0.5	2.1	0.3
1955	0.8	3.4	0.6
1958	1.2	6.3	1.3
1959	1.6	7.7	1.7
1960	1.9	10.1	2.4
1961	2.1	12.5	3.2
1962	2.4	13.5	3.7
1963	2.8	13.6	3.9
1964	2.3	15.1	4.2
1965	3.0	18.6	5.7
1966	3.1	19.7	6.7
1967	3.4	21.2	8.1
1968	3.4	21.8	9.5

Table 17. Specialists with Higher or Secondary Training, Total USSR (In Thousands)

Year	Kolkhozy All[b]	Kolkhozy Ag. Only	Sovkhozy[a] All[b]	Sovkhozy[a] Ag. Only	Total All[b]	Total Ag. Only
1941[c]	29	19	21	15	50	34
1953[d]	83	69	31	27	114	96
1960[e]	222	161	166	118	388	279
1965[f]	232	165	264	174	496	339
1966[f]	265	180	292	189	557	369
1968[f]	326	206	345	210	671	416

Notes:

[a] Sovkhozy and other state enterprises.

[b] Including economists and others with non-agricultural specialty training, plus agronomists, veterinarians, and zoo technicians.

[c] January 1.   [d] July 1.   [e] December 1.   [f] November 15.

Table 18. Workers and Employees in the Kolkhozy and Sovkhozy, Total USSR (Averages per year, in Millions)

Year	Total	Kolkhozy & Subsidiary Enterprises	Kolkhozy Only	Sovkhozy & Subsidiary Enterprises	Sovkhozy Only	Total Excluding Subsidiary Enterprises*
1928	1.1	0.8	0.7	0.3	0.3	1.0
1940	31.3	29.0	26.1	1.8	1.6	28.1
1950	30.7	27.6	25.1	2.4	2.2	27.9
1960	29.0	22.3	20.1	6.3	5.8	26.1
1961	28.1	20.7	18.7	7.4	6.8	25.5
1962	27.7	20.0	18.1	7.7	7.1	25.2
1963	27.3	19.4	17.6	7.9	7.3	24.9
1964	27.3	19.2	17.7	8.1	7.5	25.2
1965	27.5	18.9	17.6	8.6	8.0	25.6
1966	27.4	18.6	17.3	8.8	8.1	25.4
1967	27.7	18.4	...	9.3	...	24.7
1968	27.5	18.1	...	9.4	...	24.6

Note:

*Including other state agricultural enterprises.

Table 19. PRIVATE PRODUCTION[a]

Year	MEAT Million Tons	%[b]	MILK Million Tons	%[b]	EGGS (Billions) Pieces	%[b]	POTATOES %[b]	VEGETABLES %[b]	SOWN AREA Million Hectares	%[b] (All Land)
1940	3.4	72	26.1	77	11.5	94	65	48	19.5[b]	13.0[c]
1950	3.3	67	26.4	75	10.4	89	72	44	9.4	6.4
1955	2.7	..	26.0	..	16.2	..	..	..	...	...
1958	4.0	..	31.2	..	19.7	..	..	..	...	...
1959	4.2	..	30.6	..	16.7	..	..	..	...	...
1960	3.6	41	29.1	47	22.1	80	63	44	6.8	3.3
1961	3.9	..	28.5	..	23.0	..	..	..	...	...
1962	4.2	..	28.7	..	23.0	..	..	..	...	...
1963	4.3	..	27.3	..	21.4	..	..	..	...	...
1964	3.5	..	27.0	..	19.7	..	..	..	...	...
1965	4.5	40	28.7	39	19.6	67	63	41	6.6	3.2
1966	4.4	42	30.2	40	20.9	66	64	42	6.7	3.2
1967	4.5	40	31.1	39	21.3	63	63	40	6.8	3.2
1968	4.4	38	31.0	38	21.1	60	62	41	6.8	3.2

Notes:

[a]These absolute figures are derived from subtracting the totals of Tables 12 and 16 from the figures in Table 8. Although this is largely private plot production (i.e., peasant plus urban and other non-farm production) the analyst must remember that a substantial portion of the feed for the private animals is grown on the collective and state farm fields.

[b]Percentage of the total U.S.S.R. output, which is calculated from Soviet tables indicating the percent of total output produced by the Kolkhozy, Sovkhozy, and other state enterprises combined.

[c]Still in 1940 9.5% of the land (14.3 million hectares) remained in family farms.

Table 19a. LIVESTOCK PRODUCTION PER CAPITA

Year	U.S.S.R. Meat[a]	Milk	Eggs[b]	Kolkhozy Meat[a]	Milk	Eggs[b]	Sovkhozy[c] Meat[a]	Milk	Eggs[b]
1940	.024	.173	.062	.005	.029	.003	.002	.010	.001
1950	.027	.198	.066	.006	.020	.002	.003	.012	.002
1955	.032	.221	.095	.011	.070	.009	.004	.017	.003
1956	.033	.248	.099	...	...	...	...	...	...
1957	.037	.272	.111	...	...	...	...	...	...
1958	.038	.287	.113	.012	.104	.010	.006	.031	.006
1959	.043	.297	.096	.015	.113	.013	.008	.037	.008
1960	.041	.291	.129	.015	.106	.014	.009	.048	.011
1961	.040	.290	.138	.012	.100	.014	.010	.058	.015
1962	.043	.291	.137	.013	.099	.015	.011	.061	.017
1963	.046	.274	.127	.014	.091	.014	.013	.061	.017
1964	.037	.280	.118	.011	.094	.012	.010	.067	.019
1965	.044	.317	.127	.013	.110	.017	.013	.081	.025
1966	.046	.328	.137	.014	.113	.018	.013	.085	.029
1967	.049	.341	.145	.015	.118	.019	.015	.090	.035
1968	.049	.347	.150	.016	.124	.021	.014	.092	.040

Notes:

[a]Carcass weight.

[b]Million per 1,000 population.

[c]And other state enterprises.

Table 20. Sown Area: Republics (In Thousand Hectares)

	1913[a]	1940	1950	1960	1965	1967	1968
U.S.S.R.[b]	118,215	150,633	146,302	202,985	209,104	206,766	207,021
All grains	104,648	110,728	102,877	115,537	128,024	122,172	121,472
Fodder crops	3,331	18,075	20,739	37,305	33,554	35,587	60,705
Potatoes	4,209	7,696	8,534	9,144	8,612	8,331	8,301
ARMENIA[b]	346	434	471	415	400	408	403
All grains	308	340	319	222	219	211	105
Fodder crops	4	38	77	139	129	148	159
Potatoes	7	13	23	16	17	16	18
AZERBAIDZHAN[b]	962	1,124	1,057	1,292	1,150	1,218	1,305
All grains	833	797	737	699	658	676	651
Fodder crops	4	66	110	312	207	261	280
Potatoes	6	22	18	15	16	14	15
BELORUSSIA[b]	4,542	5,212	4,913	5,664	6,034	6,135	6,085
All grains	3,630	3,475	3,392	2,590	2,890	2,856	2,725
Fodder crops	159	433	302	1,675	1,738	1,922	2,016
Potatoes	583	929	875	1,027	1,003	994	989
ESTONIA[b]	697	918	813	762	772	759	774
All grains	418	572	453	273	324	319	330
Fodder crops	172	235	234	374	350	350	354
Potatoes	69	83	97	100	87	80	80
GEORGIA[b]	748	896	913	829	770	783	745
All grains	707	749	760	472	501	472	429
Fodder crops	6	52	67	269	174	213	216
Potatoes	7	25	25	22	24	23	25
KAZAKHSTAN[b]	4,194	6,746	7,759	28,432	30,422	29,904	30,302
All grains	3,894	5,795	6,019	21,932	24,297	22,686	23,090
Fodder crops	92	495	1,214	5,895	5,476	6,571	6,374
Potatoes	42	100	140	174	180	182	187
KIRGIZIA[b]	640	1,056	1,061	1,196	1,170	1,236	1,262
All grains	555	778	704	593	607	613	629
Fodder crops	40	141	205	439	376	433	444
Potatoes	4	14	16	19	24	26	27
LATVIA[b]	1,396	1,964	1,413	1,534	1,556	1,525	1,531
All grains	949	1,132	805	564	623	577	586
Fodder crops	286	609	383	745	730	752	755
Potatoes	91	139	149	159	140	136	135
LITHUANIA[b]	1,890	2,497	2,294	2,375	2,440	2,344	2,324
All grains	1,558	1,638	1,493	924	1,043	966	911
Fodder crops	80	520	446	1,095	1,078	1,088	1,128
Potatoes	179	210	225	238	209	199	196
MOLDAVIA[b]	2,072	2,057	1,895	1,886	1,931	1,910	1,860
All grains	1,981	1,672	1,382	823	968	906	806
Fodder crops	34	76	124	630	460	508	565
Potatoes	18	29	69	45	46	45	46
R.S.F.S.R.[b]	69,798[c]	92,076	88,953	120,734	123,945	122,713	122,681
All grains	62,939[c]	70,143	64,948	71,372	77,594	74,872	74,290
Fodder crops	1,360[c]	10,432	11,796	37,305	33,554	35,584	36,238
Potatoes	2,116[c]	4,078	4,970	5,108	4,723	4,536	4,501
TADZHIKISTAN[b]	494	807	837	724	765	747	748
All grains	438	567	552	361	397	350	339
Fodder crops	13	55	49	131	105	131	133
Potatoes	1	9	5	6	7	6	6
TURKMENIA[b]	318	411	368	446	517	552	544
All grains	202	183	128	71	133	119	106
Fodder crops	25	48	64	124	94	125	127
Potatoes	...	4	1	1	2	1	1
UKRAINE[b]	27,952	31,336	30,656	33,547	33,785	33,288	33,063
All grains	24,696	21,385	20,047	13,729	16,495	15,501	15,111
Fodder crops	893	4,428	5,238	13,412	10,292	11,020	11,263
Potatoes	1,080	2,018	1,904	2,186	2,108	2,050	2,047
UZBEKISTAN[b]	2,166	3,099	2,899	3,149	3,447	3,315	3,495
All grains	1,540	1,502	1,138	912	1,275	1,048	1,274
Fodder crops	163	447	430	635	415	500	453
Potatoes	6	23	17	28	26	23	26

Notes:

[a] Present boundaries.　　[b] All crops.　　[c] R.S.F.S.R., Karelo-Finnish.

Table 21. Sown Area (Continued) and Tractors: Republics (In Thousand Hectares)

	1913[a]	1940	1950	1960	1965	1967	1968
U.S.S.R.[b]	676	1,226	1,308	3,043	3,882	3,797	3,560
Winter wheat[c]	8,270	14,318	12,484	12,055	19,794	19,708	18,972
Spring wheat[c]	24,754	25,984	26,044	48,338	50,411	47,318	48,259
Tractors[d]	...	683.8	932.5	1,984.8	3,032.4	3,484.5	3,775.5
ARMENIA[b]	...	2	4	4	4	5	4
Winter wheat[c]	96	122	146	122	100	113	105
Spring wheat[c]	96	100	52	33	31	23	19
Tractors[d]	...	2.0	3.3	7.5	13.4	16.6	18.3
AZERBAIDZHAN[b]	...	...	...	...	...	...	...
Winter wheat[c]	524	449	434	176	429	473	466
Spring wheat[c]	9	22	14	7	10	3	2
Tractors[d]	...	6.5	9.4	22.4	35.5	41.4	44.2
BELORUSSIA[b]	...	...	5	29	59	50	49
Winter wheat[c]	55	76	26	60	171	219	358
Spring wheat[c]	31	186	213	102	16	9	5
Tractors[d]	...	13.4	18.6	60.7	99.4	120.8	130.8
ESTONIA[b]	...	...	...	...	...	...	...
Winter wheat[c]	5	25	16	20	18	14	17
Spring wheat[c]	4	45	45	19	11	8	6
Tractors[d]	...	1.4	3.9	11.7	18.5	21.5	23.1
GEORGIA[b]	...	6	6	5	4	4	4
Winter wheat[c]	169	233	232	166	186	176	159
Spring wheat[c]	67	39	33	10	9	8	4
Tractors[d]	...	3.7	6.2	12.6	22.3	28.6	29.8
KAZAKHSTAN[b]	...	15	20	60	67	67	66
Winter wheat[c]	116	213	304	736	805	847	862
Spring wheat[c]	2,399	3,223	3,693	17,323	17,915	16,278	17,278
Tractors[d]	...	41.3	49.3	313.7	421.0	451.0	464.5
KIRGIZIA[b]	...	15	20	35	54	53	51
Winter wheat[c]	53	243	233	225	206	247	277
Spring wheat[c]	298	207	210	114	105	86	64
Tractors[d]	...	6.2	6.8	17.3	30.5	35.6	38.1
LATVIA[b]	...	15	17	20	23	32	17
Winter wheat[c]	31	70	29	28	80	60	68
Spring wheat[c]	6	88	105	34	26	21	12
Tractors[d]	...	1.0	4.5	22.3	30.2	36.3	39.0
LITHUANIA[b]	...	13	26	32	36	30	28
Winter wheat[c]	72	142	88	94	166	107	119
Spring wheat[c]	14	61	97	14	2	1	1
Tractors[d]	...	1.0	6.8	31.1	50.2	58.1	63.3
MOLDAVIA[b]	3	4	11	68	103	106	97
Winter wheat[c]	325	447	479	358	416	366	244
Spring wheat[c]	221	92	42	0.1	3	0.2	0.1
Tractors[d]	...	1.3	9.5	20.9	39.1	49.4	57.0
R.S.F.S.R.[b]	115	336	342	133	1,669	1,630	1,507
Winter wheat[c]	3,069	5,045	4,364	5,473	9,069	9,065	9,026
Spring wheat[c]	15,088	20,427	19,795	30,227	31,473	30,433	30,569
Tractors[d]	...	461.3	617.1	1,084.8	1,646.8	1,870.8	2,032.1
TADZHIKISTAN[b]	...	...	...	...	...	...	...
Winter wheat[c]	101	230	269	198	206	207	195
Spring wheat[c]	233	180	164	52	82	47	45
Tractors[d]	...	4.1	5.2	15.1	24.9	30.1	32.6
TURKMENIA[b]	...	...	...	...	...	...	...
Winter wheat[c]	106	84	45	24	69	64	59
Spring wheat[c]	46	36	39	10	23	11	9
Tractors[d]	...	4.5	4.8	14.8	22.4	30.4	35.3
UKRAINE[b]	558	820	823	1,457	1,863	1,830	1,737
Winter wheat[c]	3,088	6,317	5,383	3,691	7,346	7,392	6,453
Spring wheat[c]	5,770	901	1,168	261	493	178	121
Tractors[d]	...	112.5	152.1	275.9	451.5	534.7	586.0
UZBEKISTAN[b]	...	...	...	...	...	...	...
Winter wheat[c]	460	616	436	384	527	358	564
Spring wheat[c]	472	407	374	132	212	212	124
Tractors[d]	...	23.6	35.0	73.0	126.7	159.2	181.4

Notes:

[a] Present boundaries.　　　　[b] Industrial beets.

[c] Western specialists argue that Soviet grain yields continue to be grossly overstated; thus such specialists consistently reduce Soviet grain figures by some 10-15%.

[d] Thousands, 15 hp. units.

Table 22. GROSS YIELD AND MINERAL FERTILIZER: REPUBLICS (In Thousand Tons)

	1913[a]	1940	1950	1960	1965	1967	1968
U.S.S.R.[b]	86,030	95,638	81,200	125,490	121,141	147,887	169,540
Potatoes	31,863	75,874	88,612	84,374	88,676	95,464	102,184
Sugar beets[c]	11,319	18,015	20,819	57,728	72,276	87,111	94,340
Fertilizer[d]	...	3,159	5,350	11,404	27,066	33,668	36,272
ARMENIA[b]	174	223	281	232	244	288	205
Potatoes	47	97	159	185	198	182	173
Sugar beets[c]	...	17	48	111	125	131	117
Fertilizer[d]	...	...	...	81	142	168	168
AZERBAIDZHAN[b]	486	567	523	725	645	729	726
Potatoes	38	82	119	114	166	122	132
Sugar beets[c]	...	...	...	...	...	...	...
Fertilizer[d]	...	...	...	197	286	328	341
BELORUSSIA[b]	2,568	2,727	2,684	2,165	3,335	3,219	3,002
Potatoes	4,024	11,879	9,537	10,641	12,116	13,573	14,851
Sugar beets[c]	...	...	70	383	856	1,176	1,017
Fertilizer[d]	...	...	...	952	1,941	2,526	2,792
ESTONIA[b]	428	655	522	363	711	695	740
Potatoes	689	1,223	1,140	1,303	1,481	1,281	1,522
Sugar beets[c]	...	...	...	...	...	...	...
Fertilizer[d]	...	...	...	301	469	493	555
GEORGIA[b]	428	538	796	629	658	729	638
Potatoes	48	139	134	200	228	255	224
Sugar beets[c]	...	72	115	136	124	182	147
Fertilizer[d]	...	...	...	250	365	456	489
KAZAKHSTAN[b]	2,162	2,502	4,747	18,693	7,595	4,408	19,485
Potatoes	178	394	1,158	1,265	1,128	1,820	1,504
Sugar beets[c]	...	385	541	1,148	1,930	2,350	2,160
Fertilizer[d]	...	...	...	267	838	755	1,052
KIRGIZIA[b]	436	588	434	649	560	883	907
Potatoes	19	105	135	113	248	283	247
Sugar beets[c]	...	628	...	...	...	...	1,548
Fertilizer[d]	...	...	...	178	399	459	534
LATVIA[b]	880	1,372	732	570	946	938	1,054
Potatoes	645	2,093	1,934	1,688	2,007	1,947	2,146
Sugar beets[c]	...	251	247	359	330	505	378
Fertilizer[d]	...	...	...	441	761	923	1,004
LITHUANIA[b]	1,449	1,536	1,172	855	1,691	1,744	1,820
Potatoes	1,375	2,726	3,122	2,259	2,601	2,801	3,027
Sugar beets[c]	...	255	349	484	569	776	657
Fertilizer[d]	...	...	...	586	983	1,116	1,120
MOLDAVIA[b]	2,008	1,810	1,299	1,601	2,494	2,046	1,862
Potatoes	119	147	605	255	321	310	300
Sugar beets[c]	15	119	274	1,322	2,019	2,323	2,981
Fertilizer[d]	...	...	...	86	281	310	367
R.S.F.S.R.[b]	50,468	55,637	46,826	76,201	69,665	89,490	109,577
Potatoes	16,079	36,424	50,086	46,689	49,795	52,906	55,330
Sugar beets[c]	1,967	3,239	3,614	20,830	20,655	30,666	28,012
Fertilizer[d]	...	...	...	3,658	10,844	12,854	14,680
TADZHIKISTAN[b]	202	324	209	256	226	202	252
Potatoes	10	38	36	31	51	47	45
Sugar beets[c]	...	...	...	...	...	...	...
Fertilizer[d]	...	...	...	312	480	543	636
TURKMENIA[b]	159	124	84	40	83	96	88
Potatoes	...	6	5	5	9	10	10
Sugar beets[c]	...	...	...	...	...	...	...
Fertilizer[d]	...	...	...	225	475	556	581
UKRAINE[b]	23,157	26,420	20,448	21,790	31,651	31,848	27,955
Potatoes	8,546	20,408	20,329	19,461	18,157	19,728	22,489
Sugar beets[c]	9,337	13,049	14,624	31,761	43,793	47,006	57,323
Fertilizer[d]	...	...	...	2,013	5,474	6,499	7,512
UZBEKISTAN[b]	1,025	615	443	721	637	572	1,229
Potatoes	46	113	113	165	170	199	184
Sugar beets[c]	...	...	...	...	...	...	...
Fertilizer[d]	...	...	...	1,721	2,550	3,205	3,047

Notes:

[a]Present boundaries.

[b]All grains. Western specialists argue that Soviet grain yields continue to be grossly overstated; thus such specialists consistently reduce Soviet grain figures by some 10-15%.

[c]Industrial.   [d]Total ingredients.

Table 23. NUMBER OF LIVESTOCK: REPUBLICS (In Thousand Head, January 1)

	1916[a]	1941	1951	1961	1966	1968	1969
U.S.S.R.[b]	58,381	54,517	57,089	75,780	93,436	97,167	95,735
Cows	28,820	27,841	24,283	34,829	40,140	41,567	41,180
Swine	23,037	27,517	24,372	58,674	59,576	50,867	49,047
Sheep & Goats	96,309	91,587	98,953	140,304	135,316	144,041	146,141
ARMENIA[b]	708	599	494	599	662	705	714
Cows	231	212	141	237	264	281	289
Swine	16	59	81	127	86	93	90
Sheep & Goats	1,217	1,221	1,309	1,983	2,222	2,367	2,273
AZERBAIDZHAN[b]	1,397	1,367	1,248	1,373	1,460	1,679	1,671
Cows	491	489	345	513	584	664	665
Swine	31	120	73	156	85	101	92
Sheep & Goats	2,394	2,907	3,360	4,884	4,035	4,713	4,708
BELORUSSIA[b]	2,293	2,844	2,746	3,666	4,704	4,892	4,850
Cows	1,610	1,956	1,382	2,037	2,364	2,504	2,513
Swine	2,444	2,520	1,623	3,164	3,688	3,189	3,222
Sheep & Goats	2,050	2,578	1,409	1,213	846	711	677
ESTONIA[b]	429	528	462	494	610	629	653
Cows	309	402	285	296	308	309	311
Swine	277	319	297	587	592	526	556
Sheep & Goats	490	325	274	267	175	168	167
GEORGIA[b]	1,301	1,607	1,473	1,486	1,514	1,567	1,501
Cows	445	575	431	585	608	633	609
Swine	377	615	498	585	574	563	569
Sheep & Goats	1,866	2,194	2,458	2,084	2,174	2,293	2,084
KAZAKHSTAN[b]	5,062	3,356	4,422	5,501	6,795	7,527	7,544
Cows	1,876	1,259	1,431	2,055	2,566	2,820	2,796
Swine	278	451	399	1,759	1,709	1,849	1,561
Sheep & Goats	18,364	8,132	17,638	28,250	30,059	33,682	35,352
KIRGIZIA[b]	519	556	662	739	857	912	954
Cows	188	219	222	293	353	389	396
Swine	27	87	89	199	224	216	214
Sheep & Goats	2,544	2,529	4,515	6,251	8,303	9,106	9,467
LATVIA[b]	718	986	812	938	1,108	1,113	1,126
Cows	518	797	496	553	589	599	589
Swine	611	588	533	1,051	913	770	838
Sheep & Goats	877	613	514	492	386	363	349
LITHUANIA[b]	934	1,054	731	1,223	1,526	1,634	1,662
Cows	673	782	504	737	828	863	858
Swine	858	1,068	723	1,720	1,731	1,569	1,751
Sheep & Goats	997	627	402	384	198	171	168
MOLDAVIA[b]	505	514	551	652	914	945	824
Cows	228	181	217	274	362	393	355
Swine	379	339	338	1,177	1,187	1,124	956
Sheep & Goats	1,248	1,464	1,021	1,738	1,676	1,600	1,465
R.S.F.S.R.[b]	32,990	27,848	30,174	38,155	48,207	50,162	49,761
Cows	17,282	14,247	13,349	17,983	29,933	21,415	21,271
Swine	11,267	12,090	11,865	29,427	29,497	25,478	24,342
Sheep & Goats	47,027	51,234	46,242	65,446	61,416	63,894	64,554
TADZHIKISTAN[b]	739	580	558	683	818	936	965
Cows	269	188	172	264	325	365	375
Swine	...	21	16	80	61	70	59
Sheep & Goats	1,930	2,174	2,755	2,585	2,431	2,886	3,003
TURKMENIA[b]	312	268	265	365	405	443	452
Cows	103	96	88	143	164	184	189
Swine	...	36	11	57	53	52	52
Sheep & Goats	4,580	2,596	3,243	4,928	4,036	4,560	4,669
UKRAINE[b]	9,132	10,748	11,182	17,632	21,324	21,165	20,158
Cows	4,116	5,816	4,811	7,928	8,827	8,975	8,754
Swine	6,469	9,101	7,765	18,194	18,920	14,995	14,480
Sheep & Goats	6,904	7,201	6,740	10,631	9,342	8,974	8,661
UZBEKISTAN[b]	1,342	1,672	1,309	2,274	2,532	2,839	2,890
Cows	481	622	410	931	1,065	1,180	1,210
Swine	3	703	61	401	256	272	266
Sheep & Goats	3,821	5,792	7,073	9,168	8,017	8,553	8,544

Notes:

[a]Present boundaries.

[b]Cattle.

Table 24. Livestock Production by Republics (In Thousand Tons)

	1913[a]	1940	1950	1960	1965	1967	1968
U.S.S.R.							
Meat[b]	4,954	4,695	4,867	8,682	9,956	11,515	11,576
Milk	29,430	33,640	35,311	61,718	72,563	79,920	82,053
Eggs[c]	11,919	12,214	11,697	27,464	29,068	33,921	35,522
ARMENIA							
Meat[b]	19	23	99	42	40	44	45
Milk	129	170	133	317	338	375	391
Eggs[c]	54	46	43	158	193	200	216
AZERBAIDZHAN							
Meat[b]	40	41	133	79	70	80	86
Milk	203	275	235	427	408	491	484
Eggs[c]	94	158	105	334	290	348	373
BELORUSSIA							
Meat[b]	219	275	222	402	508	641	656
Milk	1,429	2,005	1,643	3,219	4,124	4,640	4,992
Eggs[c]	413	612	568	868	1,106	1,335	1,401
ESTONIA							
Meat[b]	60	72	54	100	107	123	126
Milk	415	782	508	857	955	996	1,025
Eggs[c]	67	134	122	236	218	274	311
GEORGIA							
Meat[b]	49	75	51	91	93	99	100
Milk	222	358	293	487	471	505	481
Eggs[c]	119	251	156	221	305	308	344
KAZAKHSTAN							
Meat[b]	440	226	242	545	763	803	840
Milk	857	1,099	1,555	2,457	3,296	3,869	3,852
Eggs[c]	233	313	255	851	1,044	1,237	1,309
KIRGIZIA							
Meat[b]	39	41	46	100	116	119	125
Milk	91	210	213	401	482	520	541
Eggs[c]	19	47	58	163	190	215	225
LATVIA							
Meat[b]	122	123	81	152	160	186	186
Milk	673	1,537	945	1,470	1,654	1,748	1,802
Eggs[c]	136	174	205	313	346	419	431
LITHUANIA							
Meat[b]	159	134	126	212	267	364	364
Milk	832	1,383	851	1,749	2,042	2,323	2,449
Eggs[c]	264	187	266	438	541	615	637
MOLDAVIA							
Meat[b]	53	51	62	119	140	177	176
Milk	210	182	485	615	676	745	728
Eggs[c]	275	235	...	...	...	...	547
R.S.F.S.R.							
Meat[b]	2,437	2,373	2,646	4,492	5,203	5,947	5,998
Milk	19,306	17,832	21,393	34,523	40,149	44,625	45,809
Eggs[c]	7,115	6,577	6,019	15,705	16,794	19,708	20,555
TADZHIKISTAN							
Meat[b]	48	30	21	47	51	55	57
Milk	102	135	86	203	230	270	277
Eggs[c]	20	38	30	91	85	100	113
TURKMENIA							
Meat[b]	58	22	15	51	50	51	54
Milk	63	107	67	126	155	179	173
Eggs[c]	18	37	32	56	80	100	106
UKRAINE							
Meat[b]	1,122	1,127	1,195	2,068	2,221	2,645	2,571
Milk	4,667	7,114	6,804	13,995	16,629	17,494	17,835
Eggs[c]	3,005	3,272	3,490	7,187	6,941	7,863	8,257
UZBEKISTAN							
Meat[b]	89	82	57	182	167	181	192
Milk	231	451	300	872	955	1,140	1,214
Eggs[c]	87	133	95	468	566	655	697

Notes:

[a]Present boundaries. [b]Carcass weight. [c]In millions.

Table 25. KOLKHOZY ONLY (Republics, Agricultural Only)

	1940	1950	1960	1965	1967	1968
U.S.S.R.						
Number	235,450	121,353	43,981	36,276	36,187	36,172
Households[a]	18,704.3	20,455.2	17,106.0	15,414.0	15,261.0	15,067.0
Milk/Cow[b]	1,017	1,027	1,854	1,906	2,042	2,177
ARMENIA						
Number	1,030	668	760	536	524	495
Households[a]	174.0	155.2	154.0	118.0	116.0	107.0
Milk/Cow[b]	655	584	1,477	1,382	1,498	1,536
AZERBAIDZHAN						
Number	3,416	1,600	1,104	982	1,087	1,076
Households[a]	357.9	298.9	352.0	294.0	298.0	294.0
Milk/Cow[b]	408	381	834	577	629	606
BELORUSSIA						
Number	10,165	9,326	2,377	2,347	2,355	2,363
Households[a]	766.7	1,236.8	938.0	885.0	881.0	878.0
Milk/Cow[b]	833	961	1,725	1,838	2,004	2,200
ESTONIA						
Number	...	2,213	648	469	405	411
Households[a]	...	118.6	84.0	75.0	71.0	383.0
Milk/Cow[b]	...	1,659	2,676	2,934	3,056	3,213
GEORGIA						
Number	4,256	2,530	1,842	1,431	1,518	1,367
Households[a]	476.1	472.7	492.0	462.0	463.0	421.0
Milk/Cow[b]	441	468	1,286	912	979	1,066
KAZAKHSTAN						
Number	6,841	3,670	1,291	441	437	470
Households[a]	594.9	592.8	4,180.0	207.0	206.0	206.0
Milk/Cow[b]	840	818	1,785	1,718	1,890	1,804
KIRGIZIA						
Number	1,732	1,135	304	248	249	249
Households[a]	184.4	184.3	165.0	170.0	174.0	175.0
Milk/Cow[b]	638	552	1,762	1,760	1,902	1,929
LATVIA						
Number	...	1,776	1,105	782	753	755
Households[a]	...	226.9	173.0	153.0	151.0	157.0
Milk/Cow[b]	...	1,848	2,504	2,617	2,768	3,000
LITHUANIA						
Number	...	4,500	1,912	1,529	1,499	1,482
Households[a]	...	326.5	304.0	259.0	261.0	260.0
Milk/Cow[b]	...	1,322	2,163	2,502	2,862	3,087
MOLDAVIA						
Number	233	1,636	552	513	543	549
Households[a]	49.1	472.6	565.0	560.0	563.0	553.0
Milk/Cow[b]	773	1,098	2,344	1,984	2,078	2,121
R.S.F.S.R.						
Number	167,291	67,921	20,814	15,934	15,640	15,692
Households[a]	10,992.9	9,968.2	7,091.0	5,860.0	5,668.0	5,558.0
Milk/Cow[b]	1,052	1,061	1,921	1,925	2,087	2,221
TADZHIKISTAN						
Number	3,093	1,314	353	309	301	301
Households[a]	196.9	158.1	199.0	231.0	234.0	234.0
Milk/Cow[b]	284	315	1,046	781	881	923
TURKMENIA						
Number	1,540	567	234	318	324	330
Households[a]	128.0	105.4	121.0	141.0	146.0	150.0
Milk/Cow[b]	447	345	1,153	1,154	1,273	1,271
UKRAINE						
Number	28,374	19,295	9,634	9,441	9,529	9,587
Households[a]	3,990.4	5,500.6	5,375.0	5,241.0	5,243.0	5,214.0
Milk/Cow[b]	1,255	1,215	1,824	1,969	2,054	2,190
UZBEKISTAN						
Number	7,499	3,202	951	996	1,023	1,045
Households[a]	793.0	677.6	677.0	758.0	786.0	795.0
Milk/Cow[b]	382	322	1,120	887	979	1,045

Notes:

[a] Thousands.

[b] Kilograms/cow.

Table 26. Sovkhozy Only (Republics)

	1940	1950	1960	1965	1967	1968
U.S.S.R.						
Number	4,159	4,988	7,375	11,681	12,783	13,398
Workers[a]	285	303	745	663	617	...
Milk/Cow[b]	1,803	2,256	2,185	2,121	2,262	2,319
ARMENIA						
Number	14	27	83	203	232	257
Milk/Cow[b]	2,036	2,222	1,789	1,517	1,605	1,605
AZERBAIDZHAN						
Number	50	44	86	285	305	334
Milk/Cow[b]	1,285	1,155	1,541	982	1,070	1,062
BELORUSSIA						
Number	92	122	300	630	695	724
Milk/Cow[b]	2,037	2,792	2,082	1,977	2,075	2,274
ESTONIA						
Number	...	127	144	157	170	170
Milk/Cow[b]	...	3,645	2,977	3,024	3,024	3,144
GEORGIA						
Number	76	80	147	168	181	199
Milk/Cow[b]	1,524	1,393	2,042	1,509	1,559	1,470
KAZAKHSTAN						
Number	194	264	868	1,507	1,539	1,562
Milk/Cow[b]	1,001	1,470	1,782	1,684	1,885	1,797
KIRGIZIA						
Number	36	48	67	84	93	93
Milk/Cow[b]	1,444	1,934	2,011	1,857	2,035	2,027
LATVIA						
Number	...	57	162	187	196	204
Milk/Cow[b]	...	3,401	2,758	2,766	2,779	2,933
LITHUANIA						
Number	...	113	228	316	310	308
Milk/Cow[b]	...	2,775	2,475	2,597	2,767	2,934
MOLDAVIA						
Number	40	59	61	81	91	115
Milk/Cow[b]	2,027	2,168	2,664	2,240	2,315	2,397
R.S.F.S.R.						
Number	2,600	2,953	4,047	6,321	7,114	7,518
Milk/Cow[b]	1,779	2,258	2,242	2,158	2,328	2,398
TADZHIKISTAN						
Number	21	35	39	55	67	75
Milk/Cow[b]	598	1,219	1,060	1,317	1,225	1,072
TURKMENIA						
Number	26	32	49	57	51	51
Milk/Cow[b]	1,071	983	1,465	1,582	1,582	1,614
UKRAINE						
Number	929	935	902	1,343	1,418	1,463
Milk/Cow[b]	2,381	2,431	2,158	2,369	2,334	2,374
UZBEKISTAN						
Number	81	92	192	297	321	325
Milk/Cow[b]	1,401	1,931	1,251	1,255	1,321	1,423

Notes:

   [a]Averages per sovkhoz.

   [b]Kilograms/cow.

CHAPTER II TABLE SOURCE NOTES

Table 1

Collective Farms:
   1918–1930: SS-SSSR, p. 160.
   1940–1955: N.K. 1956, p. 100.
   1956–1957: N.K. 1958, p. 349.
   1958: N.K. 1958, p. 239.
   1959: Selsk, p. 36.
   1960–1962: N.K. 1962, p. 330.
   1963: N.K. 1963, p. 341.
   1964: N.K. 1964, p. 390.
   1965–1967: N.K. 1967, p. 466.
   1968: N.K. 1968, p. 313.
State Farms:
   1928: N.K. 1956, p. 100.

   1930: Selsk, p. 42.
   1940, 1950, 1955: N.K. 1956, p. 100.
   1956–1958: N.K. 1958, p. 349.
   1959: Selsk, p. 36.
   1960: N.K. 1967, p. 480
   1961–1962: N.K. 1962, p. 352.
   1963: N.K. 1963, p. 356.
   1964: N.K. 1964, p. 410.
   1965–1967: N.K. 1967, p. 480.
   1968: N.K. 1968, p. 313.
Agricultural Kolkhozy:
   1928: N.K. 1958, p. 494.
   1940, 1950: N.K. 1967, p. 325.
   1955–1958: N.K. 1958, p. 494.

1959: *Selsk*, p. 51.
1960: *N.K. 1967*, p. 325.
1961–1962: *N.K. 1962*, p. 330.
1963: *N.K. 1963*, p. 341.
1964: *N.K. 1964*, p. 390.
1965–1967: *N.K. 1967*, p. 325.
1968: *N.K. 1968*, p. 313.

TABLE 2

Tractors:
1928–1954: *N.K. 1956*, p. 144.
1955: *N.K. 1956*, p. 98.
1956–1957: *N.K. 1958*, p. 488.
1958: *N.K. 1958*, p. 348.
1959: *Selsk*, p. 10.
1960: *N.K. 1967*, p. 456.
1961: *N.K. 1963*, p. 324.
1962–1964: *N.K. 1964*, p. 382.
1965–1967: *N.K. 1967*, p. 456.
1968: *N.K. 1968*, p. 416.

Grain Combines:
1940: *N.K. 1956*, p. 146.
1950: *N.K. 1956*, p. 146.
1955: *N.K. 1956*, p. 98.
1956–1957: *N.K. 1958*, p. 489.
1958: *N.K. 1964*, p. 383.
1959: *N.K. 1962*, p. 325.
1960: *N.K. 1967*, p. 456.
1961: *N.K. 1962*, p. 325.
1962–1964: *N.K. 1964*, p. 383.
1965–1967: *N.K. 1967*, p. 456.
1968: *N.K. 1968*, p. 417.

Mineral Fertilizer:
1913: *N.K. 1960*, p. 380 and *Narodnoe Khozyaistvo: Statistichesky Sbornik*, p. 81.
1928: *SS za 50 L.*, p. 160.
1932: *N.K. 1961*, p. 380.
1940: *SS za 50 L.*, p. 160 and *Narodnoe Khozyaistvo: Statistichesky Sbornik*, p. 81.
1950: *SS za 50 L.*, p. 160 and *Narodnoe Khozyaistvo: Statistichesky Sbornik*, p. 81.
1955–1957: *N.K. 1958*, p. 444.
1958: *N.K. 1961*, p. 380.
1959: *N.K. 1960*, p. 380.
1960–1966: *SS za 50 L.*, p. 160.
1967: *N.K. 1967*, p. 412.
1968: *N.K. 1968*, p. 380.
1970: *Selskaya Zhizn*, February 4, 1971, pp. 1–2.

TABLE 3

All Crops:
1913: *N.K. 1956*, p. 106.
1920: *SS-SSSR*, p. 176.
1926–1927: *SS-SSSR*, p. 177.

1928: *N.K. 1956*, p. 106.
1930: *SS-SSSR*, p. 177.
1940: *N.K. 1956*, p. 108.
1950: *N.K. 1956*, p. 108.
1955: *N.K. 1956*, p. 108.
1956–1958: *N.K. 1958*, p. 387.
1959: *Selsk*, p. 127.
1960: *N.K. 1967*, p. 348.
1961: *N.K. 1962*, p. 252.
1962–1964: *N.K. 1964*, p. 278.
1965–1967: *N.K. 1967*, p. 348.
1968: *N.K. 1968*, p. 334.

All Grains:
1913: *N.K. 1958*, p. 386.
1920: *SS-SSSR*, p. 176.
1926–1927: *SS-SSSR*, p. 177.
1928: *N.K. 1956*, p. 108.
1930: *SS-SSSR*, p. 177.
1940: *N.K. 1956*, p. 108.
1950: *N.K. 1956*, p. 108.
1955: *N.K. 1956*, p. 108.
1956–1958: *N.K. 1958*, p. 387.
1959: *Selsk*, p. 127.
1960: *N.K. 1967*, p. 348.
1961: *N.K. 1962*, p. 252.
1962–1964: *N.K. 1964*, p. 279.
1965–1967: *N.K. 1967*, p. 348.
1968: *N.K. 1968*, p. 334.

Fodder Crops:
1913: *N.K. 1958*, p. 388.
1928: *N.K. 1956*, p. 109.
1940: *N.K. 1956*, p. 109.
1950: *N.K. 1956*, p. 109.
1955: *N.K. 1956*, p. 109.
1956–1958: *N.K. 1958*, p. 389.
1959: *Selsk*, p. 127.
1960–1962: *N.K. 1962*, p. 265.
1964: *N.K. 1964*, p. 291.
1965–1967: *N.K. 1967*, p. 348.
1968: *N.K. 1968*, p. 334.

Corn (Ripe):
1913: *N.K. 1958*, p. 402.
1920: *SS-SSSR*, p. 176.
1926–1928: *SS-SSSR*, p. 177.
1930: *SS-SSSR*, p. 177.
1940: *N.K. 1967*, p. 359.
1950: *N.K. 1967*, p. 359.
1955–1956: *N.K. 1958*, p. 403.
1957: *Selsk*, pp. 156, 157.
1958: *N.K. 1964*, p. 283.
       N.K. 1962, p. 259.
1959: *Selsk*, p. 157.
       N.K. 1962, p. 259.
1960: *N.K. 1964*, p. 283.
       N.K. 1962, p. 259.
1961: *N.K. 1962*, p. 529.
       N.K. 1962, p. 259.
1962: *N.K. 1964*, p. 283.
       N.K. 1962, p. 259.
1963: *N.K. 1964*, p. 283.
       N.K. 1963, p. 269.
1964: *Selsk*, p. 283.
1965–1967: *N.K. 1967*, p. 359.

1968: *N.K. 1968*, p. 334.
Sugar Beets:
    1913: *N.K. 1958*, p. 405.
    1920: *SS-SSSR*, p. 176.
1926–1928: *SS-SSSR*, p. 177.
    1930: *SS-SSSR*, p. 177.
    1940: *N.K. 1958*, p. 405.
    1950: *N.K. 1967*, p. 362.
    1955: *N.K. 1956*, p. 106.
1956–1958: *N.K. 1958*, p. 405.
    1959: *N.K. 1962*, p. 262.
    1960: *N.K. 1967*, p. 362.
    1961: *N.K. 1962*, p. 262.
1962–1964: *N.K. 1964*, p. 287.
1965–1967: *N.K. 1967*, p. 362.
    1968: *N.K. 1968*, p. 334.
Flax:
    1913: *N.K. 1958*, p. 407.
    1920: *SS-SSSR*, p. 176.
1926–1928: *SS-SSSR*, p. 177.
    1930: *SS-SSSR*, p. 177.
    1940: *N.K. 1958*, p. 407.
    1950: *N.K. 1967*, p. 363.
    1955: *N.K. 1956*, p. 106.
1956–1958: *N.K. 1958*, p. 407.
    1959: *N.K. 1962*, p. 263.
    1960: *N.K. 1967*, p. 363.
    1961: *N.K. 1962*, p. 263.
1962–1964: *N.K. 1964*, p. 288.
1965–1967: *N.K. 1967*, p. 363.
    1968: *N.K. 1968*, p. 334.
Winter Wheat:
    1913: *N.K. 1958*, p. 400.
    1920: *SS-SSSR*, p. 176.
1926–1928: *SS-SSSR*, p. 177.
    1955: *N.K. 1956*, p. 106.
1956–1958: *N.K. 1958*, p. 400.
    1959: *N.K. 1962*, p. 258.
    1960: *N.K. 1967*, p. 356.
    1961: *N.K. 1962*, p. 258.
1962–1964: *N.K. 1964*, p. 280.
1965–1967: *N.K. 1967*, p. 356.
    1968: *N.K. 1968*, p. 334.
Spring Wheat:
    1913: *N.K. 1958*, p. 401.
    1920: *SS-SSSR*, p. 176.
1926–1928: *SS-SSSR*, p. 177.
    1955: *N.K. 1956*, p. 106.
1956–1958: *N.K. 1958*, p. 401.
    1959: *N.K. 1962*, p. 258.
    1960: *N.K. 1967*, p. 357.
    1961: *N.K. 1962*, p. 258.
1962–1964: *N.K. 1964*, p. 281.
1965–1967: *N.K. 1967*, p. 357.
    1968: *N.K. 1968*, p. 334.
Rye:
    1913: *SS-SSSR*, p. 176.
    1920: *SS-SSSR*, p. 176.
1926–1928: *SS-SSSR*, p. 177.
    1930: *SS-SSSR*, p. 177.
    1940: *N.K. 1967*, p. 358.
    1950: *N.K. 1967*, p. 358.
    1955: *N.K. 1956*, p. 106.

    1958: *N.K. 1964*, p. 282.
    1960: *N.K. 1967*, p. 358.
1962–1964: *N.K. 1964*, p. 282.
1965–1967: *N.K. 1967*, p. 358.
    1968: *N.K. 1968*, p. 334.
Potatoes:
    1913: *N.K. 1958*, p. 409.
    1920: *SS-SSSR*, p. 176.
1926–1928: *SS-SSSR*, p. 177.
    1930: *SS-SSSR*, p. 177.
    1940: *N.K. 1958*, p. 409.
    1950: *N.K. 1967*, p. 364.
    1955: *N.K. 1956*, p. 107.
1956–1958: *N.K. 1958*, p. 409.
    1959: *N.K. 1962*, p. 264.
    1960: *N.K. 1967*, p. 364.
    1961: *N.K. 1962*, p. 264.
1962–1964: *N.K. 1964*, p. 289.
1965–1967: *N.K. 1967*, p. 364.
    1968: *N.K. 1968*, p. 334.

TABLE 4

All Grains:
    1913: *N.K. 1958*, p. 352.
    1918: *N.K. 1963*, p. 273.
1928–1932: *N.K. 1958*, p. 352.
    1950: *N.K. 1967*, p. 370.
    1955: *N.K. 1967*, p. 370.
1956–1958: *N.K. 1958*, p. 352.
1959–1967: *N.K. 1967*, p. 370.
    1968: *N.K. 1968*, p. 314.
    1970: T. I. Sokolov, "Dlya blaga
        narodov," *Ekonomicheskaya
        gazeta*, no. 1, January 1971,
        p. 3.
Corn:
    1913: *Selsk*, p. 28.
    1928: *N.K. 1958*, p. 418.
    1940: *N.K. 1967*, p. 379.
    1950: *N.K. 1967*, p. 379.
1955–1962: *N.K. 1962*, p. 270.
1963–1964: *N.K. 1964*, p. 304.
1965–1967: *N.K. 1967*, p. 379.
    1968: *N.K. 1968*, p. 318.
Sugar Beets:
    1913: *N.K. 1958*, p. 353
    1930: *N.K. 1958*, p. 353.
    1950: *N.K. 1967*, p. 386.
1955-1967: *N.K. 1967*, p. 386.
    1968: *N.K. 1968*, p. 318.
    1970: *Selskaya Zhizn*, February 4,
        1971, pp. 1–2.
Wheat:
    1913: *N.K. 1967*, p. 373.
    1930: *Selsk*, p. 197.
    1940: *N.K. 1967*, p. 373.
    1950: *N.K. 1967*, p. 373.
1955–1967: *N.K. 1967*, p. 373.
    1968: *N.K. 1968*, p. 318.
Rye:
    1913: *Selsk*, p. 202.
    1940: *N.K. 1967*, p. 377.
    1950: *N.K. 1967*, p. 377.

1955–1959: *Selsk*, p. 203.
1960: *N.K. 1967*, p. 377.
1962–1964: *N.K. 1964*, p. 302.
1965–1967: *N.K. 1967*, p. 377.
1968: *N.K. 1968*, p. 318.

Flax:
1913: *N.K. 1958*, p. 354.
1930: *N.K. 1958*, p. 354.
1950: *N.K. 1967*, p. 389.
1955: *N.K. 1967*, p. 389.
1956–1958: *N.K. 1958*, p. 354.
1959–1967: *N.K. 1967*, p. 389.
1968: *N.K. 1968*, p. 318.

Potatoes:
1913: *N.K. 1958*, p. 355.
1930: *N.K. 1958*, p. 355.
1950: *N.K. 1967*, p. 393.
1955: *N.K. 1967*, p. 393.
1956–1958: *N.K. 1958*, p. 355.
1959–1967: *N.K. 1967*, p. 393.
1968: *N.K. 1968*, p. 315.
1970: *Selskaya Zhizn*, February 4, 1971, pp. 1–2.

TABLE 5

Grain:
1913: *N.K. 1958*, p. 352.
1930: *N.K. 1958*, p. 352.
1950: *N.K. 1967*, p. 370.
1955: *N.K. 1967*, p. 370.
1956–1958: *N.K. 1958*, p. 352.
1959–1967: *N.K. 1967*, p. 370.
1968: *N.K. 1968*, p. 319.

Corn:
1913: *Selsk*, p. 28.
1926–1927: *SS-SSSR*, p. 203.
1928: *N.K. 1958*, p. 418.
1930: *SS-SSSR*, p. 203.
1940: *N.K. 1964*, p. 305.
Selsk, p. 28.
1950: *Selsk*, p. 208.
1955: *Selsk*, p. 209.
N.K. 1962, p. 270.
1956–1958: *N.K. 1958*, p. 352.
1959: *Selsk*, p. 198.
1960: *N.K. 1967*, p. 380.
N.K. 1962, p. 270.
1961: *N.K. 1962*, p. 270.
1962: *N.K. 1964*, p. 305.
N.K. 1964, p. 270.
1963–1964: *N.K. 1964*, p. 305.
1965–1967: *N.K. 1967*, p. 380.
1968: *N.K. 1968*, p. 319.

Sugar Beets:
1913: *N.K. 1958*, p. 353.
1926–1927: *SS-SSSR*, p. 211.
1930: *N.K. 1958*, p. 353.
1950: *N.K. 1967*, p. 386.
1955: *N.K. 1967*, p. 386.
1956–1958: *N.K. 1958*, p. 353.
1959–1967: *N.K. 1967*, p. 386.

1968: *N.K. 1968*, p. 319.

Winter Wheat:
1913: *Selsk*, p. 197.
1930: *Selsk*, p. 197.
1940: *N.K. 1967*, p. 375.
1950: *N.K. 1967*, p. 375.
1955: *Selsk*, p. 209.
1956–1959: *Selsk*, p. 197.
1960: *N.K. 1967*, p. 375.
1961–1962: *N.K. 1962*, p. 275.
1963–1964: *N.K. 1964*, p. 300.
1965–1967: *N.K. 1967*, p. 375.
1968: *N.K. 1968*, p. 319.

Spring Wheat:
1913: *Selsk*, p. 197.
1930: *Selsk*, p. 197.
1940: *N.K. 1967*, p. 376.
1950: *N.K. 1967*, p. 376.
1955: *Selsk*, p. 209.
1956–1959: *Selsk*, p. 197.
1960: *N.K. 1967*, p. 376.
1961–1962: *N.K. 1962*, p. 275.
1963–1964: *N.K. 1964*, p. 301.
1965–1967: *N.K. 1967*, p. 376.
1968: *N.K. 1968*, p. 319.

Flax:
1913: *N.K. 1958*, p. 354.
1930: *N.K. 1958*, p. 354.
1950: *N.K. 1967*, p. 389.
1955: *N.K. 1967*, p. 389.
1956–1958: *N.K. 1958*, p. 354.
1959–1967: *N.K. 1967*, p. 389.
1968: *N.K. 1968*, p. 319.

Potatoes:
1913: *N.K. 1958*, p. 355.
1930: *N.K. 1958*, p. 355.
1950: *N.K. 1967*, p. 393.
1955: *N.K. 1967*, p. 393.
1956–1958: *N.K. 1958*, p. 355.
1959–1967: *N.K. 1967*, p. 393.
1968: *N.K. 1968*, p. 319.

Winter Rye:
1913: *Selsk*, p. 208.
1926–1928: *SS-SSSR*, p. 203.
1930: *SS-SSSR*, p. 203.
1932: *SS-SSSR*, p. 203.
1940: *N.K. 1967*, p. 378.
1950: *N.K. 1967*, p. 378.
1955–1959: *Selsk*, p. 209.
1960: *N.K. 1967*, p. 378.
1962–1964: *N.K. 1964*, p. 303.
1965–1967: *N.K. 1967*, p. 378.
1968: *N.K. 1968*, p. 319.

TABLE 6

Cattle:
1918: *N.K. 1963*, p. 311.
1928: *N.K. 1956*, p. 118.
1930: *N.K. 1956*, p. 118.
1940: *N.K. 1956*, p. 118.
1950: *N.K. 1956*, p. 118.
1955–1968: *N.K. 1967*, p. 425.

1969: *N.K. 1968*, p. 393.
1971: *Selskaya zhizn*, February 4, 1971, pp. 1–2.
Swine:
1918: *N.K. 1963*, p. 311.
1928: *N.K. 1956*, p. 118.
1930: *N.K. 1956*, p. 118.
1940: *N.K. 1956*, p. 118.
1950: *N.K. 1956*, p. 118.
1955–1968: *N.K. 1967*, p. 425.
1969: *N.K. 1968*, p. 393.
1971: *Selskaya zhizn*, February 4, 1971, pp. 1–2.
Sheep and Goats:
1918: *N.K. 1963*, p. 311.
1928: *N.K. 1961*, p. 381.
1930, 1940, 1950: *N.K. 1956*, p. 118.
1955–1968: *N.K. 1967*, p. 425.
1969: *N.K. 1968*, p. 393.
1971: *Selskaya zhizn*, February 4, 1971, pp. 1–2.

TABLE 7

Cows (Million Head):
1918: *N.K. 1961*, p. 381.
1926–1928: *N.K. 1961*, p. 381.
1930, 1940: *N.K. 1961*, p. 381.
1950: *N.K. 1967*, p. 425.
1955–1968: *N.K. 1967*, p. 425.
1969: *N.K. 1969*, p. 393.
1971: *Selskaya zhizn*, February 4, 1971, pp. 1–2.
Milk/Cow:
1913: *SS za 50 L.*, p. 151.
1940, 1950: *N.K. 1967*, p. 446.
1955–1967: *N.K. 1967*, p. 446.
1968: *N.K. 1968*, p. 409.
1970: *Selskaya zhizn*, Febuary 4, 1971, pp. 1–2.

TABLE 8

Meat:
1913: *Selsk*, p. 31.
1928, 1930: *Selsk*, p. 328.
1940: *N.K. 1967*, p. 434.
1950: *N.K. 1958*, p. 355.
1955: *N.K. 1967*, p. 434.
1956–1958: *N.K. 1958*, p. 355.
1959: *Selsk*, p. 31.
1960–1967: *N.K. 1967*, p. 434.
1968: *N.K. 1968*, p. 320.
1969–1970: *Selskaya zhizn*, February 4, 1971, pp. 1–2.
Milk:
1913: *Selsk*, p. 31.
1928, 1930: *Selsk*, p. 328.
1940: *N.K. 1967*, p. 434.
1950: *N.K. 1958*, p. 355.
1955: *N.K. 1967*, p. 434.
1956–1958: *N.K. 1958*, p. 355.

1959: *Selsk*, p. 31.
1960–1967: *N.K. 1967*, p. 434.
1968: *N.K. 1968*, p. 320.
1969–1970: *Selskaya zhizn*, February 4, 1971.
Eggs:
1913: *Selsk*, p. 31.
1928, 1930: *Selsk*, p. 328.
1940: *N.K. 1967*, p. 434.
1950: *N.K. 1958*, p. 355.
1955: *N.K. 1967*, p. 434.
1956–1958: *N.K. 1958*, p. 355.
1960–1967: *N.K. 1967*, p. 434.
1968: *N.K. 1968*, p. 320.
1969–1970: *Selskaya zhizn*, February 4, 1971.

TABLE 9

Households:
1928: *N.K. 1956*, p. 100.
1930: *SS-SSSR*, p. 164.
1940, 1950, 1955: *N.K. 1956*, p. 100.
1956–1958: *N.K. 1958*, p. 349.
1959: *Selsk*, p. 59.
1960–1962: *N.K. 1962*, p. 331.
1963: *N.K. 1963*, p. 342.
1964: *N.K. 1964*, p. 391.
1965–1967: *N.K. 1967*, p. 467.
1968: *N.K. 1968*, p. 424.
Collective Sown Area:
1928: *Selsk*, p. 58.
1930: *SS-SSSR*, p. 164.
1940, 1950: *Selsk*, p. 59.
1955: *N.K. 1956*, p. 129.
1956–1959: *Selsk*, p. 58.
1960–1962: *N.K. 1962*, p. 331.
1963: *N.K. 1963*, p. 342.
1964: *N.K. 1964*, p. 391.
1965–1967: *N.K. 1967*, p. 470.
1968: *N.K. 1968*, p. 427.
Income (Rubles)/Household:
1940, 1950: *Selsk*, p. 65.
1955: *N.K. 1968*, p. 499.
1956–1959: *Selsk*, p. 65.
1960: *N.K. 1964*, p. 401.
1961: *N.K. 1962*, p. 342.
1962–1964: *N.K. 1964*, p. 401.
Agricultural Land (1,000 Hectares):
1928: *Selsk*, p. 58.
1940, 1950: *Selsk*, p. 59.
1955: *N.K. 1958*, p. 495.
1956–1957: *Selsk*, p. 59.
1958: *N.K. 1964*, p. 391.
1959–1962: *N.K. 1962*, 331.
1963: *N.K. 1963*, p. 342.
1964: *N.K. 1964*, p. 391.
1965–1967: *N.K. 1967*, p. 467.
1968: *N.K. 1968*, p. 424.
Tractors per farm:
1958: *N.K. 1964*, p. 391.
1963: *N.K. 1963*, p. 342.

1964: *N.K. 1964*, p. 391.
1965–1967: *N.K. 1967*, p. 467.
1968: *N.K. 1968*, p. 424.

TABLE 10

Cattle:
1929, 1941: *N.K. 1961*, p. 418.
1951, 1955: *N.K. 1958*, p. 494.
1956: *N.K. 1960*, p. 492.
1957: *N.K. 1958*, p. 494.
1958: *N.K. 1958*, p. 499.
1959: *N.K. 1965*, p. 405.
1960–1962: *N.K. 1961*, p. 418.
1963: *N.K. 1962*, p. 330.
1964: *N.K. 1963*, p. 341.
1965: *N.K. 1965*, p. 405.
1966–1968: *N.K. 1967*, p. 466.
1969: *N.K. 1968*, p. 423.
Swine:
1929, 1941: *N.K. 1961*, p. 418.
1951, 1955: *N.K. 1958*, p. 494.
1956: *N.K. 1960*, p. 492.
1957–1958: *N.K. 1958*, p. 494.
1959: *N.K. 1965*, p. 405.
1960–1962: *N.K. 1961*, p. 418.
1963: *N.K. 1962*, p. 330.
1964: *N.K. 1963*, p. 341.
1965: *N.K. 1965*, p. 405.
1966–1968: *N.K. 1967*, p. 466.
1969: *N.K. 1968*, p. 423.
Sheep and Goats:
1929, 1941: *N.K. 1961*, p. 418.
1951, 1955: *N.K. 1958*, p. 494.
1956: *N.K. 1960*, p. 492.
1957–1958: *N.K. 1958*, p. 494.
1959: *N.K. 1965*, p. 405.
1960–1962: *N.K. 1961*, p. 418.
1963: *N.K. 1962*, p. 330.
1964: *N.K. 1963*, p. 341.
1965: *N.K. 1965*, p. 405.
1966–1968: *N.K. 1967*, p. 466.
1969: *N.K. 1968*, p. 423.

TABLE 11

Cows (Number):
1929, 1941: *N.K. 1961*, p. 418.
1951, 1955: *N.K. 1958*, p. 494.
1956: *N.K. 1960*, p. 492.
1957–1958: *Selsk*, p. 279.
1959: *N.K. 1965*, p. 405.
1960–1962: *N.K. 1961*, p. 418.
1963: *N.K. 1962*, p. 330.
1964: *N.K. 1963*, p. 341.
1965: *N.K. 1965*, p. 390.
1966–1968: *N.K. 1967*, p. 466.
1969: *N.K. 1968*, p. 423.
Milk/Cow:
1940: *Selsk*, p. 372.
1950: *N.K. 1967*, p. 448.
1955: *N.K. 1960*, p. 478.

1956–1957: *Selsk*, p. 372.
1958: *N.K. 1964*, p. 375.
1959: *Selsk*, p. 372.
1960: *N.K. 1967*, p. 448.
1961: *N.K. 1961*, p. 442.
1962–1964: *N.K. 1964*, p. 375.
1965–1967: *N.K. 1967*, p. 448.

TABLE 12

Meat:
1940, 1950, 1955: *N.K. 1967*, p. 435.
1958–1962: *N.K. 1962*, p. 309.
1963–1967: *N.K. 1967*, p. 435.
1968: *N.K. 1968*, p. 400.
Milk:
1940, 1950, 1955: *N.K. 1967*, p. 435.
1958–1962: *N.K. 1962*, p. 309.
1963–1967: *N.K. 1967*, p. 435.
1968: *N.K. 1968*, p. 400.
Eggs:
1940, 1950, 1955: *N.K. 1967*, p. 435.
1958–1962: *N.K. 1962*, p. 309.
1963–1967: *N.K. 1967*, p. 435.
1968: *N.K. 1968*, p. 400.

TABLE 13

Number of Workers:
1940, 1950: *N.K. 1958*, p. 521.
1955–1958: *N.K. 1958*, p. 521.
1959: *Selsk*, p. 49.
1960–1962: *N.K. 1962*, p. 359.
1963: *N.K. 1963*, p. 359.
1964: *N.K. 1964*, p. 411.
1965–1967: *N.K. 1967*, p. 483.
Sown Area:
1940, 1950: *N.K. 1958*, p. 521.
1955–1958: *N.K. 1958*, p. 521.
1959: *Selsk*, p. 49.
1960–1962: *N.K. 1962*, p. 359.
1963: *N.K. 1963*, p. 359.
1964: *N.K. 1964*, p. 411.
1965–1967: *N.K. 1967*, p. 483.
1968: *N.K. 1968*, p. 439.
Agricultural Land:
1940, 1950: *Selsk*, p. 49.
1955: *N.K. 1956*, p. 136.
1956–1958: *Selsk*, p. 49.
1959–1963: *N.K. 1962*, p. 359.
1963: *N.K. 1963*, p. 359.
1964: *N.K. 1964*, p. 411.
1965–1967: *N.K. 1967*, p. 483.
1968: *N.K. 1968*, p. 439.
Tractors (Farms):
1940, 1950: *Selsk*, p. 49.
1956–1957: *Selsk*, p. 49.
1958–1962: *N.K. 1962*, p. 359.
1963: *N.K. 1963*, p. 359.
1964: *N.K. 1964*, p. 411.
1965–1967: *N.K. 1967*, p. 483.
1968: *N.K. 1968*, p. 439.

TABLE 14

Cattle:
- 1941: *N.K. 1961*, p. 513.
- 1951: *N.K. 1958*, p. 519.
- 1956: *N.K. 1961*, p. 513.
- 1957–1958: *N.K. 1958*, p. 519.
- 1959: *N.K. 1965*, p. 424.
- 1960–1963: *N.K. 1962*, p. 357.
- 1964: *N.K. 1963*, p. 358.
- 1965: *N.K. 1965*, p. 424.
- 1966–1968: *N.K. 1967*, p. 482.
- 1969: *N.K. 1968*, p. 438.

Swine:
- 1941: *N.K. 1960*, p. 513.
- 1951: *N.K. 1958*, p. 519.
- 1956: *N.K. 1960*, p. 513.
- 1957–1958: *N.K. 1958*, p. 519.
- 1959: *N.K. 1965*, p. 424.
- 1960–1963: *N.K. 1962*, p. 357.
- 1964: *N.K. 1963*, p. 358.
- 1965: *N.K. 1965*, p. 424.
- 1966–1968: *N.K. 1967*, p. 482.
- 1969: *N.K. 1968*, p. 438.

Sheep and Goats:
- 1941: *N.K. 1960*, p. 513.
- 1951: *N.K. 1958*, p. 519.
- 1956–1958: *N.K. 1958*, p. 519.
- 1959: *N.K. 1964*, p. 410.
- 1960–1963: *N.K. 1962*, p. 357.
- 1964: *N.K. 1963*, p. 358.
- 1965: *N.K. 1965*, p. 424.
- 1966–1968: *N.K. 1967*, p. 482.
- 1969: *N.K. 1968*, p. 438.

TABLE 15

Cows (Number):
- 1941: *N.K. 1960*, p. 513.
- 1951: *N.K. 1958*, p. 519.
- 1956: *N.K. 1960*, p. 513.
- 1957–1958: *N.K. 1958*, p. 519.
- 1959–1963: *N.K. 1962*, p. 357.
- 1964: *N.K. 1963*, p. 358.
- 1965: *N.K. 1965*, p. 424.
- 1966–1968: *N.K. 1967*, p. 482.
- 1969: *N.K. 1968*, p. 438.

Milk/Cow:
- 1940: *SS za 50 L.*, p. 51.
- 1950: *N.K. 1967*, p. 449.
- 1958: *N.K. 1965*, p. 388.
- 1960: *N.K. 1967*, p. 449.
- 1961–1962: *SS za 50 L.*, p. 151.
- 1963–1964: *N.K. 1965*, p. 388.
- 1965–1967: *N.K. 1967*, p. 449.
- 1968: *N.K. 1968*, p. 410.

TABLE 16

Meat:
- 1940, 1950, 1955: *N.K. 1967*, p. 435.
- 1958–1962: *N.K. 1962*, p. 309.
- 1963–1967: *N.K. 1967*, p. 435.
- 1968: *N.K. 1968*, p. 400.

Milk:
- 1940, 1950, 1955: *N.K. 1967*, p. 435.
- 1958–1962: *N.K. 1962*, p. 309.
- 1963–1967: *N.K. 1967*, p. 435.
- 1968: *N.K. 1968*, p. 400.

Eggs:
- 1940, 1950, 1955: *N.K. 1967*, p. 435.
- 1958–1962: *N.K. 1962*, p. 309.
- 1963–1967: *N.K. 1967*, p. 435.
- 1968: *N.K. 1968*, p. 400.

TABLE 17: SPECIALISTS

Kolkhozy (all):
- 1941, 1953, 1960, 1965, 1966: *N.K. 1967*, p. 493.
- 1968: *N.K. 1968*, p. 448.

Ag. only:
- 1941, 1953, 1960, 1965, 1966: *N.K. 1967*, p. 493.
- 1968: *N.K. 1968*, p. 448.

Sovkhozy (all):
- 1941, 1953, 1960, 1965, 1966: *N.K. 1967*, p. 493.
- 1968: *N.K. 1968*, p. 448.

Ag. only:
- 1941, 1953, 1960, 1965, 1966: *N.K. 1967*, p. 493.
- 1968: *N.K. 1968*, p. 448.

Total (all):
- 1941, 1953, 1960, 1965, 1966: *N.K. 1967*, p. 493.
- 1968: *N.K. 1968*, p. 448.

Ag. only:
- 1941, 1953. 1960, 1965, 1966: *N.K. 1967*, p. 493.
- 1968: *N.K. 1968*, p. 448.

TABLE 18: WORKERS AND EMPLOYEES

Total:
- 1928, 1940, 1950, 1960–1966: *SS za 50 L.*, pp. 163–164.
- 1967–1968: *N.K. 1968*, p. 446.

Kolkhozy and Subsidiary Enterprises:
- 1928, 1940, 1950, 1960–1966: *SS za 50 L.*, pp. 163–164.
- 1967–1968: *N.K. 1968*, p. 446.

Kolkhozy only:
- 1928, 1940, 1950, 1960–1966: *SS za 50 L.*, pp. 163–164.
- 1967–1968: *N.K. 1968*, p. 446.

Sovkhozy and Subsidiary Enterprises:
- 1928, 1940, 1950, 1960–1966: *SS za 50 L.*, pp. 163–164.
- 1967–1968: *N.K. 1968*, p. 446.

Sovkhozy only:
- 1928, 1940, 1950, 1960–1966: *SS za 50 L.*, pp. 163–164.
- 1967–1968: *N.K. 1968*, p. 446.

Total Exc. Subsidiary Enterprises:
- 1928, 1940, 1950, 1960–1966: *SS za 50 L.*, pp. 163–164.

1967–1968: *N.K. 1968*, p. 446.

TABLE 19: OTHER (PRIVATE)

Percentages of Total USSR output calculated from *N.K. 1968*, pp. 320, 338: and L. Kalenin, "Private Farming Plots," *Voprosy Ekonomiki*, November 1968, pp. 52–63.
Sown Area: *N K 1968*, p. 338.

TABLE 20: SOWN AREA: REPUBLICS

All Republics Have Same Sources:
All Crops: 1913–1967: *N.K. 1967*, p. 354.
1968: *N.K. 1968*, pp. 340, 345, 346.
All Grains: 1913–1967: *N.K. 1967*, p. 355.
1968: *N.K. 1968*, pp. 340, 345, 346.
Fodder Crops: 1913–1967: *N.K. 1967*, p. 366.
1968: *N.K. 1968*, pp. 340, 345, 346.
Potatoes: 1913–1967: *N.K. 1967*, p. 364.
1968: *N.K. 1968*, pp. 340, 345, 346.

TABLE 21: SOWN AREA AND TRACTORS

All Republics Have Same Sources:
BT: 1913–1967: *N.K. 1967*, p. 362.
1968: *N.K. 1968*, pp. 341, 344, 415.
Winter Wheat: 1913–1967: *N.K. 1967*, p. 356.
1968: *N.K. 1968*, pp. 341, 344, 415.
Spring Wheat: 1913–1967: *N.K. 1967*, p. 357.
1968: *N.K. 1968*, pp. 341, 344, 415.
Tractors: 1913–1967: *N.K. 1967*, p. 458.
1968: *N.K. 1968*, pp. 350, 361, 344, 415

TABLE 22: GROSS YIELD AND MINERAL FERTILIZER

All Republics Have Same Sources:
AG: 1913–1967: *N.K. 1967*, p. 371.
1968: *N.K. 1968*, pp. 350, 361, 367, 380.
Potatoes: 1913–1967: *N.K. 1967*, p. 394.
1968: *N.K. 1968*, pp. 350, 361, 367, 380.
Sugar Beets: 1913–1967: *N.K. 1967*, p. 387.
1968: *N.K. 1968*, pp. 350, 361, 367, 386.

Fertilizer: 1913–1967: *N.K. 1967*, p. 412.
1968: *N.K. 1968*, pp. 350, 361, 367, 380.

TABLE 23: NUMBER OF LIVESTOCK

All Republics Have Same Sources:
CT: 1916–1968: *N.K. 1967*, p. 428.
1969: *N.K. 1968*, pp. 396, 397.
Cows: 1916–1968: *N.K. 1968*, p. 429.
1969: *N.K. 1968*, pp. 396, 397.
Swine: 1916–1968: *N.K. 1967*, p. 430.
1969: *N.K. 1968*, pp. 396, 397.
Sheep and Goats: 1916–1968: *N.K. 1967*, p. 431.
1969: *N.K. 1968*, pp. 396, 397.

TABLE 24: LIVESTOCK PRODUCTION

All Republics Have Same Sources:
Meat: 1913–1967: *N.K. 1967*, p. 436.
1968: *N.K. 1968*, p. 401.
Milk: 1913–1967: *N.K. 1967*, p. 437.
1968: *N.K. 1968*, p. 401.
Eggs: 1913–1967: *N.K. 1967*, p. 438.
1968: *N.K. 1968*, p. 402.

TABLE 25: KOLKHOZY ONLY

All Republics Have Same Sources:
Number: 1940–1950: *Selsk*, p. 51.
1960: *N.K. 1960*, p. 500.
1965: *N.K. 1965*, p. 416.
1967: *N.K. 1967*, p. 474.
1968: *N.K. 1968*, pp. 430–431.
Households: 1940–1950: *Selsk*, p. 52.
1960: *N.K. 1960*, p. 500.
1965: *N.K. 1965*, p. 416.
1967: *N.K. 1967*, p. 474.
1968: *N.K. 1968*, pp. 430–431.
Milk/Cow: 1940–1950: *Selsk*, p. 372.
1960–1967: *N.K. 1967*, p. 448.
1968: *N.K. 1968*, p. 409.

TABLE 26: SOVKHOZY ONLY

All Republics Have Same Sources:
Number: 1940–1950: *Selsk*, p. 43.
1960–1967: *N.K. 1967*, p. 481.
1968: *N.K. 1968*, pp. 419, 437.
Workers: 1940–1950: *N.K. 1958*, p. 521.
1960: *N.K. 1962*, p. 359.
1965–1967: *N.K. 1967*, p. 483.
1968: *N.K. 1968*, p. 419, 437.
Milk/Cow: 1940–1950: *Selsk*, p. 373.
1960–1967: *N.K. 1967*, p. 449.
1968: *N.K. 1968*, pp. 419, 437.

PRODUCTION

STANLEY H. COHN

SINCE THE MAIN PURPOSE in presenting the statistics in this handbook is to enable the reader to obtain additional perspective on the Soviet system, it is essential that the data be comparable with those of other countries. With regard to the comparability of Soviet economic statistics, some degree of selectivity is required. Their main limitation in terms of international comparability is not the overt one of falsification, but the more subtle explanation of inconsistent methodology. Official physical production statistics, such as Tables 8 to 14 contain, are relatively homogeneous and are methodologically comparable with estimates of leading market economies. Therefore, the physical output statistics are official estimates taken from various issues of the annual economic statistical handbook (*Narodnoe Khozyaistvo SSSR*) or from the irregularly published handbooks of industrial statistics (*Promyshlennost SSSR*). The two tables on monthly incomes, Tables 15 and 16, are also reproduced directly from the official labor statistics handbook (*Trud v SSSR*).

In the case of the first seven tables on statistics of gross national product (GNP), official statistics have not been used, as the official concept of national product is a more limited one than that used in standard market economy national accounting. There are, in addition, other methodological differences which further reduce international comparability. Therefore, the time series on GNP and its major components in Tables 1 to 7 are based on estimates of Western scholars. Although the estimates are derived from Soviet data, they are presented according to the standard methodology used among market economies. Official estimates of national income show more rapid growth rates, with the differences between official and Western estimates tending to narrow over the past fifteen years.

DERIVATIONS OF GROSS NATIONAL PRODUCT TIME SERIES (TABLES 1–7)

The growth rates for the 1913 to 1928 period (Tables 1 to 3) have been obtained from Raymond Goldsmith in Simon Kuznets, "Quantitative Aspects of the Economic Growth of Nations," *Economic Development and Cultural Change,* October 1956, p. 81. The estimates for the years 1928 to 1950 are from Norman Kaplan, "The Retardation in Soviet Growth," *Review of Economics and Statistics,* November 1968, Appendix Table A-1. Estimates since 1950 are obtained from a contribution by Stanley H. Cohn, "General Growth Performance of the Soviet Economy," to a compendium published in 1970 by the U.S. Congress Joint Economic Committee, *Economic Performance and Military Burden in the Soviet Union.* They may also be found in an article by the same author, "National Income Growth Statistics," Durham, Duke University Press, 1972, in a volume entitled *Soviet Economic Statistics,* which incorporates papers presented at a conference on that theme at Duke in November 1969.

The base year, 1966, dollar value of Soviet GNP has also been derived from Cohn's contribution to the Joint Economic Committee. The population estimates used to express the GNP estimates in per capita terms have been obtained from Warren Eason, "Labor Force," in Abram Bergson and Simon Kuznets, *Economic Trends in the Soviet Union,* Harvard University Press, 1963, p. 72 and from Albert Vainshtein, *Narodny Dokhod Rossii i SSSR* (National Income of Russia and the USSR), Nauka, 1969, p. 110.

The shares of income originating in agriculture (Table 4) are obtained from Richard Moorsteen and Raymond Powell, *The Soviet Capital Stock, 1928–1962,* Homewood, Ill., Richard D. Irwin, Inc., 1966, p. 361* and from Appendix Table 2 in Cohn's contribution to the Joint Economic Committee.

The shares of GNP accounted for by private consumptions, investment, and defense (Tables 5 to 7) are derived from Abram Bergson, *The Real National Income of Soviet Russia Since 1928,* Harvard University Press, 1961, p. 237 and from the 1970 compendium of the Joint Economic Committee. The 1955 base year estimates of values of each end use are based on ruble estimates prepared by Morris Bornstein and Associates, *Soviet National Accounts for 1955,* Center for Russian Studies, University of Michigan, 1961, p. 68. Each end use is then converted to dollars on the basis of ratios estimated by Morris Bornstein, "A Comparison of Soviet and United States National Product," in Joint Economic Committee, *Comparisons of the United States and Soviet Economies,* 1959, pp. 385–386. These estimates in terms of 1955 dollars are then expressed in 1966 dollars by applying U.S. and Soviet price indexes for each end use.

* Reprinted with permission.

Table 1. GROSS NATIONAL PRODUCT (In Billions of 1966 U.S. Dollars)

Year	Billions of Dollars
1913	62
1928	66
1932	71
1937	98
1940	119
1950	140
1955	185
1956	201
1957	212
1958	230
1959	241
1960	253
1961	269
1962	278
1963	285
1964	308
1965	326
1966	348
1967	365
1968	386
1969	395

Table 2. GROSS NATIONAL PRODUCT PER CAPITA (In 1966 U.S. Dollars)

Year	Dollars
1913	447
1928	436
1932	442
1937	591
1940	603
1950	777
1955	943
1956	1,007
1957	1,043
1958	1,112
1959	1,114
1960	1,181
1961	1,234
1962	1,255
1963	1,268
1964	1,351
1965	1,414
1966	1,493
1967	1,549
1968	1,623
1969	1,641

Table 3. GROWTH OF GNP: AGGREGATE AND PER CAPITA (Average Annual Rate)

Period	Aggregate Rate	Per Capita Rate
1913-28	0.4	-0.2
1928-32	2.0	0.3
1932-37	6.6	6.0
1937-40	6.8	0.7
1940-50	1.6	2.6
1950-55	5.8	4.0
1955-60	6.5	4.6
1960-65	5.2	3.7
1965-67	5.6	4.7
1955-56	8.6	6.8
1956-57	5.5	3.6
1957-58	8.5	6.6
1958-59	4.8	2.9
1959-60	5.0	3.2
1960-61	6.2	4.5
1961-62	3.4	1.7
1962-63	2.5	1.1
1963-64	8.1	6.5
1964-65	6.0	4.7
1965-66	6.4	5.6
1966-67	5.0	3.8
1967-68	5.8	4.8
1968-69	2.3	1.1

Table 4. PERCENTAGE AND VALUE OF GNP ORIGINATING IN AGRICULTURE

Year	Percentage of G.N.P.	Value-Added (Billions of 1966 U.S. Dollars)
1928	58.6	39
1932	42.7	30
1937	41.6	41
1940	40.0	48
1950	35.9	50
1955	31.5	58
1958	31.5	72
1959	29.1	70
1960	27.6	70
1961	27.6	74
1962	25.9	72
1963	24.0	68
1964	25.0	77
1965	24.1	79
1966	24.4	85
1967	23.2	85
1968	23.4	90
1969	21.2	84

Table 5. PRIVATE CONSUMPTION: PER CAPITA VALUE AND PERCENTAGE OF GNP

Year	Percentage of G.N.P.	Per Capita (1966 U.S. Dollars)
1928	79.5	243
1937	52.5	238
1940	49.4	228
1950	53.9	285
1955	52.7	394
1958	52.1	443
1960	51.4	476
1963	49.3	504
1965	49.6	535
1967	49.6	591
1968	...	618
1969	...	641

Table 6. FIXED CAPITAL INVESTMENT: VALUE AND PERCENTAGE OF GNP

Year	Percentage of G.N.P.	Value (Billions of 1966 U.S. Dollars)
1928	25.0	5.4
1937	25.9	17.6
1940	19.2	19.7
1950	21.2	33.2
1955	24.3	60.0
1958	28.1	89.9
1960	29.9	109.9
1963	29.1	126.2
1965	30.0	149.1
1967	30.2	173.5
1968	...	187.6
1969	...	195.1

Table 7. DEFENSE: VALUE AND PERCENTAGE OF GNP

Year	Percentage of G.N.P.	Value (Billions of 1966 U.S. Dollars)
1928	2.5	1.4
1937	7.9	13.9
1940	16.1	37.1
1950	12.3	34.2
1955	13.2	45.3
1958	10.4	44.6
1960	9.6	46.0
1963	12.2	68.9
1965	10.6	68.5
1967	10.6	79.7

Table 8. ELECTRIC POWER PRODUCTION PER CAPITA

Year	Production Per Capita (Millions of Kilowatt Hours)
1913	15
1928	33
1932	84
1937	218
1940	245
1950	507
1953	709
1954	782
1955	868
1956	960
1957	1,032
1958	1,138
1959	1,259
1960	1,364
1961	1,503
1962	1,667
1963	1,835
1964	2,014
1965	2,197
1966	2,336
1967	2,494
1968	2,684
1969	2,864

Table 8a. REGIONAL DISTRIBUTION OF ELECTRIC POWER PRODUCTION (In Millions of Kilowatt Hours)

Year	RSFSR	Ukraine	Belorussia	Uzbekistan	Kazakhstan	Georgia	Azerbaidzhan
1913	1,323	543	3	3	1	20	111
1928	3,215	1,261	39	34	8	42	377
1932	9,122	3,248	177	94	67	120	618
1937	23,433	9,451	421	281	303	503	1,387
1940	30,289	12,411	508	482	632	742	1,827
1950	63,409	14,711	749	2,682	2,617	1,385	2,924
1955	115,884	30,099	1,870	3,889	5,689	2,010	4,640
1960	196,988	53,926	3,636	5,884	10,497	3,702	6,590
1965	332,784	94,616	8,411	11,489	19,226	6,042	10,417
1967	379,759	108,722	10,877	14,407	23,773	6,703	11,164
1968	411,855	116,176	12,164	15,041	27,609	7,748	11,063

Year	Lithuania	Moldavia	Latvia	Kirgizia	Tadzhikistan	Armenia	Turkmenia	Estonia
1913	6	1	15	...	...	5	3	6
1928	...	...	...	1	...	21	11	...
1932	...	3	...	12	2	54	26	...
1937	...	13	...	32	25	258	56	...
1940	41	17	134	52	62	395	84	96
1950	221	100	493	197	170	949	186	435
1955	574	258	928	517	297	2,215	413	941
1960	1,122	677	1,672	872	1,288	2,747	752	1,950
1965	3,851	3,111	1,487	2,312	1,567	2,855	1,402	7,104
1967	4,691	4,932	2,583	2,968	2,245	4,682	1,573	8,620
1968	6,026	6,827	2,630	3,111	2,556	4,997	1,667	9,191

Table 9. FUEL PRODUCTION PER CAPITA (In Equivalent 7,000 Calorie Units)

Year	Metric Tons
1913	0.4
1940	1.2
1950	1.7
1953	2.0
1954	2.2
1955	2.4
1956	2.6
1957	2.8
1958	3.0
1959	3.1
1960	3.2
1961	3.4
1962	3.5
1963	3.8
1964	4.0
1965	4.2
1966	4.4
1967	4.6
1968	4.7

Table 10. STEEL OUTPUT PER CAPITA

Year	Metric Tons
1913	.031
1928	.028
1932	.037
1937	.107
1940	.093
1950	.152
1953	.201
1954	.215
1955	.231
1956	.244
1957	.252
1958	.265
1959	.285
1960	.305
1961	.325
1962	.345
1963	.357
1964	.373
1965	.395
1966	.416
1967	.434
1968	.448

Table 11. MOTOR VEHICLE PRODUCTION (In Thousands of Units)

Year	Automobiles	Trucks	Busses
1928	*	*	*
1932	*	25	*
1937	18	180	1
1940	6	136	4
1950	65	294	1
1953	77	271	6
1954	95	301	9
1955	103	328	9
1956	98	356	10
1957	114	370	12
1958	122	375	14
1959	125	351	19
1960	139	362	23
1961	149	382	25
1962	166	382	29
1963	173	382	32
1964	185	385	33
1965	201	380	36
1966	230	408	37
1967	251	437	40
1968	280	478	42

*Less than 1000 units.

Table 12. CEMENT PRODUCTION PER CAPITA (In Metric Tons)

Year	Metric Tons
1913	.01
1928	.01
1932	.02
1937	.03
1940	.03
1950	.05
1953	.08
1954	.10
1955	.11
1956	.12
1957	.14
1958	.16
1959	.18
1960	.21
1961	.23
1962	.26
1963	.27
1964	.28
1965	.31
1966	.34
1967	.36
1968	.37

Table 13. COTTON CLOTH PRODUCTION PER CAPITA (In Millions of Square Meters)

Year	Millions of Square Meters
1913	13
1928	12
1932	11
1937	15
1940	14
1950	15
1953	20
1954	21
1955	22
1956	20
1957	20
1958	21
1959	22
1960	23
1961	22
1962	22
1963	23
1964	24
1965	24
1966	24
1967	25
1968	26

Table 14. MEAT PRODUCTION PER CAPITA (In Kilograms)

Year	Industrial Production	Total Production
1913	9	36
1928	4	...
1932	4	...
1937	6	18
1940	8	24
1950	9	27
1953	12	31
1954	13	33
1955	13	32
1956	13	40
1957	15	32
1958	16	36
1959	20	37
1960	21	42
1961	20	40
1962	22	43
1963	24	45
1964	18	36
1965	23	43
1966	25	46
1967	27	49
1968	28	49

Table 15. INCOMES BY ECONOMIC SECTOR (In Rubles per Month)

Year	Industry	Construction	State Farms	Transportation	Communications	Commerce
1940	34.0	33.9	21.0	34.7	28.1	25.0
1950	70.3	60.1	38.2	70.5	52.7	46.9
1955	78.3	74.2	46.6	77.0	55.6	52.3
1960	91.3	91.7	53.9	86.7	62.3	58.6
1961	94.5	96.8	58.0	93.1	70.6	61.0
1962	96.6	99.3	66.1	97.5	71.9	63.6
1963	98.4	101.6	67.1	99.3	72.5	64.5
1964	100.5	106.0	70.6	102.2	73.0	65.7
1965	103.0	109.4	74.5	105.5	73.9	74.9
1966	106.8	113.1	79.8	109.6	75.4	79.3
1967	111.7	118.1	84.1	115.0	78.0	82.5

Year	Housing	Health	Education	Science	Finance	Public Administration	Total Economy
1940	26.1	25.5	32.3	46.7	33.4	38.8	33.0
1950	49.1	48.5	66.7	93.0	66.4	68.3	63.9
1955	52.3	52.1	70.3	102.8	70.0	79.6	71.5
1960	57.6	58.9	69.9	104.2	70.3	85.6	80.1
1961	59.4	59.8	72.5	105.2	72.5	88.1	83.4
1962	61.0	60.8	73.8	108.1	76.8	90.1	86.2
1963	62.6	62.0	75.3	109.7	78.1	93.6	87.6
1964	64.5	65.3	78.5	112.0	79.0	95.8	90.1
1965	71.8	78.9	93.6	115.6	86.0	104.7	95.6
1966	75.5	80.7	95.5	118.6	89.3	110.4	99.2
1967	78.6	82.4	96.5	122.0	93.0	112.5	103.0

Table 16. INCOMES BY BRANCHES OF INDUSTRY (In Rubles per Month)

Year	Electric Power	Coal	Ferrous	Chemicals	Machinery Metalworking
1950	77.8	121.9	97.7	76.6	77.1
1955	85.0	126.8	102.0	83.7	84.0
1960	93.7	169.2	116.8	97.3	93.3
1961	101.5	170.7	117.2	98.2	94.7
1962	103.4	173.3	119.1	100.3	97.1
1963	105.0	177.2	121.0	101.7	98.8
1964	107.6	181.5	123.5	104.2	100.8
1965	110.7	194.6	126.1	106.8	102.9
1966	113.2	195.3	129.0	110.0	106.5

Year	Forest Products	Construction Materials	Light	Food	All Industry
1950	60.8	61.0	51.6	52.9	70.3
1955	73.6	69.1	57.6	61.0	78.3
1960	86.7	85.6	65.9	73.1	91.3
1961	91.4	89.4	71.1	80.7	94.5
1962	93.5	92.3	72.8	82.6	96.6
1963	95.2	94.6	73.9	84.3	98.4
1964	98.2	97.8	75.7	86.3	100.5
1965	100.2	100.7	77.6	89.2	103.3
1966	105.3	104.3	81.3	92.1	106.8

CHAPTER III TABLE SOURCE NOTES

TABLES 1–7

    See introduction to Chapter III

TABLE 8

    N.K. 1967, p. 230.
    Prom., p. 232.
    N.K. 1968, p. 228.

TABLE 8a

    N.K. 1967, p. 231.
    N.K. 1968, p. 229.

TABLE 9

    N.K. 1967, p. 235.
    Prom., p. 191.
    N.K. 1968, p. 233.

TABLE 10

    N.K. 1967, p. 243.
    Prom., p. 164.
    N.K. 1968, p. 241.

TABLE 11

    N.K. 1967, p. 263.
    Prom., p. 278.
    N.K. 1968, p. 261.

TABLE 12

    N.K. 1967, p. 280.
    Prom., p. 318.
    N.K. 1968, p. 276.

TABLE 13

    N.K. 1967, p. 290.
    Prom., p. 364.
    N.K. 1968, p. 286.

TABLE 14

    N.K. 1967, pp. 310, 327.
    Prom., p. 433.
    N.K. 1968, pp. 304, 315.

TABLE 15

    Trud v SSSR, pp. 138–139.

TABLE 16

    Trud v SSSR, pp. 140–144.

HEALTH

MARK G. FIELD

THE MATERIALS PRESENTED HERE were drawn from general statistical hand-books that contained some materials on health and illness in the Soviet Union and from specialized medical publications that contained primarily such materials.*

The data pertain to four areas of importance in studying the Soviet health system: vital statistics (Tables 1 to 4), morbidity (Table 5), health personnel and medical facilities (Tables 6 to 16), and medical education (Table 17).

Generally speaking, the Soviets have been much more generous with statistical data pertaining to their health resources (in manpower and facili-ties) than with data that would show the magnitude of their morbidity problem or the effectiveness of the Soviet health system in dealing with that morbidity. Vital statistics reflect only partially the activities of the health system, since these statistics are affected by a host of other factors such as diet, housing, income levels, personal habits, place of residence, and so on.

No blanket judgment can be offered on the validity and reliability of the statistical data presented here. The same general cautions that apply to statis-tics in general, and to Soviet statistics in particular, apply with equal force in this area. It is probably true that statistical data that, overall, either conform to or confirm the general claims of the Soviet regime and (or) show that Soviet accomplishments are particularly impressive when compared with similar achievements in the non-Communist world will tend to be reported more fully than those that do not. Those that fail to confirm Soviet claims will probably not be published, rather than be deliberately distorted. One might say that in the area of the health care system, particularly in human and material resources, the Soviets have every reason to be satisfied with their accomplishments, at least quantitatively, and would thus have little reluctance to publish the data. No statement can be made about the qualitative achieve-ments. Generally, the Soviet system seems to be the result of a deliberate

---

* The assistance of Judith H. Koivumaki in this work is gratefully acknowledged.

decision to place high priority on quantitative indices in order to meet the most obvious pressing needs. But in the medical area it is quite probable that, beyond a certain point, quantitative changes have an impact on quality of services, and it is quite possible that, having achieved one of the highest (perhaps the highest) per capita supply of physicians in the world, the Soviet Union may now begin to turn to a policy of increasing the quality of medical students, of medical education, of clinical services, and of medical research. In the Soviet sources there are signs that these areas are of concern to Soviet health authorities.

Table 1. AVERAGE LIFE EXPECTANCY AT BIRTH, RUSSIA AND USSR, BY SEX, URBAN AND RURAL AREAS

Years	Entire Population			Urban Population			Rural Population		
	Both Sexes	Of That Number		Both Sexes	Of That Number		Both Sexes	Of That Number	
		Men	Women		Men	Women		Men	Women
1896-1897[a]	32	31	33	..	..	..	..	..	..
1926-1927[b]	44	42	47	46	43	49	44	42	46
1950	68	64	71	..	..	..	..	..	..
1958-1959	69	64	72	68	64	71	69	65	72
1960-1961	70	65	73	69	64	72	70	66	73
1962-1963	70	65	73	69	65	72	70	66	73
1965-1966	70	66	74	70	65	73	70	66	74

Notes:

[a] Fifty provinces of European Russia.

[b] European part of Russia.

Table 2. MORTALITY, AGE-SPECIFIC, RUSSIA AND USSR

Mortality per 1,000 of Population

Age Group	1896-1897	1926	1938-1939	1958-1959	1962-1963	1963-1964
0-4	133.0	78.9	75.8	11.9	8.7	7.8
5-9	12.9	7.3	5.5	1.1	0.9	0.8
10-14	5.4	3.1	2.6	0.8	0.7	0.6
15-19	5.8	3.7	3.4	1.3	1.1	1.0
20-24	7.6	5.5	4.4	1.8	1.6	1.6
25-29	8.2	6.1	4.7	2.2	2.0	2.0
30-34	8.7	6.3	5.4	2.6	2.6	2.5
35-39	10.3	7.5	6.8	3.1	3.1	3.1
40-44	11.8	9.0	8.1	4.0	3.8	3.7
45-49	15.7	10.9	10.2	5.4	5.3	5.1
50-54	18.5	14.0	13.8	7.9	7.7	7.7
55-59	29.5	18.1	17.1	11.2	11.2	10.7
60-64	34.5	24.7	24.5	17.1	17.5	17.1
65-69	61.6	36.5	35.1	25.2	25.6	24.1
70 and older	89.0	79.5	78.9	63.8	67.7	63.6
Total Population	32.4	20.3	17.4	7.4	7.4	7.1

Table 3. Mortality, Russia and USSR, by Sex and Age (Expressed as Number per 1,000 Born Alive, Dying During Age Interval)

Age	1896-1897[a]			1926-1927[b]			1958-1959[c]		
	All	Men	Women	All	Men	Women	All	Men	Women
0	278.67	298.00	258.54	187.01	201.02	172.14	40.60	44.24	36.77
1	97.11	100.26	94.00	63.87	66.70	60.97	8.40	8.52	8.27
2	56.70	57.81	55.61	31.92	32.95	30.89	3.72	3.72	3.72
3	38.20	38.58	37.83	18.68	18.99	18.36	2.24	2.31	2.17
4	27.95	28.07	27.82	14.29	14.54	14.04	1.61	1.72	1.49
5	20.30	20.39	20.21	10.70	10.91	10.49	1.31	1.43	1.17
10	6.66	6.84	6.48	3.07	3.22	2.92	0.84	1.03	0.70
15	4.94	4.57	5.29	3.18	3.16	3.20	0.94	1.13	0.77
20	6.67	6.63	6.70	5.06	5.40	4.74	1.61	2.05	1.17
25	7.70	7.47	7.91	5.98	6.38	5.70	2.03	2.73	1.35
30	8.27	7.89	8.62	6.25	6.39	6.00	2.40	3.28	1.60
35	9.63	9.31	9.94	7.07	7.53	6.69	2.79	4.02	1.95
40	11.19	11.19	11.19	8.24	9.34	7.26	3.60	5.19	2.59
45	14.08	14.78	13.37	10.34	12.54	8.32	4.61	6.68	3.28
50	17.61	18.78	16.50	12.65	16.57	9.42	6.78	10.04	4.74
55	24.62	25.36	23.90	17.44	22.63	13.31	9.76	15.02	6.83
60	32.87	32.64	33.08	22.42	27.87	18.34	14.33	22.22	10.28
65	49.51	48.73	50.26	34.26	40.39	29.37	21.53	30.74	16.51
70	67.13	67.72	66.63	51.15	59.68	45.76	33.50	44.04	27.93
75	86.52	87.94	85.22	74.57	82.39	68.69	51.80	63.63	45.94
80	111.80	112.01	111.58	101.24	113.11	90.46	80.51	92.53	75.00

Notes:

[a] Fifty provinces of European Russia.

[b] European part of U.S.S.R.

[c] Entire territory of U.S.S.R.

Table 4. Mortality, Age-specific, and Average Life Expectancy, Both Sexes, USSR, 1958–1959

Age (both sexes)	Of 100,000 born alive, number dying during age interval	Average life expectancy	Age (both sexes)	Of 100,000 born alive, number dying during age interval	Average life expectancy
0	4,060	68.59	50	573	27.11
1	806	70.48	51	608	26.29
2	354	70.08	52	649	25.48
3	212	69.34	53	694	24.67
4	152	68.49	54	742	23.88
5	124	67.60	55	793	23.09
6	116	66.69	56	848	22.31
7	107	65.77	57	905	21.54
8	97	64.84	58	966	20.79
9	87	63.91	59	1,031	20.04
10	79	62.97	60	1,099	19.30
11	76	62.02	61	1,170	18.57
12	76	61.07	62	1,247	17.86
13	77	60.12	63	1,330	17.15
14	80	59.17	64	1,418	16.46
15	88	58.22	65	1,516	15.78
16	99	57.28	66	1,625	15.12
17	118	56.34	67	1,733	14.47
18	132	55.41	68	1,842	13.84
19	143	54.48	69	1,951	13.23
20	150	53.57	70	2,069	12.63
21	157	52.65	71	2,184	12.05
22	166	51.74	72	2,298	11.49
23	176	50.83	73	2,409	10.94
24	184	49.93	74	2,513	10.42
25	187	49.03	75	2,605	9.92
26	191	48.13	76	2,688	9.43
27	197	47.23	77	2,767	8.96
28	206	46.33	78	2,843	8.52
29	213	45.43	79	2,905	8.10
30	219	44.53	80	2,937	7.70
31	225	43.64	81	2,933	7.33
32	230	42.75	82	2,894	6.99
33	236	41.86	83	2,826	6.67
34	243	40.96	84	2,729	6.37
35	251	40.07	85	2,600	6.09
36	261	39.18	86	2,441	5.83
37	273	38.30	87	2,258	5.59
38	286	37.41	88	2,055	5.37
39	301	36.53	89	1,867	5.15
40	319	35.65	90	1,677	4.94
41	336	34.78	91	1,490	4.75
42	352	33.91	92	1,310	4.57
43	369	33.05	93	1,139	4.39
44	384	32.18	94	980	4.23
45	400	31.32	95	834	4.07
46	423	30.47	96	701	3.93
47	454	29.61	97	584	3.79
48	493	28.77	98	480	3.65
49	533	27.93	99	391	3.52
			100	314	3.40

Table 4a. MORTALITY, AGE-SPECIFIC, AND AVERAGE LIFE EXPECTANCY, MALES, USSR, 1958–1959

Age Males	Of 100,000 born alive, number dying during age interval	Average life expectancy	Age Males	Of 100,000 born alive, number dying during age interval	Average life expectancy
0	4,424	64.42	50	809	24.05
1	814	66.39	51	861	23.29
2	353	65.95	52	922	22.54
3	218	65.20	53	990	21.80
4	162	64.35	54	1,064	21.07
5	134	63.46	55	1,141	20.36
6	130	62.55	56	1,220	19.66
7	123	61.64	57	1,299	18.98
8	113	60.72	58	1,382	18.31
9	104	59.79	59	1,464	17.66
10	96	58.85	60	1,543	17.02
11	90	57.91	61	1,615	16.40
12	89	56.97	62	1,682	15.78
13	89	56.02	63	1,746	15.18
14	95	55.08	64	1,808	14.59
15	105	54.13	65	1,877	14.01
16	123	53.19	66	1,953	13.43
17	146	52.26	67	2,030	12.88
18	167	51.34	68	2,104	12.33
19	181	50.44	69	2,174	11.80
20	189	49.53	70	2,243	11.28
21	200	48.64	71	2,307	10.78
22	214	47.74	72	2,366	10.29
23	228	46.85	73	2,417	9.82
24	243	45.97	74	2,462	9.36
25	249	45.09	75	2,490	8.92
26	255	44.21	76	2,502	8.49
27	262	43.33	77	2,507	8.07
28	274	42.46	78	2,507	7.67
29	285	41.58	79	2,495	7.29
30	295	40.71	80	2,464	6.93
31	306	39.85	81	2,409	6.58
32	317	38.98	82	2,334	6.26
33	328	38.12	83	2,242	5.95
34	341	37.26	84	2,131	5.66
35	355	36.40	85	1,999	5.39
36	369	35.54	86	1,845	5.14
37	385	34.69	87	1,674	4.91
38	403	33.84	88	1,491	4.68
39	422	33.00	89	1,345	4.46
40	448	32.16	90	1,182	4.26
41	473	31.32	91	1,025	4.07
42	495	30.49	92	878	3.89
43	518	29.67	93	742	3.72
44	539	28.85	94	618	3.56
45	560	28.03	95	508	3.40
46	592	27.21	96	411	3.26
47	640	26.41	97	328	3.12
48	698	25.61	98	258	2.99
49	757	24.82	99	200	2.86
			100	152	2.74

Table 4b. MORTALITY, AGE-SPECIFIC, AND AVERAGE LIFE EXPECTANCY, FEMALES, USSR, 1958–1959

Age Females	Of 100,000 born alive, number dying during age interval	Average life expectancy	Age Females	Of 100,000 born alive, number dying during age interval	Average life expectancy
0	3,677	71.68	50	415	28.99
1	797	73.40	51	443	28.12
2	355	73.01	52	472	27.27
3	207	72.28	53	505	26.41
4	141	71.44	54	542	25.56
5	111	70.55	55	582	24.72
6	102	69.63	56	625	23.89
7	91	68.70	57	673	23.06
8	78	67.77	58	724	22.25
9	71	66.82	59	781	21.44
10	66	65.87	60	841	20.64
11	62	64.92	61	906	19.85
12	63	63.96	62	980	19.06
13	66	63.00	63	1,065	18.29
14	69	62.05	64	1,158	17.54
15	72	61.09	65	1,269	16.79
16	78	60.14	66	1,396	16.07
17	89	59.19	67	1,525	15.36
18	98	58.24	68	1,657	14.67
19	106	57.30	69	1,792	14.00
20	110	56.37	70	1,934	13.35
21	115	55.43	71	2,082	12.72
22	119	54.50	72	2,234	12.11
23	121	53.57	73	2,383	11.52
24	123	52.64	74	2,533	10.96
25	126	51.71	75	2,668	10.41
26	128	50.78	76	2,792	9.89
27	135	49.85	77	2,921	9.39
28	141	48.92	78	3,052	8.91
29	143	47.99	79	3,175	8.46
30	148	47.07	80	3,260	8.04
31	152	46.14	81	3,290	7.65
32	157	45.22	82	3,277	7.29
33	163	44.29	83	3,231	6.95
34	170	43.37	84	3,152	6.64
35	179	42.45	85	3,030	6.35
36	187	41.53	86	2,865	6.08
37	198	40.62	87	2,675	5.83
38	210	39.70	88	2,463	5.59
39	222	38.80	89	2,257	5.36
40	235	37.89	90	2,045	5.45
41	247	36.99	91	1,833	4.95
42	259	36.09	92	1,626	4.76
43	273	35.19	93	1,427	4.58
44	284	34.30	94	1,239	4.41
45	293	33.40	95	1,064	4.25
46	306	32.51	96	904	4.10
47	328	31.62	97	761	3.96
48	356	30.74	98	633	3.82
49	386	29.86	99	521	3.69
			100	424	3.56

Table 5. INFECTIOUS DISEASES, SELECTED CASES, USSR (In Absolute Numbers of Cases, in Thousands, and Cases per 100,000)

Type of Disease	1940	1950	1960	1965	1966	1967	1968
Typhoid and Paratyphoid, A,B,C[a]	121.3	48.3	47.3	25.5	27.5	23.9	23.3
Scarlet Fever	251.5	596.1	671.2	530.8	691.6	597.3	502.0
Diphtheria	177.0	83.9	53.2	4.7	3.1	2.6	2.2
Whooping Cough	453.3	315.1	554.1	190.0	145.7	114.7	119.4
Tetanus	...	2.1	2.3	1.4	1.3	1.1	0.9
Acute Poliomyelitis	1.3	2.6	7.2	0.30	0.29	0.14	0.12
Measles	1,181.9	1,045.9	2,083.3	2,128.7	1,747.2	1,798.1	1,579.8
Infectious Hepatitis (Botkin's disease)[b]	...	...	513.1	470.1	465.2	372.9	371.4
Typhus, Exanthematous Epidemic, Including Brill's Disease[c]	48.0	16.4	6.2	3.7	3.4	3.3	3.1
Malaria	3,198.6	781.3	0.4	0.3	0.3	0.3	0.3

Notes:

[a]Until June, 1965, only cases of paratyphoid A and B were registered.

[b]Including parenteral hepatitis.

[c]Beginning in 1958, basically cases of Brill's disease were seen.

Table 5. INFECTIOUS DISEASES, SELECTED CASES, USSR (Continued)

Type of Disease	Number of Cases per 100,000 of the Population						
	1940	1950	1960	1965	1966	1967	1968
Typhoid and Paratyphoid A,B,C	62	27	22	11	12	10	10
Scarlet Fever	129	331	313	230	297	254	211
Diphtheria	91	47	25	2	1.3	1.1	0.9
Whooping Cough	232	175	259	82	63	49	50
Tetanus	...	1.2	1.1	0.6	0.6	0.5	0.4
Acute Poliomyelitis	0.7	1.4	3.3	0.13	0.12	0.06	0.05
Measles	605	581	972	923	750	763	664
Infectious Hepatitis (Botkin's disease)	...	...	239	204	200	158	156
Typhus, Exanthematous Epidemic, Including Brill's Disease	25	9.1	2.9	1.6	1.5	1.4	1.3
Malaria	1,637	434	0.17	0.14	0.13	0.11	0.11

Table 6. PHYSICIANS, USSR, INCLUDING STOMATOLOGISTS AND DENTISTS, EXCLUDING THE MILITARY (In Absolute Numbers, in Thousands, and Numbers per 100,000)

Year	(a) Physicians	(b) Stomatologists	(a)+(b)	(c) Dentists	(a)+(b)+(c) "Doctors of all specialties"	$\frac{(a)+(b)+(c)}{10,000 \text{ of Population}}$	Women Physicians	$\frac{(d)}{(a)+(b)+(c)} \times 100$ Percentage of women doctors to doctors in all specialties
1913 (contemp. borders)	23.2	...	23.2	4.9	28.1	1.5	2.3	10
1913 (borders (17 Sept. 1939)	...	...	20	...	...	1.4	1.9	10
1928	...	...	63	...	...	4.0	28.4	45
1940	134.9	6.8	141.7	13.6	155.3	7.0	96.3	62
1950	236.9	10.4	247.3	17.7	265.0	14.0	204.9	77
1958	347.6	14.0	361.6	26.8	388.4	18.6	294.6	76
1959	364.3	15.2	379.5	28.5	408.0	17.9	286.1	75
1960	385.4	16.2	401.6	30.1	431.7	18.6	327.1	76
1961	408.5	17.3	425.7	32.4	458.1	19.4	315.9	74
1962	426.6	18.5	445.1	34.7	479.8	21.5	361.9	75
1963	443.3	20.2	463.5	37.3	500.8	22.1	374.2	75
1964	467.4	22.9	490.3	41.8	532.1	23.2	396.2	74
1965	485.0	25.5	510.5	43.7	554.2	23.9	408.9	74
1966	503.3	28.3	531.6	46.1	577.7	24.6	422.7	73
1967	519.5	30.9	550.4	47.8	598.2	25.3	425.3	71
1968	534.3	33.7	568.0	49.8	617.8	25.9	447.7	72

Notes:

(a) Physicians: graduates of medical institutes.

(b) Stomatologists: graduates of stomatological faculty of a medical institute, i.e., a dentist or mouth specialist with a professional degree.

(c) Dentists: in Russian zubnoi vrach (dental doctor); this is a graduate of a secondary medical school and does not hold a professional degree.

(d) For some years, the number of women doctors excludes dentists (1959, 1961). Soviet statistical tables often lump together (a), (b), and (c) as "doctors in all specialties." The percentages of women in medicine are based on the percentage of women among "doctors in all specialties."

Since these figures are exclusive of the military physicians, it can be assumed that they are underestimates, and that the number of physicians per 10,000 inhabitants is actually higher since the population estimates cover the entire population, civilian and military.

Table 7. PHYSICIANS, USSR, EXCLUDING THE MILITARY, BY REPUBLICS (In Absolute Numbers and Number of Physicians per 10,000)

Area	1913 (contemporary boundaries)[a]		1932[a]		1940[a]		1950[a]		1958[a]	
	No.	No.per 10,000	No.	No.per 10,000	No.	No.per 10,000	No.	No.per 10,000	No.	No.per 10,000
U.S.S.R.	23,205	1.5	76,027	...	141,752	7.2	247,346	13.6	361,544	17.3
Armenia	57	.6	492	...	929	6.8	2,340	17.2	3,876	22.0
Azerbaidzhan	291	1.2	1,626	...	3,083	9.2	5,892	20.1	7,965	21.5
Belorussia	911	1.3	1,880	...	4,238	4.7	6,253	8.0	10,036	12.5
Estonia	425	4.5	...c	...	874	8.3	1,399	12.7	2,595	21.7
Georgia	351	1.3	2,690	...	4,736	12.8	9,379	26.3	12,773	31.6
Kazakhstan	196	.3	929	...	2,498	3.9	6,132	9.0	11,448	12.3
Kirgizia	15	.2	224	...	533	3.4	1,669	9.5	2,714	13.1
Latvia	518	2.1	...c	...	2,069	10.9	2,843	14.6	4,876	23.3
Lithuania	352	1.2	...c	...	1,971	6.7	2,716	10.6	4,295	15.8
Moldavia	240	1.2	75	...	990	4.0	2,340	9.8	3,530	12.2
R.S.F.S.R.	13,081	1.5	46,978	...	82,165	7.4	148,920	14.5	210,425	17.9
Tadzhikistan	13	.1	243	...	589	3.8	1,199	7.7	2,117	10.7
Turkmenia	56	.5	367	...	895	6.7	1,514	12.4	2,570	17.0
Ukraine	6,571	1.9	18,715	...	33,364	8.0	48,626	13.1	72,510	17.3
Uzbekistan	128	.3	1,808	...	2,818	4.2	6,124	9.5	9,814	12.1

Area	1959[a]		1960[b]		1961[a]		1962[b]		1963[b]	
	No.	No.per 10,000	No.	No.per 10,000	No.	No.per 10,000	No.	No.per 10,000	No.	No.per 10,000
U.S.S.R.	379,501	17.9	431,700	20.0	425,745	19.4	479,800	21.5	500,800	22.1
Armenia	3,968	21.8	4,600	24.2	4,551	23.2	5,100	25.6	5,200	25.4
Azerbaidzhan	8,361	21.9	9,400	23.7	9,143	22.2	10,100	23.8	10,200	23.2
Belorussia	10,798	13.3	13,500	16.4	12,640	15.2	15,500	18.4	16,300	19.3
Estonia	2,704	22.4	2,900	23.9	2,995	24.2	3,200	26.1	3,500	27.5
Georgia	12,963	31.4	13,800	33.0	13,673	32.0	14,400	33.2	14,800	33.5
Kazakhstan	12,490	12.7	14,200	13.9	14,659	13.4	17,000	15.1	18,900	16.4
Kirgizia	2,842	13.3	3,400	15.4	3,419	14.7	4,100	17.4	4,300	17.1
Latvia	5,109	24.2	5,700	26.5	5,729	26.4	6,300	28.8	6,500	29.4
Lithuania	4,577	16.6	4,900	17.3	5,042	17.7	5,500	19.0	5,700	19.6
Moldavia	3,813	12.8	4,300	14.3	4,459	14.4	5,100	16.0	5,300	16.3
R.S.F.S.R.	220,822	18.6	251,400	20.9	246,616	20.2	276,600	22.4	286,900	23.0
Tadzhikistan	2,279	11.2	2,700	12.7	2,598	11.9	3,100	13.7	3,300	13.9
Turkmenia	2,631	16.8	3,000	18.7	3,029	18.0	3,600	20.4	3,600	19.8
Ukraine	75,526	17.8	85,600	19.9	84,603	19.4	95,600	21.7	100,600	22.6
Uzbekistan	10,618	12.7	12,300	13.8	12,589	14.0	14,600	15.4	15,700	16.0

Area	1964[b]		1965[b]		1966[b]		1967[b]		1968[b]	
	No.	No.per 10,000	No.	No.per 10,000	No.	No.per 10,000	No.	No.per 10,000	No.	No.per 10,000
U.S.S.R.	532,100	23.2	554,200	23.9	577,700	24.6	598,200	25.3	617,800	25.9
Armenia	5,700	26.6	6,000	27.3	6,300	28.2	6,700	28.8	7,100	30.1
Azerbaidzhan	10,600	23.5	11,000	23.6	11,600	24.1	11,900	24.2	12,200	24.3
Belorussia	17,800	20.9	18,800	21.8	19,800	22.6	20,400	23.2	21,300	23.9
Estonia	3,600	28.5	3,800	29.8	4,000	30.7	4,100	31.5	4,200	32.0
Georgia	15,300	34.2	15,800	34.7	16,400	35.5	16,900	36.3	16,900	35.9
Kazakhstan	21,400	18.0	22,400	18.4	23,400	18.9	24,300	19.1	25,900	20.1
Kirgizia	4,600	17.9	5,000	18.8	5,300	19.4	5,500	19.5	5,700	19.5
Latvia	6,900	30.8	7,100	31.4	7,500	32.6	7,700	33.4	7,900	33.9
Lithuania	6,100	20.8	6,400	21.5	7,000	23.1	7,400	24.3	7,800	25.2
Moldavia	5,800	17.5	6,000	17.9	6,300	18.5	6,600	18.8	6,800	19.2
R.S.F.S.R.	303,600	24.1	315,500	24.9	328,300	25.8	339,600	26.5	350,300	27.3
Tadzhikistan	3,600	14.3	3,800	14.9	4,100	15.5	4,200	15.5	4,300	15.4
Turkmenia	3,900	20.8	4,100	21.2	4,200	21.4	4,400	21.5	4,400	21.1
Ukraine	106,200	23.6	110,600	24.3	114,000	24.8	118,000	25.4	121,900	26.1
Uzbekistan	17,000	16.8	17,900	16.9	19,500	17.9	20,600	18.3	21,100	18.1

Notes:

[a] Does not include "dental doctors" (_zubnoi vrach_), that is, dentists without professional degrees.

[b] "All specialties" (includes physicians, stomatologists, and dentists or dental doctors).

[c] Since Lithuania, Latvia, and Estonia were not Soviet republics in 1932, figures for that year are not given.

Table 8. PHYSICIANS, USSR, EXCLUDING THE MILITARY, BY BASIC SPECIALTY (In Thousands)

Specialty	1940 No.	1940 %	1950 No.	1950 %	1958 No.	1958 %	1959 No.	1959 %	1960 No.	1960 %	1961 No.	1961 %
Therapists[a]	42.6	30.1	56.0	22.6	89.3	24.7	92.7	24.4	96.2	24.0	100.4	23.6
Surgeons[b]	12.6	8.9	22.5	9.1	36.4	10.1	37.7	9.9	40.5	10.1	42.9	10.1
Obstetricians-Gynecologists	10.6	7.4	16.6	6.7	26.2	7.2	27.4	7.2	28.7	7.2	30.0	7.0
Pediatricians	19.4	13.7	32.1	13.0	51.7	14.3	55.0	14.5	58.9	14.7	62.2	14.6
Oculists	3.6	2.5	5.7	2.3	9.4	2.6	9.9	2.6	10.5	2.6	11.1	2.6
Otorhinolaryngologists	2.6	1.8	4.6	1.9	8.3	2.3	8.9	2.3	9.6	2.4	10.3	2.4
Neuropathologists	3.2	2.3	5.1	2.1	9.2	2.5	9.9	2.6	10.5	2.6	11.4	2.7
Psychiatrists	2.4	1.7	3.1	1.3	5.8	1.6	6.1	1.6	6.4	1.6	7.1	1.7
Dermato-Venereologists	3.9	2.8	9.4	3.8	15.5	4.3	16.0	4.2	16.5	4.1	17.4	4.1
Roentgenologists	4.8	3.4	9.2	3.7	9.3	2.6	9.3	2.5	9.3	2.3	9.5	2.2
Phtysiatrists	2.7	1.9	6.2	2.5	13.9	3.8	14.8	3.9	15.7	3.9	17.1	4.0
Physicians specializing in physical culture	0.3	0.2	0.8	0.3	1.6	0.4	1.6	0.4	1.6	0.4	1.7	0.4
Physicians of the public-health anti-epidemic group[c]	12.5	8.8	21.9	8.9	27.9	7.7	29.2	7.7	31.5	7.8	32.9	7.7
Stomatologists	6.8	4.8	10.4	4.2	14.0	3.9	15.2	4.0	16.2	4.0	17.3	4.1
"Others"[d]	13.7	9.7	43.7	17.6	43.0	11.9	45.8	12.1	49.5	12.3	54.4	12.8
TOTAL	141.7	100.0	247.3	100.0	361.5	100.0	379.5	100.0	401.6	100.0	425.7	100.0

Specialty	1962 No.	1962 %	1963 No.	1963 %	1964 No.	1964 %	1965 No.	1965 %	1966 No.	1966 %	1967 No.	1967 %	1968 No.	1968 %
Therapists[a]	104.3	23.4	107.3	23.1	111.9	22.8	114.9	22.5	118.4	22.3	121.2	22.0	125.6	22.1
Surgeons[b]	45.4	10.2	47.6	10.3	50.4	10.3	52.5	10.3	55.1	10.4	58.0	10.5	60.2	10.6
Obstetricians-Gynecologists	31.8	7.1	32.7	7.1	34.4	7.0	35.4	7.0	36.3	6.8	37.4	6.8	38.5	6.8
Pediatricians	64.9	14.6	67.1	14.5	70.2	14.3	71.7	14.0	73.6	13.8	74.9	13.6	74.8	13.2
Oculists	11.7	2.6	12.1	2.6	12.7	2.6	13.1	2.6	13.7	2.6	14.5	2.6	15.0	2.6
Otorhinolaryngologists	10.9	2.4	11.4	2.5	12.2	2.5	12.8	2.5	13.4	2.5	14.1	2.6	14.7	2.6
Neuropathologists	12.2	2.7	12.8	2.8	13.7	2.8	14.3	2.8	25.2	2.9	16.5	2.9	16.5	3.0
Psychiatrists	7.9	1.8	8.6	1.9	9.2	1.9	10.1	2.0	10.8	2.0	11.6	2.1	12.5	2.2
Dermato-Venereologists	18.4	4.1	19.5	4.2	20.7	4.2	21.6	4.2	22.4	4.2	22.8	4.1	23.1	4.1
Roentgenologists	9.6	2.2	9.7	2.1	10.1	2.1	10.3	2.0	10.5	2.0	10.9	2.0	11.3	2.0
Phtysiatrists	18.2	4.1	19.0	4.1	20.1	4.1	20.9	4.1	21.7	4.1	22.4	4.1	23.0	4.0
Physicians specializing in physical culture	1.8	0.4	1.9	0.4	2.1	0.4	2.2	0.4	2.3	0.4	2.5	0.5	2.6	0.5
Physicians of the public-health anti-epidemic group[c]	33.7	7.6	34.2	7.4	35.7	7.3	36.3	7.1	37.5	7.1	38.1	6.9	38.7	6.8
Stomatologists	18.5	4.2	20.2	4.4	22.9	4.7	25.5	5.0	28.3	5.3	30.9	5.6	33.7	5.9
"Others"[d]	55.8	12.5	59.4	12.8	64.0	13.1	68.9	13.5	72.4	13.6	75.3	13.7	77.8	13.7
TOTAL	445.1	100.0	463.5	100.0	490.3	100.0	510.5	100.0	531.6	100.0	550.4	100.0	568.0	100.0

Notes:

[a] Includes physiotherapists, endocrinologists, infectionists.

[b] Includes traumatologists, orthopedists, oncologists, anaesthesiologists, and urologists.

[c] Includes sanitary physicians, virusologists, epidemiologists, malarialogists, bacteriologists, helminthologists, disinfectionists, other parasitologists.

[d] Does not include "dental doctors" (_zubnoi vrach_).

Table 9. SEMI-PROFESSIONAL HEALTH PERSONNEL, USSR, EXCLUDING THE MILITARY, BY SPECIALTY (In Thousands)

Personnel	1913	1930	1940	1950	1958	1959	1960	1961
TOTAL	ca.50.0	123.6	472.0	719.4	1,233.5	1,315.8	1,388.3	1,430.3
Of that number:								
Feldshers	37.8	...	82.2	160.0	267.4	308.3	334.7	341.8
Feldsher-midwives		...	12.8	42.0	75.9	77.3	76.2	78.1
Midwives	...	....	68.1	66.5	117.5	129.8	139.3	142.0
Assistants to public health physicians and epidemiologists	...	...	9.7	18.5	27.3	27.5	28.2	28.2
Nurses	10.0	...	227.7	325.0	568.5	595.4	623.5	640.1
Laboratory technicians	...	...	11.7	25.3	47.9	49.7	52.5	54.2
X-ray technicians and X-ray laboratory technicians	...	...	3.6	7.5	17.0	17.7	18.3	18.6
Dental technicians	...	...	4.9	6.7	12.0	12.9	13.9	15.1
Disinfection instructors and disinfectors	...	...	15.9	27.0	46.3	50.0	52.4	56.3
Nonspecified	...	...	35.4	43.6	53.7	47.2	49.3	55.9

Personnel	1962	1963	1964	1965	1966	1967	1968
TOTAL	1,478.5	1,523.4	1,620.4	1,691.8	1,777.5	1,860.7	1,943.6
Of that number:							
Feldshers	355.9	364.1	380.4	395.9	411.9	417.4	434.6
Feldsher-midwives	77.9	77.3	78.6	79.3	80.2	82.1	80.4
Midwives	147.2	154.3	164.7	171.4	180.3	184.8	193.2
Assistants to public health physicians and epidemiologists	28.4	28.5	30.0	30.0	30.8	31.4	32.3
Nurses	660.1	684.1	741.8	784.9	836.4	892.6	944.4
Laboratory technicians	55.4	58.3	61.5	63.7	66.0	71.7	74.8
X-ray technicians and X-ray laboratory technicians	19.2	19.7	20.7	20.6	21.1	22.6	22.2
Dental technicians	16.2	17.2	18.7	19.6	20.9	22.2	23.0
Disinfection instructors and disinfectors	58.0	58.2	61.5	64.2	67.2	68.1	68.1
Nonspecified	60.2	61.7	62.5	62.2	62.7	67.8	70.6

Table 10. PROFESSIONAL AND SEMI-PROFESSIONAL HEALTH PERSONNEL, USSR, EXCLUDING THE MILITARY (End of the Year Figures, in Thousands)

Type of Personnel	1913	1940	1950	1958	1959	1960	1961
Physicians of all specialties (including dentists)	28.1	155.3	265.0	388.4	408.0	431.7	458.1
Physicians excluding stomatologists and dentists	23.2	134.9	236.9	347.6	364.3	385.4	408.5
Stomatologists	...	6.8	10.4	14.0	15.2	16.2	17.3
Dentists	4.9	13.6	17.7	26.8	28.5	30.1	32.4
Semi-professional health personnel	46.0	472.0	719.0	1,233.0	1,312.7	1,388.0	1,430.3
Semi-professional health personnel per physician (all specialties)	1.63	3.04	2.71	3.17	3.22	3.22	3.12
Semi-professional health personnel per physician (excluding stomatologists and dentists)	1.98	3.50	3.04	3.55	3.60	3.60	3.50

Note:

Growth rate of semi-professional personnel is more rapid than that of professional manpower. Hence, the average number of semi-professional personnel per professional has increased by about 50%.

111 MARK G. FIELD

Table 10. PROFESSIONAL AND SEMI-PROFESSIONAL HEALTH PERSONNEL, USSR, EXCLUDING THE MILITARY (Continued)

Type of Personnel	1962	1963	1964	1965	1966	1967	1968
Physicians of all specialties (including dentists)	479.8	500.8	532.1	554.2	577.7	598.2	617.8
Physicians excluding stomatologists and dentists	426.6	443.3	467.4	485.0	503.3	519.5	534.3
Stomatologists	18.5	20.2	22.9	25.5	28.3	30.9	33.7
Dentists	34.7	37.3	41.8	43.7	46.1	47.8	49.8
Semi-professional health personnel	1,478.0	1,523.0	1,620.0	1,692.0	1,778.0	1,861.0	1,944.0
Semi-professional health personnel per physician (all specialties)	3.08	3.04	3.04	3.05	3.08	3.11	3.15
Semi-professional health personnel per physician (excluding stomatologists and dentists)	3.46	3.44	3.47	3.49	3.53	3.58	3.64

Table 11. TOTAL REPORTED AND PROJECTED ANNUAL AVERAGE EMPLOYMENT, NONAGRICULTURAL SECTORS, USSR

Sector	1928	1937	1940	1950	1958	1959	1960	1961
TOTAL	10,790,000	26,744,000	31,192,000	36,958,000	49,710,000	52,071,000	54,909,000	58,023,000
Public health	399,000	1,127,000	1,507,000	2,051,000	3,059,000	3,245,000	3,461,000	3,677,000
Construction	...	...	1,620,000	2,569,000	4,421,000	4,800,000	5,143,000	5,270,000
Education	...	...	2,678,000	3,315,000	4,378,000	4,556,000	4,803,000	5,165,000
Science and scientific services	...	...	362,000	714,000	1,338,000	1,474,000	1,763,000	2,011,000
Government and administration	...	...	1,837,000	1,831,000	1,294,000	1,273,000	1,245,000	1,295,000
Industry	...	...	13,079,000	14,144,000	19,675,000	20,207,000	22,291,000	23,475,000

Sector	1962	1963	1964	1965	1966	1967	1970
TOTAL	60,103,000	62,187,000	64,706,000	67,751,000	70,211,000	72,711,000	80,721,000
Public health	3,818,000	3,933,000	4,082,000	4,277,000	4,465,000	4,661,000	5,294,000
Construction	5,172,000	5,237,000	5,370,000	5,617,000	5,783,000	5,948,000	6,454,000
Education	5,521,000	5,835,000	6,204,000	6,600,000	6,931,000	7,324,000	8,470,000
Science and scientific services	2,213,000	2,370,000	2,497,000	2,624,000	2,806,000	3,018,000	3,681,000
Government and administration	1,316,000	1,308,000	1,354,000	1,460,000	1,488,000	1,509,000	1,613,000
Industry	24,297,000	25,057,000	25,933,000	27,056,000	27,689,000	28,322,000	30,302,000

Table 12. HOSPITAL (IN-PATIENT) INSTITUTIONS, USSR, EXCLUDING MILITARY HOSPITALS, BY TYPE AND NUMBER OF BEDS

Type of Hospital	1960 Number of Institutions	1960 Number of Beds (thousands)	1964 Number of Institutions	1964 Number of Beds (thousands)
Total number of hospital institutions	26,668	1,739.2	26,357	2,132.8
Of that number:				
Regional hospitals	160	71.2	176	88.7
City hospitals	4,918	561.8	4,992	668.5
Specialized hospitals (children's, infectious, anti-tuberculosis, etc.)	1,601[a]	168.2	1,936[b]	218.1
District hospitals (urban settlements and rural localities)	3,184	288.1	3,282	364.1
Micro-district hospitals	12,941	263.8	11,815	302.0
In-patient units of dispensaries, not including psychoneurological ones	2,198	100.9	2,493	150.0
In-patient units of scientific-research establishments and clinics of higher educational institutions	145	36.1	153	38.2
Maternity homes (except kolkhoz maternity units in general hospitals)	952	63.5	854	74.3
Psychiatric, psychoneurological hospitals and in-patient units of psychoneurological dispensaries	439	162.2	523	205.2
Other hospital institutions	130	23.4	133	23.7

Notes:

[a] Of these, 930 children's hospitals (including 796 for non-infectious patients).

[b] Of these, 994 children's hospitals (including 872 for non-infectious patients).

Table 13. HOSPITAL BEDS, USSR, EXCLUDING MILITARY HOSPITALS, BY REPUBLICS (In Numbers per 1,000 and Numbers per 10,000)

Area	1913 No.	1913 No.per 10,000	1940 No.	1940 No.per 10,000	1950 No.	1950 No.per 10,000	1958 No.	1958 No.per 10,000	1959 No.	1959 No.per 10,000
U.S.S.R.	207.6	13.0	790.9	40.2	1,010.7	55.7	1,532.5	73.4	1,618.1	76.2
Armenia	.2	2.1	4.1	30.1	6.5	47.6	11.6	65.7	12.2	67.1
Azerbaidzhan	1.1	4.8	12.6	37.8	17.0	57.8	24.2	65.5	25.8	67.5
Belorussia	6.4	9.3	29.6	32.6	32.0	41.2	48.9	60.8	51.9	63.8
Estonia	2.5	26.2	5.1	47.7	7.3	66.1	11.0	91.9	11.2	92.6
Georgia	2.1	8.0	13.3	36.0	19.4	54.6	27.7	68.5	28.8	69.8
Kazakhstan	1.8	3.2	25.1	39.7	35.1	52.1	72.6	78.0	76.9	78.1
Kirgizia	.1	1.2	3.8	24.1	7.1	40.3	12.9	62.3	14.6	68.1
Latvia	6.2	24.9	12.0	63.0	14.0	71.7	21.0	100.5	22.2	104.9
Lithuania	2.2	7.7	8.9	30.0	10.8	42.1	19.7	72.9	20.6	74.4
Moldavia	2.5	12.2	6.1	24.6	10.8	45.1	19.3	66.8	20.5	69.1
R.S.F.S.R.	133.4	14.8	482.0	43.3	609.8	59.2	889.8	75.7	936.6	78.7
Tadzhikistan	.04	.4	4.5	28.6	6.8	43.9	11.4	57.5	12.6	62.0
Turkmenia	.3	2.7	5.6	41.6	7.5	61.3	12.1	79.7	12.8	81.6
Ukraine	47.7	13.6	157.6	37.7	194.2	52.2	301.4	72.0	318.6	75.0
Uzbekistan	1.0	2.3	20.6	30.1	32.4	49.7	48.9	60.3	52.8	63.1

Table 13. Hospital Beds, USSR, Excluding Military Hospitals, by Republics (Continued)

Area	1960 No.	1960 No.per 10,000	1961 No.	1961 No.per 10,000	1962 No.	1962 No.per 10,000	1963 No.	1963 No.per 10,000	1964 No.	1964 No.per 10,000
U.S.S.R.	1,739.2	80.5	1,845.4	84.0	1,941.5	87.0	2,043.9	90.3	2,132.8	93.1
Armenia	13.2	69.6	14.1	72.2	15.2	75.5	15.9	76.9	16.8	78.8
Azerbaidzhan	27.4	69.1	30.1	73.0	32.8	77.6	35.3	80.5	37.8	83.4
Belorussia	55.9	68.0	61.5	74.0	66.9	79.5	71.1	84.1	75.4	88.3
Estonia	11.5	94.1	12.2	99.0	13.0	104.5	13.7	108.8	13.9	109.7
Georgia	30.3	72.2	32.1	75.2	33.5	77.2	35.0	79.4	36.3	81.0
Kazakhstan	81.3	79.7	89.3	81.6	96.4	85.6	107.5	93.4	113.8	96.1
Kirgizia	16.3	73.3	18.7	80.6	19.8	83.2	21.0	84.2	22.4	87.3
Latvia	23.0	107.3	23.9	110.2	24.6	112.8	25.3	114.0	25.7	114.6
Lithuania	21.7	77.5	22.8	79.9	23.7	82.2	24.7	84.8	25.6	86.8
Moldavia	22.0	72.3	23.5	75.8	25.2	79.5	27.1	83.5	28.9	87.4
R.S.F.S.R.	990.9	82.2	1,044.4	85.5	1,097.8	88.9	1,145.5	91.9	1,192.2	94.8
Tadzhikistan	14.2	67.1	15.7	71.6	16.8	74.3	18.2	77.5	20.8	83.8
Turkmenia	13.5	83.0	14.6	86.6	15.0	86.3	15.6	86.8	16.3	87.8
Ukraine	343.8	79.8	367.4	84.4	382.3	86.8	403.4	90.4	414.9	92.0
Uzbekistan	74.2	83.6	75.1	83.6	78.5	82.7	84.6	86.2	92.0	90.9

Area	1965 No.	1965 No.per 10,000	1966 No.	1966 No.per 10,000	1967 No.	1967 No.per 10,000	1968 No.	1968 No.per 10,000
U.S.S.R.	2,225.5	96.0	2,321.0	99.0	2,397.9	101.3	2,486.7	104.1
Armenia	17.8	81.1	18.5	82.1	19.7	85.5	20.2	85.3
Azerbaidzhan	39.8	85.3	41.5	86.5	43.3	88.1	44.3	87.8
Belorussia	80.0	92.6	83.5	95.5	85.3	96.7	87.7	98.5
Estonia	14.3	111.2	14.5	111.9	14.8	113.3	14.9	113.1
Georgia	38.2	84.0	39.3	85.3	40.4	86.7	41.4	88.0
Kazakhstan	122.1	100.7	128.5	103.6	134.5	106.1	141.2	109.7
Kirgizia	23.8	89.9	25.6	93.3	26.7	94.2	28.9	98.9
Latvia	26.2	115.9	26.6	116.5	26.9	117.1	27.1	116.8
Lithuania	26.6	89.0	28.0	92.4	29.2	95.3	30.3	97.6
Moldavia	30.1	89.3	31.5	92.0	32.5	93.2	33.5	94.9
R.S.F.S.R.	1,241.1	98.1	1,290.1	101.3	1,132.9	104.2	1,377.5	107.2
Tadzhikistan	22.4	87.2	23.5	88.8	24.9	90.9	26.3	93.1
Turkmenia	17.4	90.8	18.5	94.1	19.6	96.9	21.0	100.6
Ukraine	428.2	94.1	448.7	97.6	460.0	99.2	479.4	102.5
Uzbekistan	97.5	92.3	102.7	94.3	107.2	95.2	113.0	96.9

Table 14. HOSPITAL BEDS, USSR, BY SPECIALTY (In Thousands)

Kind of Bed	1940	1950	1958	1959	1960	1961	1962
Total No. of Beds	790.9	1,010.7	1,532.5	1,618.1	1,739.2	1,845.4	1,941.5
Of these:							
Medicine[a]	102.3	177.0	315.0	331.0	361.7	380.2	403.2
Surgery[b]	99.4	143.7	209.5	216.0	236.7	246.1	262.2
Cancer[c]	1.7	12.2	20.5	22.2	24.2	26.4	28.0
Gynecology	33.6	42.2	76.0	83.0	91.3	97.1	104.7
Tuberculosis	34.0	85.5	142.1	140.0	157.2	164.9	191.1
Of these:							
Adults	(28.7)	(75.3)	(122.3)	(120.2)	(136.3)	(142.2)	(166.3)
Children	(5.3)	(10.2)	(19.8)	(19.8)	(20.9)	(22.7)	(24.8)
Infectious diseases	94.3	125.6	156.6	159.9	166.6	170.8	172.9
Of these:							
Adults	(62.4)	(81.8)	(84.8)	(86.8)	(91.3)	(93.1)	(94.6)
Children	(31.9)	(43.8)	(71.8)	(73.1)	(75.3)	(77.7)	(78.3)
Sick children (non-infectious)	52.5	79.1	135.1	147.8	163.9	178.4	193.6
Diseases of the eyes	13.4	16.1	26.4	27.2	30.3	31.6	32.6
Otorhinolaryn-gology	6.9	8.9	15.7	17.3	20.0	22.6	24.4
Skin-venereal diseases	15.4	30.0	29.0	29.4	31.0	31.8	32.8
Psychic diseases	82.9	71.8	138.9	149.6	162.5	175.0	185.5
Neurology	10.0	15.1	24.6	26.1	30.5	32.8	37.1
For pregnant women and infants (in maternity homes and divisions of general hospitals)	113.5	122.2	162.2	167.9	175.3	181.6	185.7
Non-specialized beds	119.7	73.2	63.1	65.9	67.9	69.2	67.8

Kind of Bed	1963	1964	1965	1966	1967	1968
Total No. of Beds	2,043.9	2,132.8	2,225.5	2,321.0	2,397.9	2,486.7
Of these:						
Medicine[a]	416.7	436.7	425.9	447.2	465.0	484.5
Surgery[b]	270.6	282.3	289.4	300.6	310.7	324.6
Cancer[c]	30.6	32.4	34.5	39.7	41.0	43.2
Gynecology	109.4	114.8	125.2	134.7	139.8	114.9
Tuberculosis	225.1	241.7	259.2	265.9	271.9	274.7
Of these:						
Adults	(197.0)	(212.3)	(230.0)	(237.7)	(242.4)	(245.8)
Children	(28.1)	(29.4)	(29.2)	(30.2)	(29.5)	(28.9)
Infectious diseases	174.7	173.7	176.7	182.0	184.9	187.2
Of these:						
Adults	(95.2)	(93.5)	(100.9)	(102.1)	(102.5)	(102.4)
Children	(79.5)	(80.2)	(75.8)	(79.9)	(82.4)	(84.8)
Sick children (non-infectious)	211.9	231.1	248.5	267.8	282.0	298.4
Diseases of the eyes	33.7	34.7	35.0	35.6	35.9	37.2
Otorhinolaryn-gology	26.6	28.7	31.1	33.3	34.8	36.8
Skin-venereal diseases	33.6	34.4	36.0	41.3	43.0	45.8
Psychic diseases	196.0	205.2	215.5	225.9	234.1	246.5
Neurology	39.9	43.4	47.3	52.6	57.4	62.1
For pregnant women and infants (in maternity homes and divisions of general hospitals)	188.5	190.2	190.9	189.5	191.5	193.2
Non-specialized beds	65.9	61.1	91.7	93.7	94.8	96.3

Notes:

[a] Includes beds for physiotherapy, endocrinology.

[b] Includes beds for neurosurgery, traumatology, orthopedics, urology, stomatology.

[c] Includes beds for radiology and roentgen-radiology.

Table 15. Hospital Beds (Medical and Obstetrical) for Pregnant Women and Infants, USSR, by Republics (In Thousands)

Area	1940	1950	1958	1959	1960	1961	1962	1963	1964	1965	1966	1967	1968
U.S.S.R.	147.1	143.0	196.9	204.8	213.4	219.4	224.8	227.1	228.5	227.0	224.5	224.5	223.4
Armenia	0.7	1.2	1.9	2.1	2.2	2.3	2.4	2.4	2.4	2.7	2.7	2.8	2.9
Azerbaidzhan	2.0	2.1	2.8	3.1	3.3	3.5	3.8	4.0	4.3	4.3	4.5	4.9	5.1
Belorussia	5.4	4.4	6.1	6.3	6.7	7.1	7.4	7.4	7.5	7.5	7.4	7.1	7.1
Estonia	0.3	0.8	0.9	0.9	0.9	0.9	0.9	0.9	0.8	0.8	0.8	0.8	0.8
Georgia	1.9	2.5	3.6	3.7	3.9	4.0	4.1	4.3	4.3	4.2	4.2	4.3	4.3
Kazakhstan	4.3	4.9	10.5	11.2	11.9	12.5	13.4	13.8	14.1	14.5	15.0	15.4	15.6
Kirgizia	0.8	1.0	2.2	2.4	2.6	2.8	3.1	3.1	3.1	3.2	3.4	3.7	3.9
Latvia	0.8	1.1	1.6	1.7	1.7	1.7	1.7	1.6	1.5	1.5	1.3	1.3	1.3
Lithuania	0.4	1.7	2.3	2.4	2.4	2.5	2.5	2.4	2.5	2.5	2.5	2.5	2.5
Moldavia	0.6	1.7	3.7	4.0	4.2	4.2	4.3	4.3	4.3	4.4	4.5	4.5	4.5
R.S.F.S.R.	90.7	82.7	105.5	109.4	112.9	115.9	118.2	119.2	119.6	118.3	115.4	114.3	112.1
Tadzhikistan	0.6	0.8	1.3	1.3	1.4	1.6	1.7	1.9	2.1	2.2	2.4	2.5	2.5
Turkmenia	0.8	0.9	1.6	1.6	1.7	1.7	1.8	1.8	1.8	1.9	2.1	2.3	2.4
Ukraine	35.0	33.7	46.4	47.8	48.9	49.9	51.0	50.4	49.5	47.8	47.0	46.1	45.7
Uzbekistan	2.8	3.5	6.5	6.9	8.7	8.8	8.9	9.6	10.5	11.2	11.3	12.0	12.7

Table 16. Women's Consultation Clinics, Children's Consultation Clinics, and Polyclinics (Independent and Divisions of Other Institutions), by Republics

Area	1940	1950	1958	1959*	1960	1961*	1962	1963	1964	1965	1966	1967	1968
U.S.S.R.	8,603	11,348	14,921	15,624	16,397	17,196	17,865	18,461	18,982	19,333	19,914	20,159	20,505
Armenia	60	134	146	183	185	190	205	212	199	232	237	235	240
Azerbaidzhan	166	189	214	220	231	235	242	256	273	274	268	268	290
Belorussia	311	433	439	445	459	469	487	492	501	503	513	522	533
Estonia	57	100	114	122	123	127	124	115	116	115	123	124	121
Georgia	283	374	289	302	332	352	371	396	431	445	466	470	488
Kazakhstan	269	383	571	580	624	669	721	835	855	890	902	954	941
Kirgizia	66	152	167	192	198	202	204	219	226	220	267	268	266
Latvia	109	91	121	199	201	206	206	203	206	217	205	204	210
Lithuania	51	157	227	226	194	196	196	196	205	205	204	204	203
Moldavia	40	93	143	155	188	200	206	209	223	222	221	180	193
R.S.F.S.R.	4,917	6,462	8,870	9,054	9,460	9,939	10,270	10,504	10,733	10,956	11,246	11,313	11,442
Tadzhikistan	71	94	105	116	130	128	152	150	180	122	187	195	189
Turkmenia	106	157	136	136	136	135	148	159	158	147	157	159	163
Ukraine	1,821	2,140	2,955	3,293	3,484	3,678	3,851	3,997	4,123	4,157	4,294	4,404	4,511
Uzbekistan	276	389	424	401	452	470	482	518	553	628	624	659	715

*Figures do not include polyclinics.

Table 17. List of Higher Medical Educational Institutions, USSR, 1967

No.	Name of the Institute	Medicine	Pediatrics	Public Health	Stomatology	Pharmaceutics	Year of Founding
	Medical Institutes						
1	Azerbaidzhan, in the name of Narimanov (Baku)	+	+	+	+	+	1919
2	Altai (Barnaul)	+	-	-	-	-	1954
3	Arkhangel	+	-	-	+	-	1932
4	Andizhan	+	-	-	-	-	1955
5	Astrakhan, in the name of A.V. Lunacharsky	+	-	-	-	-	1918
6	Aktiubinsk	+	-	-	-	-	1957
7	Bashkir, in the name of 15-year VLKSM (Ufa)	+	+	-	-	-	1932
8	Blagoveshchensk	+	-	-	-	-	1952
9	Voronezh	+	+	-	+	-	1918
10	Volgograd	+	-	-	+	-	1935
11	Vladivostok	+	-	-	-	-	1958
12	Vinnitsa	+	+	-	-	-	1932
13	Vitebsk	+	-	-	-	+	1934
14	Gorky	+	+	-	-	-	1918
15	Grodnensk	+	-	-	-	-	1958
16	Dagestan (Makhachkal)	+	-	-	+	-	1932
17	Dnepropetrovsk	+	+	+	-	-	1916
18	Donets, in the name of A.M. Gorky	+	+	+	-	-	1930
19	Dushanbin, in the name of Abu Ali Ibn-Sin (Avitsenni)	+	+	-	+	-	1939
20	Yerevan	+	+	+	+	-	1922
21	Ivanov	+	+	-	-	-	1930
22	Izhevsk	+	-	-	-	-	1933
23	Irkutsk	+	-	+	+	+	1919
24	Ivano-Frankov	+	-	-	-	-	1945
25	Kazan, order of Red Banner of Labor, in the name of C.V. Kurashov	+	+	+	+	-	1814
26	Kazakh (Alma-Ata)	+	+	+	-	+	1931
27	Kalinin	+	-	-	-	-	1954
28	Karaganda	+	+	+	-	-	1950
29	Kaunas	+	-	-	-	+	1950
30	Kemerov	+	-	+	+	-	1956
31	Kiev, order of Red Banner of Labor, in the name of A.A. Bogomollts	+	+	+	+	-	1841
32	Kirgiz (Frunze)	+	+	+	+	-	1939
33	Kishinev	+	+	+	+	+	1945
34	Krasnoyarsk	+	+	-	-	-	1942
35	Kuban, in the name of the Red Army (Krasnodar)	+	-	-	+	-	1920
36	Kuibishev	+	-	-	-	-	1919
37	Kursk	+	-	-	-	-	1935
38	First Leningrad, in the name of I.P. Pavlov	+	-	-	+	-	1897
39	Leningrad, pediatric	-	+	-	-	-	1935
40	Leningrad, public health	-	-	+	-	-	1907
41	L'vov	+	+	-	+	+	1773
42	Lugan	+	-	-	-	-	1956
43	Minsk	+	+	+	+	-	1919
44	First Moscow, order of Lenin and Red Banner of Labor, in the name of I.M. Sechenov	+	-	+	-	+	1765
45	Second Moscow, order of Lenin, in the name of N.I. Pirogov	+	+	-	-	-	1906
46	Novosibirsk	+	+	-	-	-	1935
47	Odessa	+	+	-	+	-	1900
48	Omsk, in the name of M.I. Kalinin	+	+	+	+	-	1920
49	Orenburg	+	-	-	-	-	1944
50	Perm	+	-	+	+	-	1930
51	Riga	+	-	-	+	+	1930
52	Rostov	+	+	+	-	-	1915
53	Riazan, in the name of I.P. Pavlov	+	+	+	-	-	1950
54	Samarkand, in the name of I.P. Pavlov	+	+	-	-	-	1930
55	Saratov	+	+	-	-	-	1908
56	Sverdlov	+	+	+	-	-	1920
57	Semipalatinsk	+	+	-	-	-	1953
58	Simferopol	+	+	-	-	-	1918
59	Smolensk	+	-	-	+	-	1920
60	Stavropol	+	-	-	+	-	1938
61	Severo-Osetin (Ordzhonikidze)	+	-	-	-	-	1939
62	Tashkent	+	+	+	+	-	1919
63	Tbilisi	+	+	+	+	+	1918
64	Tomsk	+	+	-	-	+	1888
65	Turkmen (Ashkhabad)	+	-	-	+	-	1932
66	Ternopol	+	-	-	-	-	1957
67	Tiumen	+	-	-	-	+	1963
68	Khabarovsk	+	+	-	-	+	1930
69	Kharkov	+	+	+	-	-	1805

Table 17. LIST OF HIGHER MEDICAL EDUCATIONAL INSTITUTIONS, USSR, 1967 (Continued)

		Faculties						
No.	Name of the Institute	Medicine	Pediatrics	Public Health	Stomatology	Pharmaceutics	Year of Founding
70	Chelizbinsk.............................	+	–	–	–	–	1944
71	Chernovits.............................	+	–	–	+	–	1944
72	Chita..................................	+	–	–	+	–	1953
73	Tselinograd............................	+	–	–	–	–	1964
74	Yaroslav...............................	+	–	–	–	–	1919
	Medical Stomatological Institutes						
1	Moscow.................................	–	–	–	+	–	1935
2	Kharkov................................	–	–	–	+	–	1821
	Pharmaceutical Institutes						
1	Zaporozhe..............................	–	–	–	–	+	1921
2	Leningrad, chemico-pharmaceutical..........	–	–	–	–	+	1937
3	Perm...................................	–	–	–	–	+	1929
4	Piatigorsk.............................	–	–	–	–	+	1943
5	Tashkent...............................	–	–	–	–	+	1937
6	Kharkov................................	–	–	–	–	+	1921

Medical faculties, parts of universities: 1) Vilnius, 2) Iakutsk, 3) Petrozavodsk, 4) Uzhgorod, 5) Tartu.

Note:

In general, professional education in the health care field in the U.S.S.R. is offered in five areas, three in medicine, one in dentistry (stomatology), and one in pharmacology. These areas are called faculties; the three medical faculties are: therapeutic, pediatric, and public health (sanitary-hygiene). A medical school is called a "medical institute" and is considered a higher educational institution. A medical institute may offer training in all five faculties, but in most instances it has less than these five faculties. There are, in addition, separate medical stomatological institutes (schools of dental medicine) and pharmacological institutes. Medical, dental, and pharmacological institutes are not parts of universities, except in the five instances listed at the bottom of the table. The formal course of study lasts six years in the medical faculties, and five in the others. Admission of students is upon completion of high school (middle education), normally at age 18.

CHAPTER IV TABLE SOURCE NOTES

TABLE 1

Zdravookhranenie v SSSR, Moscow (1960), p. 45; SS za 50 L., p. 260.

TABLE 2

"Zdravookhranenie," Malaya Meditsinskaya Entsiklopedia, vol. 3, col. 889, Moscow (1966).

TABLE 3

Itogi vsesoyuznoi perepisi naselenia 1959, USSR, Summary Volume, Moscow (1962), p. 258.

TABLE 4

Itogi vesesoyuznoi perepisi naselenia 1959, USSR, Summary Volume, Moscow (1962), pp. 262–263.

TABLE 4a

Itogi vsesoyuznoi perepisi naselenia 1959, USSR, Summary Volume, Moscow (1962), pp. 264–265, 13.

TABLE 4b

Itogi vsesoyuznoi perepisi naselenia 1959, USSR, Summary Volume, Moscow (1962), pp. 266–267,13.

TABLE 5

N.K. 1967, p. 851.
N.K. 1968, p. 736.

TABLE 6

Zdravookhranenie v SSSR, Moscow (1960), p. 50.
N.K. 1959, p. 787.

N.K. *1961*, pp. 743–744.
N.K. *1962*, pp. 615, 617.
N.K. *1963*, pp. 623–625.
N.K. *1964*, pp. 733–735.
"Vrach," *Malaya Meditsinskaya Entsiklopedia*, vol. 2, col. 438, Moscow (1966).
N.K. *1967*, pp. 843–845.
N.K. *1968*, pp. 729–731.

TABLE 7

Zdravookhranenie v SSSR, Moscow (1960), pp. 81, 82.
N.K. *1959*, p. 788.
N.K. *1961*, p. 743.
N.K. *1963*, p. 624.
N.K. *1964*, p. 734.
N.K. *1967*, p. 844.
N.K. *1968*, p. 730.

TABLE 8

N.K. *1959*, p. 787.
N.K. *1961*, p. 744.
N.K. *1963*, p. 625.
N.K. *1964*, p. 735.
N.K. *1965*, p. 745.
N.K. *1967*, p. 845.
N.K. *1968*, p. 731.

TABLE 9

XXV Let Sovetskogo Zdravookhranenie, ed. G. A. Miterev, Moscow (1944), p. 231.
N.K. *1959*, p. 789.
N.K. *1961*, p. 745.
N.K. *1963*, p. 626.
N.K. *1964*, p. 736.
N.K. *1967*, p. 846.
N.K. *1968*, p. 732.

TABLE 10

N.K. *1961*, pp. 744–745.
N.K. *1963*, p. 623.
N.K. *1964*, p. 733.
N.K. *1967*, p. 843.
N.K . *1968*, p. 729.

TABLE 11

Estimates and Projections of the Labor Force and Civilian Employment in the U.S.S.R.: 1950–1975, U.S. Department of Commerce, Bureau of the Census, U.S. Government Printing Office (1967), International Population Reports, Series P-91, no. 15, p. 26.
Zdravookhranenie v SSSR, Moscow (1957), p. 50. N.K. *1967*, pp. 648–649.

TABLE 12

"Zdravookhranenie," *Malaya Meditsinskaya Entsiklopedia*, vol. 3, cols. 903–904, Moscow (1966).

TABLE 13

N.K. *1959*, p. 791.
N.K. *1961*, pp. 746–747.
N.K. *1963*, pp. 627–628.
N.K. *1964*, p. 738.
"Zdravookhranenie," *Malaya Meditsinskaya Entsiklopedia*, vol. 3, cols. 900, 901, Moscow (1966).
N.K. *1967*, p. 848.
N.K. *1968*, p. 734.

TABLE 14

N.K. *1961*. p. 747.
N.K. *1963*, p. 630.
N.K. *1964*, p. 740.
N.K. *1967*, p. 850.
N.K. *1968*, p. 735.

TABLE 15

N.K. *1959*, p. 792.
N.K. *1961*, p. 748.
N.K. *1963*, p. 631.
N.K. *1964*, p. 741
N.K. *1967*, p. 852.
N.K. *1968*, p. 737.

TABLE 16

N.K. *1961*, p. 748.
N.K. *1963*, p. 631.
N.K. *1964*, p. 741
N.K. *1967*, p. 852.
N.K. *1968*, p. 737.

TABLE 17

"Meditsinskoe Obrazovanie," *Malaya Meditsinskaya Entsiklopedia*, vol. 5, cols. 781–782, Moscow (1967).

HOUSING

HENRY W. MORTON

THE CRITICAL NEED to supply a rapidly growing population with comfortable, good quality housing of sufficient quantity is a worldwide problem. Its application to the USSR will be briefly discussed.

The Soviet Union inherited a poorly developed housing fund from Tsarist Russia. Most of the housing, in towns and in the countryside, before 1917 consisted mainly of small wooden single-story one-family houses lacking almost completely in utilities.[1]

Under Soviet rule the housing shortage became more acute. The Stalinist policy of rapid industrialization based on forced collectivization of agriculture, begun in 1929, brought millions of peasants from rural areas to the cities. The scope of this mass migration is indicated in the following figures. In 1926, 26.3 million people or 18 percent of the population lived in urban areas. By 1939 these figures had increased to 63.1 million and 33 percent, and by 1968 to 134.2 million and 56 percent, respectively. In 1926 three cities had a population of over 500,000. In 1939 this total increased to 11 and by 1968 there were 34 such cities.[2]

At the same time, the scale of housing construction by the state failed to keep up with the rapid rate of urban growth until the last years of Stalin's rule because the primary concentration of capital investment during his years in power (1929 to 1953) was in heavy industry. Thus the amount of urban housing available to citizens sharply declined. Lastly, the war against Germany (1941 to 1945) saw widespread destruction of housing in the European part of the USSR, and many cities and towns had to be almost completely rebuilt.

Despite an intensive building program which was begun in the mid-1950's— in the decade between 1959 and 1968, the USSR built more housing units than any other country,[3] which enabled 87.7 million of its citizens (37 percent of the population) to move into newly built dwellings (Tables 12 and 14)— housing remained a primary domestic problem of the nation. This is reflected in a careful reading of Soviet housing statistics.

Housing in the USSR is not measured in units or in density of occupancy per room, but in square meters of "living space" (zhilaya ploshchad). This includes bedrooms and living rooms, but not kitchens, bathrooms, and storage areas. Living and nonliving space together make up the aggregate "housing space" (Obshchaya ploshchad) of a dwelling. Each republic, according to law, sets the "sanitary housing norm" for its citizens. For the Russian Republic, as well as for most of the others, it is 9 square meters of *living space*.[4]

Yet, except for isolated instances, housing statistics released for the USSR, for the republics, and for major urban centers as well as for other categories are not given in square meters of living space, the measurement every citizen goes by, but in square meters of aggregate housing space.

To calculate living space from housing space data D. L. Broner, a leading Soviet writer on housing, applied a correction factor of .7 to the published statistics of aggregate housing space. By using his correction factor, we find that in 1968 of the major cities only Moscow satisfied the per capita sanitary norm with 9.7 square meters of living space; and of the republics, only Estonia with 9.4 square meters and Latvia with 9.2 square meters fulfilled the minimum standard.[5] The average number of square meters of living space for the urban dweller in the USSR for 1968 was 7.4, significantly below the sanitary norm.[6]

Housing statistics released by the Soviet government have become more plentiful and sophisticated in recent years. Yet only certain categories have been chosen for publication, and many of these list no data prior to 1960.

Still unavailable, for instance, is a listing for the total housing fund for the USSR and the republics. Specifically omitted has been the housing fund for rural areas. No figures have been published which specify the average number of rooms per apartment (or small house); density of occupancy per room; how many families live in separate apartments (otdelnaya kvartira) compared with those who share their quarters, particularly kitchen and toilet facilities with other families; and what percent of the total population lives in barracks or hostel type housing. Few data have been published which spell out the availability of utility services, an important measurement of housing quality, to the public; what sketchy figures are available apply only to urban housing. At the end of 1968 in state-owned housing, in urban centers, and settlements (which amounted to 68 percent of the total with cooperative housing included) almost 100 percent of the units were electrified, 71 percent had running water, 68 percent had sewage systems, 66 percent had central heating, and 56 percent had gas.[7]

The private sector continues to be a significant factor in Soviet housing. In 1968 2½ times as many square meters of housing space in urban centers and settlements were privately owned as had been in 1913—the last prerevolutionary year for which figures are available. Thus in 1968 almost one-third or 32 percent of all urban housing was still in private hands (Chart 1). The total number of housing in the private sector would increase well over 50 percent if statistics on rural housing were published. Most of the houses in the countryside, where 104,766,000 Soviet citizens, or 44 percent of the population, lived in 1968 are in private hands. Also noteworthy is that the share of the private housing fund in urban areas differs sharply among republics, ranging from a high of 49 percent in Georgia (for 1968) to a low of 23 percent in Latvia (Chart 5).

The private sector has also played an important role in housing construction. Of all square meters of housing space built from 1918 through 1968, 51.4 percent was constructed privately or by nonstate agencies.[8] Included in this figure was housing built by collective farms (which legally are cooperatives), by collective farmers, and by rural intelligentsia (Table 16). In 1968, 38.4 percent of all housing construction was non-state built. This included construction of private housing—13.9 percent; of collective farmers and rural intelligentsia housing—19.2 percent; and of cooperative housing—6.3 percent (Tables 6 and 15).

Cooperative housing construction figures begin with the year 1963 because in 1962, housing cooperatives, which had been experimented with earlier in Soviet history, were again officially encouraged—at the expense of private housing construction.[9] The granting of land sites for private housing in capitals of republics and credits to support such construction were discontinued; both became difficult to obtain in large urban centers. This was probably a principal reason behind the decline of the urban private housing fund and urban private housing construction in proportion to the state's in the 1960's.

Population figures used in tables are official estimates except for census years of 1926, 1939, and 1959.

NOTES

1. Timothy Sosnovy, "Housing Conditions and Urban Development in the U.S.S.R.," *New Directions in the Soviet Economy*, Part II-B, Washington, D.C., U.S. Government Printing Office, 1966, pp. 534–535.
2. *N.K. 1959*, p. 9 and *N.K. 1968*, pp. 1, 23–32.
3. This is in absolute numbers but not on a per capita basis.
4. See Article 316 in Whitmore Gray and Raymond Stults (translators), *Civil Code of the Russian Soviet Federated Socialist Republic*, Ann Arbor, University of Michigan Law School, 1965, p. 82. For the Ukraine it is 13.65 square meters of living space per person.
5. D. L. Broner, *Zhilishchny vopros i statistika* (The Housing Question and Statistics), Moscow, Statistika, 1966, p. 8 in Donald D. Barry, "Housing in the USSR," *Problems of Communism*, XVIII, 3 (May–June) 1969, p. 2. Using the corrections factor of .7 leads to a slight overestimation of the real living space—at least for Moscow, for which we have the aggregate living space statistic for 1968 of 61,300,000 square meters. (*N.K. 1968*, p. 583). By dividing the estimated population of Moscow for 1968, which was 6,642,000, into 61,300,000 square meters of living space, we find that the average living space per Muscovite was 9.2 square meters or .05 percent lower than the estimate based on Broner's correction factor.
6. Defining what constitutes urban has not remained constant and differs, often sharply, by republic. In the 1926 census the urban population included those living in an officially designated town or city (gorod) and in a settlement of an urban type (poselki gorodskogo tipa) provided that it had not fewer than 500 inhabitants and that more than half of the labor force was engaged in nonagricultural pursuits. The 1939 census (which was never fully published) held, in the main, to the criteria of the 1926 census. In the 1959 census an officially designated town or city varied in size from 12,000 to 5,000 by republic, and urban settlements from 3,000 to 1,000. See Robert A. Lewis and Richard H. Rowland, *Urbanization in Russia and the USSR: 1897–1966*, New York, mimeographed (n.d.), p. 4; and Maurice F. Parkins, *City Planning in Soviet Russia*, Chicago, University of Chicago Press, 1953, pp. 3–4.
7. D. L. Broner, "Zhilishchnyia problema v trudykh i gosudarstvennoi deyatelnosti V. I. Lenina," ("Lenin and the Housing Question, in His Writings and in His Activities as Governmental Leader), *Vestnik Statistiki*, no. 3, 1970, p. 11.
8. 1,143,200,000 square meters of housing space was built by private individuals and nonstate agencies compared with 1,082,900,000 square meters of housing space built by state and housing cooperatives. See Table 16.
9. *Pravda*, August 7, 1962.

Table 1. URBAN HOUSING: STATE AND PRIVATE SHARE (In Million Square Meters of Housing Space)

Year	Total City Housing Fund (mil. sq. meters)	State Housing	% State	Private Housing	% Private
1913	180	...	0	180	100.0
1926	216	103	47.7	113	52.3
1940	421	267	63.4	154	36.6
1950	513	340	66.3	173	33.7
1952	557	371	66.6	186	33.4
1955	640	432	67.5	208	32.5
1956	673	454	67.5	219	32.5
1957	723	486	67.2	237	32.8
1958	832	500	60.1	332	39.9
1959	896	541	60.4	355	39.6
1960	958	583	60.9	375	39.1
1961	1,017	626	61.6	391	38.4
1962	1,074	670	62.4	404	37.6
1963	1,130	716	63.4	414	36.6
1964	1,182	759	64.2	423	35.8
1965	1,238	806	65.1	432	34.9
1966	1,290	854	66.2	436	33.8
1967	1,350	906	67.1	444	32.9
1968	1,410	959	68.0	451	32.0

Table 2. AGGREGATE AND PER CAPITA URBAN HOUSING

Year	Urban Housing Fund Aggregate Housing Space (mil. sq. meters)	% of 1913	Urban Population (millions)	% of 1913	Average Housing Space Per Person (sq. meters)	% of 1913
1913	180	100.0	28.5	100.0	6.3	100.0
1940	421	233.1	64.9	288.1	6.5	103.2
1950	513	284.2	73.0	256.6	7.0	111.1
1960	958	531.3	108.3	380.6	8.9	141.3
1965	1,238	686.1	124.7	438.5	9.9	157.1
1967	1,350	748.3	130.9	460.2	10.3	163.5
1968	1,410	781.7	134.2	471.6	10.5	166.7

Table 3. Aggregate (in Million Square Meters of Housing Space) and
per Capita Housing, by Republics

Republic	1958 Urban Population[a]	1958 Housing Fund[b]	1958 Per Capita[c]	1959 Housing Fund	1960 Housing Fund	1960 Per Capita	1961 Urban Population	1961 Housing Fund	1961 Per Capita
U.S.S.R.	99,978	832,000	8.3	896,000	958,000	8.8	111,844	1,017,000	9.1
Armenia	882	6,700	7.6	7,200	7,700	7.9	1,030	8,400	8.2
Azerbaidzhan	1,767	14,000	7.9	14,700	15,800	8.1	2,031	16,600	8.2
Belorussia	2,481	20,700	8.3	22,600	24,400	8.8	2,911	26,100	9.0
Estonia	676	7,400	10.9	7,700	8,100	11.5	731	8,600	11.8
Georgia	1,713	16,300	9.5	17,000	17,900	9.8	1,919	19,200	10.0
Kazakhstan	4,037	30,200	7.5	33,100	36,300	7.8	4,883	39,100	8.0
Kirgizia	696	4,900	7.0	5,400	5,700	7.4	859	6,400	7.5
Latvia	1,174	14,100	12.0	14,500	15,000	12.2	1,273	15,700	12.3
Lithuania	1,046	9,800	9.4	10,300	10,600	9.4	1,166	11,100	9.5
Moldavia	643	5,100	7.9	5,500	6,100	8.4	752	6,500	8.6
R.S.F.S.R.	61,611	496,500	8.1	534,900	570,800	8.6	68,207	606,200	8.9
Tadzhikistan	646	5,000	7.7	5,400	5,700	7.9	756	6,000	7.9
Turkmenia	700	5,700	8.1	6,000	6,500	8.4	807	6,900	8.6
Ukraine	19,147	174,800	9.1	189,600	203,700	9.8	21,334	215,000	10.1
Uzbekistan	2,759	20,500	7.4	22,100	23,700	7.8	3,185	24,900	7.8

Republic	1962 Urban Population	1962 Housing Fund	1962 Per Capita	1963 Urban Population	1963 Housing Fund	1963 Per Capita	1964 Urban Population	1964 Housing Fund	1964 Per Capita
U.S.S.R.	115,088	1,074,000	9.3	118,531	1,130,000	9.5	121,673	1,182,000	9.7
Armenia	1,069	9,000	8.4	1,124	9,800	8.7	1,175	10,500	8.9
Azerbaidzhan	2,104	17,500	8.3	2,186	18,600	8.5	2,265	19,500	8.6
Belorussia	3,037	27,700	9.1	3,146	29,300	9.3	3,270	30,800	9.4
Estonia	751	9,100	12.1	768	9,500	12.4	788	9,900	12.6
Georgia	1,968	20,300	10.3	2,018	21,100	10.5	2,085	22,000	10.5
Kazakhstan	5,096	42,100	8.3	5,313	45,400	8.5	5,576	48,600	8.7
Kirgizia	894	6,800	7.6	936	7,100	7.6	972	7,500	7.7
Latvia	1,303	16,200	12.4	1,337	16,700	12.5	1,367	17,300	12.7
Lithuania	1,203	11,700	9.7	1,245	12,400	10.0	1,289	13,100	10.2
Moldavia	783	7,000	8.9	819	7,500	9.2	858	8,000	9.3
R.S.F.S.R.	70,039	641,200	9.2	71,974	673,800	9.4	73,559	703,200	9.6
Tadzhikistan	778	6,300	8.1	820	6,700	8.2	865	7,100	8.2
Turkmenia	844	7,200	8.5	874	7,600	8.7	908	7,900	8.7
Ukraine	21,859	226,300	10.4	22,495	237,800	10.6	23,093	248,100	10.7
Uzbekistan	3,360	26,000	7.7	3,476	27,200	7.8	3,603	28,500	7.9

Republic	1965 Urban Population	1965 Housing Fund	1965 Per Capita	1966 Housing Fund	1967 Urban Population	1967 Housing Fund	1967 Per Capita	1968 Urban Population	1968 Housing Fund	1968 Per Capita
U.S.S.R.	124,751	1,238,000	9.9	1,290,000	130,935	1,350,000	10.3	134,177	1,410,000	10.5
Armenia	1,209	11,200	9.3	11,800	1,288	12,500	9.7	1,333	13,000	9.8
Azerbaidzhan	2,329	20,400	8.8	21,300	2,486	22,200	8.9	2,546	23,100	9.1
Belorussia	3,403	32,400	9.5	34,300	3,691	36,500	9.9	3,847	38,700	10.1
Estonia	804	10,200	12.7	10,600	830	10,900	13.1	844	11,300	13.4
Georgia	2,140	22,800	10.7	23,800	2,238	24,900	11.1	2,292	25,900	11.3
Kazakhstan	5,784	51,300	8.9	53,900	6,254	56,900	9.1	6,479	60,000	9.3
Kirgizia	1,020	7,800	7.6	8,200	1,102	8,600	7.8	1,148	9,100	7.9
Latvia	1,400	17,800	12.7	18,400	1,453	19,000	13.1	1,484	19,600	13.2
Lithuania	1,336	13,800	10.3	14,600	1,431	15,400	10.8	1,486	16,200	10.9
Moldavia	953	9,000	9.4	9,400	1,031	10,100	9.8	1,077	10,700	9.9
R.S.F.S.R.	75,073	736,500	9.8	769,100	78,113	803,300	10.3	79,738	838,200	10.5
Tadzhikistan	914	7,500	8.2	8,000	1,018	8,500	8.3	1,049	9,000	8.6
Turkmenia	939	8,400	8.9	8,800	995	9,300	9.3	1,025	1,700	9.5
Ukraine	23,714	258,900	10.9	269,400	24,951	280,800	11.3	25,612	292,800	11.4
Uzbekistan	3,733	29,600	7.9	28,300	4,054	30,800	7.6	4,217	32,600	7.7

Notes:

[a] Urban population in millions.

[b] Housing fund in million square meters.

[c] Per capita - square mile.

Table 4. AGGREGATE AND PER CAPITA HOUSING FUND FOR FIFTEEN LARGEST CITIES (In Million Square Meters of Housing Space)

City	1925 Housing Fund[a]	1939 Population[b]	1939 Housing Fund	1939 Per Capita	1955 Population	1955 Housing Fund	1955 Per Capita
Moscow	16,500	4,183	28,165	6.7	4,839	35,400	7.3
Leningrad	21,027	3,385	25,700	7.6	3,176	25,300	8.0
Kiev	5,028	847	6,650	7.9	991	7,700	7.8
Baku	3,057	775	5,830	7.5	901	6,600	7.3
Kharkov	3,246	833	6,564	7.9	876	6,700	7.6
Gorky	1,378	644	4,275	6.6	877	5,900	6.7
Tashkent	1,986	550	4,025	7.3	778	4,700	6.0
Kuibyshev	1,360	390	2,435	6.2	760	4,600	6.1
Novosibirsk	665	404	2,440	6.0	731	4,300	5.9
Sverdlovsk	891	423	2,881	6.8	707	4,900	6.9
Tbilisi	2,869	519	4,609	8.9	625	5,400	8.6
Donetsk	714	466	3,180	6.8	635	4,500	7.1
Chelyabinsk	394	273	1,725	6.3	612	3,800	6.2
Dnepropretrovsk	2,062	527	3,860	7.3	576	4,400	7.6
Kazan	1,465	398	2,640	6.6	565	3,500	6.2

City	1958 Population	1958 Housing Fund	1958 Per Capita	1959 Housing Fund	1960 Housing Fund	1961 Population	1961 Housing Fund	1961 Per Capita
Moscow	43,270	43,270	8.6	46,160	58,861	6,296	63,948	10.2
Leningrad	3,321	27,780	8.4	28,852	30,544	3,498	32,372	9.3
Kiev	1,104	8,885	8.0	10,586	11,503	1,208	12,411	10.3
Baku	971	7,135	7.3	8,215	8,601	1,067	9,035	8.5
Kharkov	934	7,445	8.0	8,697	9,022	990	9,335	9.4
Gorky	942	6,870	7.3	7,664	8,085	1,025	8,565	8.4
Tashkent	912	5,285	5.8	7,426	7,681	1,002	8,043	8.0
Kuibyshev	806	5,550	6.9	6,243	6,649	881	7,060	8.0
Novosibirsk	886	5,420	6.1	7,052	7,541	985	8,072	8.2
Sverdlovsk	779	5,935	7.6	6,651	7,212	853	7,713	9.0
Tbilisi	695	5,680	8.2	6,135	6,368	743	6,674	9.0
Donetsk	699	5,640	8.1	6,950	7,602	760	8,075	10.6
Chelyabinsk	689	4,830	7.0	5,757	6,223	751	6,731	9.0
Dnepropretrovsk	660	4,995	7.6	6,320	6,659	722	6,899	9.6
Kazan	647	4,015	6.2	4,945	5,261	711	5,584	7.9

City	1962 Population	1962 Housing Fund	1962 Per Capita	1963 Population	1963 Housing Fund	1963 Per Capita	1964 Population	1964 Housing Fund	1964 Per Cap.
Moscow	6,354	68,631	10.8	6,408[c]	72,214	11.3	6,443[c]	75,827	11
Leningrad	3,552	34,084	9.6	3,607	35,698	9.9	3,641	37,341	10
Kiev	1,248	13,518	10.8	1,308[c]	14,512	11.1	1,348[c]	15,428	11
Baku	1,086	9,576	8.8	1,128[c]	10,122	9.0	1,348[c]	10,506	7
Kharkov	1,006	9,760	9.7	1,048	10,380	9.9	1,070	10,879	10
Gorky	1,042	9,030	8.9	1,066	9,454	8.9	1,085	9,766	9
Tashkent	1,029	8,430	8.2	1,073[c]	8,835	8.2	1,106[c]	9,236	8
Kuibyshev	901	7,457	8.3	928	7,838	8.4	948	8,335	8.
Novosibirsk	990	8,581	8.7	1,013	9,101	9.0	1,029	9,457	9.
Sverdlovsk	869	8,148	9.4	897	8,520	9.5	919	8,865	9.
Tbilisi	768	6,980	9.1	794[c]	7,295	9.2	812[c]	7,630	9.
Donetsk	774	8,580	11.1	794	9,041	11.4	809	9,427	11.
Chelyabinsk	689	7,218	10.5	790	7,580	9.6	805	7,859	9.
Dnepropretrovsk	667	7,238	10.9	721	7,542	10.5	735	7,889	10.
Kazan	725	5,888	8.1	743	6,121	8.2	762	6,362	8.

City	1965 Population	1965 Housing Fund	1965 Per Capita	1966 Population	1966 Housing Fund	1966 Per Capita
Moscow	6,463	79,466	12.3	6,507	83,553	12.8
Leningrad	3,665	39,182	10.7	3,706	41,003	11.1
Kiev	1,367	16,390	12.0	1,413	17,308	12.2
Baku	1,164	11,020	9.5	1,196	11,508	9.6
Kharkov	1,092	11,381	10.4	1,125	11,897	10.6
Gorky	1,100	10,191	9.3	1,120	10,722	9.6
Tashkent	1,199	9,676	8.1	1,239	7,654	6.2
Kuibyshev	969	8,657	8.9	992	9,117	9.2
Novosibirsk	1,049	9,903	9.4	1,064	10,344	9.7
Sverdlovsk	940	9,199	9.8	961	9,709	10.1
Tbilisi	823	7,891	9.6	842	8,241	9.8
Donetsk	823	9,815	11.9	840	10,194	12.1
Chelyabinsk	820	8,257	10.1	836	8,628	10.3
Dnepropretrovsk	790	8,238	10.4	776	8,594	11.1
Kazan	804	6,603	8.2	821	6,929	8.4

Notes:

[a] Housing fund in million square meters.

[b] Population in millions.

[c] For July 1.

Table 4. Aggregate and per Capita Housing Fund for Fifteen Largest Cities (Continued)

City	1967 Population	Housing Fund	Per Capita	1968 Population	Housing Fund	Per Capita
Moscow	6,590[c]	87,324	13.3	6,642	91,388	13.8
Leningrad	3,752	42,627	11.4	3,798	44,759	11.8
Kiev	1,476[c]	18,274	12.4	1,507	19,092	12.7
Baku	1,224[c]	11,924	9.7	1,236	12,367	10.0
Kharkov	1,148	12,484	10.9	1,170	13,157	11.2
Gorky	1,139	11,248	9.9	1,159	11,671	10.1
Tashkent	1,324[c]	9,008	6.8	1,354	9,794	7.2
Kuibyshev	1,014	9,588	9.5	1,038	9,989	9.6
Novosibirsk	1,079	10,941	10.1	1,098	11,440	10.4
Sverdlovsk	981	10,191	10.4	1,001	10,552	10.5
Tbilisi	866[c]	8,600	9.9	879	8,878	10.1
Donetsk	855	10,570	12.4	866	10,954	12.6
Chelyabinsk	851	9,019	10.6	871	9,368	10.8
Dnepropretrovsk	797	8,919	11.2	859	9,254	10.8
Kazan	837	7,225	8.6	850	7,582	8.9

Notes:

[a]Housing fund in million square meters.

[b]Population in millions.

[c]For July 1.

Table 5. Urban Housing Fund Owned by State and Private Sectors, by Republics (In Million Square Meters of Housing Space)

Republic	Urban Housing Space	State Housing Space	% State	Private Housing Space	% Private
U.S.S.R.					
1960	958	583	60.9	375	39.1
1965	1,238	806	65.1	432	34.9
1966	1,290	854	66.2	436	33.8
1967	1,350	906	67.1	444	32.9
1968	1,410	959	68.0	451	32.0
Armenia					
1960	7.7	3.1	40.3	4.6	59.7
1965	11.2	6.0	53.6	5.2	46.4
1966	11.8	6.5	55.1	5.3	44.9
1967	12.5	7.2	57.6	5.3	42.4
1968	13.0	7.7	59.2	5.3	40.8
Azerbaidzhan					
1960	15.8	9.8	62.0	6.0	38.0
1965	20.4	13.5	66.2	6.9	33.8
1966	21.3	14.2	66.7	7.1	33.3
1967	22.2	14.9	67.1	7.3	32.9
1968	23.1	15.6	67.5	7.5	32.5
Belorussia					
1960	24.4	12.7	52.0	11.7	48.0
1965	32.4	18.9	58.3	13.5	41.7
1966	34.3	20.5	59.8	13.8	40.2
1967	36.5	22.3	61.1	14.2	38.9
1968	38.7	24.2	62.5	14.5	37.5
Estonia					
1960	8.1	6.1	75.3	2.0	24.7
1965	10.2	7.5	73.5	2.7	26.5
1966	10.6	7.8	73.6	2.8	26.4
1967	10.9	8.1	74.3	2.8	25.7
1968	11.3	8.5	75.2	2.8	24.8
Georgia					
1960	17.9	8.2	45.8	9.7	54.2
1965	22.8	11.2	49.1	11.6	50.9
1966	23.8	11.8	49.6	12.0	50.4
1967	24.9	12.5	50.2	12.4	49.8
1968	25.9	13.2	51.0	12.7	49.0

Table 5. URBAN HOUSING FUND OWNED BY STATE AND PRIVATE SECTORS, BY REPUBLICS (Continued)

Republic	Urban Housing Space	State Housing Space	% State	Private Housing Space	% Private
Kazakhstan					
1960	36.3	17.9	49.3	18.4	50.7
1965	51.3	29.7	57.9	21.6	42.1
1966	53.9	32.0	59.4	21.9	40.6
1967	56.9	34.7	61.0	22.2	39.0
1968	60.0	37.4	62.3	22.6	37.7
Kirgizia					
1960	5.7	2.4	42.1	3.3	57.9
1965	7.8	3.8	48.7	4.0	51.3
1966	8.2	4.2	51.2	4.0	48.8
1967	8.6	4.5	52.3	4.1	47.7
1968	9.1	4.9	53.8	4.2	46.2
Latvia					
1960	15.0	11.3	75.3	3.7	24.7
1965	17.8	13.5	75.8	4.3	24.2
1966	18.4	14.0	76.1	4.4	23.9
1967	19.0	14.6	76.8	4.4	23.2
1968	19.6	15.1	77.0	4.5	23.0
Lithuania					
1960	10.6	6.6	62.3	4.0	37.7
1965	13.8	9.2	66.7	4.6	33.3
1966	14.6	9.9	67.8	4.7	32.2
1967	15.4	10.6	68.8	4.8	31.2
1968	16.2	11.3	69.8	4.9	30.2
Moldavia					
1960	6.1	2.8	45.9	3.3	54.1
1965	9.0	4.6	51.1	4.4	48.9
1966	9.4	4.9	52.1	4.5	47.9
1967	10.1	5.4	53.5	4.7	46.5
1968	10.7	5.9	55.1	4.8	44.9
R.S.F.S.R.					
1960	570.8	385.4	67.5	185.4	32.5
1965	736.5	526.7	71.5	209.8	28.5
1966	769.1	557.2	72.4	211.9	27.6
1967	803.3	589.3	73.4	214.0	26.6
1968	838.2	622.5	74.3	215.7	25.7
Tadzhikistan					
1960	5.7	2.7	47.4	3.0	52.6
1965	7.5	4.3	57.3	3.2	42.7
1966	8.0	4.6	57.5	3.4	42.5
1967	8.5	5.1	60.0	3.4	40.0
1968	9.0	5.5	61.1	3.5	38.9
Turkmenia					
1960	6.5	3.5	53.8	3.0	46.2
1965	8.4	5.2	61.9	3.2	38.1
1966	8.8	5.6	63.6	3.2	36.4
1967	9.3	6.0	64.5	3.3	35.5
1968	9.7	6.3	64.9	3.4	35.1
Ukraine					
1960	203.7	101.9	50.0	101.8	50.0
1965	258.9	138.5	53.5	120.4	46.5
1966	269.4	146.5	54.4	122.9	45.6
1967	280.8	154.8	55.1	126.0	44.9
1968	292.8	163.4	55.8	129.4	44.2
Uzbekistan					
1960	23.7	8.6	36.3	15.1	63.7
1965	29.6	13.5	45.6	16.1	54.4
1966	28.3	13.8	48.7	14.5	51.2
1967	30.8	16.0	51.9	14.8	48.1
1968	32.6	17.6	54.0	15.0	46.0

Table 6. Housing Built by State Including Cooperatives; Collective Farms, Collective Farmers, and Rural Intelligentsia; and Privately (In Million Square Meters of Housing Space)

Year	Total Number of Housing Built	Built By State Including Cooperatives	Built Privately By Workers and Salaried Employees	Built By Collective Farms, Collective Farmers and Rural Intelligentsia
1918-1968	2,226.1	1,082.9	429.9	713.3
1918-1928	203.0	23.7	27.5	151.8
1929-1932 1st 5 Yr. Plan	56.9	32.6	7.6	16.7
1933-1937 2nd 5 Yr. Plan	67.3	37.2	7.1	23.0
1938-July 1941 Part of 3rd 5 Yr. Plan	81.6	34.4	10.8	36.4
July 1941-1945	102.5	41.3	13.6	47.6
1946-1950 4th 5 Yr. Plan	200.9	72.4	44.7	83.8
1951-1955	240.5	113.0	65.1	62.4
1956-1960	474.1	224.0	118.8	136.3
1961-1965	490.6	300.4	94.0	96.2
1961	102.7	56.6	23.6	22.5
1962	100.0	59.8	20.7	19.5
1963	97.6	61.9	17.4	18.3
1964	92.7	58.9	16.2	17.6
1965	97.6	63.2	16.1	18.3
1966	102.1	65.9	15.9	20.3
1967	104.5	68.7	15.6	20.2
1968	102.1	69.3	14.2	18.6

Table 7. Percentage of Housing Built by State Including Cooperatives; Collective Farms, Collective Farmers, and Rural Intelligentsia; and Privately (In Million Square Meters of Housing Space)

Year	Total	State Including Cooperatives	% State	Private	% Private	Collective Farms, Collective Farmers and Rural Intelligentsia	% Collective Farms, etc.
1960	109,600	55,800	50.9	27,000	24.6	26,800	24.5
1961	102,700	56,600	55.1	23,600	23.0	22,500	21.9
1962	100,000	59,800	59.8	20,700	20.7	19,500	19.5
1963	97,600	61,900	63.4	17,400	17.8	18,300	18.8
1964	92,700	58,900	63.5	16,200	17.5	17,600	19.0
1965	97,600	63,200	64.8	16,100	16.5	18,300	18.8
1966	102,100	65,900	64.5	15,900	15.6	20,300	19.9
1967	104,500	68,700	65.7	15,600	14.9	20,200	19.3
1968	102,100	69,300	67.9	14,200	13.9	18,600	18.2

Table 8. Percentage of Housing Built by State Including Cooperatives; Collective Farms, Collective Farmers, and Rural Intelligentsia; and Privately, by Republics

Republic	Housing Units Built (Thousand)	Housing Space Built (Mil.Sq.M.)	% State Built (Sq.M.)	% Privately Built (Sq.M.)	% Collective Farms, Collective Farmers & Rural Intelligentsia (Sq.M.)
U.S.S.R.					
1960	2,591	109,600	50.9	24.6	24.5
1965	2,222	97,600	64.0	16.5	10.0
1966	2,291	102,100	15.6	15.6	19.9
1967	2,312	104,500	65.7	14.9	19.3
1968	2,233	102,100	67.9	13.9	18.2
Armenia					
1960	22	924	40.4	21.1	38.5
1965	27	1,295	62.9	18.6	18.5
1966	26	1,276	55.6	21.2	23.2
1967	25	1,274	60.0	18.7	21.3
1968	22	1,036	65.3	15.2	19.5
Azerbaidzhan					
1960	50	1,837	35.6	14.5	49.9
1965	41	1,646	54.8	18.5	26.7
1966	42	1,661	53.6	16.5	29.9
1967	40	1,609	52.1	18.6	29.3
1968	41	1,776	50.1	17.2	32.7
Belorussia					
1960	76	3,237	35.6	33.2	31.2
1965	74	3,282	52.2	23.2	24.6
1966	79	3,691	51.0	22.0	27.0
1967	85	4,015	50.5	21.8	27.7
1968	87	4,166	52.2	21.5	26.3
Estonia					
1960	11	537	66.3	27.6	6.1
1965	12	529	79.2	14.0	6.8
1966	12	524	75.2	16.0	8.8
1967	12	555	77.5	12.3	10.3
1968	14	632	78.2	11.4	10.4
Georgia					
1960	31	1,749	32.1	24.0	43.9
1965	28	1,559	43.0	28.8	28.2
1966	30	1,772	42.4	25.7	31.9
1967	29	1,777	44.1	28.4	27.5
1968	27	1,691	38.4	28.5	33.1
Kazakhstan					
1960	164	7,379	59.2	27.1	13.7
1965	139	6,300	76.8	15.2	8.0
1966	137	6,189	75.5	15.5	9.0
1967	143	6,514	77.5	14.7	7.8
1968	131	6,002	79.5	13.3	7.2
Kirgizia					
1960	23	930	35.2	31.3	33.5
1965	22	1,022	41.3	22.7	36.0
1966	25	1,163	36.8	23.2	40.0
1967	25	1,250	38.0	24.2	37.8
1968	27	1,278	38.6	24.3	37.2
Latvia					
1960	16	741	67.2	17.9	14.8
1965	16	709	81.2	12.1	6.6
1966	19	826	82.4	10.8	6.8
1967	19	827	81.7	10.3	8.0
1968	21	889	82.3	9.1	8.5
Lithuania					
1960	15	753	50.9	22.4	26.7
1965	25	1,143	69.5	17.3	13.2
1966	27	1,240	71.7	15.0	13.3
1967	29	1,368	68.1	12.7	19.0
1968	30	1,496	61.5	15.8	22.7
Moldavia					
1960	38	1,616	21.3	18.6	60.1
1965	24	1,062	39.9	16.4	43.7
1966	26	1,361	32.8	15.5	51.7
1967	31	1,562	37.2	16.3	46.5
1968	28	1,395	39.0	17.8	43.2

Table 8. Percentage of Housing Built Privately; by State Including Cooperatives; and Collective Farms, Collective Farmers, and Rural Intelligentsia, by Republics (Continued)

Republic	Housing Units Built (Thousand)	Housing Space Built (Mil.Sq.M.)	% State Built (Sq.M.)	% Privately Built (Sq.M.)	% Collective Farms, Collective Farmers & Rural Intelligentsia (Sq.M.)
R.S.F.S.R.					
1960	1,554	63,553	57.7	23.0	19.2
1965	1,298	54,859	73.2	13.3	13.4
1966	1,307	55,738	74.1	12.7	13.2
1967	1,313	56,700	75.2	11.9	12.9
1968	1,286	56,031	77.8	10.5	11.7
Tadzhikistan					
1960	20	791	40.6	14.0	45.4
1965	22	916	53.4	6.8	39.8
1966	22	1,018	37.4	8.3	54.3
1967	24	1,124	46.7	9.5	43.8
1968	23	1,083	44.2	11.0	44.8
Turkmenia					
1960	22	932	42.0	19.4	38.6
1965	17	808	55.6	12.4	32.1
1966	18	965	51.4	13.4	35.2
1967	18	921	52.7	11.2	36.2
1968	17	904	51.2	12.3	36.5
Ukraine					
1960	468	20,838	39.6	29.3	31.1
1965	403	18,892	46.8	24.0	29.2
1966	419	19,903	47.7	22.0	30.3
1967	409	19,542	49.5	21.2	29.3
1968	374	18,532	52.3	20.1	27.6
Uzbekistan					
1960	81	3,740	29.8	25.7	44.5
1965	78	3,607	47.4	16.8	35.8
1966	102	4,807	52.5	11.8	35.7
1967	110	5,426	52.7	13.3	34.0
1968	105	5,093	51.9	15.2	32.9

Table 9. Percentage of Housing Space (in Million Square Meters) Built by Urban and Rural Areas in the USSR

Year	Total	State	Private	Collective Farmers
1960	109.6	55.8	27.0	26.8
Urban/% Urban	59.0/53.8%	44.6/79.9%	14.4/53.3%	...
Rural/% Rural	50.6/46.2%	11.2/20.1%	12.6/46.7%	26.8/100%
1961	102.7	56.6	23.6	22.5
Urban/% Urban	56.1/54.6%	43.7/77.2%	12.4/52.5%	...
Rural/% Rural	46.6/45.4%	12.9/22.8%	11.2/47.5%	22.5/100%
1962	100.0	59.8	20.7	19.5
Urban/% Urban	58.9/58.9%	47.5/79.4%	11.4/55.1%	...
Rural/% Rural	41.1/41.1%	12.3/20.6%	9.3/44.9%	19.5/100%
1963	97.6	61.9	17.4	18.3
Urban/% Urban	58.4/59.8%	48.6/78.5%	9.8/56.3%	...
Rural/% Rural	39.2/40.2%	13.3/21.5%	7.6/43.7%	18.3/100%
1964	92.7	58.9	16.2	17.6
Urban/% Urban	57.5/62.0%	48.3/82.0%	9.2/56.8%	...
Rural/% Rural	35.2/38.0%	10.6/18.0%	7.0/43.2%	17.6/100%
1965	97.6	63.2	16.1	18.3
Urban/% Urban	60.7/62.2%	52.7/83.4%	8.0/49.7%	...
Rural/% Rural	36.9/37.8%	10.5/16.6%	8.1/50.3%	18.3/100%
1966	102.1	65.9	15.9	20.3
Urban/% Urban	63.4/62.1%	55.7/84.5%	7.7/48.4%	...
Rural/% Rural	38.7/37.9%	10.2/15.5%	8.2/51.6%	20.3/100%
1967	104.5	68.7	15.6	20.2
Urban/% Urban	66.1/63.3%	58.3/84.9%	7.8/50.0%	...
Rural/% Rural	38.4/36.7%	10.4/15.1%	7.8/50.0%	20.2/100%
1968	102.1	69.3	14.2	18.6
Urban/% Urban	66.1/64.7%	58.9/85.0%	7.2/50.7%	...
Rural/% Rural	36.0/35.3%	10.4/15.0%	7.0/49.3%	18.6/100%

Table 10.   Average Square Meters of Housing Space per Housing Unit
Built by Republics

Republic	1960	1965	1966	1967	1968
U.S.S.R.	42.3	43.8	44.6	45.2	45.7
Armenia	43.0	48.3	48.7	50.2	46.9
Azerbaidzhan	36.8	39.8	39.6	40.3	42.6
Belorussia	42.4	44.5	46.8	47.3	48.0
Estonia	40.4	44.1	45.6	47.0	46.5
Georgia	56.6	55.5	59.3	62.1	63.3
Kazakhstan	45.0	45.3	45.1	45.6	45.8
Kirgizia	40.1	46.5	47.1	49.4	48.0
Latvia	46.3	44.3	43.5	44.5	42.7
Lithuania	50.5	45.2	46.3	46.5	50.2
Moldavia	42.5	44.1	52.1	51.0	50.4
R.S.F.S.R.	40.9	42.2	42.6	43.2	43.6
Tadzhikistan	39.7	42.2	46.9	46.3	48.0
Turkmenia	43.0	49.0	53.6	50.3	52.3
Ukraine	44.5	46.8	47.5	47.8	49.6
Uzbekistan	46.2	46.1	47.0	49.5	48.3

Table 11.   Housing Space per Capita Built by Republics (In Square Meters
of Housing Space)

Republic	1960	1965	1966	1967	1968
U.S.S.R.	.51	.42	.44	.44	.43
Armenia	.49	.59	.57	.48	.44
Azerbaidzhan	.46	.35	.35	.32	.36
Belorussia	.39	.38	.42	.45	.47
Estonia	.44	.41	.40	.42	.48
Georgia	.42	.34	.38	.38	.36
Kazakhstan	.71	.52	.50	.51	.47
Kirgizia	.42	.39	.42	.43	.44
Latvia	.35	.31	.36	.36	.38
Lithuania	.27	.38	.41	.44	.48
Moldavia	.53	.32	.40	.44	.40
R.S.F.S.R.	.53	.43	.44	.44	.44
Tadzhikistan	.38	.36	.38	.40	.38
Turkmenia	.57	.42	.49	.45	.43
Ukraine	.48	.42	.43	.42	.40
Uzbekistan	.43	.34	.44	.47	.44

Table 12. PERCENTAGE OF HOUSING UNITS AND SQUARE METERS OF HOUSING SPACE BUILT BY REPUBLICS

Republic	1960			1965		
	% of Housing Units Built	% of Sq.M. Housing Space Built	% of Population By Republics	% of Housing Units Built	% of Sq.M. Housing Space Built	% of Population By Republics
U.S.S.R.	....	....	....	....	....	....
Armenia	.8	.8	.9	1.2	1.3	.9
Azerbaidzhan	1.9	1.7	1.8	1.9	1.7	2.0
Belorussia	2.9	3.0	3.8	3.3	3.4	3.7
Estonia	.4	.5	.6	.5	.5	.6
Georgia	1.2	1.6	1.9	1.3	1.6	2.0
Kazakhstan	6.3	6.7	4.8	6.2	6.5	5.2
Kirgizia	.9	.8	1.0	1.1	1.0	1.1
Latvia	.6	.7	1.0	.7	.7	1.0
Lithuania	.6	.7	1.3	1.1	1.2	1.3
Moldavia	1.5	1.5	1.4	1.1	1.1	1.5
R.S.F.S.R.	60.0	58.0	55.8	58.3	56.2	54.6
Tadzhikistan	.8	.7	1.0	1.0	.9	1.1
Turkmenia	.8	.9	.8	.7	.8	.8
Ukraine	18.1	19.0	19.9	18.1	19.4	19.6
Uzbekistan	3.1	3.4	4.0	3.5	3.7	4.6

Republic	1966			1967		
	% of Housing Units Built	% of Sq.M. Housing Space Built	% of Population By Republics	% of Housing Units Built	% of Sq.M. Housing Space Built	% of Population By Republics
U.S.S.R.	....	....	....	....	....	....
Armenia	1.1	1.2	1.0	1.1	1.2	1.0
Azerbaidzhan	1.8	1.6	2.0	1.7	1.5	2.1
Belorussia	3.4	3.6	3.7	3.7	3.8	3.7
Estonia	.5	.5	.6	.5	.5	.6
Georgia	1.3	1.7	2.0	1.2	1.7	2.0
Kazakhstan	6.0	6.1	5.3	6.2	6.2	5.4
Kirgizia	1.1	1.1	1.2	1.2	1.2	1.1
Latvia	.8	.8	1.0	.8	.8	1.0
Lithuania	1.2	1.2	1.3	1.3	1.3	1.3
Moldavia	1.1	1.3	1.5	1.3	1.5	1.5
R.S.F.S.R.	57.1	54.6	54.3	56.8	54.3	53.9
Tadzhikistan	.9	1.0	1.1	1.1	1.1	1.2
Turkmenia	.7	.9	.8	.8	.9	.9
Ukraine	18.3	19.5	19.6	17.7	18.7	19.6
Uzbekistan	4.5	4.7	4.7	4.7	5.2	4.8

Republic	1968		
	% of Housing Units Built	% of Sq. M. Housing Space Built	% of Population By Republics
U.S.S.R.	....	....	....
Armenia	1.0	1.0	1.0
Azerbaidzhan	1.9	1.7	2.1
Belorussia	3.9	4.1	3.7
Estonia	.6	.6	.6
Georgia	1.2	1.7	2.0
Kazakhstan	5.9	5.9	5.4
Kirgizia	1.2	1.3	1.2
Latvia	.9	.9	1.0
Lithuania	1.3	1.5	1.3
Moldavia	1.2	1.4	1.5
R.S.F.S.R.	57.6	54.9	53.8
Tadzhikistan	1.0	1.1	1.2
Turkmenia	.8	.9	.9
Ukraine	16.7	18.2	19.6
Uzbekistan	4.7	5.0	4.9

Table 13. INCREASE IN URBAN HOUSING (In Million Square Meters of Housing Space)

Republic	Increase in Urban Housing	New Construction	Transferral of Rural Into Urban Settlements	Loss of Housing Due to Razing & Other Causes
U.S.S.R.				
1960	62,286	59,030	9,089	5,833
1961	58,350	56,114	7,831	5,595
1962	57,728	58,858	5,389	6,519
1963	56,097	58,469	4,954	7,326
1964	51,545	57,459	3,556	9,470
1965	55,560	60,597	5,919	10,956
1966	52,240	63,400	2,880	14,040
1967	59,942	66,108	3,082	9,248
1968	60,181	66,086	3,774	9,679
1960-1968	513,929	546,121	46,474	78,666
Including (1960-1968)				
Armenia	5,791	5,929	531	669
Azerbaidzhan	8,383	8,407	971	995
Belorussia	16,111	15,993	1,633	1,515
Estonia	3,609	3,986	153	530
Georgia	8,821	7,674	1,931	784
Kazakhstan	26,892	27,772	3,091	3,971
Kirgizia	3,726	3,431	583	288
Latvia	5,187	5,271	377	461
Lithuania	6,015	6,625	49	659
Moldavia	5,190	4,346	1,234	390
R.S.F.S.R.	303,331	331,871	24,455	52,995
Tadzhikistan	3,552	3,374	592	414
Turkmenia	3,625	4,073	209	657
Ukraine	103,026	102,506	9,381	8,861
Uzbekistan	10,623	14,816	1,284	5,477

Table 14. COOPERATIVE HOUSING BUILT (IN THOUSAND SQUARE METERS OF HOUSING SPACE) AS PERCENTAGE OF TOTAL HOUSING BUILT AND PER CAPITA BY REPUBLIC

Republic	1963 Sq. Meters of Co-ops Built (Thous.Sq.M.)	1963 % of Total Housing Space Built	1963 Per Capita Built (Sq.M.)	1964 Sq. Meters of Co-ops Built (Thous.Sq.M.)	1964 % of Total Housing Space Built	1964 Per Capita Built (Sq.M.)
U.S.S.R.	1,840	1.9	.008	4,791	5.2	.02
Armenia	...	...	...	26	...	.01
Azerbaidzhan	...	...	...	23	...	.005
Belorussia	89	...	.01	154	...	.02
Estonia	5	...	.004	30	...	.02
Georgia	34	...	.008	103	...	.002
Kazakhstan	35	...	.003	64	...	.005
Kirgizia	8	...	.003	14	...	.005
Latvia	23	...	.01	49	...	.02
Lithuania	54	...	.02	94	...	.03
Moldavia	17	...	.005	38	...	.01
R.S.F.S.R.	1,277	...	.01	3,493	...	.03
Tadzhikistan	3	...	.001	1	...	.0004
Turkmenia	...	...	...	0.4	...	.002
Ukraine	286	...	.006	659	...	.01
Uzbekistan	9	...	.0009	43	...	.004

Republic	1965 Sq. Meters of Co-ops Built (Thous.Sq.M.)	1965 % of Total Housing Space Built	1965 Per Capita Built (Sq.M.)	1966 Sq. Meters of Co-ops Built (Thous.Sq.M.)	1966 % of Total Housing Space Built	1966 Per Capita Built (Sq.M.)
U.S.S.R.	6,513	6.7	.03	6,743	6.6	.03
Armenia	96	7.4	.04	46	3.6	.02
Azerbaidzhan	65	3.9	.01	49	3.0	.01
Belorussia	288	8.8	.03	285	7.7	.03
Estonia	45	8.5	.04	41	7.8	.03
Georgia	87	5.6	.02	111	6.3	.02
Kazakhstan	118	1.9	.009	129	2.1	.01
Kirgizia	23	2.3	.009	18	1.5	.007
Latvia	75	10.6	.003	95	11.5	.04
Lithuania	158	1.4	.05	170	13.7	.06
Moldavia	46	4.3	.01	57	4.2	.02
R.S.F.S.R.	4,487	8.2	.04	4,505	8.1	.04
Tadzhikistan	19	2.1	.007	4	.04	.001
Turkmenia	1	.01	.0005	2	.02	.001
Ukraine	916	4.8	.02	1,141	5.7	.02
Uzbekistan	89	2.5	.008	90	1.9	.008

Table 14. Cooperative Housing Built (in Thousand Square Meters of Housing Space) as Percentage of Total Housing Built and per Capita by Republic (Continued)

Republic	1967			1968		
	Sq. Meters of Co-ops Built (Thous.Sq.M.)	% of Total Housing Space Built	Per Capita Built (Sq.M.)	Sq. Meters of Co-ops Built (Thous.Sq.M.)	% of Total Housing Space Built	Per Capita Built (Sq.M.)
U.S.S.R.	6,538	6.3	.03	6,442	6.3	.03
Armenia	37	2.9	.04	90	8.7	.04
Azerbaidzhan	65	4.0	.01	66	3.7	.01
Belorussia	316	7.9	.04	302	7.2	.03
Estonia	50	9.0	.05	62	9.8	.05
Georgia	134	7.5	.03	85	5.0	.02
Kazakhstan	115	1.8	.009	109	1.8	.008
Kirgizia	18	1.4	.006	38	3.0	.01
Latvia	87	10.5	.04	77	8.7	.03
Lithuania	191	14.0	.06	153	10.2	.05
Moldavia	85	5.4	.02	66	4.7	.02
R.S.F.S.R.	4,222	7.4	.03	4,196	7.5	.03
Tadzhikistan	26	2.3	.007	19	1.8	.006
Turkmenia	3	.03	.002	4	.04	.002
Ukraine	1,093	5.6	.02	1,108	6.0	.02
Uzbekistan	96	1.8	.008	67	1.3	.005

Table 15. Per Capita Investment in Housing Construction by Republics (in Million Rubles)

Republic	1958		1960		1963	
	Total Investment	Per Capita (Rubles)	Total Investment	Per Capita (Rubles)	Total Investment	Per Capita (Rubles)
U.S.S.R.	7,536.0	36.1	8,209	38.0	7,714.0	34.1
Armenia	56.8	32.2	61	32.2	84.4	40.8
Azerbaidzhan	94.8	25.6	111	27.9	111.5	25.4
Belorussia	193.6	24.0	211	25.7	203.0	24.0
Estonia	36.0	30.1	44	36.0	43.4	34.5
Georgia	89.8	22.2	112	26.7	110.5	25.0
Kazakhstan	403.2	43.3	550	53.0	567.6	49.3
Kirgizia	48.7	23.6	59	26.5	56.2	22.6
Latvia	51.4	24.6	56	26.1	58.4	26.3
Lithuania	44.3	16.3	53	18.9	72.4	24.9
Moldavia	67.8	23.5	78	25.7	61.2	18.9
R.S.F.S.R.	4,898.9	41.7	5,192	43.1	4,782.6	38.4
Tadzhikistan	45.1	22.8	48	22.8	56.2	24.0
Turkmenia	41.5	27.4	52	32.0	48.5	26.9
Ukraine	1,273.5	30.4	1,385	32.1	1,277.6	28.6
Uzbekistan	191.0	23.6	197	22.7	180.4	18.4

Republic	1964		1965		1966	
	Total Investment	Per Capita (Rubles)	Total Investment	Per Capita (Rubles)	Total Investment	Per Capita (Rubles)
U.S.S.R.	7,394.0	32.3	8,162	35.2	8,957	38.2
Armenia	85.7	40.2	96	43.8	104	46.2
Azerbaidzhan	103.7	23.0	109	23.4	116	24.2
Belorussia	213.4	25.0	238	27.6	273	31.2
Estonia	44.7	35.1	47	36.6	55	42.5
Georgia	102.5	22.9	115	25.3	136	29.5
Kazakhstan	503.4	42.5	585	48.3	593	47.8
Kirgizia	61.3	23.9	68	25.7	78	28.4
Latvia	57.3	25.6	68	30.1	79	34.6
Lithuania	75.3	25.5	93	31.1	109	36.0
Moldavia	64.6	19.6	72	21.4	85	24.8
R.S.F.S.R.	4,584.4	36.5	5,019	39.7	5,362	42.1
Tadzhikistan	54.2	21.8	64	24.9	66	24.9
Turkmenia	48.5	26.0	51	26.7	65	33.1
Ukraine	1,191.5	26.4	1,295	28.5	1,439	31.3
Uzbekistan	203.5	20.1	242	22.9	397	36.4

Republic	1967		1968	
	Total Investment	Per Capita (Rubles)	Total Investment	Per Capita (Rubles)
U.S.S.R.	9,643	40.5	10,120	42.4
Armenia	106	45.4	113	47.8
Azerbaidzhan	123	24.7	133	26.4
Belorussia	319	36.0	347	39.0
Estonia	59	45.1	72	54.7
Georgia	140	29.9	145	30.8
Kazakhstan	650	50.7	652	50.6
Kirgizia	87	30.2	98	33.5
Latvia	87	37.7	98	42.2
Lithuania	126	40.9	143	46.1
Moldavia	103	29.3	103	29.2
R.S.F.S.R.	5,712	44.6	6,040	47.0
Tadzhikistan	78	28.1	88	31.2
Turkmenia	69	33.4	67	32.1
Ukraine	1,491	32.0	1,535	32.8
Uzbekistan	493	43.0	482	41.3

Table 16. PERCENTAGE OF TOTAL HOUSING CONSTRUCTION BUDGET ALLOCATED TO REPUBLICS

Republic	1950	1958	1960	1963	1964	1966	1967	1968
Budget U.S.S.R.	2,023 (billion rubles)	7,536 (billion rubles)	8,209 (billion rubles)	7,714 (billion rubles)	7,394 (billion rubles)	8,957 (billion rubles)	9,643 (billion rubles)	10,120 (billion rubles)
Armenia	.9%	.8%	.7%	1.1%	1.2%	1.2%	1.0%	1.1%
Azerbaidzhan	1.6%	1.3%	1.4%	1.4%	1.4%	1.3%	1.3%	1.3%
Belorussia	3.3%	2.6%	2.6%	2.6%	2.9%	3.0%	3.3%	3.4%
Estonia	.5%	.5%	.5%	.6%	.6%	.6%	.6%	.7%
Georgia	1.9%	1.2%	1.4%	1.4%	1.4%	1.5%	1.5%	1.4%
Kazakhstan	4.9%	5.4%	6.7%	7.4%	6.8%	6.6%	6.7%	6.4%
Kirgizia	.8%	.6%	.7%	.7%	.8%	.9%	.9%	1.0%
Latvia	.5%	.7%	.7%	.8%	.8%	.9%	.9%	1.0%
Lithuania	.4%	.6%	.6%	.9%	1.0%	1.2%	1.3%	1.4%
Moldavia	.5%	.9%	1.0%	.8%	.9%	.9%	1.1%	1.0%
R.S.F.S.R.	62.3%	65.0%	63.2%	62.0%	62.0%	59.9%	59.2%	59.7%
Tadzhikistan	.7%	.6%	.6%	.7%	.7%	.7%	.8%	.9%
Turkmenia	1.0%	.6%	.6%	.6%	.7%	.7%	.7%	.7%
Ukraine	18.5%	16.9%	16.9%	16.6%	16.1%	16.1%	15.5%	15.2%
Uzbekistan	2.4%	2.5%	2.4%	2.3%	2.8%	4.4%	5.1%	4.8%

Table 17. HOUSING UNITS BUILT PER 1,000 PEOPLE IN THE USSR

Year	Total Housing Units Built (millions)	Units Per 1,000 People
1950	1,073	...
1958	2,382	11.4
1959	2,711	12.8
1960	2,591	12.0
1961	2,435	11.8
1962	2,383	10.7
1963	2,322	10.3
1964	2,184	9.5
1965	2,227	9.6
1966	2,291	9.8
1967	2,312	9.7
1968	2,233	9.3

CHAPTER V TABLE SOURCE NOTES

TABLE 1

N.K. *1958*, p. 641.
N.K. *1961*, p. 614.
N.K. *1963*, p. 515.
N.K. *1964*, p. 610.
N.K. *1965*, p. 615.
N.K. *1968*, p. 580.

TABLE 2

D. L. Broner, "Zhilishchnaya problema v trudykh i gosudarstvennoi deyatelnosti V.I. Lenina," *Vestnik Statistiki,* no. 3, 1970, p. 10.

TABLE 3

N.K. *1960*, pp. 10, 613.
N.K. *1961*, p. 615.
N.K. *1963*, p. 515.
N.K. *1964*, p. 610.
N.K. *1965*, p. 615.
N.K. *1967*, p. 682.
N.K. *1968*, pp. 10, 580.

TABLE 4

N.K. *1956*, p. 24.
N.K. *1959*, p. 35.
N.K. *1960*, p. 614.

N.K. 1963, p. 516.
N.K. 1968, pp. 23, 583.

Table 5

N.K. 1968, pp. 580, 581.

Table 6

N.K. 1968, p. 573.

Table 7

N.K. 1968, p. 574.

Table 8

N.K. 1968, pp. 575, 577, 578.

Table 9

N.K. 1968, p. 574.

Table 10

N.K. 1968, pp. 575, 576.

Table 11

N.K. 1960, p. 8.
N.K. 1967, p. 16.
N.K. 1968, pp. 9, 576.

Table 12

N.K. 1960, p. 8.
N.K. 1967, p. 16.
N.K. 1968, pp. 9, 575, 576.

Table 13

N.K. 1968, p. 582.

Table 14

N.K. 1963, p. 9.
N.K. 1964, p. 9.
N.K. 1967, p. 16.
N.K. 1968, pp. 9, 575, 579.

Table 15

N.K. 1964, p. 606.
N.K. 1968, p. 516.

Table 16

N.K. 1964, p. 606.
N.K. 1968, p. 576.

Table 17

N.K. 1964, p. 609.
N.K. 1968, p. 575.

EDUCATION

A: JONATHAN POOL AND JEREMY AZRAEL
B: JAAN PENNAR, IVAN I. BAKALO, AND
   GEORGE Z. F. BEREDAY

THE SOVIET REGIME is justifiably proud of the educational progress that has taken place in the USSR during the fifty-odd years of Communist rule. These years have seen the development of a comprehensive network of schools for both young people and adults. Mass illiteracy has been eradicated, and most non-Russian youths can read and write Russian in addition to their native tongues. Universal compulsory education, which was first introduced after the Bolshevik Revolution, has been extended to eight years and is slated to reach ten years in the near future. Already over 50 percent of all Soviet students continue their education beyond the eighth grade (the terminal point of their so-called "incomplete secondary education"), and roughly 40 percent manage to graduate from either specialized secondary or general (ten year) secondary schools. Of these graduates, in turn, approximately 20 percent go on to higher education, thereby qualifying for candidate membership in the multitudinous ranks of the "new Soviet intelligentsia."

These are indeed impressive accomplishments. However, they do not add up to quite the educational miracle that is sometimes alleged to have occurred. In the first place, the Tsarist empire was not an educational wasteland, and many of the Bolshevik achievements of the 1920's and 1930's were foreshadowed in the particularly rapid educational development that took place during the last years of Tsarist rule. In the second place, most peasant children (including the vast majority of Central Asian natives) received only four years of formal education until well after World War II. In the third place, even today, somewhere between 10 and 20 percent of all Soviet students fail to complete the eighth grade, and the dropout rate in rural areas approaches 30 percent. In the fourth place, approximately 40 percent of the students in grades 9 and 10 and over 50 percent of the students in institutions of higher education are part-time students who receive distinctly inferior training. In the fifth place, many Soviet institutions of higher education offer narrowly specialized training of a sort that would not qualify for university status in the West. Finally, the student body of the better Soviet universities and institutes is drawn predominantly from the ranks of the "state bourgeoisie" and is no more democratic in its composition than comparable groups in the West.

The reason for emphasizing these points is not to detract from real Soviet successes but to forestall certain misleading interpretations of the data in the following tables. Almost all these data are drawn from official Soviet statistical handbooks, and one of the major purposes of these handbooks is to celebrate the achievements of the Communist regime. As a result, they characteristically omit or conceal "unpleasant" information, especially information about the true state of affairs under Stalin, when figures on educational development were grossly inflated. These distortions can be identified and at least partially corrected by careful scrutiny of other, less accessible, Soviet sources as well as by the exercise of a certain amount of analytical ingenuity. However, there is no way to generate completely reliable aggregate data to replace or supplement the official figures, and for the purposes at hand, it has seemed advisable to allow these figures to stand but to introduce them with some appropriate cautionary notes. With these caveats in mind, the tables that follow can be safely used for many kinds of comparative analysis.

Table A.1. LITERACY: PERCENTAGE OF POPULATION AGED 9–49

Territory	Both Sexes			Male			Female		
	1926	1939	1959	1926	1939	1959	1926	1939	1959
URBAN & RURAL									
U.S.S.R.	56.6	87.4	98.5	71.5	93.5	99.3	42.7	81.6	97.8
Armenia	38.7	83.9	98.4	53.7	92.7	99.2	22.7	74.7	97.6
Azerbaidzhan	28.2	82.8	97.3	36.1	88.8	98.8	19.2	76.1	96.0
Belorussia	59.7	80.8	99.0	79.1	90.7	99.5	41.3	71.4	98.6
Estonia	...	98.6	99.6	...	98.9	99.7	...	98.3	99.5
Georgia	53.0	89.3	99.0	61.2	93.4	99.4	44.6	85.2	98.6
Kazakhstan	25.2	83.6	96.9	35.4	90.3	98.8	14.5	75.8	95.1
Kirgizia	16.5	79.8	98.0	23.9	84.9	99.0	8.4	74.4	97.0
Latvia	...	92.7	99.0	...	94.6	99.4	...	91.0	98.8
Lithuania	...	76.7	98.5	...	78.7	98.9	...	75.0	98.1
Moldavia	...	45.9	97.8	...	59.0	99.1	...	33.1	96.6
R.S.F.S.R.	60.9	89.7	98.5	77.1	96.0	99.3	46.4	83.9	97.7
Tadzhikistan	3.8	82.8	96.2	6.4	87.4	98.0	0.9	77.5	94.6
Turkmenia	14.0	77.7	95.4	18.3	83.0	97.7	8.8	71.9	93.4
Ukraine	63.6	88.2	99.1	81.1	93.9	99.6	47.2	82.9	98.8
Uzbekistan	11.6	78.7	98.1	15.3	83.6	99.0	7.3	73.3	97.3
URBAN									
U.S.S.R.	80.9	93.8	98.7	88.0	97.1	99.5	73.9	90.7	98.1
Armenia	68.8	91.9	98.3	76.7	96.3	99.2	59.6	87.2	97.6
Azerbaidzhan	58.7	89.1	97.3	68.9	94.4	99.0	47.0	83.7	95.8
Belorussia	85.7	93.8	99.1	91.9	97.2	99.6	79.1	90.6	98.7
Estonia	...	99.3	99.7	...	99.5	99.8	...	99.1	99.6
Georgia	80.3	94.7	99.0	84.6	96.9	99.5	75.8	92.6	98.5
Kazakhstan	61.0	87.5	96.9	70.3	93.4	98.9	51.6	80.8	95.2
Kirgizia	41.3	85.6	97.9	50.3	89.5	99.1	31.0	81.0	96.8
Latvia	...	96.1	99.4	...	97.1	99.6	...	95.2	99.2
Lithuania	...	83.9	98.9	...	84.9	99.3	...	82.9	98.5
Moldavia	...	70.9	96.9	...	80.3	98.6	...	61.7	95.5
R.S.F.S.R.	85.0	94.9	98.6	91.9	98.1	99.6	78.4	91.8	98.2
Tadzhikistan	19.5	86.8	95.7	29.2	90.5	97.9	6.6	82.2	93.7
Turkmenia	65.6	85.4	95.7	73.8	89.4	98.1	51.4	81.0	93.5
Ukraine	82.1	94.2	99.1	90.0	97.6	99.7	74.2	91.0	98.7
Uzbekistan	39.8	86.8	98.0	49.6	90.4	99.0	28.6	82.8	97.1
RURAL									
U.S.S.R.	50.6	84.0	98.2	67.3	91.6	99.1	35.4	76.8	97.5
Armenia	30.5	80.1	98.4	47.0	90.9	99.3	13.3	68.8	97.6
Azerbaidzhan	13.7	78.5	97.4	20.5	85.3	98.7	5.8	70.6	96.1
Belorussia	53.7	77.1	99.0	75.9	88.9	99.4	33.3	65.8	98.6
Estonia	...	98.2	99.1	...	98.6	99.4	...	97.8	99.4
Georgia	43.7	86.5	99.0	53.0	91.6	99.3	34.3	81.3	98.7
Kazakhstan	21.6	81.9	96.8	31.9	89.1	98.7	10.6	73.7	95.0
Kirgizia	13.0	78.3	98.1	20.1	83.7	99.0	5.3	72.7	97.2
Latvia	...	90.8	98.5	...	93.2	99.0	...	88.5	98.1
Lithuania	...	74.4	98.2	...	76.6	98.6	...	72.5	97.9
Moldavia	...	41.7	98.0	...	55.4	99.3	...	28.4	97.0
R.S.F.S.R.	55.0	86.7	98.0	73.3	94.8	99.1	38.8	79.3	97.1
Tadzhikistan	2.0	81.8	96.5	3.6	86.6	98.0	0.3	76.5	95.1
Turkmenia	4.6	73.2	95.2	7.6	79.2	97.3	1.3	66.5	93.2
Ukraine	58.7	85.0	99.1	78.6	91.9	99.5	40.3	78.5	98.9
Uzbekistan	3.5	76.1	98.2	5.5	81.4	98.9	1.2	70.2	97.5

Note:

1926 figures are for U.S.S.R. boundaries before 1939; 1939 - postwar boundaries.

Table A.2. KINDERGARTENS AND COMBINED NURSERY SCHOOL–KINDERGARTENS

Year	U.S.S.R.	Armenia	Azerbaidzhan	Belorussia	Estonia	Georgia	Kazakhstan[a]	Kirgi...
1927-28[b]	2,132	...	...	90	...	...	...	...
1940	23,999	286	909	823	91	664	545	101
1950	25,624	238	539	425	127	514	669	170
1955	31,596	258	549	597	170	569	835	219
1956	33,788	274	562	613	181	579	913[c]	235
1957	34,366	311	573	640	184	554	1,182[c]	235
1958	36,795	329	609	692	210	606	1,348	285
1959	39,890	354	644	772	229	627	1,534	298
1960	43,569	416	668	877	244	669	1,803	338
1961	48,557	470	696	988	277	710	2,416	376
1962	52,662	551	741	1,120	313	761	2,832	410
1963	57,561	564	810	1,249	335	838	3,291	436
1964	62,314	651	886	1,377	381	921	3,550	504
1965	67,537	666	943	1,525	432	997	4,143	547
1966	72,103	717	953	1,660	467	1,091	4,434	586
1967	75,099	769	1,160	1,768	491	1,186	4,614	639
1968	78,340	820	1,171	1,865	520	1,253	4,838	675

Year	Latvia	Lithuania	Moldavia	R.S.F.S.R.	Tadzhikistan	Turkmenia	Ukraine	Uzbeki...
1927-28[b]	...	...	...	1,387	0	40	343	
1940	87	249	58	15,409	103	502	3,384	7
1950	154	197	112	17,775	150	463	3,312	7
1955	248	245	176	22,063	164	454	3,945	1,1
1956	244	254	186	23,466	165	473	4,187	1,4
1957	241	256	190	23,807	197	483	4,204	1,3
1958	260	264	211	25,491	197	512	4,449	1,3
1959	282	278	230	27,716	238	534	4,790	1,3
1960	305	298	263	30,123	252	544	5,283	1,4
1961	337	323	351	32,840	292	641	5,878	1,9
1962	380	376	433	35,040	306	673	6,498	2,2
1963	425	422	475	37,627	322	707	7,666	2,3
1964	469	482	558	40,462	334	717	8,712	2,3
1965	516	544	618	43,401	349	698	9,713	2,4
1966	572	588	638	45,924	375	808	10,612	2,6
1967	608	623	698	47,813	384	695	11,229	2,4
1968	639	654	760	49,856	403	689	11,715	2,4

Notes:

[a] Figures from 1940 through 1963 have been adjusted to correspond with borders after transfer of part of Kazakhstan to Uzbekistan on January 26, 1963.

[b] Figures for 1927-28 are for kindergartens and "children's hearths," and for boundaries as of 1932.

[c] Adjustment estimated by interpolation.

Table A.3. CHILDREN ENROLLED IN KINDERGARTENS AND COMBINED NURSERY SCHOOL–KINDERGARTENS (In Thousands)

Year	U.S.S.R.	Armenia	Azerbaidzhan	Belorussia	Estonia	Georgia	Kazakhstan[a]	Kirgizia
1940	1,171.5	14.5	43.8	45.5	5.2	38.7	21.2	3.7
1950	1,168.8	10.3	21.9	19.9	5.4	24.0	26.1	6.6
1953	1,438.3	10.5	23.6	25.3	6.7	27.1	32.8	8.0
1955	1,730.9	13.2	26.2	34.2	8.0	30.6	42.8	10.8
1956	1,882.0	14.5	27.1	37.8	9.1	32.2	46.8[b]	13.0
1957	2,095.1	16.7	29.9	42.8	10.1	33.7	62.9[b]	14.8
1958	2,354.1	19.2	32.9	48.1	12.3	36.6	74.0	18.8
1959	2,671.1	22.8	36.8	57.6	13.9	40.7	88.8	21.4
1960	3,115.1	29.8	40.2	70.4	16.0	46.3	111.1	26.2
1961	3,627.2	35.7	45.6	85.2	19.1	51.0	146.8	30.6
1962	4,171.7	41.3	50.9	102.1	22.3	56.7	185.1	35.2
1963	4,813.0	46.3	58.2	121.5	25.3	65.6	241.7	40.0
1964	5,496.0	53.8	67.1	143.4	30.5	72.5	292.6	49.6
1965	6,207.3	62.0	76.6	168.5	35.3	83.6	360.2	55.8
1966	6,778.0	68.8	83.1	188.7	39.5	91.9	404.3	61.5
1967	7,191.6	75.7	95.0	204.0	42.6	98.5	436.7	68.2
1968	7,537.0	81.6	95.1	217.2	46.4	103.4	469.1	73.6

Notes:

[a] See Note a, Table A.2.

[b] See Note c, Table A.2.

Table A.3. Children Enrolled in Kindergartens and Combined Nursery School–Kindergartens (Continued)

Year	Latvia	Lithuania	Moldavia	R.S.F.S.R.	Tadzhikistan	Turkmenia	Ukraine	Uzbekistan[a]
1940	5.5	13.3	3.0	751.9	3.1	16.0	172.2	33.9
1950	7.0	6.5	4.2	829.8	5.2	15.3	155.8	30.8
1953	10.0	8.0	6.4	1,028.3	7.0	20.6	185.0	39.0
1955	11.7	9.3	8.9	1,226.4	9.6	23.1	219.1	57.0
1956	12.1	10.0	9.6	1,326.9	10.8	25.3	236.7	70.1[b]
1957	13.1	11.0	11.1	1,474.6	13.6	27.5	261.2	72.1[b]
1958	14.8	12.4	13.1	1,653.8	15.8	29.0	292.2	81.1
1959	16.6	13.9	15.8	1,868.8	19.3	30.6	330.7	93.4
1960	19.6	16.0	19.8	2,149.7	23.3	34.8	399.4	112.5
1961	23.3	18.4	25.8	2,458.6	27.9	38.1	479.0	138.1
1962	28.6	24.3	34.4	2,774.7	30.7	43.9	573.6	167.9
1963	33.3	29.3	41.0	3,140.5	34.8	47.3	702.9	185.3
1964	39.4	35.6	49.7	3,522.0	39.4	54.5	841.3	204.6
1965	45.9	42.9	57.5	3,913.3	47.0	59.8	971.5	227.4
1966	52.1	50.5	62.7	4,213.4	52.4	66.4	1,086.5	256.2
1967	56.4	57.2	69.4	4,435.7	54.3	63.8	1,173.0	261.1
1968	60.4	64.2	76.0	4,620.2	55.7	62.3	1,234.2	277.6

Table A.3a. Children Enrolled in Kindergartens and Combined Nursery School–Kindergartens per 1,000 Population

Year	U.S.S.R.	Armenia	Azerbaidzhan	Belorussia	Estonia	Georgia	Kazakhstan	Kirgizia
1940	6.0	11.0	13.3	5.0	4.9	10.7	3.5	2.4
1950	6.6	7.7	7.7	2.6	4.9	6.9	4.0	3.9
1955	8.9	8.6	8.0	4.4	6.9	8.1	5.6	5.7
1956	9.5	9.1	8.0	4.8	7.8	8.3	5.7	6.8
1957	10.4	10.2	8.6	5.4	8.6	8.6	7.4	7.6
1958	11.5	11.3	9.2	6.0	10.4	9.2	8.5	9.4
1959	12.8	12.9	10.0	8.1	11.7	10.1	9.7	10.4
1960	14.7	16.3	10.5	8.7	13.4	11.2	11.5	12.3
1961	16.8	18.9	11.5	10.4	15.8	12.2	14.4	13.8
1962	19.0	21.1	12.4	12.3	18.1	13.3	17.2	15.2
1963	21.6	23.1	13.8	14.4	20.3	15.1	21.5	16.8
1964	24.3	26.0	15.3	17.0	24.2	16.4	25.4	19.9
1965	27.1	29.1	17.0	19.8	27.7	18.7	30.4	21.0
1966	29.2	31.4	17.8	21.9	30.7	20.2	33.4	23.2
1967	30.7	33.6	19.8	23.3	32.9	21.4	35.2	24.8
1968	31.8	35.4	19.3	24.6	35.6	22.2	37.0	26.0

Year	Latvia	Lithuania	Moldavia	R.S.F.S.R.	Tadzhikistan	Turkmenia	Ukraine	Uzbekistan
1940	2.9	4.6	1.2	6.8	2.0	12.3	4.2	5.1
1950	3.6	2.5	1.8	8.2	3.4	12.8	4.3	4.9
1955	5.8	3.6	3.4	11.1	5.5	17.2	5.6	7.8
1956	6.0	3.8	3.6	11.8	6.0	18.5	6.0	9.4
1957	6.4	4.1	4.1	12.9	7.3	19.5	6.5	9.4
1958	7.1	4.7	4.7	14.3	8.2	19.9	7.1	10.2
1959	7.9	5.1	5.5	15.9	9.8	20.2	7.9	11.3
1960	9.3	5.8	6.7	18.1	11.5	22.2	9.4	13.2
1961	10.9	6.6	8.5	20.4	13.3	23.5	11.1	15.6
1962	13.2	8.5	11.1	22.7	14.1	26.1	13.2	18.3
1963	15.2	10.2	12.9	25.4	15.4	27.2	16.0	19.5
1964	17.8	12.2	15.3	28.2	16.8	30.2	18.9	20.8
1965	20.5	14.6	17.4	31.3	18.9	32.1	21.5	22.4
1966	23.0	16.9	18.6	33.3	20.4	34.7	23.9	24.2
1967	24.7	18.9	20.3	34.8	20.5	32.5	25.5	24.0
1968	26.3	21.0	21.8	36.1	20.4	30.7	26.6	24.6

Note: See Notes to Table A.3.

Table A.4.   PERSONS WITH SECONDARY EDUCATION (In Thousands)

Territory	Both Sexes		Male		Female	
	1939	1959	1939	1959	1939	1959
U.S.S.R.						
Total	14,689	54,930	8,053	25,711	6,636	29,218
Urban	9,806	34,458	4,954	15,531	4,852	18,927
Rural	4,884	20,472	3,099	10,180	1,784	10,292
Armenia						
Total	104	508	67	251	37	257
Urban	69	307	40	146	28	161
Rural	36	201	27	105	9	96
Azerbaidzhan						
Total	235	967	152	519	83	449
Urban	172	562	100	282	71	280
Rural	63	405	51	236	11	169
Belorussia						
Total	595	1,814	349	845	247	969
Urban	340	922	172	401	168	520
Rural	255	892	176	444	79	449
Estonia						
Total	136	364	68	155	68	209
Urban	92	264	43	112	49	152
Rural	44	100	25	43	19	57
Georgia						
Total	401	1,271	217	548	185	686
Urban	262	695	130	307	132	388
Rural	140	576	87	277	53	299
Kazakhstan						
Total	365	2,215	254	1,143	111	1,072
Urban	190	1,209	118	588	72	621
Rural	175	1,007	136	555	38	452
Kirgizia						
Total	47	470	30	248	17	223
Urban	28	215	16	104	12	111
Rural	19	255	14	143	6	112
Latvia						
Total	265	722	148	318	116	404
Urban	225	501	126	217	99	284
Rural	40	221	22	102	18	120
Lithuania						
Total	184	476	115	216	69	260
Urban	138	317	87	141	52	176
Rural	46	159	29	74	18	85
Moldavia						
Total	97	535	56	271	41	263
Urban	49	211	25	97	23	114
Rural	49	324	31	174	18	150
R.S.F.S.R.						
Total	8,291	30,904	4,364	13,967	3,927	16,937
Urban	5,727	20,818	2,801	9,185	2,927	11,633
Rural	2,564	10,086	1,563	4,782	1,001	5,304
Tadzhikistan						
Total	40	426	28	237	12	189
Urban	27	181	18	92	10	89
Rural	13	245	10	145	2	100
Turkmenia						
Total	58	388	37	202	21	187
Urban	46	205	27	103	19	102
Rural	12	183	10	99	1	85
Ukraine						
Total	3,625	11,973	2,012	5,730	1,613	6,243
Urban	2,266	7,220	1,148	3,343	1,117	3,877
Rural	1,359	4,753	863	2,387	496	2,366
Uzbekistan						
Total	246	1,897	157	1,026	89	870
Urban	176	932	102	411	73	420
Rural	70	1,065	55	615	15	450

Note:

    1926 figures are for U.S.S.R. boundaries before 1939; 1939 -
postwar boundaries.

Table A.4a. PERSONS WITH SECONDARY EDUCATION PER 1,000 POPULATION

Republic	1939[a]	1959
U.S.S.R.	75.7	263.0
Armenia	78.8	288.2
Azerbaidzhan	71.8	261.5
Belorussia	65.8	225.2
Estonia	129.0	307.2
Georgia	111.0	314.3
Kazakhstan	60.3	242.0
Kirgizia	30.8	227.5
Latvia	140.5	345.0
Lithuania	62.9	175.6
Moldavia	39.3	185.4
R.S.F.S.R.	75.3	262.9
Tadzhikistan	26.2	215.2
Turkmenia	44.6	129.0
Ukraine	87.7	286.0
Uzbekistan	37.0	229.6

Note:

[a]Population figures are for 1940.

Table A.5. PRIMARY AND GENERAL SECONDARY SCHOOLS (Includes Evening and Adult Schools)

Year	U.S.S.R.	Armenia	Azerbaidzhan	Belorussia	Estonia	Georgia	Kazakhstan[a]	Kirgizia
1914-15	123,687	459	976	7,682	1,780	1,765	2,000	107
1940-41	198,821	1,218	4,436	12,294	1,255	4,783	7,915	1,698
1950-51	222,093	1,405	4,233	12,715	1,243	4,800	9,370	1,910
1955-56	213,023	1,388	4,272	12,446	1,190	4,533	9,538	1,900
1958-59	215,163	1,382	4,211	12,411	1,199	4,558	10,083	1,902
1959-60	220,568	1,435	4,300	12,772	1,193	4,585	10,125	1,923
1960-61	224,457	1,494	4,433	13,063	1,211	4,665	10,271	1,979
1961-62	228,235	1,550	4,569	12,985	1,255	4,651	10,371	2,035
1962-63	226,728	1,590	4,856	12,967	1,267	4,634	10,523	2,074
1963-64	221,149	1,597	5,186	12,884	1,226	4,672	10,360	2,008
1964-65	218,384	1,604	5,378	13,366	1,156	4,683	10,406	2,064
1965-66	214,290	1,574	5,491	13,000	1,068	4,673	10,578	2,056
1966-67	210,238	1,562	5,618	12,966	1,020	4,685	10,523	1,985
1967-68	206,253	1,529	5,647	12,394	967	4,642	10,439	1,939
1968-69	201,920	1,505	5,643	12,011	932	4,620	10,337	1,936

Year	Latvia	Lithuania	Moldavia	R.S.F.S.R.	Tadzhikistan	Turkmenia	Ukraine	Uzbekistan[a]
1914-15	2,227	1,702	1,314	77,367	10	58	26,069	171
1940-41	1,626	2,865	1,864	116,914	2,789	1,528	32,132	5,504
1950-51	1,659	3,721	3,051	131,324	2,996	1,381	35,961	6,324
1955-56	1,647	4,011	2,782	124,497	2,784	1,281	34,216	6,538
1958-59	1,623	4,143	2,487	125,461	2,800	1,348	34,511	7,044
1959-60	1,615	4,184	2,514	127,835	2,885	1,429	36,437	7,336
1960-61	1,648	4,257	2,569	129,119	2,935	1,467	37,660	7,686
1961-62	1,627	4,859	2,802	128,367	2,901	1,530	40,518	8,215
1962-63	1,550	5,007	2,576	127,431	2,864	1,537	39,603	8,249
1963-64	1,511	4,748	2,509	125,035	2,758	1,566	37,002	8,087
1964-65	1,421	4,589	2,547	123,009	2,779	1,590	35,405	8,387
1965-66	1,382	4,404	2,552	119,746	2,834	1,603	34,613	8,716
1966-67	1,336	4,318	2,393	117,002	2,823	1,620	33,594	8,793
1967-68	1,302	4,274	2,316	114,301	2,847	1,649	32,858	9,149
1968-69	1,254	4,134	2,253	111,796	2,923	1,646	31,850	9,080

Notes:

[a]Figures from 1914-15 through 1963-64 have been adjusted to correspond with borders after transfer of part of Kazakhstan to Uzbekistan on January 26, 1963.

Table A.6. PUPILS ENROLLED IN PRIMARY AND GENERAL SECONDARY SCHOOLS
OF ALL TYPES (In Thousands)

Year	U.S.S.R.	Armenia	Azerbaidzhan	Belorussia	Estonia	Georgia	Kazakhstan	Kirgizia
1940-41	183.2	252.3	212.3	192.0	114.8	212.4	189.6	218.6
1950-51	194.6	236.8	230.9	201.7	142.2	211.2	206.8	199.9
1955-56	154.7	194.1	195.6	166.3	139.2	185.1	173.9	172.9
1956-57	152.6	182.2	189.3	159.5	142.9	179.1	162.8	169.3
1957-58	152.0	176.3	184.3	157.4	143.1	177.6	161.3	167.3
1958-59	153.6	173.3	183.9	157.7	145.2	165.8	170.6	171.0
1959-60	159.9	177.0	195.2	163.4	150.2	161.7	175.3	174.3
1960-61	170.5	185.4	189.9	169.7	154.6	170.3	184.9	186.2
1961-62	180.9	195.0	195.5	178.9	158.0	178.0	194.6	197.7
1962-63	193.2	210.0	210.9	189.6	164.4	188.3	209.3	211.1
1963-64	200.3	224.2	226.7	196.0	168.0	197.7	216.9	224.7
1964-65	206.3	237.8	241.0	204.5	170.0	204.5	228.1	234.0
1965-66	210.5	247.9	252.6	208.8	170.5	209.2	237.0	236.6
1966-67	207.8	252.2	257.1	204.9	167.3	204.1	236.4	247.8
1967-68	208.6	260.1	264.9	205.7	164.6	206.5	238.9	250.6
1968-69	207.9	265.4	270.5	207.4	161.0	208.6	241.8	254.9

Year	Latvia	Lithuania	Moldavia	R.S.F.S.R.	Tadzhikistan	Turkmenia	Ukraine	Uzbekist
1940-41	128.3	165.6	178.3	187.4	206.6	193.6	165.2	199.4
1950-51	151.8	167.1	210.0	191.2	213.4	187.1	195.0	215.0
1955-56	145.3	166.9	153.3	148.2	190.1	173.1	149.8	188.6
1956-57	145.1	161.9	155.4	147.3	183.1	170.0	147.0	182.4
1957-58	140.9	157.9	160.9	148.4	178.7	170.5	145.1	177.5
1958-59	137.6	159.1	163.9	151.4	178.1	169.9	144.1	175.5
1959-60	135.7	162.3	174.0	159.5	184.9	172.2	147.9	176.7
1960-61	138.7	164.1	183.6	171.5	193.3	178.3	158.3	185.8
1961-62	141.0	169.0	199.4	182.2	200.3	187.8	169.4	196.0
1962-63	149.3	178.4	211.2	194.0	209.3	201.6	183.0	208.5
1963-64	152.3	179.6	220.7	200.7	217.9	213.6	188.3	220.5
1964-65	154.3	182.9	227.6	206.2	228.1	223.0	191.0	232.1
1965-66	155.7	190.6	231.9	209.7	234.9	233.6	192.3	244.4
1966-67	151.6	188.2	226.5	206.9	238.2	237.9	186.4	245.3
1967-68	152.7	187.7	225.7	206.4	248.7	246.7	185.4	256.2
1968-69	152.7	185.7	224.2	204.1	255.5	251.9	182.4	264.8

Note:
    See Notes to Table A.6.

Table A.6a. Pupils Enrolled in Primary and General Secondary Schools of All Types per 1,000 Population

Year	U.S.S.R.	Armenia	Azerbaidzhan	Belorussia	Estonia	Georgia	Kazakhstan[a]	Kirgizia
1914-15	9,656	35	73	489	92	157	105	7
1927-28	11,638	83[c]	176	485[c,d]	...	290	271[b]	42
1940-41	35,552	333	695	1,737	121	767	1,148	334
1950-51	34,752	319	660	1,555	156	738	1,349	343
1953-54	32,157	315	639	1,413	157	700	1,327	328
1955-56	30,070	298	641	1,290	161	704	1,321	326
1956-57	30,127	290	639	1,252	166	694	1,331	325
1957-58	30,623	289	642	1,245	168	697	1,379	328
1958-59	31,483	295	661	1,256	172	659	1,492	341
1959-60	33,364	312	685	1,308	178	666	1,605	360
1960-61	36,187	338	725	1,382	185	703	1,789	398
1961-62	39,086	369	776	1,471	192	747	1,986	439
1962-63	42,442	411	868	1,577	203	804	2,250	489
1963-64	44,682	450	959	1,649	209	858	2,443	534
1964-65	46,664	492	1,056	1,729	214	903	2,626	583
1965-66	48,255	529	1,141	1,782	217	938	2,809	629
1966-67	48,170	553	1,199	1,769	215	928	2,866	657
1967-68	48,902	586	1,272	1,799	213	952	2,966	689
1968-69	49,195	612	1,330	1,829	210	972	3,066	723

Year	Latvia	Lithuania	Moldavia	R.S.F.S.R.	Tadzhikistan	Turkmenia	Ukraine	Uzbekistan[a]
1914-15	172	118	92	5,684	0.4	7	2,607	18
1927-28	...	183[c,e]	...	7,544	14	33	2,448[c,d]	145[b]
1940-41	242	380	440	20,633	315	252	6,830	1,325
1950-51	295	430	481	19,399	322	224	7,134	1,347
1953-54	299	444	450	17,569	329	227	6,593	1,367
1955-56	292	436	399	16,381	334	232	5,882	1,372
1956-57	293	428	412	16,533	331	233	5,841	1,359
1957-58	290	421	438	16,921	334	240	5,864	1,367
1958-59	286	424	460	17,510	344	248	5,935	1,400
1959-60	284	440	502	18,744	366	261	6,193	1,460
1960-61	293	453	545	20,398	393	279	6,722	1,584
1961-62	302	474	606	21,968	420	305	7,301	1,730
1962-63	324	509	656	23,681	457	339	7,964	1,910
1963-64	333	517	700	24,777	493	372	8,296	2,092
1964-65	342	532	738	25,709	535	402	8,524	2,279
1965-66	349	556	766	26,374	583	435	8,671	2,476
1966-67	343	562	763	26,187	613	455	8,468	2,592
1967-68	349	568	773	26,277	660	485	8,522	2,791
1968-69	351	569	781	26,100	699	511	8,459	2,983

Notes:

[a] See Note a, Table A.2.

[b] See Note c, Table A.2.

[c] Figure excludes evening schools.

[d] Figure excludes Western part of republic, annexed from Poland in 1939.

[e] Figure is for 1928-29.

Table A.6b. Primary and Secondary Pupils as Percentage of Population Aged 5–19

Year	Percentage of Population Aged 5-19
1950	64%
1955	57%
1956	56%
1957	56%
1958	58%
1959	62%
1960	67%
1961	72%
1962	76%
1963	77%
1964	76%
1965	75%
1966	72%

Table A.7. VOCATIONAL SECONDARY SCHOOLS

Year	U.S.S.R.	Armenia	Azerbaidzhan	Belorussia	Estonia	Georgia	Kazakhstan[a]	Kirgiz
1914-15	450	1	3	15	4	5	7	0
1927-28	1,037	12	37	30	..	46	24	4
1933-34	2,861	43	72	81	..	171	88	14
1940-41	3,773	62	91	128	17	192	118	33
1945-46	3,169	51	69	94	46	126	92	25
1950-51	3,424	44	81	107	47	119	112	29
1953-54	3,726	44	80	124	48	118	125	28
1955-56	3,753	45	79	123	46	105	134	28
1956-57	3,642	44	75	116	46	99	135	30
1957-58	3,498	39	75	114	44	100	143	31
1958-59	3,346	37	72	106	35	92	141	30
1959-60	3,330	33	67	108	33	92	140	27
1960-61	3,328	38	66	102	34	81	139	27
1961-62	3,416	41	68	101	34	85	140	28
1962-63	3,521	42	69	105	34	86	144	29
1963-64	3,626	42	69	112	34	87	154	30
1964-65	3,717	43	69	121	35	87	161	32
1965-66	3,820	45	71	122	35	89	167	36
1966-67	3,980	53	78	126	37	92	179	36
1967-68	4,075	57	78	126	37	92	182	36
1968-69	4,129	59	78	127	37	94	184	36

Year	Latvia	Lithuania	Moldavia	R.S.F.S.R.	Tadzhikistan	Turkmenia	Ukraine	Uzbekis
1914-15	11	13	5	297	0	0	88	1
1927-28	..	..	..	672	3	10	158	41
1933-34	..	..	2	1,693	24	34	567	72
1940-41	41	24	22	2,188	30	36	693	98
1945-46	70	37	26	1,881	24	25	532	71
1950-51	66	45	36	2,005	32	26	584	91
1953-54	64	55	39	2,204	34	31	632	100
1955-56	65	66	37	2,220	33	37	635	100
1956-57	68	68	32	2,164	31	33	599	102
1957-58	64	59	32	2,054	29	25	590	99
1958-59	62	61	31	1,958	25	23	588	85
1959-60	59	72	31	1,948	22	23	595	80
1960-61	56	76	32	1,961	22	23	595	76
1961-62	55	76	31	2,018	23	23	611	82
1962-63	54	75	31	2,078	24	24	641	85
1963-64	54	75	34	2,127	28	25	669	86
1964-65	52	77	36	2,175	29	26	682	92
1965-66	52	76	38	2,229	30	27	697	106
1966-67	54	82	44	2,293	32	28	717	129
1967-68	54	83	46	2,334	32	29	740	149
1968-69	55	83	47	2,362	35	29	747	156

Table A.8. NUMBER OF STUDENTS ENROLLED IN VOCATIONAL SECONDARY SCHOOLS (In Thousands)

Year	U.S.S.R.	Armenia	Azerbaidzhan	Belorussia	Estonia	Georgia	Kazakhstan[a]	Kirgizia
1914-15	54.3	0.1	0.5	1.4	0.2	0.5	0.3	0
1927-28	189.4	1.7	7.4	5.3	...	7.7	3.6	0.4
1940-41	974.8	8.9	17.4	35.0	2.1	26.1	30.3	6.0
1950-51	1,297.6	10.3	20.3	41.8	10.4	23.8	41.9	10.6
1953-54	1,645.5	13.5	24.2	47.5	15.3	26.0	55.0	11.8
1955-56	1,960.4	17.0	29.3	60.2	16.1	30.2	67.4	13.6
1956-57	2,012.2	16.5	29.6	60.6	15.6	30.9	71.9	14.4
1957-58	1,941.1	14.7	28.6	57.3	13.7	29.7	75.3	14.8
1958-59	1,875.9	14.0	26.3	55.7	12.6	26.8	75.1	15.8
1959-60	1,907.8	13.7	25.9	57.4	13.4	27.0	80.8	16.3
1960-61	2,059.5	14.8	27.0	62.6	15.4	26.3	86.0	17.2
1961-62	2,369.7	17.8	31.0	73.0	18.5	28.5	96.9	19.2
1962-63	2,667.7	20.1	36.8	83.0	21.3	30.1	112.5	21.5
1963-64	2,982.8	23.1	43.2	94.0	23.8	33.0	127.2	24.4
1964-65	3,326.0	26.6	49.3	108.6	25.8	35.5	149.6	27.2
1965-66	3,659.3	31.4	55.8	122.1	27.6	37.8	169.9	31.8
1966-67	3,993.9	36.0	65.0	134.8	27.1	43.2	193.4	35.4

Note:

[a]See Note a, Table A.2.

Table A.8. Number of Students Enrolled in Vocational Secondary Schools (Continued)

Year	Latvia	Lithuania	Moldavia	R.S.F.S.R.	Tadzhikistan	Turkmenia	Ukraine[a]	Uzbekistan
1914-15	1.3	1.5	0.5	35.4	0	0	12.5	0.1
1927-28	...	...	...	123.2	0.3	1.5	31.2	7.1
1940-41	9.6	6.4	4.1	594.0	5.9	7.7	196.2	25.1
1950-51	17.7	11.5	12.8	810.0	10.8	7.6	227.7	40.4
1953-54	21.0	17.6	16.6	1,016.3	11.9	10.7	308.8	49.3
1955-56	25.1	22.3	18.5	1,201.0	13.4	13.6	374.6	58.1
1956-57	25.7	22.8	17.7	1,243.6	13.7	14.5	374.9	59.8
1957-58	23.9	22.2	16.9	1,199.0	13.6	14.2	359.3	57.9
1958-59	23.5	23.7	15.9	1,154.6	12.2	13.3	351.1	55.3
1959-60	23.9	27.7	16.3	1,162.2	11.5	12.7	364.5	54.5
1960-61	24.7	32.3	17.2	1,260.3	11.9	12.3	398.2	53.3
1961-62	27.9	37.8	20.1	1,453.4	13.5	13.9	454.8	63.4
1962-63	30.5	43.6	22.0	1,641.2	14.9	15.1	501.8	73.3
1963-64	34.4	49.4	25.3	1,843.3	16.4	17.0	549.0	79.3
1964-65	36.6	54.3	28.7	2,062.4	20.1	19.2	593.7	88.4
1965-66	38.3	57.5	33.1	2,259.3	23.0	21.9	645.9	103.9
1966-67	41.2	60.9	39.8	2,423.9	27.2	25.3	718.7	122.0

Table A.9. Institutions of Higher Education

Year	U.S.S.R.	Armenia	Azerbaidzhan	Belorussia	Estonia	Georgia	Kazakhstan	Kirgizia
1914-15	105	0	0	0	4	1	0	0
1927-28	148	2	3	4	...	6	1	0
1933-34	714	7	13	18	...	17	15	3
1940-41	817	9	16	25	5	21	20	6
1945-46	789	13	17	24	5	20	24	6
1950-51	880	15	20	29	7	19	26	7
1953-54	818	13	14	29	7	19	26	10
1955-56	765	12	14	23	7	19	25	9
1956-57	767	12	15	24	6	19	26	9
1957-58	763	11	15	24	6	19	27	9
1958-59	766	11	15	25	6	19	27	9
1959-60	753	11	12	24	6	18	27	8
1960-61	739	10	12	24	6	18	28	8
1961-62	731	10	12	25	6	18	28	8
1962-63	738	11	12	25	6	18	32	8
1963-64	742	11	11	25	6	18	37	8
1964-65	754	11	11	26	6	18	39	8
1965-66	756	11	11	27	6	18	39	8
1966-67	767	12	12	28	6	18	41	8
1967-68	785	12	12	28	6	18	43	9
1968-69	794	12	12	28	6	18	43	9

Year	Latvia	Lithuania	Moldavia	R.S.F.S.R.	Tadzhikistan	Turkmenia	Ukraine	Uzbekistan
1914-15	1	0	0	72	0	0	27	0
1927-28	..	..	0	90	0	0	39	3
1933-34	..	..	3	428	5	5	173	27
1940-41	7	7	6	481	6	5	173	30
1945-46	8	10	6	456	7	6	154	33
1950-51	11	11	8	516	8	6	160	37
1953-54	10	12	9	473	8	6	147	35
1955-56	9	12	7	444	8	6	134	36
1956-57	9	12	8	443	8	6	138	32
1957-58	9	12	8	441	7	6	138	31
1958-59	9	12	8	441	7	6	140	31
1959-60	9	12	8	438	7	4	138	31
1960-61	10	12	6	430	6	4	135	30
1961-62	10	11	6	425	6	4	133	29
1962-63	10	11	6	426	7	4	133	29
1963-64	10	11	6	427	7	5	131	29
1964-65	10	11	7	432	7	5	132	31
1965-66	10	11	7	432	7	5	132	32
1966-67	10	11	7	435	7	5	132	35
1967-68	10	11	8	442	7	5	136	38
1968-69	10	11	8	449	7	5	138	38

Table A.10. NUMBER OF STUDENTS ENROLLED IN INSTITUTIONS OF HIGHER EDUCATION (In Thousands)

Year	U.S.S.R.	Armenia	Azerbaidzhan	Belorussia	Estonia	Georgia	Kazakhstan	Kirgizia
1914-15	127.4	0	0	0	3.3	0.3	0	0
1927-28	168.5	1.6	4.5	4.6	...	10.5	0.1	0
1940-41	811.7	11.1	14.6	21.5	4.8	28.5	10.4	3.1
1950-51	1,247.4	15.1	28.6	31.6	8.8	35.0	31.2	8.6
1955-56	1,867.0	19.4	34.7	50.5	11.9	38.0	49.2	13.6
1956-57	2,001.0	20.2	34.6	52.3	11.9	39.9	55.2	14.8
1957-58	2,099.1	20.4	34.0	54.8	12.0	41.7	58.8	15.1
1958-59	2,178.9	19.6	36.0	57.0	12.1	48.2	65.2	15.8
1959-60	2,267.0	19.1	34.6	56.8	12.9	51.1	70.2	17.1
1960-61	2,396.1	20.2	36.0	59.3	13.5	56.3	77.1	17.4
1961-62	2,639.9	22.1	39.0	66.2	15.1	60.1	86.1	19.7
1962-63	2,943.7	25.9	45.1	75.7	16.6	65.9	98.0	23.1
1963-64	3,260.7	29.1	53.0	86.3	17.9	69.8	113.3	25.1
1964-65	3,608.4	33.7	58.7	96.3	19.9	74.8	132.0	29.0
1965-66	3,860.5	38.9	67.0	104.0	21.4	76.6	144.7	32.2
1966-67	4,123.2	43.3	78.3	115.9	21.9	81.4	163.1	36.7
1967-68	4,310.9	48.5	87.4	124.8	22.7	86.0	176.1	40.5
1968-69	4,469.7	51.8	95.0	131.5	22.8	89.3	188.4	43.9

Year	Latvia	Lithuania	Moldavia	R.S.F.S.R.	Tadzhikistan	Turkmenia	Ukraine	Uzbekistan
1914-15	2.1	0	0	86.5	0	0	35.2	0
1927-28	...	...	0	114.2	0	0	29.1	3.9
1940-41	9.9	6.0	2.5	478.1	2.3	3.0	196.8	17.1
1950-51	14.2	11.4	8.7	796.7	7.1	6.6	201.6	42.2
1955-56	15.7	22.7	17.2	1,176.1	14.4	12.2	325.9	65.5
1956-57	16.2	24.0	17.8	1,266.7	16.3	13.0	346.6	71.5
1957-58	18.2	24.6	17.0	1,326.5	17.1	13.4	367.2	78.3
1958-59	18.3	24.4	16.2	1,365.7	18.2	12.9	381.1	88.2
1959-60	18.9	25.4	18.0	1,417.3	18.9	12.8	401.6	92.3
1960-61	21.6	26.7	19.2	1,496.7	20.0	13.1	417.7	101.3
1961-62	24.7	29.8	21.6	1,645.5	21.2	14.0	460.6	114.2
1962-63	27.4	33.3	24.8	1,827.0	22.0	14.8	517.6	126.5
1963-64	29.2	38.0	28.8	2,013.6	23.6	17.0	576.8	139.2
1964-65	31.4	42.8	33.4	2,212.9	26.9	18.5	643.8	154.3
1965-66	33.1	46.4	36.3	2,353.9	30.4	19.8	690.0	165.8
1966-67	36.0	50.7	40.6	2,470.5	34.7	22.7	739.1	188.3
1967-68	38.8	53.4	43.1	2,555.5	37.9	24.6	766.9	204.7
1968-69	40.1	54.5	45.4	2,622.5	40.9	27.3	792.2	224.1

Table A.10a. NUMBER OF STUDENTS ENROLLED IN INSTITUTIONS OF HIGHER EDUCATION PER 100,000 POPULATION

Year	U.S.S.R.	Armenia	Azerbaidzhan	Belorussia	Estonia	Georgia	Kazakhstan	Kirgizia
1914-15	80.1	...	...	...	...	...	...	...
1940-41	418.3	840.9	446.5	237.8	457.1	789.0	171.8	202.9
1950-51	698.6	1,121.0	1,000.4	409.9	802.2	1,001.7	478.4	442.4
1955-56	960.3	1,263.8	1,058.9	651.0	1,028.5	999.2	647.7	721.5
1956-57	1,011.1	1,268.8	1,025.2	666.2	1,024.1	1,029.4	675.3	770.8
1957-58	1,042.2	1,244.7	975.9	692.8	1,022.2	1,062.7	695.3	770.0
1958-59	1,063.3	1,151.6	1,001.4	715.9	1,021.1	1,212.6	745.3	792.4
1959-60	1,085.6	1,083.4	935.6	705.2	1,088.6	1,263.6	766.9	827.7
1960-61	1,129.0	1,108.1	943.2	728.2	1,127.8	1,363.5	796.7	814.2
1961-62	1,221.6	1,168.1	982.4	805.0	1,249.0	1,432.0	843.5	887.0
1962-63	1,340.0	1,323.5	1,095.7	910.2	1,344.1	1,543.3	911.5	997.0
1963-64	1,461.6	1,449.9	1,252.7	1,025.8	1,438.9	1,608.3	1,005.7	1,056.0
1964-65	1,594.9	1,628.8	1,356.3	1,139.0	1,563.2	1,694.2	1,146.7	1,163.7
1965-66	1,684.4	1,822.9	1,483.0	1,218.8	1,681.1	1,708.7	1,220.8	1,211.0
1966-67	1,778.5	1,974.5	1,678.8	1,342.5	1,704.3	1,790.2	1,345.3	1,384.4
1967-68	1,839.2	2,152.7	1,820.1	1,427.3	1,754.3	1,865.1	1,418.7	1,473.3
1968-69	1,888.4	2,246.3	1,932.1	1,490.9	1,748.5	1,941.0	1,486.0	1,548.0

Year	Latvia	Lithuania	Moldavia	R.S.F.S.R.	Tadzhikistan	Turkmenia	Ukraine	Uzbekistan
1940-41	524.9	205.1	101.3	434.3	150.8	230.4	476.1	287.4
1950-51	730.5	443.1	379.9	785.4	470.5	551.4	551.0	673.7
1955-56	781.1	868.7	661.0	1,064.0	819.6	910.5	829.9	900.3
1956-57	802.0	907.7	671.2	1,128.3	901.6	948.2	872.1	959.7
1957-58	883.9	922.4	624.5	1,163.4	914.9	951.7	908.4	1,016.8
1958-59	880.2	915.6	577.3	1,180.7	942.0	883.6	925.5	1,105.5
1959-60	903.0	936.9	623.9	1,205.9	954.6	844.3	959.2	1,117.2
1960-61	1,032.0	967.0	646.7	1,258.6	983.8	837.1	983.6	1,188.4
1961-62	1,153.1	1,063.1	710.8	1,365.0	1,011.0	862.1	1,069.0	1,293.6
1962-63	1,263.0	1,167.2	798.5	1,496.5	1,007.8	880.0	1,189.1	1,381.0
1963-64	1,335.8	1,320.4	907.9	1,631.3	1,042.9	975.9	1,309.4	1,467.0
1964-65	1,416.3	1,471.8	1,030.2	1,774.6	1,146.6	1,026.1	1,442.3	1,571.1
1965-66	1,477.0	1,573.4	1,198.0	1,871.6	1,224.8	1,063.4	1,529.6	1,636.7
1966-67	1,591.5	1,697.9	1,205.5	1,952.1	1,348.0	1,186.6	1,623.8	1,781.6
1967-68	1,698.0	1,764.7	1,258.4	2,007.3	1,428.0	1,251.3	1,668.4	1,878.7
1968-69	1,745.0	1,778.7	1,303.1	2,050.3	1,494.9	1,345.5	1,694.5	1,989.1

Table A.11. Students Enrolled in Institutions of Higher Education by Branch (Including Extension–Correspondence Students, In Thousands)

Year	Construction & Production	Transport & Communications	Agriculture	Economics & Law	Health & Sports	Education	Art	Total
1914-15	24.9		4.6	11.4	5.0	81.5		127.4
1928-29	52.3		26.9	16.5	25.6	39.1	6.4	166.8[a]
1940-41	168.4	36.2	52.1	36.3	109.8	398.6	10.3	811.7
1950-51	272.8	47.9	104.1	89.2	111.5	607.0	14.9	1,247.4
1954-55	489.2	83.4	173.3	105.8	144.9	719.7	14.2	1,730.5
1955-56	550.6	99.0	195.9	106.7	158.8	741.6	14.4	1,867.0
1958-59	847.0		232.0	158.0	183.0	715.0	15.0	2,150.0[b]
1959-60	768.1	145.1	261.4	153.9	184.4	737.2	16.9	2,267.0
1960-61	873.1	146.7	246.5	161.9	188.9	759.6	19.4	2,396.1
1965-66	1,528.3	221.6	377.1	264.1	238.8	1,198.7	32.0	3,860.6
1966-67	1,625.6	234.1	398.9	290.8	259.5	1,279.0	35.3	4,123.2
1967-68	1,707.1	240.1	414.2	308.9	276.8	1,326.7	37.1	4,310.9
1968-69	1,773.1	246.1	428.0	328.5	294.4	1,360.3	39.3	4,469.7

Notes:

[a] Officially reported total is 176.6.

[b] Officially reported total is 2,179.0.

Table A.12. Females as Percentage of Students Enrolled in Institutions of Higher Education

Year	Percentage
1927-28	28%
1933-34	33%
1940-41	58%
1945-46	77%
1950-51	53%
1955-56	52%
1956-57	51%
1957-58	49%
1958-59	47%
1959-60	45%
1960-61	43%
1961-62	42%
1962-63	42%
1963-64	43%
1964-65	43%
1965-66	44%
1966-67	45%
1967-68	46%
1968-69	47%

Table A.13. Evening, Extension, and Correspondence Students as Percentage of Students Enrolled in Institutions of Higher Education

Year	U.S.S.R.	Armenia	Azerbaidzhan	Belorussia	Estonia	Georgia	Kazakhstan	Kirgizia
1957-58	43	38	38	37	33	38	38	33
1958-59	46	41	41	41	35	44	38	35
1959-60	49	44	44	45	41	49	41	37
1960-61	52	46	49	46	44	55	45	38
1961-62	54	47	52	48	46	59	46	42
1962-63	56	49	55	51	49	63	47	46
1963-64	58	50	58	52	50	66	49	48
1964-65	58	49	59	52	50	67	53	51
1965-66	59	49	60	53	51	67	53	52
1966-67	58	48	59	51	50	65	52	51
1967-68	56	47	58	49	49	64	51	51
1968-69	55	45	57	47	48	62	50	50

Table A.13. EVENING, EXTENSION, AND CORRESPONDENCE STUDENTS AS PERCENTAGE OF STUDENTS ENROLLED IN INSTITUTIONS OF HIGHER EDUCATION (Continued)

Year	Latvia	Lithuania	Moldavia	R.S.F.S.R.	Tadzhikistan	Turkmenia	Ukraine	Uzbekistan
1957-58	36	36	42	46	40	38	40	39
1958-59	37	36	42	48	41	35	44	42
1959-60	41	39	45	51	44	37	50	44
1960-61	42	42	46	53	43	39	52	49
1961-62	46	44	46	56	45	39	56	53
1962-63	48	46	47	57	47	39	58	55
1963-64	49	48	49	58	49	45	60	57
1964-65	50	50	54	59	51	45	60	58
1965-66	51	51	55	59	54	46	61	59
1966-67	48	51	52	58	53	44	60	58
1967-68	46	51	51	57	52	43	59	57
1968-69	45	50	49	55	48	43	57	54

Table A.14. GRADUATES OF HIGHER EDUCATION

Territory	Both Sexes		Male		Female	
	1939	1959	1939	1959	1939	1959
U.S.S.R.						
Total	1,177.1	3,777.5	799.2	1,933.2	377.9	1,844.3
Urban	956.2	3,169.4	628.5	1,594.9	327.7	1,574.5
Rural	220.9	608.1	170.7	338.4	50.2	269.8
Armenia						
Total	7.5	48.8	5.1	27.0	2.4	21.8
Urban	6.4	40.9	4.2	21.6	2.2	19.3
Rural	1.1	7.9	0.9	5.4	0.2	2.5
Azerbaidzhan						
Total	21.6	77.2	16.2	45.7	5.4	31.5
Urban	18.7	65.8	13.6	36.6	5.1	29.2
Rural	2.9	11.4	2.6	9.1	0.3	2.4
Belorussia						
Total	33.0	95.7	22.7	48.1	10.3	47.6
Urban	23.4	73.3	14.6	36.1	8.8	37.2
Rural	9.6	22.4	8.1	12.0	1.5	10.4
Estonia						
Total	8.7	25.2	6.9	12.5	1.8	12.7
Urban	7.2	21.7	5.6	10.7	1.6	11.0
Rural	1.5	3.5	1.3	1.8	0.2	1.7
Georgia						
Total	39.7	153.4	27.5	81.7	12.2	71.7
Urban	31.9	119.8	21.2	62.1	10.7	57.8
Rural	7.8	33.6	6.3	19.7	1.5	13.9
Kazakhstan						
Total	27.5	114.0	20.9	64.7	6.6	49.3
Urban	15.2	82.5	10.6	44.4	4.6	38.1
Rural	12.2	31.5	10.3	20.3	2.0	11.2
Kirgizia						
Total	3.3	27.2	2.4	15.2	0.8	12.0
Urban	2.3	18.8	1.7	9.8	0.6	9.0
Rural	0.9	8.4	0.7	5.4	0.2	3.0

Table A.14. Graduates of Higher Education (Continued)

Territory	Both Sexes 1939	1959	Male 1939	1959	Female 1939	1959
Latvia						
Total	13.9	44.4	11.5	20.7	2.4	23.7
Urban	12.5	39.3	10.3	18.1	2.2	21.1
Rural	1.4	5.1	1.2	2.5	0.2	2.6
Lithuania						
Total	6.4	35.4	4.9	18.6	1.5	16.8
Urban	4.8	30.7	3.9	16.0	0.9	14.7
Rural	1.6	4.7	1.0	2.6	0.6	2.1
Moldavia						
Total	7.3	29.5	5.0	15.3	2.4	14.2
Urban	4.4	21.6	2.7	10.9	1.7	10.7
Rural	2.9	7.9	2.2	4.4	0.7	3.5
R.S.F.S.R.						
Total	709.5	2,265.9	472.2	1,128.5	237.3	1,137.4
Urban	595.6	1,939.0	387.0	959.5	208.6	979.5
Rural	113.9	326.9	85.1	169.0	28.7	158.0
Tadzhikistan						
Total	3.0	20.7	2.2	12.5	0.7	8.2
Urban	2.2	16.0	1.7	8.8	0.6	7.2
Rural	0.7	4.6	0.6	3.7	0.2	1.0
Turkmenia						
Total	4.0	19.8	3.0	12.0	1.1	7.8
Urban	3.6	15.6	2.5	8.5	1.0	7.1
Rural	0.5	4.2	0.4	3.6	0.04	0.7
Ukraine						
Total	272.0	715.4	184.7	368.5	87.3	346.9
Urban	211.5	603.4	137.6	307.9	74.0	295.5
Rural	60.4	112.1	47.1	60.7	13.3	51.4
Uzbekistan						
Total	19.7	104.9	14.1	62.3	5.7	42.6
Urban	16.4	80.9	11.3	43.9	5.1	37.0
Rural	3.3	24.0	2.8	18.4	0.6	5.6

Table A.14a. Graduates of Higher Education per 1,000 Population

Republic	1939[a]	1959
U.S.S.R.	6.1	18.1
Armenia	5.7	27.7
Azerbaidzhan	6.6	20.9
Belorussia	3.7	11.9
Estonia	8.3	21.3
Georgia	11.0	37.9
Kazakhstan	4.5	12.5
Kirgizia	2.2	13.2
Latvia	7.4	21.2
Lithuania	2.2	13.1
Moldavia	3.0	10.2
R.S.F.S.R.	6.4	19.3
Tadzhikistan	2.0	10.5
Turkmenia	3.1	13.1
Ukraine	6.6	17.1
Uzbekistan	3.0	12.7

Note:
[a] Population figures for 1940 are used.

Table A.15. STUDENT–TEACHER RATIO IN PRIMARY AND GENERAL SECONDARY SCHOOLS OF ALL TYPES

GRADUATES OF HIGHER EDUCATION AS PERCENTAGE OF TEACHERS IN REGULAR PRIMARY AND GENERAL SECONDARY SCHOOLS

Year	Student–Teacher Ratio
1914–15	34
1927–28	33
1940–41	29
1950–51	24
1953–54	20
1955–56	17
1956–57	17
1957–58	16
1958–59	17
1959–60	17
1960–61	18
1961–62	18
1962–63	19
1963–64	19
1964–65	19
1965–66	19
1966–67	19
1967–68	19
1968–69	19

Year	% Teachers With Higher Education
1914–15	...
1927–28	...
1940–41	...
1950–51	14.2
1953–54	...
1955–56	23.5
1956–57	...
1957–58	26.8
1958–59	28.9
1959–60	31.6
1960–61	34.4
1961–62	35.9
1962–63	...
1963–64	38.3
1964–65	40.0
1965–66	41.5
1966–67	42.9
1967–68	45.0
1968–69	47.1

Table B.1. PERCENTAGE OF POPULATION AND PERCENTAGE OF STUDENTS IN INSTITUTIONS OF HIGHER EDUCATION BY REPUBLIC

Republic	1927–28 Pop.	1927–28 Students	1940–41 Pop.	1940–41 Students	1960–61 Pop.	1960–61 Students	1965–66 Pop.	1965–66 Students
U.S.S.R.	100.0	100.0	100.0	100.0	100.0	100.0	100.0	100.0
Armenia	0.6	1.0	0.7	1.4	0.9	0.9	0.9	1.0
Azerbaidzhan	1.6	2.7	1.7	1.8	1.9	1.5	2.0	1.7
Belorussia	3.4	2.8	4.7	2.6	3.8	2.5	3.7	2.7
Estonia	...	...	0.5	0.6	0.5	0.6	0.6	0.6
Georgia	1.8	6.2	1.8	3.5	1.9	2.3	2.0	2.0
Kazakhstan	4.1	0.0	3.1	1.3	4.8	3.2	5.2	3.7
Kirgizia	0.7	...	0.8	0.4	1.0	0.7	1.1	0.8
Latvia	...	...	1.0	1.2	1.0	0.9	1.0	0.9
Lithuania	...	...	1.5	0.7	1.3	1.1	1.3	1.2
Moldavia	0.1	0.0	1.3	0.3	1.4	0.8	1.5	0.9
R.S.F.S.R.	63.0	67.7	56.8	58.9	55.8	62.5	54.6	61.0
Tadzhikistan	0.7	...	0.8	0.3	1.0	0.8	1.1	0.8
Turkmenia	0.7	...	0.7	0.4	0.7	0.6	0.8	0.5
Ukraine	20.1	17.3	21.3	24.2	19.9	17.4	19.6	17.9
Uzbekistan	3.2	2.3	3.3	2.4	4.1	4.2	4.6	4.3

Note: The population percentage for 1927–28 is based on the 1926 census, that for 1940–41 -- on the 1939 figures.

Table B.2. NATIONAL COMPOSITION OF STUDENTS IN INSTITUTIONS OF HIGHER EDUCATION (In Percentages)

Nationality	1927-28	1950-51[a]	1960-61	1966-67	Percentage of Population 1926 Census	1959 Census
All nationalities of the U.S.S.R.	100.00	100.00	100.00	100.00	100.00	100.00
Armenians	2.02	2.21	1.53	1.64	1.07	1.34
Azerbaidzhanis	1.13	1.59	1.19	1.55	1.16	1.41
Bashkirs	...	...	0.26	0.31	...	0.47
Belorussians	2.91	2.04	2.66	2.97	3.22	3.79
Chuvash	...	...	0.34	0.39	...	0.70
Dagestanis	...	...	0.31	0.40	...	0.45
Estonians	...	0.83	0.54	0.46	...	0.47
Georgians	2.37	2.58	2.02	1.87	1.24	1.29
Jews	...	...	3.22	2.58	...	1.09
Kazakhs	0.18	1.17	1.70	1.84	2.70	1.73
Kirgiz	0.06	0.37	0.41	0.45	0.52	0.46
Latvians	...	0.96	0.69	0.55	...	0.67
Lithuanians	...	1.02	1.08	1.12	...	1.11
Maris	...	...	0.10	0.10	...	0.24
Moldavians	0.12	0.19	0.50	0.64	0.19	1.06
Mordvinians	...	...	0.18	0.26	...	0.62
Russians	56.08	60.84	61.77	60.51	52.88	54.65
Tadzhiks	0.06	0.27	0.50	0.48	0.66	0.67
Tatars	...	...	1.66	1.77	...	2.38
Turkmens	0.06	0.27	0.40	0.43	0.46	0.48
Udmurts	...	...	0.13	0.15	...	0.30
Ukrainians	14.55	12.80	14.34	14.31	21.22	17.84
Uzbeks	0.30	1.48	2.23	2.72	2.66	2.88

Note:

[a]Not including students at correspondence courses.

Table B.3. NATIONAL COMPOSITION OF THE POPULATION OF UNION REPUBLICS COMPARED WITH THE NATIONAL COMPOSITION OF POST-GRADUATE STUDENTS (In Percentages)

Nationality	National Composition of the Population According to the 1959 Census	National Composition of Post-Graduate Students According to 1960 Figures
All nationalities of the U.S.S.R.	100.00	100.00
Armenians	1.34	1.98
Azerbaidzhanis	1.41	2.77
Belorussians	3.79	2.45
Estonians	0.47	1.09
Georgians	1.29	2.30
Kazakhs	1.73	1.61
Kirgiz	0.46	0.50
Latvians	0.67	0.75
Lithuanians	1.11	1.13
Moldavians	1.06	0.40
Russians	54.65	58.53
Tadzhiks	0.67	0.87
Turkmens	0.48	0.63
Ukrainians	17.84	11.10
Uzbeks	2.88	3.04

Table B.4. NATIONAL COMPOSITION OF SCIENTIFIC WORKERS BY REPUBLIC, 1960

Republic	Total Number	Of Indigenous Nationality Total Number	Of Indigenous Nationality Percentage
Armenia	4,275	4,000	93.5
Azerbaidzhan	7,226	4,669	64.6
Belorussia	6,840	3,209	47.0
Estonia	2,227	1,758	78.9
Georgia	9,137	7,650	83.0
Kazakhstan	9,623	2,064	21.4
Kirgizia	2,315	573	24.7
Latvia	3,348	2,189	65.4
Lithuania	3,320	2,776	83.6
Moldavia	1,999	516	25.8
R.S.F.S.R.	242,872	193,193	79.5
Tadzhikistan	2,154	727	33.7
Turkmenia	1,836	677	36.9
Ukraine	46,657	22,523	48.3
Uzbekistan	10,329	3,552	34.4

Table B.5. NATIONAL COMPOSITION OF SCIENTIFIC WORKERS IN SELECTED YEARS

Nationality	Number of Scientific Workers 1950	Number of Scientific Workers 1960	Number of Scientific Workers 1966	Percentage 1950	Percentage 1960	Percentage 1966
Total Number	162,500	354,158	712,400	100.00	100.00	100.00
Armenians	3,900	8,001	15,200	2.40	2.26	2.13
Azerbaidzhanis	1,900	4,972	9,800	1.17	1.43	1.38
Bashkirs	...	391	990	...	0.11	0.14
Belorussians	2,700	6,358	13,900	1.66	1.80	1.95
Chuvash	...	606	1,296	...	0.17	0.18
Dagestanis	...	454	1,203	...	0.13	0.17
Estonians	1,200	2,048	3,700	0.74	0.58	0.52
Georgians	4,300	8,306	13,700	2.65	2.32	1.92
Jews	...	33,529	55,070	...	9.47	7.73
Kazakhs	700	2,290	5,300	0.43	0.65	0.74
Kirgiz	100	586	1,200	0.06	0.17	0.17
Latvians	1,500	2,662	4,800	0.92	0.75	0.67
Lithuanians	1,200	2,959	5,900	0.74	0.83	0.83
Maris	...	109	211	...	0.03	0.03
Moldavians	100	590	1,700	0.06	0.17	0.24
Mordvinians	...	351	779	...	0.10	0.11
Russians	98,900	229,547	470,500	60.86	64.81	66.04
Tadzhiks	200	866	1,600	0.12	0.24	0.22
Tatars	...	3,691	8,455	...	1.04	1.19
Turkmens	100	707	1,400	0.06	0.20	0.19
Udmurts	...	188	409	...	0.05	0.06
Ukrainians	14,700	35,426	75,300	9.05	10.00	10.57
Uzbeks	800	3,748	7,900	0.49	1.05	1.11

Table B.6. Percentage of Doctors and Candidates of Science among Research Workers and Faculty

Republic	1950 Doctors	1950 Candidates of Science	1965 Doctors	1965 Candidates of Science
U.S.S.R.	5.1	28.0	2.2	20.2
Armenia	5.6	32.9	3.3	26.2
Azerbaidzhan	3.7	27.0	2.7	24.3
Belorussia	4.5	21.9	1.7	21.1
Estonia	4.9	14.4	2.3	28.0
Georgia	6.6	35.8	4.5	28.8
Kazakhstan	2.9	23.3	1.3	18.0
Kirgizia	2.9	19.5	1.9	24.2
Latvia	2.7	11.7	1.3	22.1
Lithuania	2.5	7.7	0.9	21.0
Moldavia	4.1	22.1	1.7	25.7
R.S.F.S.R.	5.5	29.0	2.3	19.4
Tadzhikistan	2.8	21.7	1.3	20.8
Turkmenia	4.3	20.9	1.5	23.2
Ukraine	4.0	27.3	2.0	20.5
Uzbekistan	3.5	26.4	1.9	23.8

Table B.7. Expenditures for Education and Culture from USSR Budget and Union Republican Budgets

Republic	Population in Thousands 1960	Population in Thousands 1965	Budget Allocations in Millions of Rubles 1960	Budget Allocations in Millions of Rubles 1965	Per 100 Population 1960	Per 100 Population 1965
U.S.S.R. Total	216,151	231,868	10,305.4	17,510.4	4,768	7,552
Of this, from union rep.	...	...	2,225.3	4,733.5	...	...
Armenia	1,893	2,194	92.2	166.7	4,871	7,598
Azerbaidzhan	3,973	4,660	148.4	256.7	3,735	5,509
Belorussia	8,226	8,633	299.2	486.6	3,637	5,636
Estonia	1,221	1,285	67.1	97.7	5,495	7,603
Georgia	4,200	4,548	181.9	270.9	4,331	5,956
Kazakhstan	10,387	12,129	378.0	701.6	3,639	5,784
Kirgizia	2,225	2,652	85.6	147.1	3,847	5,547
Latvia	2,142	2,262	101.1	150.6	4,719	6,644
Lithuania	2,804	2,986	116.4	188.6	4,151	6,316
Moldavia	3,040	3,368	90.9	169.7	2,990	5,038
R.S.F.S.R.	120,554	126,561	4,681.5	7,152.9	3,883	5,651
Tadzhikistan	2,104	2,579	86.8	144.5	4,125	5,603
Turkmenia	1,626	1,914	63.7	109.6	3,918	5,726
Ukraine	43,091	45,516	1,396.4	2,221.4	3,241	4,880
Uzbekistan	8,665	10,581	290.9	512.3	3,357	4,841

Table B.8. EXPENDITURES FOR INSTITUTIONS OF HIGHER EDUCATION

Republic	Number of Students in Thousands			Budget Allocations in Millions of Rubles			Expenditure Per Student		
	1950	1960	1965	1950	1960	1965	1950	1960	1965
U.S.S.R. Total	1,247	2,396	3,860	721.0	1,167.0	1,593.8	578	487	413
From rep. budgets	...	...	...	485.3	56.1	235.2	...	...	...
Armenia	15	20	39	4.2	11.9	17.8	278	589	458
Azerbaidzhan	28	36	67	6.4	17.5	23.3	224	486	348
Belorussia	32	59	104	7.7	29.3	41.9	244	494	403
Estonia	9	14	21	1.6	8.4	9.9	182	622	462
Georgia	35	56	77	9.5	26.6	25.4	271	472	332
Kazakhstan	31	77	145	8.9	35.8	49.0	285	464	338
Kirgizia	8	17	32	3.4	9.3	10.8	395	534	335
Latvia	14	22	33	2.4	12.6	11.5	170	583	347
Lithuania	11	27	46	2.1	15.4	18.8	184	577	405
Moldavia	9	19	36	1.6	8.2	13.0	184	427	360
R.S.F.S.R.	797	1,497	2,354	129.9	698.9	844.2	163	467	358
Tadzhikistan	7	20	30	3.1	9.2	10.3	437	460	338
Turkmenia	7	13	20	2.6	7.9	6.5	394	603	328
Ukraine	202	418	690	42.2	182.1	228.2	209	435	331
Uzbekistan	42	101	166	10.1	37.8	48.0	240	373	290

CHAPTER VI (A) TABLE SOURCE NOTES*

TABLE A.1

Itogi vsesoyuznoi perepisi naselenia 1959 goda—USSR, Moscow (1962), pp. 88–89.

TABLE A.2

N.K. Kazakhstan, Alma Ata (1968), pp. 356–357.
N.K. Srednei Azii 1963, Tashkent, (1964), p. 318.
N.K. SSSR, Moscow and Leningrad, (1932), pp. 508–510.
N.K. 1958, pp. 822–823.
N.K. 1961, p. 686.
N.K. 1963, p. 564.
N.K. 1965, p. 686.
N.K. 1967, pp. 786–787.
N.K. 1968, p. 676.

TABLE A.3

N.K. Kazakhstan, Alma Ata (1968), p. 357.
N.K. Srednei Azii 1963, Tashkent (1964), p. 318.
N.K. 1958, p. 823.
N.K. 1961, p. 687.
N.K. 1963, p. 565.
N.K. 1965, p. 687.

N.K. 1967, p. 787.
N.K. 1968, p. 677.

TABLE A.4

Itogi vsesoyuznoi perepisi naselenia 1959 goda, Moscow (1962), Table 21.

TABLE A.5

Central Asian Review, 11:161 (no. 2, 1963).
N.K. Kazakhstan, Alma Ata (1968), pp. 316–317.
N.K. 1960, pp. 760–761.
N.K. 1961, pp. 684–685.
N.K. 1962, p. 558.
N.K. 1963, p. 562.
N.K. 1965, p. 684.
N.K. 1967, p. 785.
N.K. 1968, p. 675.
N.K. Uzbekskoi SSR za 50 Let, Tashkent (1967), p. 217.
Uzbekistan za 50 Let, Tashkent (1966), p. 146.

TABLE A.6

Dostizhenie Sovetskogo Azerbaidzhana za 40 Let, Baku (1960), p. 194.

* Figures from 1958–1959 through 1963–1964 have been adjusted to correspond with borders after the transfer of part of Kazakhstan to Uzbekistan on January 26, 1963. The transfer did not affect figures prior to 1958–1959. In 1971, this territory was reassigned by Kazakhstan.

Kairov, I. A. et al., eds., *Narodnoe obrazovanie v SSSR*, Moscow (1958), p. 195.
N.K. Armenia, Erevan (1957), p. 149.
N.K. Kazakhstan, Alma Ata (1957), pp. 284–285.
N.K. Kazakhstan, Alma Ata (1968), pp. 316–317.
N.K. Srednei Azii 1963, Tashkent (1964), p. 317.
N.K. 1958, pp. 808–811.
N.K. 1961, p. 685.
N.K. 1963, p. 563.
N.K. 1965, p. 685.
N.K. 1967, p. 785.
N.K. 1968, p. 675.
N.K. Tadzhikistan, Stalinabad (1957), pp. 288–289.
N.K. Turkmenia, Ashkhabad (1957), p. 131.
N.K. Uzbekistan, Tashkent (1957), p. 175.
Narodnoe obrazovanie v Belorusskoi SSR, Minsk (1961), p. 112.
Prokofyev, M. A., *Narodnoe obrazovanie v SSSR*, Moscow (1967), p. 430.
Sovetskaya Gruzia k 50-letiyu Velikoi Oktyabrskoi Sotsialisticheskoi Revolyutsii, Tbilisi (1967), p. 219.
Sovetsky Kirgizstan za 40 Let, Frunze (1966), p. 137.
SS za 50 L., pp. 274, 307–337.
Uzbekistan za 7 Let, Tashkent (1966), p. 146.

Table A.6b

Age-group population data from "Population Policy and Demographic Trends in the Soviet Union," by James W. Brackett and John W. DePauw, *The Human Resources*. Part III of *New Directions in the Soviet Economy*, Joint Economic Committee of the United States Congress, Washington (1966), pp. 666–667.

Table A.7

N.K. 1958, pp. 833–834.
N.K. 1961, p. 692.
N.K. 1963, p. 570.
N.K. 1965, p. 692.
N.K. 1967, p. 793.
N.K. 1968, p. 684.
SS za 50 L., pp. 276, 307–337.
Uzbekistan za 7 Let, Tashkent (1966), p. 149.
Vysshee obrazovanie v SSSR, Moscow (1962), pp. 242–243.

Table A.8

N.K. 1958, pp. 833–834.
N.K. 1961, p. 692.
N.K. 1963, p. 570.
N.K. 1965, p. 692.
N.K. 1967, p. 793.
N.K. 1968, p. 684.
Vysshee obrazovanie v SSSR, Moscow (1961), pp. 242–243.
Poluboyarinov, M., "Public Education in the USSR in Figures: A Brief Survey," *The Soviet Review*, 9(2):33 (Summer 1968).
N.K. Srednei Azii v 1963, Tashkent (1964), p. 320.
N.K. Kazakhstan, Alma Ata (1968), pp. 334–335.
Uzbekistan za 7 Let, Tashkent (1966), p. 149.

Table A.9

N.K. 1958, pp. 831–832.
N.K. 1961, p. 691.
N.K. 1963, p. 569.
N.K. 1965. p. 681.
N.K. 1967, p. 792.
N.K. 1968, p. 633.
SS za 50 L., pp. 276, 307–337.
Vysshee obrazovanie v SSSR, Moscow (1961), pp. 106–109.

Table A.10

Chutkerashvili, E. V., *Razvitie vysshego obrazovania v SSSR*, Moscow (1961), p. 187.
N.K. 1958, pp. 831–832.
N.K. 1961, p. 691.
N.K. 1963, p. 569.
N.K. 1965, p. 691.
N.K. 1967, p. 792.
N.K. 1968, p. 683.
Poluboyarinov, M., "Public Education in the USSR in Figures: A Brief Survey," *The Soviet Review*, 9(2):33 (Summer 1968).
Vysshee obrazovanie v SSSR, Moscow (1961), pp. 196–109.

Table A.11

Nicholas DeWitt, *Educational and Professional Employment in the USSR*, Washington, U.S. Government Printing Office (1961), pp. 638–639.
N.K. 1967, p. 791.
N.K. 1968, p. 682.
Vysshee obrazovanie v SSSR, Moscow (1961), p. 81.

TABLE A.12

Iu. S. Borisov, *Izmenenie sotsialnogo sostava v vysshikh i srednykh spetsialnykh uchebnykh zavedeniakh (1917–1940 gg.),* in M. P. Kim et al., eds., *Kulturnaya revolyutsia v SSSR: 1917–1965 gg.,* Moscow (1967), p. 140.
N.K. 1958, p. 840.
N.K. 1961, p. 699.
N.K. 1963, p. 578.
N.K. 1965, p. 700.
N.K. 1967, p. 802.
N.K. 1968, p. 693.
SS za 50 L., p. 282.
Vysshee obrazovanie v SSSR, Moscow (1961), p. 86.
Zhenshchiny i deti v SSSR, Moscow (1969), p. 56.

TABLE A.13

N.K. 1961, p. 693.
N.K. 1963, p. 572.
N.K. 1965, p. 694.
N.K. 1967, p. 795.
N.K. 1968, p. 686.
Vysshee obrazovanie v SSSR, Moscow (1961), pp. 164–165.

TABLE A.14

Itogi vsesoyuznoi perepisi naselenia 1959 goda, USSR, Moscow, (1962), Table 21.

TABLE A.15

Poluboyarinov, M., "Public Education in the USSR in Figures: A Brief Survey," *The Soviet Review,* 9(2):33 (Summer 1968).

CHAPTER VI (B) TABLE SOURCE NOTES

TABLES B.1 to B.7

Jaan Pennar, Ivan I. Bakalo, and George Z. F. Bereday, *Modernization and Diversity in Soviet Education,* New York, Praeger, 1971.

ELITE RECRUITMENT AND MOBILIZATION

ELLEN MICKIEWICZ

THE COMMUNIST PARTY of the Soviet Union is unquestionably the country's most powerful elite. By the tenets of the political doctrine from which it gains its legitimacy, it is the only leader, the vanguard, for the masses of workers and peasants who are under its guidance. It is by no means a mass organization, although its ranks have been increasing, and it now embraces almost 10 percent of the adult population of the Soviet Union. It is rather an elite organization, membership in which is the result of special qualifications and entails responsibilities and obligations of moral and political leadership as well as the honor and rewards of being among the select. However, it is clear than only a small proportion of the Party's membership is able to serve in decision-making positions, formulate ideologically appropriate pronouncements, and staff the bureaucracy of the Party, the secretariat. This is the core political elite, the men of the *apparat,* and it is generally thought to encompass the paid party functionaries. Perhaps the difficulty of reconciling the existence of what John Armstrong has called a "bureaucratic elite"[1] with the Party's professed egalitarianism leads to suppression of the data; we have not been able to find a precise figure for the number of such Party professionals. Although we have data on the number of Party members occupied in various sorts of services, as opposed to production (Table 11), and although we know how the level of education of these functionaries has changed over the years (Tables 13, 14, and 15), we still cannot point to an exact number of secretaries.[2] Perhaps for analogous reasons, in order to understate the overwhelming dominance of the Russian Federated Republic, data for the Russian Republic are often omitted. Where possible, in Tables 2 and 20, figures for the RSFSR were arrived at by interpolation.

Very little information is available on the training of Party functionaries. Table 16 contains cumulative figures for graduates of the schools in the system of professional Party instruction, but information is scarce about the number of these graduates still in the Party and in responsible *apparat* positions. Thus, it is not yet possible to determine the role of these schools in the recruitment and advancement of Party officials. It is almost as difficult to gather information about the administration, teaching faculty (called propagandists), and enrollment of the vast network of Party schools for the political education of nonapparatus, or rank and file, Party members. Table 17 brings together from many sources data bearing on the staffing and enrollment of this system. The next table focuses on the Evening University of Marxism-Leninism, the institution responsible for the preparation and certification of the propagandists.

For some of the other tables it might be useful to explain certain of the categories used: In Table 1, "candidates" refers to new, or probationary, members, all of whom must spend one year in the Party before attaining full membership. Table 2 presents information about each convening of the Party Congress, theoretically the highest and most authoritative component of the Party. Its moribund condition during Stalin's rule indicates, however, that actual authority was located elsewhere, and, in fact, the Politburo (or, as it has been called, the Presidium) has been the most powerful body within the Party. Party statutes do, nonetheless, contain a provision that the Congress must be convened "at least once in five years."[3]

Tables 20 to 23 present data on some of the most important mass organizations, or auxiliaries of the Party. The Komsomol, or Young Communist League, is the organization that embraces youth between the ages of fourteen and twenty-eight. It is sometimes assumed that it effectively penetrates that age group with membership coverage of 90 percent or more. Table 24 indicates, however, that this goal has not been achieved, even when the relevant age group has been narrowed down to ages fifteen to twenty-four. In fact, substantial increases in the membership rate are of very recent origin and might attest to the interest on the part of Stalin's successors in the growth of this organization. Similarly impressive is the rate of growth of the trade unions, when calculated as a proportion of the able-bodied age-group of the population. Perhaps most complete coverage in a mobilization campaign is achieved by elections to the Supreme Soviet, the bicameral national legislature. As seen in Table 22, extraordinarily high percentages of eligible voters turn out every four years in response to a campaign of agitation and propaganda, both mass and personal, that blankets the country. Another agency for mass mobilization is the Znanie (Knowledge) Society, a Party coordinated lecture bureau whose audience has risen to over five times the population of the Soviet Union. Even if one discounts the probable inflation factor in these figures, the scope of the organization and growth of its audience are impressive.

The best guide to information on the Communist Party of the Soviet Union are the journals *Partynaya Zhizn* (Party Life), *Kommunist,* and, for Party education, *Politicheskoe Samoobrazovanie* (Political Self-Education). The yearbooks of the *Great Soviet Encyclopedia* are very useful, as are reference books for Party secretaries, one of which, *CPSU: Reference Guide to Party Construction* (Moscow, 1969), is particularly informative. The best sources in English for the history and functions of the Party are *Communist Party Membership in the U.S.S.R. 1917–1967,* by T. H. Rigby (Princeton University Press, 1968) and Leonard Schapiro's *The Communist Party of the Soviet Union* (New York, Random House, 1959).

NOTES

1. John A. Armstrong, *The Soviet Bureaucratic Elite,* New York, Praeger, 1959.
2. Rigby estimates that there are 300,000 secretaries. Fainsod estimated only

100,000 to 200,000 in 1962. These figures are presented by F. C. Barghoorn, *Politics in the USSR*, Boston, Little, Brown, 1966, p. 38.
3. The Party Statutes are available in English—edited by Jan F. Triska and entitled *Soviet Communism: Programs and Rules,* San Francisco, Chandler, 1962. The change from four to five years was made in 1971.

Table 1. CPSU MEMBERSHIP

Year (Jan. 1)	Members	Candidates	Total
1917[a]	24,000	none	24,000
1918[b]	350,000	none	350,000
1919[a]	390,000	none	390,000
1920[a]	611,978	...[c]	611,978
1926	639,652	440,162	1,079,814
1927	786,288	426,217	1,212,505
1928	914,307	391,547	1,305,854
1929	1,090,508	444,854	1,535,362
1930	1,184,651	493,259	1,667,910
1940	1,982,743	1,417,232	3,339,975
1950	5,510,787	829,396	6,340,183
1953	6,067,027	830,197	6,897,224
1954	6,402,284	462,579	6,864,863
1955	6,610,238	346,867	6,957,105
1956	6,767,644	405,877	7,173,521
1957	7,001,114	493,459	6,340,183
1958	7,296,559	546,637	7,843,196
1959	7,662,356	616,775	8,239,131
1960	8,017,249	691,418	8,708,667
1961	8,472,396	803,430	9,275,826
1962	9,051,934	839,134	9,891,068
1963	9,581,149	806,047	10,387,196
1964	10,182,916	839,453	11,022,369
1965	10,811,443	946,726	11,758,169
1966	11,546,287	809,021	12,357,308
1967	12,135,103	549,030	12,684,133
1968	13,640,000	681,600	14,321,600
1969	13,395,253	616,531	14,011,784

Notes:
[a] March.
[b] October.
[c] Not available.

Table 2. CPSU MEMBERSHIP: REPUBLICS

Year	Armenia Members	Candidates	Azerbaidzhan Members	Candidates	Belorussia Members	Candidates	Estonia Members	Candidates	Georgia Members	Candidates
1956	69,263	2,245	118,629	7,266	144,482	15,635	23,229	2,581	184,464	6,975
1957	71,581	2,820	123,709	7,690	155,844	16,903	24,798	2,893	189,257	7,529
1958	73,855	3,217	129,063	8,470	168,716	19,193	26,966	3,550	194,415	8,751
1959	76,835	3,515	135,001	8,729	183,855	19,592	29,431	3,951	199,651	8,933
1960	80,395	4,667	142,801	10,420	202,068	23,473	33,186	4,662	207,768	9,098
1961	84,727	4,436	151,626	12,027	223,699	25,969	37,450	5,003	214,499	9,825
1962	88,999	4,549	160,491	12,899	243,464	23,306	41,181	4,538	221,083	9,778
1963	93,659	4,836	171,560	13,236	266,248	25,987	45,230	4,574	229,083	9,508
1964	98,884	5,421	183,993	14,546	290,752	28,444	49,393	5,443	236,726	11,649
1965	105,062	5,295	197,036	14,933	320,622	22,421	54,599	4,495	245,988	12,431
1966	110,441	4,094	211,256	10,438	343,174	16,421	58,311	3,411	255,915	9,815
1967	114,057	4,771	219,130	12,271	358,727	20,494	60,715	4,180	263,087	11,593
1968	118,097	4,962	228,185	12,741	377,311	20,175	64,032	3,577	271,165	11,815

Note:
[a] Includes candidates.

Table 2. CPSU MEMBERSHIP: REPUBLICS (Continued)

Year	Kazakhstan Members	Candi- dates	Kirgizia Members	Candi- dates	Latvia Members	Candi- dates	Lithuania Members	Candi- dates	Moldavia Members	Candi- dates
1956	269,294[a]	...	49,605	3,682	48,452	5,495	42,229[a]	...	43,222[a]	...
1957	283,851[a]	...	51,594	4,138	52,167	5,138	44,821[a]	...	46,399[a]	...
1958	312,000[a]	...	58,300[a]	...	55,654	5,760	49,114[a]	...	49,997[a]	...
1959	318,000[a]	...	61,646[a]	...	59,530[a]	...	54,324[a]	...	54,320[a]	...
1960	345,000[a]	...	65,866[a]	...	65,947[a]	...	60,551[a]	...	59,900[a]	...
1961	373,648[a]	...	69,789[a]	...	70,235	6,407	66,234[a]	...	65,100[a]	...
1962	364,567	33,459	73,341[a]	...	76,357	5,629	71,061[a]	...	69,954[a]	...
1963	418,331[a]	...	71,943	6,412	81,506	6,662	69,522	7,968	69,849	6,874
1964	410,716	39,770	77,617	7,104	87,566	8,176	76,518	9,848	76,056	9,323
1965	443,565	38,017	84,266	7,404	95,734	7,072	85,568	8,399	93,794[a]	...
1966	474,304	23,761	90,703	7,588	101,851	5,502	93,124	6,255	93,886	5,738
1967	489,394	27,667	93,630	3,850	106,130	6,565	98,173	7,245	98,077	5,209
1968	538,923[a]	...	96,206	4,453	111,370	6,292	104,172	6,962	107,145[a]	...

Year	R.S.F.S.R. Members	Candi- dates	Tadzhikistan Members	Candi- dates	Turkmenia Members	Candi- dates	Ukraine Members	Candi- dates	Uzbekistan Members	Candi- dates
1956	4,914,004[a]	...	35,156	3,896	36,846	2,398	911,162	76,981	145,279	11,050
1957	5,159,681[a]	...	37,145	4,443	38,114	2,811	911,162	76,981	157,706	15,398
1958	5,121,735[a]	...	37,145	4,443	39,539	3,231	1,162,997	119,535	168,369	19,181
1959	5,337,643[a]	...	43,146	5,079	41,385	3,767	1,256,700	131,788	182,369	19,941
1960	5,656,581[a]	...	46,341	5,673	43,822	4,068	1,256,700	131,788	223,937	23,955
1961	5,931,763[a]	...	50,016	5,837	46,582	3,705	1,432,806	147,365	211,559	25,519
1962	6,443,471[a]	...	53,165	5,328	48,772	3,562	1,568,135	...	238,898	25,081
1963	6,690,892[a]	...	57,016	5,602	51,336	3,280	1,565,823	121,175	265,841	23,163
1964	7,026,015[a]	...	61,039	6,585	53,638	3,568	1,683,300	146,000	288,358	25,921
1965	7,130,916[a]	...	66,488	6,795	56,711	4,003	1,833,362	128,046	315,349	23,377
1966	8,221,433[a]	...	71,534	4,467	59,808	2,871	1,959,215	84,976	335,969	17,872
1967	8,025,915[a]	...	74,024	4,383	61,318	2,858	2,033,792	105,008	352,218	19,652
1968	9,464,066[a]	...	76,200	4,987	63,101	3,155	2,123,283	106,476	369,685	23,064

Table 3. CPSU CONGRESSES

Year	Place	No. Delegates	% Party
1898	Minsk	9	...
1903	Brussels/ London	57	...
1905	London	38	...
1906	Stockholm	134	...
1907	London	342	...
1917 (Aug.)	Petrograd	267	1.1
1918	Petrograd	104	.027
1919	Moscow	403	.115
1920	Moscow	716	.117
1921	Moscow	990	.135
1922	Moscow	687	.130
1923	Moscow	825	.165
1924	Moscow	1,164	.247
1925	Moscow	1,306	.163
1927	Moscow	1,669	.138
1930	Moscow	2,159	.129
1934	Moscow	1,961	.073
1939	Moscow	2,035	.088
1952	Moscow	1,359	.020
1956	Moscow	1,430	.020
1959	Moscow	1,367	.017
1961	Moscow	4,799	.049
1966	Moscow	4,942	.039

Table 4. CPSU MEMBERSHIP: ETHNIC REPRESENTATION

Nationality	1961	% Party	1965	% Party	1967	% Party
U.S.S.R.	9,626,700[a]	100.1	11,758,200[a]	100.0	12,684,133	100.1
Russians	6,116,700	63.5	7,335,200	62.4	7,846,292	61.9
Ukrainians	1,412,200	14.7	1,813,400	15.4	1,983,090	15.6
Belorussians	287,000	3.0	386,000	3.3	424,360	3.3
Georgians	170,400	1.8	194,300	1.7	209,196	1.6
Armenians	161,200	1.7	187,900	1.6	200,605	1.6
Kazakhs	149,200	1.5	181,300	1.5	199,196	1.6
Uzbeks	142,700	1.5	193,600	1.6	219,196	1.7
Azerbaidzhanis	106,100	1.1	141,900	1.2	162,181	1.3
Lithuanians	42,800	0.4	61,500	0.5	71,316	0.6
Latvians	33,900	0.4	44,300	0.4	49,559	0.4
Tadzhiks	32,700	0.3	41,900	0.4	46,593	0.4
Kirgiz	27,300	0.3	35,000	0.3	39,053	0.3
Turkmen	27,300	0.3	32,400	0.3	35,781	0.3
Moldavians	26,700	0.3	40,300	0.3	46,593	0.4
Estonians	24,400	0.3	33,900	0.3	37,705	0.3
Others	866,100	9.0	1,035,300	8.8	1,113,263	8.8

Note:

[a] Soviet official sources give these totals, which differ somewhat from the official totals given in Table 1.

Table 5. CPSU MEMBERSHIP: AGE

Year	Under 25	% Total	26-40	% Total	41-50	% Total	Over 50	% Total
1927	303,126	25	739,628	61	133,376	11	36,375	
1965	823,072	7	5,526,339	47	2,939,542	25	2,469,216	2
1967	634,207	5	5,898,122	47	3,247,138	25	2,904,666	2

Table 6. CPSU MEMBERSHIP: SEX

Year	Men	% Party	Men as % Population	Women	% Party	Women as % Population
1920	...	...	...	45,297	7.5	...
1922	487,142	92.2	...	41,212	7.8	...
1924	425,272	90.1	...	46,728	9.9	...
1927	1,066,056	87.9	48.3[a]	148,306	12.2	51.7[a]
1929	1,325,017	86.3	...	201,345	13.7	...
1937	1,688,406	85.2	...	293,059	14.8	...
1947	5,325,885	81.8	...	1,102,424	18.2	...
1950	5,027,765	79.3	...	1,312,418	20.7	...
1957	6,018,142	80.3	45.0[b]	1,477,678	19.7	55.0[b]
1961	7,466,138	80.5	...	1,809,688	19.5	...
1962	7,948,988	80.4	...	1,942,080	19.6	...
1963	8,336,825	80.3	...	2,050,371	19.7	...
1964	8,827,365	80.1	...	2,195,004	19.9	...
1965	9,385,708	79.8	...	2,372,461	20.2	...
1967	10,037,059	79.1	...	2,647,074	20.9	...
1968	10,379,536	78.8	...	2,792,464	21.2	...

Notes:

[a] 1926.

[b] 1959.

Table 7. CPSU Membership: Level of Education

Year	Higher	% Total	Unfinished Higher	% Total	Secondary	% Total	Unfinished Secondary and Below	% Total
1927	9,614	.8	...	...	104,714	8.6	1,098,177	90.6
1937	108,256	5.5	48,563	2.5	227,612	11.5	1,597,266	80.5
1947	453,288	7.5	136,149	2.3	1,324,896	21.9	3,219,047	68.3
1957	869,582	11.6	267,158	3.6	1,696,114	22.6	6,118,719	62.2
1965	1,763,262	15.0	301,255	2.6	3,542,005	30.1	6,151,647	52.3
1967	2,097,055	16.5	325,985	2.6	3,993,119	31.5	6,151,647	49.4

Table 8. CPSU Membership: Number of Years in Party

Year	Up to 10	% Total	10-30	% Total	Over 30	% Total
1957	3,312,601	44.2	3,889,683	51.9	292,289	3.9
1961	3,710,330	40.0	...	...	...	...
1962	3,875,517	39.0	5,558,780	56.2	474,771	4.8
1965	5,032,496	42.8	6,031,941	51.3	693,732	5.9
1967	6,126,436	48.3	5,923,490	46.7	634,207	5.0

Table 9. CPSU Membership: Social Position

Year	Workers	% Total	Peasants (Collective Farmers)	% Total	White Collar and Others	% Total
1922	234,589	44.4	141,071	26.7	152,694	28.9
1923	224,096	44.9	128,269	25.7	146,735	29.4
1924	207,680	44.0	135,936	28.8	128,384	27.2
1925	454,623	56.7	212,478	26.5	134,703	16.8
1926	613,334	56.8	279,672	25.9	186,808	17.3
1927	668,256	55.1	331,096	27.3	213,454	17.6
1928	741,725	56.8	299,041	22.9	265,088	20.3
1929	942,712	61.4	333,174	21.7	259,476	16.9
1930	1,095,675	65.3	338,937	20.2	243,296	14.5
1957	2,398,263	32.0	1,296,561	17.3	3,799,749	50.7
1960	3,753,435	43.1	1,889,781	21.7	3,065,451	35.2
1961	3,369,345	34.5	1,665,419	17.5	4,591,936	48.0
1964	4,111,344	37.3	1,818,691	16.5	5,092,334	46.2
1966	6,672,946	37.8	2,001,884	16.2	5,684,362	46.0
1967	4,832,655	38.1	2,029,461	16.0	5,822,017	45.9
1968	5,110,736	38.8	2,081,176	15.8	5,980,088	45.4

Table 10. CPSU Membership: Occupation—Agriculture and Nonagricultural

	Non-Agricultural						Agricultural			
Year	Industry	% Party	Construction	% Party	Transport	% Party	Collectives	% Party	State Farms	% Party
1937	537,843	27.1	43,104	2.2	176,550	8.9	186,904	9.4	52,220	2.6
1947	1,188,758	19.6	78,128	1.3	364,492	6.0	761,194	12.6	91,109	1.5
1957	1,786,273	23.8	205,132	2.7	550,268	7.3	931,340	12.4	132,762	1.8
1967	3,195,718	25.2	666,380	5.3	838,019	6.6	1,330,316	10.5	837,543	6.6
1968	3,347,650	25.4	721,130	5.5	859,037	6.5	1,375,316	10.4	875,002	6.6

Table 11. CPSU MEMBERSHIP: OCCUPATION—PRODUCTION AND SERVICES

| Year | Production | | | | | |
	Total	Industry & Construction	Transport & Communications	Agriculture	Trade & Supply	Other Branches
1947						
Number	4,200,019	1,724,792	562,827	1,416,145	387,322	108,934
%	69.4	28.5	9.3	23.4	6.4	1.8
1957						
Number	5,373,609	2,443,231	756,952	1,768,719	374,729	29,978
%	71.7	32.6	10.1	23.6	5.0	0.4
1967						
Number	9,297,470	4,642,393	1,141,572	2,815,878	558,102	139,526
%	73.3	36.6	9.0	22.2	4.4	1.1
1968						
Number	9,668,248	4,886,812	1,145,964	2,911,012	579,568	144,892
%	73.4	37.1	8.7	22.1	4.4	1.1

| Year | Services | | | |
	Total	Science, Health, Culture	Civil Service & Public Orgs.	Communal Living Services
1947				
Number	1,851,882	671,761	1,119,602	60,519
%	30.6	11.1	18.5	1.0
1957				
Number	2,120,964	959,305	1,071,724	89,935
%	28.3	12.8	14.3	1.2
1967				
Number	3,386,664	2,092,882	1,128,888	164,894
%	26.7	16.5	8.9	1.3
1968				
Number	3,503,752	2,160,208	1,159,136	184,408
%	26.6	16.4	8.8	1.4

Table 12. CPSU MEMBERSHIP: CANDIDATES TAKEN INTO PARTY

| Year | Workers | Peasants (Collective Farmers) | White Collar and Others | Economic Specialists | Komsomol Memb |
		% Candidates		% White Collar Candidates	% Candidate
1952–1955	27.2	16.4	56.4	48.7	24.3
1956–1961	40.6	19.4	40.0	65.1	47.6
1962–1966	47.6	14.0	38.4	72.4	39.4
1967	52.2	14.0	33.8	77.4	45.0 (1971)

Table 13.

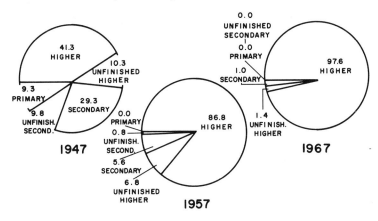

13. CPSU: EDUCATION OF SECRETARIES OF REPUBLIC, OBLAST, AND KRAI ORGANIZATIONS

Table 14.

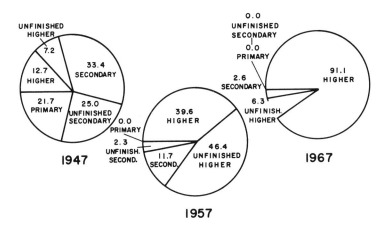

14. CPSU: EDUCATION OF SECRETARIES OF OKRUG, CITY AND DISTRICT ORGANIZATIONS

Table 15.

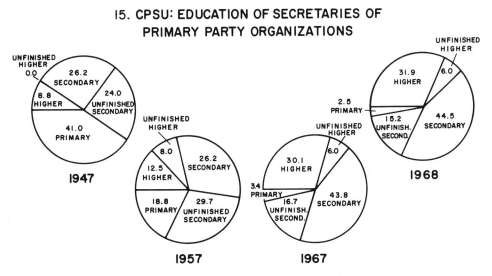

15. CPSU: EDUCATION OF SECRETARIES OF PRIMARY PARTY ORGANIZATIONS

Table 16. CPSU GRADUATES OF PARTY INSTRUCTION SCHOOLS, 1946–1966

Academy of Social Sciences[a]	Higher Party School[a]	Higher Party Correspondence School[a]	Higher Party Schools[b]	Party Schools[c]	Soviet-Party Schools[d]	Total	% C.P.S.U. (1967)
2,920	6,791	33,744	24,774	60,570	31,649	126,704	.10

Notes:

    [a]Administered by Central Committee, C.P.S.U.

    [b]Administered by Republics, Krais, Oblasts (1957-1966).

    [c]Administered by Republics, Krais, Oblasts (1946-1966).

    [d]Administered by Oblasts, Districts.

Table 17. DISTRIBUTION OF PROPAGANDA PERSONNEL

Year	Propagandists	Location	In Propaganda System C.P.S.U. Members	Students	Party Members Per Prop. Ratio	Students Per Prop Ratio
1964/65	1,100,000	U.S.S.R.	11,022,369	36,000,000	9:1	30:1
1965/66	900,000	U.S.S.R.	12,357,108	12,000,000	13:1	13:1
1967/68	1,000,000	U.S.S.R.	13,180,000	14,500,000	13:1	14:1
1968/69	1,100,000	U.S.S.R.	...	15,000,000	...	13:1
		SUB-NATIONAL FIGURES				
1967/68	6,300	Armenia	200,605	...	31:1	...
1967/68	1,795	Georgia	209,196	...	116:1	...
1965/66	43,907	Uzbekistan	193,600	...	4:1	...
1967/68	75,000	Moscow	730,000 (March,1966)	850,000	9:1	11:1

Note:

    "Non-Party activists" are also included in the propaganda system.

Table 18. EVENING UNIVERSITIES OF MARXISM–LENINISM

Year	Location	Number of Universities	Enrollment
1948	U.S.S.R.	188	100,000
1964/65	U.S.S.R.	...	200,000
1965/66	U.S.S.R.	302	230,000
1967/68	U.S.S.R.	326	220,000
	SUB-NATIONAL FIGURES		
1965/66	Moscow	...	20,000
1940-1965 (cumulative)	Moscow	...	90,000
1965-66	Kiev	...	2,500
1965/66	Riga	...	2,600
1941-1965 (cumulative)	Riga	...	12,000

Note:

    Not all of those studying at these universities become propagandists; there are also divisions, or faculties, which prepare the "generalists" of the Party organizations.

Table 19. CPSU: Primary Party Organizations

Year	Total Number	P.P.O. with up to 15 Communists	15-49 Communists	50-100 Communists	More than 100 Communists
1922	32,281	...	...	...	...
1927	38,978	...	...	...	...
1937	102,475	...	...	...	...
1947	296,568	65.5%	29.2%	3.7%	1.6%
1957	344,325	57.5%	36.4%	4.2%	1.9%
1967	337,915	...	...	...	...
1968	349,060	40.4%	42.7%	10.9%	6.0%

Table 20. Komsomol Membership

Year	U.S.S.R.	Armenia	Azerbaidzhan	Belorussia	Estonia	Georgia	Kazakhstan	Kirgizia
1918	22,100	...	...	...	...	...	...	...
1919	96,096	...	...	...	...	...	...	...
1920	482,342	...	...	...	...	...	...	...
1921	475,000	...	...	...	...	...	...	...
1922	303,944	...	...	...	...	...	...	...
1924	702,000	...	...	...	...	...	...	...
1926	1,750,000	...	...	...	...	...	...	...
1928	1,960,000	...	...	...	...	...	...	...
1931	2,897,000	...	...	...	...	...	...	...
1936	3,981,777	...	...	...	...	...	...	...
1949	9,283,289	...	...	...	...	...	...	...
1954	18,825,327	...	...	...	...	...	...	...
1956	18,000,000	170,000	...	629,250	60,000	...	627,288	136,013
1957	18,500,000	174,456	327,000	621,358	60,404	338,000	674,011	136,218
1958	18,000,000	173,470	332,237	613,896	63,341	338,693	707,502	136,670
1959	...	172,441	333,867	608,771	67,133	340,000	759,000	140,300
1960	19,000,000	177,611	335,614	620,658	73,507	342,873	800,000	142,900
1961	19,095,000	181,237	344,702	628,233	80,548	366,000	846,607	151,109
1962	20,000,000	192,300	373,742	675,713	91,266	374,500	868,843	165,800
1963	21,000,000	206,031	395,070	739,799	98,817	391,138	909,826	183,793
1964	22,500,000	215,802	410,925	788,896	104,285	402,250	925,420	196,000
1965	23,000,000	221,393	418,188	811,180	107,913	406,747	964,246	204,827
1966	23,000,000	218,595	411,099	790,685	106,321	396,333	949,570	200,262
1967	23,000,000	220,306	417,612	805,685	103,520	406,079	969,819	197,243
1968	24,000,000	234,293	431,987	860,233	104,860	428,116	1,033,915	217,988
1969	25,500,000	251,138	454,000	916,230	107,997	452,004	1,124,858	237,008

Year	Latvia	Lithuania	Moldavia	R.S.F.S.R.	Tadzhikistan	Turkmenia	Ukraine	Uzbekistan
1956	120,500	...	...	...	...	100,000	3,000,000	593,000
1957	118,000	116,010	137,000	12,099,131	114,000	104,000	2,896,319	584,093
1958	120,000	125,000	143,300	11,432,044	118,660	110,000	2,981,698	603,489
1959	125,000	131,012	149,000	...	122,859	113,588	3,057,110	614,848
1960	130,000	144,674	162,000	12,038,040	128,244	115,125	3,154,581	634,173
1961	153,163	159,612	172,200	11,842,669	134,310	122,675	3,240,935	671,000
1962	162,180	180,597	188,600	12,299,184	146,014	130,698	3,449,563	701,000
1963	175,268	204,943	212,769	12,778,635	151,966	141,160	3,647,350	763,435
1964	184,103	226,311	239,795	13,845,085	154,716	147,684	3,858,539	800,189
1965	190,117	244,791	255,469	14,014,622	160,768	156,141	3,983,795	859,803
1966	190,074	249,870	266,018	14,132,198	162,094	156,381	3,923,650	846,850
1967	190,890	253,501	267,785	14,089,270	160,960	157,857	3,920,586	838,887
1968	196,847	263,358	283,880	14,583,337	175,977	165,434	4,109,266	910,509
1969	205,361	272,867	305,112	15,505,163	192,777	178,707	4,306,499	990,279

Table 21. TRADE UNION MEMBERSHIP

Year	U.S.S.R.	Armenia	Azerbaidzhan	Belorussia	Estonia	Georgia	Kazakhstan	Kirgizi
1918	2,638,800	...	...	...	...	...	...	...
1919	3,422,000	...	...	...	...	...	...	...
1920	4,227,000	...	...	...	...	...	...	...
1921	8,485,800	...	...	...	...	...	...	...
1922	5,100,000	...	...	...	...	...	...	...
1924	6,400,000	...	...	...	...	...	...	...
1926	9,236,000	...	...	...	...	...	...	...
1928	11,000,000	...	...	...	...	...	...	...
1932	16,500,000	...	...	...	...	...	...	...
1949	28,500,000	...	...	...	...	...	...	...
1954	40,420,000	...	...	...	...	...	...	...
1956	45,338,478	290,000	598,498	1,185,000	346,000	670,510	1,681,800	266,400
1957	49,496,340	335,000	635,260	1,339,000	346,000	730,000	1,935,000	232,980
1958	51,676,180	336,000	648,180	1,436,000	365,400	752,000	2,000,000	317,000
1959	53,987,526	367,549	683,246	1,583,000	399,500	810,000	2,216,675	360,163
1960	54,796,452	384,496	742,265	1,500,000	424,000	850,000	2,579,878	407,853
1961	62,809,755	449,460	796,000	2,000,000	455,429	942,580	2,743,247	436,300
1962	65,364,772	470,800	813,211	2,000,000	456,386	974,109	2,851,456	465,700
1963	68,940,059	516,300	844,392	2,100,000	445,678	1,020,821	3,345,500	499,100
1964	73,133,506	572,900	977,399	2,300,000	514,115	1,072,591	3,350,000	521,300
1965	78,573,776	634,544	1,076,000	2,608,110	545,851	1,213,737	3,353,000	635,000
1966	83,030,244	687,299	1,148,300	2,809,065	565,791	1,245,304	4,109,000	650,000
1967	86,056,308	733,889	1,204,219	2,948,423	583,146	1,290,835	4,261,227	714,000
1968	88,643,348	792,953	1,241,700	3,090,359	570,186	1,380,025	4,418,000	750,000
1969	91,979,672	826,110	1,302,000	3,233,599	617,674	1,424,153	4,530,000	790,200

Year	Latvia	Lithuania	Moldavia	R.S.F.S.R.	Tadzhikistan	Turkmenia	Ukraine	Uzbek
1956	540,000	464,270	299,000	29,500,000	206,000	220,000	8,127,000	944
1957	600,000	500,000	330,000	32,105,100	227,000	220,000	8,861,000	1,100
1958	640,000	523,000	345,700	33,121,900	255,000	230,000	9,448,000	1,268
1959	670,000	548,000	380,000	34,429,200	265,000	270,737	9,686,456	1,318
1960	671,700	640,000	424,800	34,429,200	295,000	292,050	9,700,000	1,455
1961	770,000	711,000	497,000	39,887,400	300,000	303,339	11,000,000	1,518
1962	785,360	735,000	525,000	41,000,000	333,000	314,750	12,000,000	1,640
1963	862,646	757,000	532,900	43,634,600	349,000	299,122	12,000,000	1,733
1964	899,880	784,000	623,000	46,202,200	392,720	341,401	12,700,000	1,882
1965	937,585	892,577	700,000	48,609,100	434,814	393,472	14,500,000	2,039
1966	1,046,351	945,278	796,000	50,579,500	466,958	404,600	15,300,000	2,276
1967	1,023,004	1,054,500	858,228	52,069,000	495,255	423,248	16,000,000	2,397
1968	1,128,637	1,157,854	909,236	53,723,700	516,698	437,000	16,000,000	2,527
1969[a]	1,132,250	1,185,000	953,526	55,367,600	524,560	455,600	17,000,000	2,637

Table 22. VOTING

Election Year	Eligible	Total Voted	%
1937	94,138,159	91,113,153	98.60
1946	101,717,686	101,450,936	99.00
1950	111,116,373	111,090,010	99.98
1954	120,750,816	120,727,826	99.98
1958	133,836,325	133,796,091	99.97
1962	140,022,359	139,957,809	99.95

Election Year	Council of the Union				Council of Nationalities			
	Voted For	%	Against	Invalid	Voted For	%	Against	Invalid
1937	89,844,271	98.60	632,074	636,808	89,063,169	97.80	562,402	1,487,582
1946	100,621,225	99.18	819,699	10,012	100,603,567	99.16	818,955	28,414
1950	110,788,377	99.73	300,146	1,487	110,782,009	99.72	306,382	1,619
1954	120,479,249	99.79	247,897	680	120,539,860	99.84	187,357	609
1958	133,214,652	99.57	580,641	798	133,431,524	99.73	363,736	831
1962	139,210,431	99.47	746,563	815	139,391,455	99.60	564,155	706
1966	143,570,976	99.76	345,643	412	143,595,678	99.80	289,298	381

Table 23. ANNUAL NUMBER OF LECTURES GIVEN BY "ZNANIYE" SOCIETY AND ESTIMATED AUDIENCE (In Millions)

Year	Total Number of Lectures	Total Estimated Audience
1958	5.6	389
1959	7.3	513
1960	10.0	630
1961	12.0	710
1962	12.8	698
1963	13.3	687
1964	14.6	747
1965	15.1	743
1966	15.5	775
1967	16.2	829
1968	17.0	887

Table 24. AVERAGE ANNUAL LETTERS RECEIVED BY NEWSPAPERS

Newspaper	1955-57 Letters Received	1958-59 Letters Received	% Change Over Previous Period	1960-64 Letters Received	% Change Over Previous Period
Pravda	250[a]	299[a]	+20	247	-17
Izvestia	52[a]	76[a]	+46	215	+182
Komsomol Pravda	86[a]	206[a]	+140	194	-6
Pravda Ukraine	25	27[a]	+8	30[a]	+11
Soviet Ukraine	25	22[a]	-12	23	+5
Pravda of the East	...	13.6	...	16[a]	+22
Moscow Pravda	30[a]	...	...	41.8[a]	+39[b]
Volgograd Pravda	7.5	...	...	25[a]	+233[b]
Kiev Pravda	5.8[a]	12	+107	12[a]	0
Kursk Pravda	13.5	15.9	+18	20[a]	+26

Notes:

[a]The largest (instead of average) annual figure is used for the time period.

[b]Change from 1955-57.

Table 25. AVERAGE ANNUAL LETTERS TO NEWSPAPERS (In Thousands)

1956-57

Newspaper	Letters Received	Letters Published	Percentage[a] Published of Letters Received
Soviet Russia	...	...	..
Soviet Belorussia	15.0	3.0	20
Worker's Paper (Kiev)	14.5	5.0	34
Uzbekistan Soviet	14.6	5.9	40
Kaliningrad Pravda	13.8	4.0	29
Stavropol Pravda	13.1	3.9	30
Young Leninist (Stavropol)	8.0	3.2	40
Gorky Pravda	...	...	32[b]

1959-60

Newspaper	Letters Received	Letters Published	Percentage[a] Published of Letters Received
Soviet Russia	...	...	..
Soviet Belorussia	23.0	10.0	43
Worker's Paper (Kiev)	28.5	7.1	25
Uzbekistan Soviet	17.0	7.7	45
Kaliningrad Pravda	16.5	5.5	33
Stavropol Pravda	16.5	4.3	26
Young Leninist (Stavropol)	8.5	3.5	41
Gorky Pravda	...	...	..

1963-66

Newspaper	Letters Received	Letters Published	Percentage[a] Published of Letters Received
Soviet Russia	...	...	13.5[c]
Soviet Belorussia	50.0	12.0	24.0
Worker's Paper (Kiev)	14.7	3.4	23.0
Uzbekistan Soviet	13.4	9.2	69.0
Kaliningrad Pravda	15.0	4.6	31.0
Stavropol Pravda	18.3	4.7	26.0
Young Leninist (Stavropol)	8.1	2.5	31.0
Gorky Pravda	...	...	...

Notes:

[a]Rounded to nearest whole number.

[b]For 1957.

[c]For 1966.

Table 26. PARTICIPATION AS PERCENTAGE OF RELEVANT AGE GROUP AND RATE OF INCREASE

					Rate of Increase		
Year	C.P.S.U. Members[a]	Komsomol[b]	Trade Union Members	Znanie Audience[a] (for lectures)	C.P.S.U. Members	Komsomol	Trade Union
1950	6.1	24.1[d]	27.6[d]	...	...	...	...
1954	...	47.1	36.4	...	...	...	...
1955	6.1	...	...	...	...	...	...
1956	6.2	45.0	39.6	...	.1	...	...
1957	5.3	44.4	42.0	...	-.9	-.6	2.4
1958	6.5	45.0	43.2	312.3	1.2	.6	1.2
1959	6.8	...	43.8	410.8	.3	...	.6
1960	7.2	53.2	46.9	506.5	.4	8.2	3.1
1961	7.7	53.5	52.3	570.0	.5	.3	5.4
1962	8.2	58.0	54.8	553.4	.5	4.5	2.5
1963	8.5	63.0	55.9	527.7	.3	5.0	1.1
1964	9.0	69.8	57.4	552.2	.5	6.8	1.5
1965	9.5	71.3	60.8	529.3	.5	1.5	3.4
1966	9.8	71.3	63.2	535.7	.3	0.0	2.4

Notes:

[a] Age-Group: 25 and over.

[b] Age-Group: 15-24.

[c] Age-Group: "Able-Bodied" - 16-59 (males)/ 54 (females).

[d] Membership in 1949.

CHAPTER VII TABLE SOURCE NOTES

TABLE 1

KPSS, p. 7.

TABLE 2

B. S. E. Ezhegodnik, 1957–1969. RSFSR figures are interpolated.

TABLE 3

KPSS, p. 29.

TABLE 4

Partynaya zhizn, no. 1 (January 1962), p. 49.
Partynaya zhizn, no. 10 (May 1965), p. 12.
Partynaya zhizn, no. 19 (October 1967), pp. 14–15.

TABLE 5

T. H. Rigby, *Communist Party Membership in the USSR*, Princeton, Princeton University Press (1968), p. 354.
KPSS, p. 19.

TABLE 6

KPSS, p. 23.

Rigby, p. 361.
Partynaya zhizn, no. 10 (May 1965), p. 13.

TABLE 7

KPSS, p. 15. Note: In the 1927 data from the census, communists with unfinished higher education were placed in the category of persons with secondary education.

TABLE 8

Partynaya zhizn, no. 1 (January 1962), p. 49.
Partynaya zhizn, no. 10 (May 1965), p. 13.
Partynaya zhizn, no. 19 (October 1967), p. 15.

TABLE 9

Rigby, p. 116.
Partynaya zhizn, no. 1 (January 1962), p. 45.
Partynaya zhizn, no. 19 (October 1967), p. 13.

TABLE 10

KPSS, p. 71.

TABLE 11

KPSS, p. 69.

TABLE 12

KPSS, pp. 79–81.
Izvestia, March 31, 1971, p. 8.

TABLE 13

KPSS, p. 95.

TABLE 14

KPSS, p. 97.

TABLE 15

KPSS, p. 99.

TABLE 16

KPSS, p. 101.

TABLES 17–18

Ellen Mickiewicz, "The Modernization of Party Propaganda in the USSR," *The Slavic Review,* June 1971.

TABLE 19

KPSS, p. 117.

TABLE 20

B. S. E. Ezhegodnik, 1957–1969. RSFSR figures are interpolated.

TABLE 21

B. S. E. Ezhegodnik, 1957–1969.
KPSS, p. 115.

TABLE 22

Pravda, December 17, 1937, p. 1.
Pravda, February 14, 1946, p. 1.
Pravda, March 18, 1954, p. 1.
Pravda, March 19, 1958, p. 1.
Pravda, March 21, 1962, p. 1.
Pravda, June 14, 1966, p. 1.
Pravda, June 15, 1966, p. 1.

TABLE 23

B. S. E. Ezhegodnik, 1959–1968.

TABLE 24

V. N. Alferov, *Vozniknovenie i razvitie rabselkorovskogo dvizhenia v SSSR,* Moscow (1970), p. 272.

TABLE 25.

Alferov, pp. 234, 273.

TABLE 26

Population data from: James W. Brackett and John W. DePauw, "Population Policy and Demographic Trends in the Soviet Union," *New Directions in the Soviet Economy,* Joint Economic Committee, U.S. Congress, Washington, U.S. Government Printing Office (1966), pp. 662–663.

COMMUNICATIONS

GAYLE D. HOLLANDER

THERE ARE MANY PROBLEMS with Soviet statistics. However, since Westerners are not allowed to collect data inside the USSR, our only sources of concrete quantitative information about Soviet communications are those published by the regime itself. The Soviet specialist has no choice but to learn the skills of finding one's way around in the material and interpreting it in the most scholarly manner possible.

Often Soviet data are not in the form one would like for purposes of comparison with data from other societies. For example, figures on Soviet mass media are rarely in "per capita" form. One must calculate this from data on the population and the media themselves. Data are not reported in a consistent manner; often years are omitted for political reasons, not the least of which is that output did not measure up to the regime's expectations. The categories used by Soviet data collectors or reporters are also problematic; they are those preferred by Soviet standards, and they tend to present the rosiest picture possible. For example, figures on "book" publishing include both books and pamphlets, so that volume and variety appear greater than they are. Categories feature subject matter most important from a political point of view: Books on Marxism and Leninism are listed separately, and other important categories are often lumped together. Frequently, categories are ill-defined, or not defined at all. One is left guessing as to what the peculiarly Soviet delineation represents. There is a general lack of explanatory comment, though in recent years more notes at the beginning or end of the article or volume have appeared.

Since Soviet society, and its economy in particular, is organized on a centralized basis, the statistics published are those available in Moscow. Although these may be quite accurate reflections of the sum total of figures reported from various subdivisions, one can never be certain about what distortions may have crept in from the provinces: There is a general human tendency to inflate production figures in order to report fulfillment or over-fulfillment of an economic plan.

There are some specific problems with various individual pieces of information. For example, the figures reported on the number of telephones represent only those instruments under the control of the Ministry of Communications, but there are many additional telephones controlled by other departments and enterprises, not to mention military units. Figures for total radio broadcasting installations do not exist, although those for the receiving network are easy to obtain. Finally, estimates of audience size are not accompanied by an explanation on the method of estimation.

Generally, the main problem in working with Soviet statistics on mass communication is learning to recognize political influence and taking it into consideration. Distortions usually stem from selective suppression, not open falsification, so that in time one can learn to recognize the patterns of distortion and correct them by careful comparison with occasional data.

Quantitative data on Soviet communications facilities have become much more accessible during the post-Stalin period. For systematic figures at regular time intervals, the best sources are the *National Economy* series published for each year (generally in the following year) by the Central Statistical Administration, and the *Press of the U.S.S.R.* series, also published each year, formerly by the Ministry of Culture and now by the State Committee on the Press of the Council of Ministers, USSR. The latter series has also produced two summary volumes, for forty- and fifty-year periods, but data for some years are omitted from these so that the annual volumes must be consulted for a coherent picture. The *Ezhegodnik,* or yearbook, of the Great Soviet Encyclopedia, is also helpful, particularly for data on foreign cultural contacts; this information, however, is much less consistently published than that on internal development because of fluctuations in foreign relations. Several other volumes, among them compilations made especially for the Fiftieth Anniversary of the Bolshevik Revolution in 1967, have also been very useful.

For less systematic, but often more detailed and revealing, data on Soviet communications it is often extremely useful to comb the pages of the two major national dailies, *Pravda* and *Izvestia,* and to search the professional journals relating to mass media, most notable among which are *Sovietskoe Radio I Televidenie* (Soviet Radio and Television) and *Zhurnalist* (Journalist). All these usually carry feature articles on Press Day and Radio Day in early May of each year, and they often contain valuable information about other media as well. Since this type of source is not consistent in terms of time period, statistical base, and media covered, I have not used it here, but it is an important enough source of communications data for the non-Soviet specialist to be aware of it.

Table A.1. TOTAL LENGTH OF RAILROAD TRACKS

Date	Total Length (Thousands of Kilometers)	Of Which Electric
1913[a]	58.5	...
1928	76.9	...
1932	81.8	0.06
1940	106.1	1.9
1950	116.9	3.0
1958	122.8	9.5
1959	124.4	11.6
1960	125.8	13.8
1961	126.6	15.7
1962	127.7	18.1
1963	128.6	20.4
1964	129.3	22.5
1965	131.4	24.9
1966	132.5	27.0
1967	133.3	29.1
1968	133.6	30.8

Note:

[a]Pre-1939 boundaries.

Table A.2. TOTAL LENGTH OF ROADS (In Thousands of Kilometers)

Year	Total	Hard Surface
1913[a]	...	24.3
1928	...	32.0
1930	1,000.0 (approx.)	40.0
1940	1,531.2	143.4
1950	1,550.4	177.3
1958	1,442.6	235.9
1959	1,370.2	251.0
1960	1,365.6	270.8
1961	1,336.2	289.9
1962	1,336.4	311.0
1963	1,332.0	330.0
1964	1,340.3	351.7
1965	1,363.5	379.0
1966	1,363.6	405.6
1967	1,368.4	433.0
1968	1,368.6	433.0

Note:

[a]Pre-1939 boundaries.

Table A.3.   PASSENGER KILOMETERS BY TYPE OF TRANSPORTATION (In Billions)

Year	Railroad	Ocean	River	Auto	Air	Total
1913[a]	25.2	1.0	1.4	...	...	27.6
1928	24.5	0.3	2.1	...	0.0	26.9
1932	83.7	1.0	4.5	0.7	0.01	89.9
1940	98.0	0.9	3.8	3.4	0.2	106.3
1950	88.0	1.2	2.7	5.2	1.2	98.3
1958	158.4	1.4	4.0	42.6	6.4	212.8
1959	164.4	1.4	4.1	50.7	9.1	229.7
1960	170.8	1.3	4.3	61.0	12.1	249.5
1961	176.3	1.4	4.4	69.3	16.4	267.8
1962	189.3	1.3	4.6	82.2	20.3	297.7
1963	192.0	1.4	4.7	95.2	25.3	318.6
1964	195.1	1.3	4.7	107.7	30.9	339.7
1965	201.6	1.5	4.9	120.5	38.1	366.6
1966	219.4	1.6	5.2	137.0	45.1	408.3
1967	234.4	1.6	5.3	153.0	53.5	447.8
1968	254.1	1.7	5.5	168.5	62.1	491.9

Note:
[a]Pre-1939 boundaries.

Table A.4.   URBAN TRANSPORT FACILITIES AND ANNUAL NUMBER OF PASSENGERS (In Millions)

Year	Number of Pieces			Number of Passengers		
	Streetcar	Trolley	Metro	Streetcar	Trolley	Metro
1940	11,391	795	278	7,283	294	377
1950	10,731	1,771	539	5,157	945	629
1958	15,119	4,189	1,010	7,195	2,672	1,068
1959	16,178	4,730	1,096	7,450	2,805	1,073
1960	17,115	5,385	1,159	7,842	3,055	1,148
1961	17,878	6,083	1,254	7,780	3,139	1,233
1962	18,785	6,892	1,364	7,937	3,353	1,301
1963	19,700	7,871	1,464	7,990	3,580	1,441
1964	20,385	8,983	1,581	8,221	3,947	1,569
1965	20,921	10,174	1,691	8,239	4,293	1,652
1966	21,334	11,294	1,865	8,193	4,713	1,822
1967	21,611	12,367	1,979	8,131	5,039	1,947
1968	21,863	13,670	2,153	7,971	5,330	2,072

Table B.1. OFFICES OF COMMUNICATION[a] (In Thousands)

Year	Total	Rural
1913	11	3
1940	51	44
1950	51	43
1958	60	47
1959	61	48
1960	63	49
1961	65	50
1962	66	50
1963	68	..
1964	70	52
1965	72	54
1966	74	55
1967	76	56
1968	78	..

Note:
[a]Houses post office, inter-city telephone station, telegraph, and some subscription offices for periodical publications.

Table B.2. DOMESTIC MAIL FLOW (In Millions of Pieces)

Year	Letters	Periodicals	Packages	Telegrams
1913	615	358	9.8	36
1928	522	1,320	13.6	28
1940	2,580	6,698	45.0	141
1950	2,607	5,877	44.0	154
1958	3,985	12,121	88.0	223
1959	4,103	13,125	91.0	230
1960	4,171	14,403	91.0	241
1961	4,075	15,562	98.0	245
1962	4,239	16,595	107.0	252
1963	4,538	18,060	120.0	254
1964	4,938	20,110	131.0	257
1965	5,241	22,599	128.0	273
1966	5,659	25,497	138.0	300
1967	6,296	28,344	151.0	323
1968	6,954	29,498	159.0	339

Table B.2a. DOMESTIC MAIL FLOW PER CAPITA

Year	Letters	Periodicals	Packages	Telegrams
1913[a]	44.15	2.57	.07	.26
1928	3.47	8.77	.09	.19
1940	13.29	34.51	.23	.73
1950	14.60	32.92	.25	.86
1958	19.45	59.15	.43	1.09
1959	19.65	62.85	.44	1.10
1960	19.65	67.85	.43	1.14
1961	18.85	71.99	.45	1.13
1962	19.29	75.53	.49	1.15
1963	20.34	80.95	.54	1.14
1964	21.83	88.88	.58	1.14
1965	22.88	98.64	.56	1.19
1966	24.41	109.98	.60	1.29
1967	26.86	120.94	.64	1.38
1968	29.38	124.63	.67	1.43

Note:

[a] Pre-Soviet boundaries.

Table B.3. TELEPHONE

Year	Telephones Under Jurisdiction of Ministry of Communications (Thousands)			Of Those, Dial Telephones (Thousands)			Inter-Urban Calls (Millions)
	Total	Urban	Rural	Total	Urban	Rural	
1913	300	300	...	...	...	...	7
1928	...	...	...	...	...	...	15
1940	1,225	1,044	181	414	414.0	...	92
1950	1,410	1,231	179	573	572.3	0.4	103
1958	2,370	2,032	338	1,180	1,155.0	25.0	163
1959	2,513	2,132	381	1,311	1,273.0	38.0	172
1960	2,697	2,284	413	1,472	1,417.0	55.0	185
1961	2,932	2,484	448	1,686	1,614.0	72.0	197
1962	3,215	2,732	483	1,958	1,857.0	101.0	210
1963	3,550	...	...	2,174	...	...	219
1964	3,900	3,166	734	2,704	2,475.0	229.0	227
1965	4,459	3,715	744	3,291	2,986.0	305.0	257
1966	5,072	4,266	806	3,932	3,549.0	383.0	283
1967	5,780	4,898	882	4,671	4,197.0	474.0	314
1968	6,591	5,596	995	5,527	4,938.0	589.0	343

Note:

In 1962 the total number of telephones (excluding military, but including "departments" other than the Ministry of Communications) was 6 million; in 1968 the number of such telephones was 9.7 million.

Table B.3a. TELEPHONES PER 1,000 POPULATION

Year	Telephones Under Jurisdiction of Ministry of Communications			Of Those, Dial Telephones			Inter-Urban Calls
	Total	Urban	Rural	Total	Urban	Rural	
1913	2.2	12.1	...	...	...	...	50
1940	6.3	16.5	1.4	2.1	6.6	...	470
1950	7.9	17.7	1.6	3.2	8.2	...	580
1958	11.6	21.3	3.1	5.8	12.1	.2	800
1959	12.0	21.3	3.5	6.3	12.7	.4	820
1960	12.7	22.0	3.8	6.9	13.7	.5	870
1961	13.6	22.9	4.2	7.8	14.9	.7	910
1962	14.6	24.4	4.5	8.9	16.6	.9	960
1963	15.9	...	...	9.7	...	...	980
1964	17.2	26.7	6.8	12.0	20.9	2.1	1,000
1965	19.5	30.5	6.9	14.4	24.5	2.8	1,120
1966	21.9	34.2	7.5	17.0	28.4	3.6	1,220
1967	24.7	38.2	8.3	19.9	32.8	4.5	1,340
1968	27.9	42.7	9.4	23.4	37.7	5.6	1,453

Table B.4. FILM PROJECTORS AND MOVIE ATTENDANCE (Commercial Screenings)

Year	No. of Projectors (Thousands)			No. of Rural Projectors (Thousands)			No. Individual Visits (Millions)		
	Total	Stationary	Mobile	Total	Stationary	Mobile	Total	Urban	Rural
1914	1.5	...	...	0.1	...	...	106	...	...
1928	7.3	...	1.4	2.4	...	1.3	106	...	...
1933	25.6	14.3	.2	17.6	...	...	...	...	...
1940	28.0	15.5	12.5	19.5	8.0	11.5	883	...	...
1950	42.0	21.6	20.4	32.2	13.0	19.2	1,144	799	345
1958	78.0	45.7	32.3	61.7	31.5	30.2	3,392	...	...
1959	90.9	59.0	31.9	73.6	43.8	29.8	3,512	...	...
1960	103.4	75.6	27.8	84.6	58.6	26.0	3,611	2,277	1,334
1961	113.9	90.5	23.4	95.0	73.0	22.0	3,849	...	...
1962	120.5	99.0	21.5	100.8	80.7	20.1	3,870	...	...
1963	131.0	113.0	18.0	110.6	93.9	16.7	3,877	...	...
1964	139.3	123.9	15.4	118.0	103.9	14.1	4,123	...	...
1965	145.4	131.6	13.8	123.1	110.6	12.5	4,279	...	...
1966	149.7	136.8	12.9	127.1	115.5	11.6	4,192	2,443	1,749
1967	152.8	140.9	11.9	129.8	119.1	10.7	4,495	2,702	1,793
1968	154.9	144.0	11.0	131.3	121.5	9.8	4,715	2,842	1,873

Table B.5. PRODUCTION OF FILMS

Year	Full-Length			Shorts			
	Total	Feature	Documentary and Popular Science	Total	Feature and Animated	Documentary	Scientific, Technical, Educational
1928	200	...	..	...	..	...	...
1930	...	...	..	...	..	...	...
1940	54	38	16	198	19	47	132
1950	36	15	21	332	15	98	219
1958	130	108	22	660	39	294	327
1959	145	117	28	750	43	350	357
1960	139	108	31	799	47	358	394
1961	137	112	25	828	62	330	436
1962	116	94	22	734	60	270	404
1963	133	102	31	781	54	282	445
1964	164	124	40	852	44	322	486
1965	167	131	36	920	56	314	550
1966	159	128	31	999	62	320	617
1967	175	140	35	1,134	66	353	715
1968	163	133	30	1,183	75	404	704

Table B.6. TELEVISION BROADCASTING NETWORK

Year	Total Stations	Of Which, Centers and Major Relay Stations
1940	2	2
1950	2	2
1952	3	3
1958	139	62
1959	210	84
1960	275	100
1961	347	116
1962	397	130
1963	418	148
1964	586	168
1965	653	185
1966	748	200
1967	890	223
1968	999	243

Table B.7. GROWTH OF RADIO AND TELEVISION RECEIVING NETWORK (In Millions of Sets)

Year	Wave Radio	Wired Radio	Total Radio	Television
1928	0.070	0.022	0.092	...
1932	0.097	1.4	1.497	...
1940	1.1	5.9	7.0	0.0004
1950	3.6	9.7	13.3	0.01
1958	21.7	27.1	48.8	2.5
1959	24.7	29.2	53.9	3.6
1960	27.8	30.8	58.6	4.8
1961	30.5	32.1	62.6	6.5
1962	32.8	33.1	65.9	8.3
1963	32.8	34.6	67.4	10.4
1964	36.7	34.6	71.3	12.8
1965	38.2	35.6	73.8	15.7
1966	39.8	37.0	76.8	19.0
1967	41.8	38.9	70.7	22.7
1968	44.5	41.0	85.5	26.8

Table B.7a. RADIO AND TELEVISION SETS PER 1,000 POPULATION

Year	Total Radio	Wave Radio	Wired Radio	Television
1928	0.62	0.47	0.15	...
1940	41.74	5.67	36.07	...
1950	74.49	20.16	54.33	0.06
1958	238.13	105.89	132.24	12.20
1959	258.11	118.28	139.83	17.24
1960	276.04	130.95	145.09	22.61
1961	289.60	141.10	148.50	30.07
1962	299.91	149.27	150.64	37.77
1963	302.11	147.02	155.09	46.60
1964	315.14	162.21	152.93	56.57
1965	322.13	166.74	155.39	68.53
1966	331.26	171.67	159.59	81.95
1967	344.33	178.35	165.98	96.85
1968	361.23	188.01	173.22	113.23

Table B.8. BOOK PUBLISHING: TOTAL AND BY REPUBLIC

Year		Total	Armenia	Azerbaidzhan	Belorussia	Estonia
1913[a]	Titles (th)	26.2	...	...	...	...
	Copies (mill)	86.7	...	...	...	...
1928	Titles (th)	34.8	...	...	...	...
	Copies (mill)	270.5	...	...	...	...
1932	Titles (th)	51.7	...	...	...	...
	Copies (mill)	555.1	...	...	...	...
1940	Titles (th)	45.8	.7	1.1	.8	.3
	Copies (mill)	462.2	2.8	5.0	10.4	2.1
1950	Titles (th)	43.1	.8	1.0	.6	.9
	Copies (mill)	820.5	4.9	8.0	12.5	5.4
1958	Titles (th)	63.6	1.1	1.1	1.2	1.1
	Copies (mill)	1,103.2	7.3	8.3	14.5	7.1
1959	Titles (th)	69.1	1.2	1.1	1.3	1.1
	Copies (mill)	1,168.7	7.1	10.3	17.1	8.0
1960	Titles (th)	76.1	1.2	1.3	1.6	1.5
	Copies (mill)	1,239.6	6.9	9.9	14.2	8.8
1961	Titles (th)	74.0	1.1	1.3	1.6	1.6
	Copies (mill)	1,119.4	6.8	10.9	18.9	8.0
1962	Titles (th)	79.1	1.2	1.5	1.6	1.8
	Copies (mill)	1,248.8	7.5	12.6	17.1	8.3
1963	Titles (th)	77.6	1.2	1.4	1.6	1.9
	Copies (mill)	1,261.8	7.3	10.9	15.0	9.9
1964	Titles (th)	78.2	1.1	1.6	2.0	2.0
	Copies (mill)	1,252.9	7.6	12.4	16.8	10.0
1965	Titles (th)	76.1	1.0	1.5	1.9	1.9
	Copies (mill)	1,279.2	7.2	11.0	23.0	10.5
1966	Titles (th)	72.9	1.0	1.6	1.7	1.9
	Copies (mill)	1,260.5	7.8	12.6	21.0	10.4
1967	Titles (th)	74.0	1.1	1.3	1.8	1.6
	Copies (mill)	1,243.5	8.3	11.4	21.5	9.1
1968	Titles (th)	75.7	1.1	1.3	1.9	1.9
	Copies (mill)	1,334.0	9.9	10.7	21.0	10.9
1969	Titles (th)	74.3	1.1	1.0	2.0	1.7
	Copies (mill)	1,215.5	10.2	9.9	24.0	11.4

Year	Georgia	Kazakhstan	Kirgizia	Latvia	Lithuania	Moldavia
1913[a]	...	...	...	...	...	...
	...	...	...	...	...	...
1928	...	...	...	...	...	...
	...	...	...	...	...	...
1932	...	...	...	...	...	...
	...	...	...	...	...	...
1940	1.6	.8	.4	.4	.4	.1
	5.6	5.8	1.3	2.9	3.8	1.4
1950	1.4	.8	.4	1.3	1.0	.5
	8.2	11.5	2.9	9.3	8.1	4.5
1958	2.0	1.7	.8	1.6	1.8	.8
	11.3	16.4	5.1	12.6	11.7	6.4
1959	2.2	1.8	.7	2.0	2.1	.8
	12.8	15.9	4.1	12.8	12.8	6.6
1960	2.5	1.4	.8	2.4	2.2	1.0
	13.2	15.8	5.0	13.2	13.8	8.0
1961	2.6	1.5	.9	2.5	1.9	1.3
	12.4	16.0	5.0	13.2	13.8	9.3
1962	2.3	1.5	.8	2.3	2.0	1.4
	13.0	15.4	4.1	11.9	12.4	8.9
1963	2.5	1.5	.8	2.3	2.0	1.4
	12.0	17.0	4.3	12.3	12.2	8.8
1964	2.6	1.4	1.0	2.3	2.0	1.3
	13.5	18.4	5.0	13.2	14.2	8.9
1965	2.3	1.7	1.0	1.9	2.2	1.2
	12.8	17.6	5.0	13.9	14.8	8.4
1966	2.2	1.7	.8	1.8	2.3	1.3
	15.0	19.6	5.3	13.3	15.8	10.7
1967	2.2	1.9	.9	1.9	2.0	1.5
	15.2	19.9	5.0	13.2	14.5	11.8
1968	2.1	1.9	.9	2.0	2.2	1.5
	14.9	22.3	5.4	15.1	15.1	11.3
1969	2.3	2.0	.8	2.0	2.1	1.3
	17.4	23.0	5.7	14.9	14.5	10.2

Note:

[a] Pre-1939 boundaries.

Table B.8. BOOK PUBLISHING: TOTAL AND BY REPUBLIC (Continued)

Year	R.S.F.S.R.	Tadzhikistan	Turkmenia	Ukraine	Uzbekistan
1913[a]	...	...	...	...	...
	...	...	...	...	...
1928	...	...	...	...	...
	...	...	...	...	...
1932	...	...	...	...	...
	...	...	...	...	...
1940	32.5	.4	.3	4.8	1.2
	353.5	2.8	2.2	51.4	11.2
1950	28.5	.3	.3	4.1	.9
	646.8	2.8	2.3	77.6	15.7
1958	41.0	.5	.6	6.6	1.6
	859.4	3.7	3.2	116.2	20.0
1959	44.7	.6	.6	6.8	1.8
	933.0	3.7	3.3	99.4	21.8
1960	48.9	.7	.6	7.9	1.9
	990.2	3.9	3.6	113.1	20.0
1961	45.6	.7	.6	8.7	2.0
	851.8	4.1	3.1	120.9	24.6
1962	50.9	.7	.7	8.3	2.0
	981.2	4.3	4.2	121.4	26.4
1963	50.3	.5	.5	7.6	2.0
	1,002.3	4.2	3.7	116.3	25.5
1964	50.5	.7	.5	7.5	1.7
	988.6	5.4	4.1	112.3	22.7
1965	49.0	.6	.5	7.2	2.1
	1,007.7	5.0	4.1	110.7	27.5
1966	46.3	.6	.5	7.5	1.7
	983.5	4.8	4.9	109.7	25.9
1967	48.0	.7	.4	6.9	1.8
	957.7	5.2	4.9	115.7	30.3
1968	48.4	.7	.4	7.6	1.8
	1,029.0	6.1	4.7	126.5	30.9
1969	47.1	.65	.3	8.0	1.9
	1,005.2	5.3	4.3	126.0	33.5

Table B.8a. BOOK PUBLISHING PER 1,000 POPULATION (In Number of Copies)

Year	U.S.S.R.	Armenia	Azerbaidzhan	Belorussia	Estonia	Georgia	Kazakhstan	Kirgizia
1940	2,382	2,121	1,527	1,150	1,992	1,550	958	851
1950	4,595	3,638	2,798	1,622	4,923	2,347	1,763	1,690
1958	5,383	4,289	2,309	1,821	5,992	2,843	1,875	2,558
1959	5,597	4,027	2,785	2,123	6,751	3,165	1,737	1,985
1960	5,839	3,785	2,494	1,744	7,352	3,197	1,633	2,340
1961	5,180	3,594	2,746	2,298	6,617	2,955	1,568	2,251
1962	5,683	3,832	3,061	2,056	6,721	3,045	1,432	1,770
1963	5,656	3,637	2,576	1,783	7,958	2,765	1,509	1,809
1964	5,538	3,673	2,830	1,987	7,943	3,058	1,599	2,006
1965	5,581	3,374	2,435	2,695	8,248	2,855	1,485	1,886
1966	5,437	3,557	2,702	2,433	8,093	3,299	1,617	1,999
1967	5,305	3,684	2,374	2,459	7,032	3,297	1,603	1,819
1968	5,636	4,293	2,176	2,381	8,359	3,198	1,759	1,904

Table B.8a. BOOK PUBLISHING PER 1,000 POPULATION (Continued)

Year	Latvia	Lithuania	Moldavia	R.S.F.S.R.	Tadzhikistan	Turkmenia	Ukraine	Uzbekistan
1940	1,538	1,299	567	3,211	1,836	1,690	1,243	1,685
1950	4,784	3,148	1,965	6,376	1,856	1,922	2,121	2,506
1958	6,061	4,390	2,281	7,430	1,915	2,192	2,822	2,507
1959	6,116	4,722	2,288	7,938	1,869	2,177	2,374	2,639
1960	6,247	4,998	2,695	8,327	1,918	2,300	2,663	2,346
1961	6,163	4,923	3,060	7,066	1,955	1,909	2,806	2,787
1962	5,484	4,346	2,865	8,037	1,970	2,497	2,789	2,882
1963	5,627	4,239	2,774	8,120	1,856	2,124	2,640	2,687
1964	5,954	4,883	2,745	7,928	2,301	2,274	2,516	2,312
1965	6,270	5,019	2,543	8,012	2,015	2,274	2,455	2,715
1966	5,880	5,291	3,177	7,771	1,866	2,561	2,410	2,451
1967	5,777	4,792	3,445	7,523	1,959	2,492	2,517	2,781
1968	6,571	4,928	3,243	8,045	2,230	2,316	2,727	2,743

Table B.9. BOOKS AND PAMPHLETS BY SUBJECT MATTER (In Millions of Copies)

	Subject	1913	1940	1950	1958	1959	1960	1961	1962
1.	Political and Social-Economic	17.7	88.2	216.8	170.0	181.7	169.9	182.1	229.0
2.	Natural Science, Mathematics	1.1	58.8	103.3	112.0	128.0	123.1	171.3	168.4
3.	Technology, Industry, Transport, Communications, Communal Affairs	1.2	35.3	65.5	111.3	145.1	180.5	140.5	138.6
4.	Agriculture	3.0	23.9	43.1	53.9	46.5	48.0	44.7	47.7
5.	Trade, Public Diet	...	5.5	25.3	9.5	14.5	58.7	10.3	11.9
6.	Health, Medicine	1.6	13.5	21.8	36.4	35.0	40.1	30.7	36.0
7.	Physical Culture, Sports	...	3.1	6.9	9.7	11.1	11.7	10.1	7.9
8.	Culture, Education, Science	1.4	19.3	24.7	37.4	42.1	40.8	43.0	46.7
9.	Linguistics	0.9	66.7	77.4	89.6	92.2	96.1	86.7	105.7
10.	Literary Criticism	...	17.4	22.0	30.6	22.5	30.1	31.6	35.7
11.	Fiction and Poetry	15.9	46.6	178.9	398.3	400.1	385.9	318.6	354.0
	Of Which, Foreign	...	5.1	16.6	80.8	80.8	79.4	54.3	49.0
12.	Art	1.5	7.5	7.4	13.8	16.7	18.8	19.0	19.6
13.	Press, Library Science, Bibliography	4.9	4.2	4.9	10.9	11.6	13.9	12.0	16.2

	Subject	1963	1964	1965	1966	1967	1968	1969
1.	Political and Social-Economic	168.6	176.3	189.8	199.1	211.4	203.4	202.0
2.	Natural Science, Mathematics	179.6	179.2	188.5	184.9	180.0	197.6	182.1
3.	Technology, Industry, Transport, Communications, Communal Affairs	154.9	135.4	142.0	124.2	148.0	145.4	153.9
4.	Agriculture	47.6	44.7	37.4	35.2	34.7	33.3	33.3
5.	Trade, Public Diet	10.2	8.6	14.2	10.8	10.8	15.2	12.6
6.	Health, Medicine	38.7	41.9	44.4	38.8	30.1	30.4	30.7
7.	Physical Culture, Sports	11.5	11.9	11.7	14.4	12.8	14.8	13.0
8.	Culture, Education, Science	44.8	42.8	42.2	39.8	42.2	40.2	45.1
9.	Linguistics	116.9	115.5	106.7	102.1	104.8	111.6	103.5
10.	Literary Criticism	38.3	35.8	32.4	34.9	34.5	40.6	43.3
11.	Fiction and Poetry	385.3	395.1	411.8	419.1	368.3	422.8	429.9
	Of Which, Foreign	51.0	55.6	55.4	47.9	39.2	40.3	36.0
12.	Art	20.1	20.7	21.7	22.6	22.8	24.4	22.2
13.	Press, Library Science, Bibliography	13.7	13.5	14.6	12.9	11.6	15.4	10.1

Table B.10a. BOOK PUBLISHING BY CONTENT

Year	Political, Socio-Econ.[a] No. (th)	C.P.I. (mill)	Marxism-Leninism No. (th)	C.P.I. (mill)	C.P.S.U. No. (th)	C.P.I. (mill)	Social Sci., Philosophy No. (th)	C.P.I. (mill)	History No. (th)	C.P.I. (mill)
1913	9.9	17.7	...	...	...	...	...	...	...	...
1928	10.5	60.5	...	...	...	...	...	...	...	...
1932	14.6	186.8	...	...	...	...	...	...	...	...
1940	7.4	88.2	.6	11.8	.9	11.7	.2	4.0	.8	12.1
1950	7.4	216.8	...	...	...	...	...	...	...	...
1958	8.9	170.0	.5	9.4	1.2	28.7	.5	10.0	1.4	34.7
1959	9.9	181.7	.4	8.3	1.7	42.3	.6	7.9	1.4	28.8
1960	11.1	169.9	.8	16.1	1.5	22.3	.6	8.5	1.7	32.6
1961	10.2	182.0	.4	10.5	1.7	59.7	.6	7.1	1.3	25.0
1962	11.1	229.0	.4	8.9	2.1	46.9	.6	9.2	1.3	48.0
1963	10.6	168.7	.3	9.2	1.7	28.9	.7	11.7	1.3	40.2
1964	9.9	176.3	.4	9.2	1.3	25.3	.6	9.3	1.7	48.3
1965	10.1	189.8	.5	13.6	1.0	19.8	.7	13.6	1.4	55.4
1966	9.5	199.1	.5	12.7	1.1	44.3	.7	11.5	1.5	46.6
1967	10.7	211.4	.5	17.4	1.0	29.0	.8	12.3	1.8	59.2
1968	9.9	203.4	.7	21.4	1.1	23.0	.8	15.4	1.5	51.1
1969	10.0	202.0	1.1	34.8	.9	13.9	.8	12.9	1.3	47.1

Note:
[a] C.P.I. = Copies Per Issue.

Table B.10b. BOOK PUBLISHING BY CONTENT

Year	Works of Marx and Engels Titles	Copies (th)	Works of Lenin Titles	Copies (th)	Mass Political Literature Titles	Copies (mill)
1940	..	...	...	...	3,360	63.9
1950	..	...	...	...	4,120	139.4
1958	35	1,176	210	3,049	4,739	114.9
1959	64	1,548	158	2,798	5,657	125.0
1960	50	1,064	205	4,496	6,058	116.7
1961	39	1,660	147	4,849	6,141	139.2
1962	39	1,273	130	3,133	5,532	149.8
1963	42	1,074	108	3,347	5,272	107.0
1964	47	1,475	168	3,623	4,507	97.5
1965	43	1,509	149	5,203	4,177	98.4
1966	47	2,017	148	2,227	3,997	131.8
1967	43	1,640	190	7,310	4,762	123.9
1968	81	2,827	182	8,634	4,312	115.8
1969	37	1,810	321	19,043	3,984	110.6

Table B.11. PUBLICATION OF TEXTBOOKS (In Millions of Copies)

Year	General Education Schools	Specialized Secondary Schools	Higher Educational Institutions	Professional- Technical Schools	Other
1940	125.5	17.8	9.7	...	...
1958	146.7	8.7	22.7	2.3	5.4
1959	220.4	5.6	16.9	2.4	4.3
1960	154.4	9.6	24.5	2.2	...
1961	261.0	5.6	19.0	2.5	5.0
1962	291.5	7.0	24.1	3.7	6.5
1963	311.7	9.3	27.2	3.9	8.6
1964	305.3	8.2	23.6	3.2	8.6
1965	310.4	9.0	24.6	3.0	8.0
1966	284.6	11.9	22.5	2.6	8.8
1967	300.6	9.0	25.3	3.0	9.0
1968	316.8	13.0	29.6	4.4	11.4
1969	298.0	9.4	27.7	4.4	12.2

Table B.12. NEWSPAPER PUBLICATION: NUMBER AND COPIES PRINTED PER ISSUE BY ADMINISTRATIVE LEVEL

Year	National		Republic		Krai, Oblast Okrug		Autonomous Oblast & Okrug	
	No. of Papers	Copies Per Issue (th)	No. of Papers	Copies Per Issue (th)	No. of Papers	Copies Per Issue (th)	No. of Papers	Copies Per Issue (th)
1913	..	...	...	...	...	...	...	...
1928	..	...	...	...	...	...	...	...
1932	..	...	...	...	...	...	...	...
1940	46	8,769	135	5,284	321	6,978	119	1,197
1950	23	9,423	137	4,819	310	7,349	71	838
1958	24	18,906	176	10,581	324	10,703	107	1,607
1959	24	19,984	180	11,170	320	11,002	108	1,706
1960	25	23,524	180	13,187	305	11,380	96	1,691
1961	22	25,881	177	13,870	310	11,768	97	1,743
1962	23	31,075	173	14,430	307	12,032	96	1,809
1963	23	33,433	148	15,492	282	12,754	92	1,884
1964	23	36,821	148	17,441	256	12,535	95	2,096
1965	23	45,161	154	18,728	258	12,855	95	2,231
1966	26	50,771	155	17,565	252	13,670	97	2,532
1967	26	54,894	155	19,457	281	15,350	96	2,588
1968	26	55,977	157	21,097	289	16,295	96	2,819
1969	28	59,223	160	22,532	293	17,577	96	2,982

Year	City		Production Administration of Collective & State Farms		Raion	
	No. of Papers	Copies Per Issue (th)	No. of Papers	Copies Per Issue (th)	No. of Papers	Copies Per Issue (th)
1913	...	...	...	...	...	...
1928	...	...	...	...	...	...
1932	...	...	...	...	...	...
1940	251	1,802	...	...	3,502	8,647
1950	346	1,493	...	...	4,193	6,903
1958	460	3,109	...	...	4,148	7,927
1959	448	3,377	...	...	3,816	8,644
1960	449	3,576	...	...	3,397	8,630
1961	469	3,857	...	...	3,239	8,870
1962	490	3,818	1,098	9,221	115	254
1963	421	4,265	1,751	10,773	20	34
1964	252	4,387	1,666	10,119	...	...
1965	566	6,820	...	...	2,388	11,302
1966	589	7,900	...	...	2,541	11,559
1967	591	8,754	...	...	2,769	12,835
1968	597	9,329	...	...	2,793	13,417
1969	616	10,099	...	...	2,810	13,889

Table B.12. Newspaper Publication: Number and Copies Printed per Issue by Administrative Level (Continued)

Year	Lower Press (House Organs) No. of Papers	Copies Per Issue (th)	Individual Collective Farms No. of Papers	Copies Per Issue (th)	Total No. of Papers	Copies Per Issue (th)
1913	...	...	...	...	1,055	3,300
1928	...	...	...	...	1,197	9,400
1932	...	...	...	...	7,536	35,500
1940	4,432	5,678	...	...	8,806	38,355
1950	2,751	5,139	...	...	7,831	35,964
1958	2,447	4,862	2,777	1,628	10,733	59,323
1959	2,413	4,543	3,018	1,946	10,327	62,372
1960	2,352	4,691	2,740	1,882	9,544	93,892
1961	2,378	4,739	2,419	1,671	9,111	72,399
1962	2,469	4,291	1,941	1,357	6,712	78,287
1963	2,430	4,434	1,624	1,151	6,791	84,220
1964	2,627	4,622	1,528	1,073	6,595	89,094
1965	2,769	4,908	1,434	1,025	7,687	103,030
1966	2,868	5,370	1,439	1,019	7,967	110,386
1967	3,169	6,013	1,437	1,027	8,524	120,918
1968	3,349	6,515	1,447	1,032	8,754	126,481
1969	3,511	7,350	1,510	1,101	9,024	134,753

Table B.12a. Newspaper and Magazine Circulation per 1,000 Population

Year	All Newspapers	National Newspapers	Magazines (Per Million)
1940	200	50	13
1950	200	50	15
1958	290	90	24
1959	300	100	24
1960	444	111	26
1961	340	120	17
1962	360	140	27
1963	380	150	30
1964	390	160	33
1965	450	200	41
1966	480	220	53
1967	520	230	57
1968	534	237	57
1969	564	248	61

Table B.13. NEWSPAPER PUBLICATION BY LANGUAGE CATEGORY

Year	Total[a] No. of Papers	Total[a] Copies Per Issue (th)	In Russian No. of Papers	In Russian Copies Per Issue (th)	In Other U.S.S.R. Languages No. of Papers	In Other U.S.S.R. Languages Copies Per Issue (th)	In Foreign Languages No. of Papers	In Foreign Languages Copies Per Issue (th)
1913	859	...	775	...	59	...	25	...
1928	1,197	9,451	861	6,680	321	2,729	15	42
1940	8,806	38,400	6,499	28,200	2,275	10,000	32	200
1950	7,831	35,964	5,323	27,886	2,487	8,032	21	46
1958	7,686	57,695	7,662	57,468	2,521	12,298	24	227
1959	7,585	60,426	7,562	60,180	2,494	13,756	23	246
1960	6,804	66,700	4,665	51,400	2,121	15,100	18	200
1961	6,674	70,445	4,619	54,460	2,055	15,985	18	283
1962	4,771	76,930	3,392	59,907	1,363	16,724	16	299
1963	5,167	83,069	3,641	64,255	1,511	18,428	15	386
1964	5,067	88,011	3,625	68,111	1,427	19,427	15	483
1965	6,253	102,005	4,427	80,115	1,809	21,346	17	544
1966	6,528	109,400	4,554	85,000	1,957	23,800	17	600
1967	7,087	119,891	4,886	92,303	2,182	26,955	19	633
1968	7,307	125,449	5,065	95,727	2,224	29,105	18	617
1969	7,514	133,652	5,223	101,379	2,271	31,565	20	708

Note:

[a]Excluding Collective Farm Newspapers.

Table B.14. NEWSPAPER PUBLICATION BY SUBJECT MATTER (Including National, Republic, and Oblast Levels)

Year		Komsomol	Pioneer	Industry & Constr.	Transport	Agriculture	Culture, Lit., Art	Teacher	Physical Culture, Sport
1950	No.	72	21	2	105	8	11	10	5
	C.P.I.[a] (th)	2,628	2,154	50	377	836	652	399	180
1958	No.	107	24	12	79	7	17	14	10
	C.P.I. (th)	6,168	4,982	577	800	1,215	1,949	876	662
1959	No.	112	25	9	79	7	16	14	11
	C.P.I. (th)	6,943	5,663	542	875	1,140	1,235	1,942	833
1960	No.	117	23	6	71	7	16	15	12
	C.P.I. (th)	7,718	7,494	605	952	1,153	1,242	1,081	1,101
1961	No.	120	23	6	71	7	16	14	12
	C.P.I. (th)	7,722	8,192	745	1,123	1,498	1,142	1,019	1,161
1962	No.	120	23	6	65	7	18	14	12
	C.P.I. (th)	8,262	10,545	757	977	2,135	1,140	1,199	1,282
1963	No.	125	24	6	11	6	15	16	11
	C.P.I. (th)	8,969	10,686	830	117	3,189	1,227	1,364	1,377

Year		Komsomol	Pioneer	Industry & Constr.	Transport	Agriculture	Culture, Lit., Art	Teacher	Physical Culture, Sport
1964	No.	108	24	6	21	6	16	15	11
	C.P.I. (th)	9,000	12,377	965	145	4,642	1,139	1,441	1,513
1965	No.	115	25	5	23	6	16	15	14
	C.P.I. (th)	11,518	13,237	937	681	6,907	1,171	1,613	2,172
1966	No.	115	26	5	27	6	16	15	14
	C.P.I. (th)	12,176	14,896	515	887	7,080	1,265	1,759	2,873
1967	No.	129	27	5	34	6	17	15	14
	C.P.I. (th)	13,175	17,118	1,102	887	7,723	1,479	1,819	3,326
1968	No.	132	28	5	38	6	17	15	14
	C.P.I. (th)	14,054	16,881	1,143	966	7,528	1,647	1,811	3,577
1969	No.	131	28	6	44	6	17	15	14
	C.P.I. (th)	14,724	18,503	1,850	1,141	7,683	1,723	1,928	3,715

Note:

[a]C.P.I. = Copies Per Issue.

Table B.15. MAGAZINE PUBLICATION[a]

Year	Number of Magazines	Average Number of Copies Printed Per Issue (Thousands)
1940	681	26.6
1950	430	27.7
1958	875	49.4
1959	908	52.1
1960	923	57.3
1961	950	38.9
1962	979	59.4
1963	997	68.0
1964	1,005	76.2
1965	1,044	94.5
1966	1,069	123.1
1967	1,115	135.9
1968	1,135	135.8
1969	1,185	144.5

Note:

[a]Excluding other types of periodical publications (i.e., serials).

Table C.1. FOREIGN CULTURAL CONTACTS: "REPRESENTATIVES OF SCIENCE, EDUCATION, AND CULTURE" TO AND FROM USSR

Year	Total From U.S.S.R.	Total To U.S.S.R.	Total To U.S.S.R. From Socialist Countries	Total From U.S.S.R. To Socialist Countries
1958	7,936	1,607	3,867	3,149
1959	11,051	11,100	...	...
1960	16,000	16,000	7,400	7,000
1961	18,300	19,900	7,000	8,000
1962	16,500	17,700	6,000	6,000
1963	17,680	19,630	...	...
1964	20,000	20,000	7,327	8,515
1965	28,000	20,000	10,740	11,661
1966	29,400	22,000	14,600	15,800
1967	35,000	...	...	...

Table C.2. FOREIGN CULTURAL CONTACTS: ATHLETES, JOURNALISTS, AND SCIENTISTS TO AND FROM USSR

Year	Athletes		Journalists[a]		Scientists[b]	
	From U.S.S.R.	To U.S.S.R.	From U.S.S.R.	To U.S.S.R.	From U.S.S.R.	To U.S.S.R.
1958	3,000	2,000	...	...	2,011	2,833
1959	3,901	4,336	...	...	1,701	1,564
1960	...	...	...	...	2,408	3,700
1961	...	...	108	105	1,674	4,000
1962	...	...	147	143	1,501	1,428
1963	4,360	3,704	50	147	2,064	1,841
1964	5,036	3,393	141	294	2,287	3,200
1965	6,368	4,250	220	270	2,942	4,326
1966	7,952	5,070	300	380	3,459	9,305
1967	...	...	400	600	4,522	3,590
1968	...	...	1,000	600	...	...

Notes:
[a] Under the auspices of the Union of Journalists, U.S.S.R.
[b] Under the auspices of the Academy of Sciences, U.S.S.R.

Table C.3. TOURISM

Year	U.S.S.R. To U.S.	U.S. To U.S.S.R.
1956	0	1,500
1957	0	2,500
1958	66	5,000
1959	200	10-12,000
1960	500	10-12,000
1961	450	8-10,000
1962	77	8-10,000
1963	140	8-10,000
1964	204	10,000
1965	114	10-12,000
1966	102	18-20,000
1967	141	20-22,000
1968	115	25,000
1969	165	20,000
1970	260	50,000

Note:
    Figures for American tourists in the Soviet Union are estimates by United States official sources.

Table C.4. ATTENDANCE AT U.S. AND USSR EXHIBITS

	Attendance
1959 American National Exhibition in Moscow	2,700,000
1959 Soviet Exhibition in New York	over 1,000,000

Soviet Exhibits in the U.S.

Children's Books and Illustrations June through August 1961	115,000
Medicine and Medical Services September through December 1961	175,000
Children's Artistic and Technical Work January through April 1962	110,000
Technical Books March through June 1963	65,000
Graphic Arts November through February 1964	87,000
Public Health December 1964 through March 1965	50,000
Children's Creative Activities September 1965 through January 1966	170,000
Education in the U.S.S.R. November 1966 through February 1967	180,000

U.S. Exhibits in the U.S.S.R.

Plastics U.S.A. May through September 1961	375,000
Transportation U.S.A. October through December 1961	172,500
Medicine U.S.A. March through July 1962	206,590
Technical Books U.S.A. January through June 1963	140,430
Graphic Arts U.S.A. October 1963 through May 1964	1,602,488
Communications U.S.A. July 1964 through January 1965	768,851
Hand Tools U.S.A. August through December 1966	716,912
Industrial Design U.S.A. February through June 1967	831,000

Table D.1. MASS LIBRARIES AND BOOKS IN THEM

Year	Number of Libraries (Thousands)			Books In Them (Millions of Copies)		
	Total	Urban	Rural	Total	Urban	Rural
1913	12.6	2.3	10.3	8.9	4.7	4.2
1928	28.9	8.0	20.9	72.2	46.8	25.4
1932	32.9	9.1	23.8	91.3	60.3	31.0
1940	95.4	18.5	76.9	184.5	120.6	64.2
1950	123.1	20.8	102.3	244.2	145.4	98.8
1958	137.6	29.0	108.6	752.6	368.7	383.9
1959	137.6	32.8	104.8	803.3	403.7	399.6
1960	135.7	35.3	100.4	845.2	432.0	413.2
1961	134.4	35.4	99.0	896.5	461.8	434.7
1962	132.2	36.1	96.1	920.7	477.6	443.1
1963	126.2	35.6	90.6	948.0	498.4	449.6
1964	127.0	36.1	90.9	1,001.9	528.8	473.1
1965	127.1	37.0	90.1	1,051.7	564.5	487.2
1966	123.6	37.4	86.2	1,105.3	598.8	506.5
1967	123.4	37.3	86.1	1,154.3	629.8	524.5
1968	124.9	37.2	87.6	1,198.0	654.0	544.0

Table D.2. CLUBS AND HOUSES OF CULTURE (In Thousands)

Year	Total	Urban	Rural
1913	0.2	0.1	0.1
1928	34.5	4.5	30.0
1932	53.2	5.4	47.8
1940	118.0	10.0	108.0
1950	125.4	9.3	116.1
1958	128.5	12.9	115.6
1959	129.5	13.5	116.0
1960	128.6	14.1	114.5
1961	128.2	14.5	113.7
1962	126.9	14.6	112.3
1963	124.1	14.6	109.5
1964	126.5	14.9	111.6
1965	127.0	15.7	111.3
1966	128.9	16.6	112.3
1967	129.0	17.0	112.0
1968	131.7	17.9	113.8

CHAPTER VIII TABLE SOURCE NOTES

TABLE A.1

1913, 1928, 1932, 1940, 1950, 1960–1967: *N.K. 1967*, p. 516.
1958, 1959: *N.K. 1965*, p. 460.
1968: *B. S. E. Ezhegodnik*, 1969, p. 77.

TABLE A.2

1913: *SS za 50 L.*, p. 180.
1928: *The USSR Economy* (1957), p. 183.
1930: *Soviet Union Yearbook, 1930*, p. 236.
1940, 1950, 1960, 1965–1967: *N.K. 1967*, pp. 574–575.
1958, 1964: *N.K. 1965*, pp. 492–493.
1963: *B. S. E. Ezhegodnik*, 1965, p. 79.
1968: *B. S. E. Ezhegodnik*, 1969, p. 78.

TABLE A.3

1913, 1928, 1932, 1940, 1950, 1960–1967: *N.K. 1967*, p. 514.
1958, 1959: *N.K. 1965*, p. 458.
1968: *N.K. 1968*, p. 460.

TABLE A.4

1940, 1950, 1958, 1960, 1964–1965: *N.K. 1965*, p. 509.
1966–1967: *N.K. 1967*, p. 587.
1959, 1961–1962: *N.K. 1962*, p. 421.
1968: *N.K. 1968*, p. 499.

TABLE B.1

1913, 1940, 1960, 1966: *SS za 50 L.*, p. 183.

1950, 1965, 1967: *N.K. 1967*, p. 593.
1958, 1964: *N.K. 1965*, p. 513.
1959, 1961, 1962: *N.K. 1962*, p. 422.
1968: *N.K. 1968*, p. 507.

TABLE B.2

1913, 1928: *The USSR Economy* (1957), p. 184.
1940, 1950, 1960, 1965, 1966–1967: *N.K. 1967*, p. 184.
1958, 1959, 1961, 1962: *N.K. 1965*, p. 423.
1963: *B. S. E. Ezhegodnik 1964*, p. 77.
1964: *N.K. 1965*, p. 514.
1968: *B. S. E. Ezhegodnik 1969*, p. 78.

TABLE B.3

1913: *SS za 50 L.*, p. 183.
1928: *The USSR Economy*, p. 184.
1940, 1950, 1960, 1966, 1967: *N.K. 1967*, pp. 593–594.
1958, 1959, 1960, 1961, 1962: *N.K. 1962*, p. 422.
1964: *N.K. 1965*, p. 514.
1968: *N.K. 1968*, pp. 505–506.

TABLE B.4

SS za 50 L., p. 288.
1940, 1950, 1965, 1966, 1967: *N.K. 1967*, pp. 829–830.
1958, 1959, 1960, 1961, 1962: *N.K. 1962*, pp. 602–603.
1929, 1933: *Cultural Progress in the USSR* (1958), pp. 300–301.
1968: *N.K. 1968*, pp. 715–716.

TABLE B.5

1940, 1950, 1960, 1965, 1966, 1967:
  N.K. 1967, p. 831.
1958, 1959, 1961, 1962: *N.K. 1962*,
  p. 603.
1963: *N.K. 1963*, p. 611.
1964: *N.K. 1965*, p. 731.
1968: *N.K. 1968*, p. 717.

TABLE B.6

1952, 1958, 1959, 1960, 1961, 1962:
  N.K. 1962, p. 422.
1940, 1950, 1964, 1965: *N.K. 1965*,
  p. 514.
1963: *B. S. E. Ezhegodnik 1964*, p. 77.
1966, 1967: *N.K. 1967*, p. 594.
1968: *B. S. E. Ezhegodnik 1969*, p. 78.

TABLE B.7

1913, 1940, 1960, 1966: *SS za 50 L.*,
  p. 184.
1950, 1965, 1967: *N.K. 1967*, pp. 597–
  598.
1958, 1959, 1961, 1962: *N.K. 1962*,
  p. 422.
1964: *N.K. 1965*, p. 514.
1928, 1932: *Razvitiye Svyazi v SSSR*,
  p. 220.
1963: *B. S. E. Ezhegodnik 1963*, p. 77.
1968: *B. S. E. Ezhegodnik 1969*, p. 78.

TABLE B.8

1913–1960: *Pechat SSSR 1960*, pp. 19,
  21–22.
1963: *Pechat SSSR 1963*, pp. 21, 71, 89,
    97, 103, 109, 115, 121, 126, 131,
    136, 141, 146, 152, 158, 164.
1964: *Pechat SSSR 1964* pp. 21, 85, 114,
    128, 140, 154, 167, 181, 196, 208,
    220, 231, 243, 256, 269, 281.
1966: *Pechat SSSR 1966*, pp. 3, 75.
1967: *Pechat SSSR 1967*, pp. 3, 75.
1965: *Pechat SSSR 1965*, pp. 3, 77.
1961: *B. S. E. Ezhegodnik 1962*,
  pp. 102–103.
1962: *B. S. E. Ezhegodnik 1963*, p. 99.
1968: *B. S. E. Ezhegodnik 1968*, p. 100.
1969: *Pechat SSSR 1969*, pp. 75, 77.

TABLE B.9

1913, 1940, 1960, 1966: *SS za 50 L.*,
  p. 292.
*From *Pechat SSSR za 50 L.*, p. 174.
1961: *Pechat SSSR 1961*, pp. 24–26.
1962: *Pechat SSSR 1962*, pp. 29–31.
1963: *Pechat SSSR 1963*, p. 40.
1964: *Pechat SSSR 1964*, p. 31.
1965: *Pechat SSSR 1965*, p. 15.
1967: *Pechat SSSR 1967*, pp. 15–17.

1950, 1958, 1959: *Pechat SSSR 1960*,
  pp. 67–69.
1968: *Pechat SSSR 1968*, pp. 15–17.
1969: *Pechat SSSR 1969*, pp. 15–17.

TABLE B.10a

1940, 1960, 1966: *Pechat SSSR za 50
  L.*, p. 175.
*1950, 1958, 1959: *Pechat SSSR 1960*,
  p. 67.
1961: *Pechat SSSR 1961*, p. 28.
1963: *Pechat SSSR 1963*, pp. 27, 30.
1964: *Pechat SSSR 1964*, pp. 31, 34.
1965: *Pechat SSSR 1965*, pp. 15, 18.
1967: *Pechat SSSR 1967*, pp. 15, 18.
1962: *Pechat SSSR 1962*, pp. 29, 32.
1958: *Pechat SSSR 1958*, p. 72.
1959: *Pechat SSSR 1959*, p. 72.
1913, 1928, 1932: *Pechat SSSR za 40
  L.*, p. 63.
1968: *Pechat SSSR 1968*, pp. 15–18.
1969: *Pechat SSSR 1969*, p. 18.

TABLE B.10b

1940, 1950, 1960: *Pechat SSSR 1960*,
  p. 70.
1958: *Pechat SSSR 1958*, p. 70.
1959: *Pechat SSSR 1959*, p. 70.
1961: *Pechat SSSR 1961*, pp. 26, 40.
1962: *Pechat SSSR 1962*, pp. 28, 44.
1963: *Pechat SSSR 1963*, pp. 26, 42.
1964: *Pechat SSSR 1964*, pp. 30, 50.
1965: *Pechat SSSR 1965*, pp. 14, 34.
1966: *Pechat SSSR 1966*, pp. 14, 34.
1967: *Pechat SSSR 1967*, pp. 14, 36.
1968: *Pechat SSSR 1968*, pp. 14, 50.
1969: *Pechat SSSR 1969*, pp. 14, 50.

TABLE B.11

1940: *Pechat SSSR za 40 L.*, p. 183.
1958: *Pechat SSSR 1958*, p. 104.
1959: *Pechat SSSR 1959*, p. 100.
1960: *Pechat SSSR 1960*, p. 104.
1961: *Pechat SSSR 1961*, p. 43.
1962: *Pechat SSSR 1962*, pp. 46–47.
1963: *Pechat SSSR 1963*, p. 44.
1964: *Pechat SSSR 1964*, p. 52.
1965: *Pechat SSSR 1965*, p. 38.
1966: *Pechat SSSR 1966*, pp. 37–38.
1967: *Pechat SSSR 1967*, pp. 36–37.
1968: *Pechat SSSR 1968*, pp. 36–38.
1969: *Pechat SSSR 1969*, pp. 36–38.

TABLE B.12

1940, 1950, 1960, 1965, 1966, 1967:
  Pechat SSSR 1967, p. 65.
1958, 1959: *Pechat SSSR 1960*, p. 154.
1962, 1963, 1958*: *Pechat SSSR 1963*,
  p. 59.
1964: *Pechat SSSR 1964*, p. 74.

1961: *B. S. E. Ezhegodnik 1961*, p. 104.
1959**: *B. S. E. Ezhegodnik 1959*, p. 91.
1913, 1928, 1930: *Cultural Progress in the USSR*, Moscow (1958), p. 323.
1968, 1969: *Pechat SSSR 1969*, p. 65.

TABLE B.13

1913, 1940, 1960, 1966: *Pechat SSSR za 50 L.*, pp. 190–191.
1928, 1950, 1956: *Pechat SSSR za 40 L.*, p. 126.
1958: *Pechat SSSR 1958*, p. 163.
1959: *Pechat SSSR 1959*, p. 163.
1961: *Pechat SSSR 1961*, p. 61.
1963: *Pechat SSSR 1963*, p. 63.
1964: *Pechat SSSR 1964*, p. 77.
1965: *Pechat SSSR 1965*, p. 67.
1967: *Pechat SSSR 1967*, pp. 68–69.
1968: *Pechat SSSR 1968*, pp. 68–69.
1969: *Pechat SSSR 1969*, pp. 68–69.

TABLE B.14

1950: *Pechat SSSR za 40 L.*, p. 125.
1958: *Pechat SSSR 1958*, p. 166.
1959: *Pechat SSSR 1959*, p. 166.
1960: *Pechat SSSR 1960*, p. 166.
1961: *Pechat SSSR 1961*, p. 62.
1962: *Pechat SSSR 1962*, p. 64.
1963: *Pechat SSSR 1963*, p. 62.
1964: *Pechat SSSR 1964*, p. 77.
1965: *Pechat SSSR 1965*, p. 71.
1966: *Pechat SSSR 1966*, p. 71.
1967: *Pechat SSSR 1967*, p. 70.
1968: *Pechat SSSR 1968*, p. 70.
1969: *Pechat SSSR 1969*, p. 70.

TABLE B.15

1940, 1960, 1966: *Pechat SSSR za 50 L.*, p. 189.
1950, 1965, 1967: *Pechat SSSR 1967*, p. 56.
1958: *Pechat SSSR 1966*, p. 56.
1963, 1964: *Pechat SSSR 1964*, p. 68.
1962: *Pechat SSSR 1963*, p. 54.
1959: *Pechat SSSR 1960*, p. 126.
1961: *B. S. E. Ezhegodnik 1963*, p. 103.
1968, 1969: *Pechat SSSR 1969*, p. 56.

TABLE C.1

1958: *B. S. E. Ezhegodnik 1958*, p. 90.
1959: *B. S. E. Ezhegodnik 1959*, pp. 89–90.
1960: *B. S. E. Ezhegodnik 1960*, p. 84.
1961: *B. S. E. Ezhegodnik 1961*, p. 102.
1962: *B. S. E. Ezhegodnik 1962*, p. 98.
1963: *B. S. E. Ezhegodnik 1963*, p. 98.
1964: *B. S. E. Ezhegodnik 1964*, p. 99.
1965: *B. S. E. Ezhegodnik 1965*, p. 104.
1966: *B. S. E. Ezhegodnik 1966*, p. 111.
1967: *B. S. E. Ezhegodnik 1967*, p. 110.

TABLE C.2

Columns 1, 2
1958: *B. S. E. Ezhegodnik 1958*, p. 90.
1959: *B. S. E. Ezhegodnik 1959*, pp. 89–90.
1960: *B. S. E. Ezhegodnik 1960*, p. 84.
1961: *B. S. E. Ezhegodnik 1961*, p. 102.
1962: *B. S. E. Ezhegodnik 1962*, p. 98.
1963: *B. S. E. Ezhegodnik 1963*, p. 98.
1964: *B. S. E. Ezhegodnik 1964*, p. 99.
1965: *B. S. E. Ezhegodnik 1965*, p. 104.
1966: *B. S. E. Ezhegodnik 1966*, p. 111.
1967: *B. S. E. Ezhegodnik 1967*, p. 110.

Columns 3, 4
1961: *B. S. E. Ezhegodnik 1961*, p. 28.
1962: *B. S. E. Ezhegodnik 1962*, p. 24.
1963: *B. S. E. Ezhegodnik 1963*, p. 25.
1964: *B. S. E. Ezhegodnik 1964*, p. 24.
1965: *B. S. E. Ezhegodnik 1965*, p. 35.
1966: *B. S. E. Ezhegodnik 1966*, p. 14.
1968: *B. S. E. Ezhegodnik 1968*, p. 34.

Columns 5, 6
1958: *B. S. E. Ezhegodnik 1958*, p. 72.
1959: *B. S. E. Ezhegodnik 1959*, p. 71.
1960: *B. S. E. Ezhegodnik 1960*, p. 69.
1961: *B. S. E. Ezhegodnik 1961*, p. 69.
1962: *B. S. E. Ezhegodnik 1962*, p. 82.
1963: *B. S. E. Ezhegodnik 1963*, p. 82.
1964: *B. S. E. Ezhegodnik 1964*, p. 83.
1965: *B. S. E. Ezhegodnik 1965*, p. 104.
1966: *B. S. E. Ezhegodnik 1966*, p. 94.
1967: *B. S. E. Ezhegodnik 1967*, p. 94.

TABLE C.3

U.S. Department of State, *Exchanges with the Soviet Union and Eastern Europe*, Washington, D.C., for the appropriate years.

TABLE C.4

The editor is grateful to Professor Frederick C. Barghoorn for making these data available.

TABLE D.1

1913, 1928, 1932, 1940, 1950, 1960, 1965, 1966, 1967: *N.K. 1967*, p. 817.
1958, 1963, 1964: *N.K. 1965*, p. 717.
1959, 1961, 1962: *N.K. 1962*, p. 589.
1967: *SS za 50 L.*, p. 589.
1968: *N.K. 1968*, p. 703.

TABLE D.2

1913, 1928, 1932, 1940, 1950, 1960, 1965: *N.K. 1967*, p. 844.
1958, 1963, 1964: *N.K. 1965*, p. 724.
1959, 1961, 1962: *N.K. 1962*, p. 596.
1967: *SS za 50 L.*, p. 287.
1968: *N.K. 1968*, p. 710.

CHAPTER IX

INTERNATIONAL INTERACTIONS

ROGER KANET

THE COMPILATION AND USE of statistics on the external transactions of the Soviet Union present a number of serious problems. First of all, there is the question of finding the material itself and the problem of missing data. Although data on Soviet foreign trade are now readily available, detailed information on economic and technical assistance—in particular that concerning dispersements rather than promised aid—is not readily available in Soviet sources. A second major problem with the data that are available is reliability.

The use of either Western or Soviet sources for information on Soviet external transactions has its dangers. For example, U.S. government data on Communist Party membership and Western information on the military strength of the various communist countries are, at best, approximations based on educated guessing. The Soviets, on the other hand, tend to ignore historical data that are no longer politically acceptable. In *Vneshnyaya torgovlya SSSR: Statistichesky Sbornik, 1918–1966 gg.,* for example, all references to past trade with either Albania or South Africa were deleted, although the trade figures do appear in earlier compilations of Soviet trade statistics.

Yet another problem in employing data from Communist countries concerns the rate of exchange for monetary values. For example, in order to provide information on the trade of the members of the Council for Mutual Economic Assistance that would be comparable, it was necessary to translate the trade statistics into a common currency. The decision was made to use the official exchange rate for each country, even though unofficial rates of exchange are much different.

In spite of these and other problems in the compilation of the tables that follow—and the reader should be aware of these problems—the information can be employed for comparative purposes, so long as the user is aware of its limitations. In many respects its limitations are probably much less serious than those of similar data from developing countries—though the reasons for the limitations may be somewhat different.

The first set of tables on "Soviet Trade Statistics" is based entirely on

197

Soviet sources. As noted above, there exists the problem of "missing data"; however, the compiler has attempted to fill in such gaps in recently published Soviet materials by referring to older Soviet sources. Nonetheless, some trade remains unaccounted for, and the total of the figures given for Soviet trade with various geographical regions does not always equal the figure given for total Soviet trade in a given year.

The materials on Soviet, East European, and Chinese economic and technical assistance are based on data provided by the U.S. Department of State. These figures have been used because they (1) are very close to those provided by the Soviet Union and (2) have the great advantage of being relatively complete.

The statistical data on the Council for Mutual Economic Assistance come primarily from United Nations materials which, in turn, are provided by the various governments. The problem of rates of exchange has already been referred to. In addition, figures provided by countries concerning bilateral trade do not always agree. For example, the Albanians reported total trade with Bulgaria in 1955 as $3.11 million, and Bulgarian figures for trade with Albania in the same year are $2.82 million. Part of the discrepancy, at least, is accounted for by the fact that official rates of exchange were employed in computing the dollar equivalents.

The final set of information on World Communist Party membership is taken largely from State Department estimates. For parties in power the figures are based on official claims. For those parties not in power—particularly the smaller ones in Asia and Africa—the figures are rough estimates.

In the following tables all monetary figures are in new rubles. At the official exchange rate, one ruble equals $1.11.

Table A.1. TSARIST RUSSIAN TRADE, 1913 (In Million Rubles)

	Total	Exports	Imports
Total Trade[a]	2,895.0	1,520.0	1,375.0
Europe	2,426.0	1,353.8	1,072.2
Asia	339.1	132.6	206.5
Africa	14.9	9.0	5.9
North and South America	94.2	14.3	79.9
Australia and Oceania	.5	.1	.4

Note:
  [a]Individual figures do not add up to total because of
missing data.

Table A.2. SOVIET TRADE (In Millions of Rubles)

Year	Total Trade			Europe			Asia		
	Total	Exports	Imports	Total	Exports	Imports	Total	Exports	Imports
1918	88.9	6.4	82.5	21.7	5.8	15.9	4.6	0.0	4.6
1920	23.6	1.1	22.5	18.8	0.1	18.7	0.4	0.0	0.4
1926-27	1,192.2	632.7	559.5	766.2	473.1	293.1	172.9	81.3	91.6
1927-28	1,362.1	620.7	741.4	744.4	403.7	340.7	254.7	116.4	138.3
1937	523.7	295.1	228.6	292.2	217.5	74.7	98.0	44.3	53.7
1940	485.2	239.7	245.5	249.4	154.2	95.2	66.9	34.2	32.7
1950	2,925.5	1,615.2	1,310.3	2,019.3	1,076.4	942.9	754.4	462.8	291.6
1958	7,783.9	3,869.3	3,914.6	5,286.1	2,722.2	2,563.9	2,068.2	923.0	1,145.2
1959	9,471.2	4,905.3	4,565.9	6,401.4	3,438.9	2,962.5	2,567.7	1,212.4	1,355.3
1960	10,072.9	5,007.3	5,065.6	7,091.1	3,681.5	3,409.6	2,315.2	1,093.2	1,222.0
1961	10,643.5	5,398.6	5,244.9	7,620.7	3,965.1	3,655.6	1,890.1	862.2	1,027.9
1962	12,137.4	6,327.5	5,809.9	8,797.7	4,540.3	4,257.4	1,942.7	849.2	1,093.5
1963	12,898.1	6,545.2	6,352.9	9,532.6	4,827.1	4,705.5	1,923.0	918.3	1,004.7
1964	13,877.6	6,915.0	6,962.6	10,142.1	5,178.4	4,963.7	1,890.1	936.6	953.5
1965	14,597.9	7,349.5	7,248.4	10,651.5	5,355.7	5,295.8	1,965.3	1,028.1	937.2
1966	15,078.6	7,957.0	7,121.6	10,893.4	5,723.7	5,169.7	2,033.4	1,103.6	929.8
1967	16,366.6	8,684.0	7,682.6	12,213.0	6,149.9	6,063.1	1,998.8	1,213.5	785.3
1968	18,039.9	9,570.9	8,469.0	13,672.3	6,529.5	7,142.8	2,170.9	1,374.4	796.5
1969	19,784.0	10,489.4	9,294.1	14,925.2	7,465.4	7,459.8	2,445.4	1,425.1	1,020.3

Year	Africa			North and South America			Australia and Oceania		
	Total	Exports	Imports	Total	Exports	Imports	Total	Exports	Imports
1918	0.0	...	...	11.8	0.6	11.2	0.0	...	...
1920	0.0	...	...	0.8	0.0	0.8	0.0	...	...
1926-27	20.9	4.6	16.3	156.9	18.8	138.1	12.2	0.0	12.2
1927-28	33.0	7.4	25.6	220.0	22.6	197.4	22.8	0.0	22.8
1937	2.3	4.4	0.0	25.5	11.7	13.8	0.1	0.0	0.1
1940	0.2	0.2	0.0	95.8	19.2	76.6	0.0	...	...
1950	52.7	19.4	33.3	52.2	43.5	8.7	26.3	1.6	24.7
1958	202.8	83.5	119.3	125.2	56.6	68.6	5.3	0.4	4.9
1959	246.2	88.1	158.1	132.4	51.5	80.9	5.7	0.2	5.5
1960	271.1	89.8	181.3	311.2	122.8	188.4	39.6	0.4	39.2
1961	284.4	160.9	123.5	724.1	412.8	311.3	34.5	0.6	33.9
1962	271.6	148.3	123.3	686.6	382.7	303.9	29.5	0.4	29.1
1963	382.0	199.9	182.1	811.2	412.8	398.4	54.4	1.9	52.5
1964	382.0	222.1	159.9	1,128.0	378.5	749.5	126.8	1.3	125.5
1965	519.5	296.0	223.5	1,117.4	425.7	691.7	99.5	1.8	97.7
1966	475.2	275.6	199.6	1,296.5	520.7	769.8	50.0	1.1	48.9
1967	574.1	356.2	217.9	1,162.9	579.9	583.0	32.0	1.6	30.4
1968	561.1	297.7	263.4	1,127.1	638.3	488.8	46.5	1.6	44.9
1969	733.5	373.2	360.3	1,081.6	649.2	432.4	60.7	2.3	58.4

Year	Trade With Socialist Countries			C.M.E.A. Members Only		
	Total	Exports	Imports	Total	Exports	Imports
1918	...	...	...	...	...	...
1920	...	...	...	...	...	...
1926-27	...	...	...	...	...	...
1927-28	...	...	...	...	...	...
1937	...	...	...	...	...	...
1940	...	...	...	...	...	...
1950	2,372.8	1,350.2	1,022.6	1,678.6	899.5	779.1
1958	5,740.4	2,822.6	2,917.8	4,073.2	2,088.1	1,985.1
1959	7,135.8	3,718.5	3,417.3	4,923.0	2,655.5	2,267.5
1960	7,370.8	3,790.3	3,580.5	5,343.3	2,806.0	2,537.3
1961	7,621.1	3,889.0	3,732.1	5,837.4	3,078.1	2,759.3
1962	8,523.7	4,414.7	4,109.0	6,973.2	3,687.6	3,285.6
1963	9,077.3	4,589.5	4,487.8	7,628.3	3,849.6	3,778.7
1964	9,678.0	4,866.2	4,811.8	8,233.2	4,176.1	4,057.1
1965	10,048.3	4,999.4	5,048.9	8,471.3	4,210.2	4,261.1
1966	10,023.1	5,285.6	4,737.5	8,437.0	4,365.0	4,072.0
1967	11,089.2	5,738.1	5,351.1	9,340.8	4,701.6	4,639.2
1968	12,151.1	6,420.7	5,730.4	10,374.1	5,247.0	5,127.1
1969	12,940.4	6,913.9	6,026.5	11,213.0	5,755.2	5,457.8

Table A.3. SOVIET TRADE: SELECTED TRADING PARTNERS (In Million Rubles)

Year	United States Total	United States Exports	United States Imports	Great Britain Total	Great Britain Exports	Great Britain Imports	France Total	France Exports	France Imports
1918	11.8	0.6	11.2	11.0	1.6	9.4	1.5	0.0	1.5
1920	0.8	0.0	0.8	4.7	0.0	4.7	0.1	0.0	0.1
1926-27	132.8	18.4	114.4	252.2	172.9	79.3	59.8	42.4	17.4
1927-28	169.1	21.9	147.2	159.5	122.2	37.3	59.9	31.8	28.1
1937	64.6	22.8	41.8	105.4	94.7	10.7	19.5	14.8	4.7
1940	95.3	19.2	76.1	2.4	0.1	2.3	0.4	0.3	0.1
1950	50.4	43.2	7.2	128.2	92.0	36.2	6.5	2.9	3.6
1958	27.7	23.5	4.2	196.6	131.0	65.6	150.9	78.4	72.5
1959	39.1	23.1	16.0	230.9	149.1	81.8	169.4	79.0	90.4
1960	76.1	22.2	53.9	270.5	173.2	97.3	183.3	66.4	116.9
1961	67.5	21.9	45.6	319.5	204.1	115.4	179.9	71.5	108.4
1962	40.0	15.7	24.3	297.4	191.8	105.6	215.9	76.9	139.0
1963	47.4	22.3	25.1	310.4	193.5	116.9	151.0	93.2	63.8
1964	164.9	18.6	146.3	307.6	214.7	92.9	157.6	95.3	62.3
1965	89.2	31.0	58.2	398.8	262.0	136.8	202.4	99.5	102.9
1966	90.0	42.0	57.0	449.0	297.0	152.0	261.4	117.1	144.3
1967	91.7	34.5	56.3	450.5	272.8	177.7	299.5	130.0	169.5
1968	89.5	38.6	50.9	575.7	330.0	245.7	388.4	123.5	264.9
1969	159.6	54.5	105.1	600.5	384.2	216.3	417.4	126.8	290.6

Year	Italy Total	Italy Exports	Italy Imports	China Total	China Exports	China Imports	Japan Total	Japan Exports	Japan Imports
1918	0.0	0.0	0.0	4.6	0.0	4.6	0.0	0.0	0.0
1920	1.0	0.0	1.0	0.0	0.0	0.0	0.0	0.0	0.0
1926-27	32.1	29.5	2.6	38.2	14.7	23.5	17.9	15.1	15.1
1927-28	27.5	20.3	7.2	54.7	19.2	35.5	18.0	13.8	4.2
1937	3.3	2.8	0.5	12.9	6.0	6.9	11.2	2.0	9.2
1940	0.5	0.3	0.2	26.2	8.8	17.4	1.0	0.2	0.8
1950	33.7	14.6	19.1	518.9	349.4	169.5	4.2	3.6	0.6
1958	66.4	34.7	31.7	1,363.7	570.6	793.1	33.9	17.9	16.0
1959	117.7	70.2	47.5	1,849.4	859.1	990.3	51.1	30.0	21.1
1960	173.7	92.4	81.3	1,498.7	735.4	763.3	123.9	68.5	55.4
1961	203.6	117.2	86.4	826.9	330.6	493.3	161.6	101.7	59.9
1962	206.9	118.2	88.7	674.8	210.1	464.7	232.9	101.7	131.2
1963	245.5	123.0	122.5	540.2	168.5	371.7	260.4	111.5	148.9
1964	209.5	121.0	88.5	404.6	121.8	282.8	322.1	148.2	173.9
1965	224.7	133.2	91.5	375.5	172.5	203.0	326.1	166.5	159.6
1966	225.5	139.6	85.9	286.6	157.8	128.8	416.6	214.8	201.8
1967	347.9	208.9	139.0	96.3	45.2	51.1	466.8	317.7	149.1
1968	396.5	208.9	187.6	86.4	53.4	33.0	518.6	352.1	166.5
1969	493.5	208.4	285.1	51.1	25.0	26.1	558.7	321.3	237.4

Year	Germany (1918-40) West Germany (1950-69) Total	Exports	Imports	Finland Total	Finland Exports	Finland Imports	India Total	India Exports	India Imports
1918	0.8	0.5	0.3	...	...	...	...	...	...
1920	5.0	0.0	5.0	...	...	...	...	...	...
1926-27	264.3	137.6	126.7	...	...	...	...	...	...
1927-28	346.7	151.8	194.9	...	...	...	...	...	...
1937	52.2	18.2	34.0	...	...	...	...	...	...
1940	196.3	125.1	71.2	...	...	...	...	...	...
1950	0.0	0.0	0.0	54.9	27.9	27.0	6.2	2.1	4.1
1958	124.0	59.1	64.9	228.9	105.4	123.5	162.8	117.0	45.8
1959	188.4	80.3	108.1	258.0	130.1	127.9	115.7	61.2	54.5
1960	286.2	106.9	179.3	264.1	134.3	129.8	104.0	42.4	61.6
1961	268.3	106.9	161.4	251.0	123.2	127.8	146.1	85.9	60.2
1962	304.9	121.0	183.9	355.9	161.8	194.1	176.8	112.3	64.5
1963	252.1	118.0	134.1	384.5	196.4	188.1	285.0	199.7	85.3
1964	290.0	112.4	177.6	349.6	198.5	151.1	351.6	211.3	140.3
1965	248.5	128.7	119.8	408.3	190.9	217.4	362.9	193.5	169.4
1966	292.3	166.9	125.4	426.7	231.4	195.3	346.0	174.0	172.0
1967	319.0	172.5	146.5	460.8	219.5	241.3	308.8	146.1	162.7
1968	393.9	189.3	204.6	458.9	219.6	239.3	329.6	165.0	164.6
1969	496.8	198.8	298.0	500.8	236.2	264.6	353.5	154.2	199.3

Table A.3. SOVIET TRADE: SELECTED TRADING PARTNERS (Continued)

Year	U.A.R. (Egypt) Total	Exports	Imports	Czechoslovakia Total	Exports	Imports	East Germany Total	Exports	Imports
1918	...	...	...	...	...	...	...	...	...
1920	...	...	...	...	...	...	...	...	...
1926-27	...	...	...	...	...	...	...	...	...
1927-28	...	...	...	...	...	...	...	...	...
1937	...	...	...	...	...	...	...	...	...
1940	...	...	...	...	...	...	...	...	...
1950	44.0	19.3	24.7	379.8	198.4	181.4	311.3	167.2	144.1
1958	175.3	78.9	96.4	863.0	402.1	460.9	1,454.1	719.8	734.3
1959	162.6	79.2	83.4	1,066.4	542.7	523.7	1,727.6	927.1	800.5
1960	172.0	62.8	109.2	1,154.9	567.7	587.2	1,782.7	946.5	836.2
1961	184.4	97.8	86.6	1,215.3	587.4	627.9	1,876.5	1,088.2	788.3
1962	158.7	93.0	65.7	1,435.9	693.6	742.3	2,201.8	1,235.4	966.4
1963	232.9	121.7	111.2	1,619.6	764.1	855.5	2,355.8	1,182.5	1,173.3
1964	250.5	139.3	111.2	1,682.7	810.7	872.0	2,441.6	1,246.7	1,194.9
1965	334.9	187.8	147.1	1,765.2	833.3	931.9	2,382.9	1,226.7	1,156.2
1966	313.8	178.8	135.0	1,632.1	804.6	827.5	2,380.3	1,266.1	1,114.2
1967	383.8	253.2	130.6	1,754.7	870.7	884.0	2,545.7	1,274.3	1,271.4
1968	331.8	178.2	153.6	1,825.3	934.3	891.0	2,800.6	1,355.8	1,444.8
1969	419.7	214.4	205.3	2,001.9	998.7	1,003.2	3,031.5	1,565.1	1,466.4

Year	Poland Total	Exports	Imports	Cuba Total	Exports	Imports
1918	...	...	...	...	...	...
1920	...	...	...	...	...	...
1926-27	...	...	...	...	...	...
1927-28	...	...	...	...	...	...
1937	...	...	...	...	...	...
1940	...	...	...	...	...	...
1950	406.3	217.3	189.0	...	...	...
1958	577.7	339.1	238.6	13.9	0.0	13.9
1959	722.7	437.8	284.9	6.7	0.0	6.7
1960	789.7	441.7	348.0	160.6	67.2	93.4
1961	906.8	477.6	429.2	539.0	258.3	280.7
1962	1,042.5	534.7	507.8	540.7	330.1	210.6
1963	1,149.4	596.3	553.1	507.8	359.8	148.0
1964	1,240.1	594.0	646.1	588.6	329.4	259.2
1965	1,356.6	654.0	702.6	645.9	337.9	308.0
1966	1,382.8	722.9	659.9	689.2	431.9	257.3
1967	1,633.1	820.9	812.2	842.0	506.5	335.3
1968	1,873.5	945.1	928.4	811.8	561.8	250.0
1969	2,090.9	1,079.1	1,011.8	770.1	561.6	208.5

Table A.4. MAJOR TRADING PARTNERS OF THE SOVIET UNION (In Percentage of Soviet Trade)

Year	U.S.	G.B.	France	Italy	China	Germany	W. Germany	Finland	India	U.A.R. (Egypt)	Czechoslovakia	E. Germany	Poland	Cuba	Bulgaria	Hungary	Mongolia	Rumania
1918	13.3	12.4	1.7	...	5.2	0.9	...	...	...	...	...	...	...	...	...	...	...	...
1920	3.4	19.9	0.4	4.2	...	21.2	...	...	...	...	...	...	...	...	...	...	...	...
1925-26	10.5	24.0	4.1	3.9	3.3	19.7	...	...	...	...	...	...	...	...	...	...	...	...
1930	14.6	17.2	3.5	3.0	2.5	21.8	...	...	...	...	...	...	...	...	...	...	...	...
1940	19.7	0.5	0.1	0.1	5.4	40.4	...	...	...	...	...	...	...	...	...	...	...	...
1946	23.7	2.8	2.7	...	5.3	...	...	4.8	0.7	0.1	4.3	6.4	15.1	0.0	9.5	1.5	4.9	3.7
1950	1.7	4.4	0.2	...	17.7	...	0.0	1.9	0.2	1.5	13.0	10.6	13.9	0.0	5.1	6.5	2.5	7.8
1955	0.4	3.7	1.5	...	21.4	...	0.8	3.6	0.2	0.4	11.5	15.2	11.1	0.6	3.8	5.0	2.7	7.4
1960	0.8	2.7	1.8	...	14.9	...	2.8	2.6	1.0	1.7	11.5	17.7	7.8	1.6	5.6	4.0	1.3	4.8
1966	0.7	3.0	1.7	...	1.9	...	1.9	2.8	2.3	2.1	10.8	15.8	9.2	4.5	8.1	6.1	1.3	4.7
1967	0.6	2.8	1.8	...	0.6	...	1.9	2.8	1.9	2.3	10.7	15.5	10.0	5.2	8.4	6.5	1.4	4.5
1968	0.5	3.2	2.8	...	0.5	...	1.9	2.8	1.8	1.8	10.1	15.5	10.4	4.5	9.2	6.7	1.2	4.4
1969	0.8	3.0	2.1	...	0.3	...	2.5	2.5	1.8	2.1	10.1	15.3	10.6	3.9	8.7	6.5	1.1	4.2

Table A.5. PERCENTAGE OF SOVIET TRADE WITH SOCIALIST COUNTRIES

Year	Trade With Socialist Countries			C.M.E.A. Members Only		
	Total	Imports	Exports	Total	Imports	Exports
1946	54.4	57.8	51.6	40.5	46.1	35.8
1947	60.7	62.5	58.9	38.9	40.0	37.8
1948	60.1	58.7	61.6	43.4	40.6	45.6
1949	72.0	75.8	68.3	51.9	52.5	51.3
1950	81.1	83.5	78.0	57.3	55.6	59.4
1951	81.0	81.9	80.0	57.8	56.8	59.1
1952	81.0	83.5	78.2	59.2	59.8	58.5
1953	83.1	85.1	81.0	59.2	57.4	61.1
1954	79.4	82.2	76.6	54.8	53.9	55.8
1955	79.3	79.5	79.0	53.2	52.3	54.3
1956	75.6	75.5	75.7	49.5	48.9	50.2
1957	73.6	75.4	71.7	53.6	58.1	48.6
1958	73.7	72.9	74.5	52.3	53.9	50.7
1959	75.3	75.8	74.8	51.9	54.1	49.6
1960	73.1	75.6	70.6	53.0	56.0	50.0
1961	71.6	72.0	71.1	54.8	57.0	52.6
1962	70.2	69.7	70.7	57.4	58.2	56.5
1963	70.3	70.1	70.6	59.1	58.8	59.4
1964	69.7	70.3	69.1	59.3	60.3	58.2
1965	68.8	68.0	69.6	58.0	57.2	58.7
1966	66.4	66.4	66.5	55.9	54.8	57.2
1967	67.7	66.0	69.6	57.0	54.1	60.3
1968	67.4	67.1	67.7	57.5	54.8	60.5
1969	65.4	65.9	64.8	56.7	54.9	58.7

Table A.6.   MAJOR COMMODITIES IN SOVIET TRADE

EXPORTS

(In Percent of Total Value of Soviet Exports)

Commodity[a]	1946	1950	1955	1960	1966	1968
TOTAL	100.0	100.0	100.0	100.0	100.0	100.0
Machinery and Equipment	5.8	11.8	17.5	20.5	20.8	21.6
Fuels and Electrical Power	5.4	3.9	9.6	16.2	16.4	16.1
Ores and Ore Concentrates, Metals, Cable, and Wire	9.5	11.3	17.6	20.4	20.1	18.5
Non-metallic Minerals	0.2	0.6	0.6	0.6	1.1	...
Chemical Products, Fertilizer, Rubber	5.0	4.3	3.1	3.5	3.8	4.1
Wood Products, Pulp and Paper Articles	4.3	3.1	5.1	5.5	7.0	6.4
Unfinished and Semi-Finished Textiles	15.0	11.2	10.1	6.4	5.2	4.5
Furs and Fur Products	11.2	2.3	1.1	0.8	0.8	0.5
Foodstuffs	29.8	20.6	12.0	13.1	9.2	10.3
Consumer Goods	7.4	4.9	3.0	2.9	2.4	2.7

IMPORTS

(In Percent of Total Value of Soviet Imports)

Commodity[a]	1946	1950	1955	1960	1966	1968
TOTAL	100.0	100.0	100.0	100.0	100.0	100.0
Machinery and Equipment	28.5	21.5	30.2	29.8	32.4	36.9
Fuels and Electrical Power	11.8	11.8	8.3	4.2	2.4	2.0
Ores and Ore Concentrates, Metals, Cable, and Wire	9.9	15.0	16.5	16.8	8.7	9.2
Chemical Products, Fertilizer, Rubber	1.9	6.9	3.4	6.0	6.4	6.0
Wood Products, Pulp and Paper Articles	3.9	3.8	3.0	1.9	1.9	2.1
Unfinished and Semi-Finished Textiles	6.6	7.7	5.4	6.5	4.8	3.9
Foodstuffs	15.7	17.5	20.2	12.1	19.6	13.6
Consumer Goods	7.2	7.4	4.8	17.2	16.4	19.9

Note:

[a]These are selected commodities; they do not account for the total value of imports or exports.

Table A.7.   NUMBER OF SOVIET TRADING PARTNERS

Year	Total Number of Countries With Which the Soviet Union Traded	Number of Countries With Which the Soviet Union Had Trade and Payment Agreements
1918	9	1
1938	41	21
1946	39	20
1950	42	29
1955	59	35
1958	70	50
1959	76	52
1960	79	52
1961	80	55
1962	83	56
1963	91	65
1964	91	69
1965	97	72
1966	98	73

Table A.8.   PER CAPITA VALUE OF SOVIET TRADE

Year	Population (Millions)	Total Trade (Million Rubles)	Per Capita Trade (Rubles)	Exports (Million Rubles)	Per Capita Exports (Rubles)	Imports (Million Rubles)	Per Capita Imports (Rubles)
1918	143.5	88.9	.62	6.4	.04	82.5	.57
1920	139.9	23.6	.17	1.1	.01	22.5	.16
1925-26	140.6	1,144.6	8.14	551.5	3.92	593.1	4.22
1930	154.9	1,643.0	10.61	812.7	5.25	830.3	5.36
1935	160.0	477.4	2.98	288.1	1.80	189.3	1.18
1940	193.8[a]	485.2	2.50	239.7	1.24	245.5	1.26
1945	170.0	561.5	3.30	301.8	1.76	259.7	1.53
1950	181.5	2,019.3	11.13	1,076.4	5.93	942.9	5.20
1955	197.4	5,838.5	29.58	3,084.0	15.62	2,754.5	13.95
1960	216.1	10,643.5	49.25	5,398.6	24.98	5,244.9	24.27
1965	230.5	14,597.9	63.33	7,349.5	31.86	7,248.4	31.45
1968	238.0	18,039.9	75.80	9,570.9	40.21	8,469.0	35.58
1969	241.0	19,784.0	82.09	10,489.9	43.53	9,294.1	38.56

Note:
[a]From 1940, includes territories annexed by the Soviet Union in 1939-1940.

Table A.9.   GROWTH OF SOVIET TRADE (1960 = 100)

Year	Total	Exports	Imports
1946	14	11	17
1947	14	12	14
1948	22	21	22
1949	24	24	25
1950	31	33	28
1951	37	39	35
1952	45	47	42
1953	48	50	46
1954	54	55	53
1955	55	59	51
1956	61	62	60
1957	69	74	64
1958	76	76	77
1959	97	100	93
1960	100	100	100
1961	106	110	103
1962	122	128	115
1963	129	133	126
1964	135	139	131
1965	146	153	138
1966	155	174	137
1967	169	189	149
1968	187	209	166

Table B.1.   COMMUNIST ECONOMIC CREDITS AND GRANTS EXTENDED TO LESS DEVELOPED COUNTRIES (In Million Current U.S. Dollars)

Country	1954-69				1967			
	Total	U.S.S.R.	Eastern Europe	Com. China	Total	U.S.S.R.	Eastern Europe	Com. China
TOTAL	10,466	6,825	2,692	949	407	269	89	49
Africa	1,648	993	359	296	47	9	17	21
Algeria	304	232	22	50	...	...	..	..
Cameroon	8	8	...	...	...	...	..	..
Central African Rep.	4	...	...	4	...	...	..	..
Congo (Brazzaville)	34	9	...	25	...	...	..	..
Ethiopia	119	102	17	...	...	...	..	..
Ghana	231	89	102	40	...	...	..	..
Guinea	215	165	25	25	...	...	..	..
Kenya	62	44	...	18	...	...	..	..
Mali	102	56	23	23	...	...	..	..
Mauritania	7	3	...	4	7	3	..	4
Morocco	79	44	35	...	...	...	..	..
Nigeria	14	...	14	...	...	...	..	..
Senegal	7	7	...	...	...	...	..	..
Sierra Leone	28	28	...	...	...	...	..	..
Somalia	94	66	6	22	...	...	..	..
Sudan	102	64	38	...	17	...	17	..
Tanzania	79	20	6	53	...	...	..	..
Tunisia	105	34	71	...	...	...	..	..
Uganda	31	16	...	15	...	...	..	..
Zambia	23	6	...	17	23	6	..	17

Country	1954-69				1967			
	Total	U.S.S.R.	Eastern Europe	Com. China	Total	U.S.S.R.	Eastern Europe	Com. China
Far East	956	411	306	239	0	0	0	0
Burma	124	14	26	84	...	...	..	..
Cambodia	80	25	17	50	...	...	..	..
Indonesia	740	372	263	105	...	...	..	..
Latin America	474	207	267	0	70	55	15	0
Argentina	54	45	9	...	...	...	..	..
Brazil	312	85	227	...	...	...	..	..
Chile	60	55	5	...	55	55	..	..
Colombia	2	2	...	...	...	...	..	..
Ecuador	10	...	10	...	5	...	5	..
Uruguay	30	20	10	...	10	...	10	..
Peru	6	...	6	...	...	...	..	..
Near East & South Asia	7,388	5,214	1,760	414	290	205	57	28
Afghanistan	737	697	12	28	5	5	..	..
Ceylon	123	30	52	41	...	...	..	..
Greece	84	84	...	...	...	...	..	..
India	1,980	1,593	387	...	25	...	25	..
Iran	839	508	331	...	10	...	10	..
Iraq	432	305	127	...	...	...	..	..
Nepal	82	20	...	62	...	...	..	..
Pakistan	438	265	64	109	7	...	...	7
South Yemen	12	...	...	12	...	...	..	..
Syria	443	233	194	16	...	...	..	..
Turkey	390	376	14	...	200	200	..	..
United Arab Republic	1,679	1,011	562	106	43	...	22	21
Yemen	149	92	17	40	...	...	..	..

Country	1968				1969			
	Total	U.S.S.R.	Eastern Europe	Com. China	Total	U.S.S.R.	Eastern Europe	Com. China
TOTAL	724	307	361	56	894	462	432	0
Africa	51	...	51	..	146	135	11	0
Algeria	...	...	...	..	...	...	...	..
Cameroon	...	...	...	..	...	...	...	..
Central African Rep.	...	...	...	..	...	...	...	..
Congo (Brazzaville)	...	...	...	..	...	...	...	..
Ethiopia	...	...	...	..	...	...	...	..
Ghana	...	...	...	..	...	...	...	..
Guinea	...	...	...	..	92	92	...	..
Kenya	...	...	...	..	...	...	...	..
Mali	...	...	...	..	1	1	...	..
Mauritania	...	...	...	..	...	...	...	..
Morocco	...	...	...	..	...	...	...	..
Nigeria	...	...	...	..	...	...	...	..
Senegal	...	...	...	..	...	...	...	..
Sierra Leone	...	...	...	..	...	...	...	..
Somalia	...	...	...	..	...	...	...	..
Sudan	...	...	...	..	53	42	11	..
Tanzania	...	...	...	..	...	...	...	..
Tunisia	51	...	51	..	...	...	...	..
Uganda	...	...	...	..	...	...	...	..
Zambia	...	...	...	..	...	...	...	..

Table B.1. Communist Economic Credits and Grants Extended to Less Developed Countries (Continued)

Country	1968				1969			
	Total	U.S.S.R.	Eastern Europe	Com. China	Total	U.S.S.R.	Eastern Europe	Com. China
Far East	0	0	0	0	12	0	12	0
Burma	...	...	...	..	...	...	...	..
Cambodia	...	...	...	..	12	...	12	..
Indonesia	...	...	...	..	...	...	...	..
Latin America	12	2	10	0	31	20	11	0
Argentina	5	...	5	..	...	...	...	..
Brazil	...	...	...	..	...	...	...	..
Chile	5	...	5	..	...	...	...	..
Colombia	2	...	...	..	...	...	...	..
Ecuador	...	...	...	..	5	...	5	..
Uruguay	...	...	...	..	20	20	...	..
Peru	...	...	...	..	6	...	6	..
Near East & South Asia	661	305	300	56	705	307	398	0
Afghanistan	127	127	...	..	...	...	...	..
Ceylon	...	...	...	..	...	...	...	..
Greece	...	...	...	..	...	...	...	..
India	...	...	...	..	32	...	32	..
Iran	453	178	275[a]	..	200	...	200	..
Iraq	...	...	...	..	248	121	127	..
Nepal	2	...	...	2	...	...	...	..
Pakistan	42	...	...	42	28	20	8	..
South Yemen	12	...	...	12	...	...	...	..
Syria	25	...	25	..	25	...	25	..
Turkey	...	...	...	..	172	166	6	..
United Arab Republic	...	...	...	..	...	...	...	..
Yemen	...	...	...	..	...	...	...	..

Note:

[a] The $200 million Czechoslovak credit to Iran was finalized in 1969.

Table B.2. Communist Military Aid Extensions, Cumulative by Country (In Million U.S. Dollars)

Area and Country	Aid Extended
Total	5,510
Africa[a]	360
Algeria	250
Congo (B)	Negl.[b]
Ghana	10
Guinea	10
Mali	Negl.[b]
Morocco	40
Somalia	30
Tanzania	10
Uganda	10
Near East and South Asia	3,800
Afghanistan	250
Cyprus	30
India	610
Iran	110
Iraq	650
Pakistan	40
Syria	460
U.A.R.	1,550[c]
Yemen	100
Far East	1,350
Cambodia	10
Indonesia	1,340

Notes:

[a] Nigeria also received some communist military equipment during 1968.

[b] Negligible indicates less than $5 million.

[c] An estimated $2.5 billion dollars in military aid was sent to the U.A.R. in the 15 months after the June 1967 Arab-Israeli War.

Table B.3. COMMUNIST ECONOMIC TECHNICIANS IN LESS DEVELOPED COUNTRIES[a]

Country	1960	1962	1965	1966	1967[b]	1968[b]	1969[b]
Africa	545	1,785	7,855	10,785	10,875	11,100	11,575
Asia	2,940	3,870	4,950	6,180	900	450	400
Latin America	75	70	75	85	115	70	70
Near East[b] (and South Asia)	6,510	9,620	4,840	4,165	9,950	9,300	9,925
TOTAL	10,070	15,345	17,720	21,215	21,840	20,920	21,970

Notes:

[a]Minimum estimates of persons present for a period of one month or more.

[b]The method of compiling figures was changed in 1967. For the earlier years, Asia includes South Asia and in 1967 the countries of South Asia are listed under "Near East (and South Asia)."

Table B.4. COMMUNIST ECONOMIC TECHNICIANS IN LESS DEVELOPED COUNTRIES

	Totals			U.S.S.R.			Eastern Europe			Communist China		
Country	1967	1968	1969	1967	1968	1969	1967	1968	1969	1967	1968	1969
Africa	10,875	11,100	11,575	3,800	3,300	3,650	4,000	5,100	4,950	3,075	2,700	2,975
Far East	900	450	400	225	200	250	100	50	50	575	200	100
Latin America	115	70	70	15	20	20	100	50	50	0	0	0
Near East and South Asia	9,950	9,300	9,925	7,000	6,300	5,950	2,050	2,000	2,100	900	1,000	1,875
TOTAL	21,840	20,920	21,970	11,040	9,820	9,870	6,250	7,200	7,150	4,550	3,900	4,950

Table B.5. ACADEMIC STUDENTS STUDYING IN COMMUNIST COUNTRIES[a]

Country	Year	Total in Communist Countries	U.S.S.R.	Eastern Europe	Communist China
TOTAL	1963	12,800	7,720	4,790	290
	1965	15,915	10,435	5,025	455
	1966	14,710	11,215	3,080	415
	1967	14,425	10,275	4,150	...
	1968	15,750	11,780	3,970	...
	1969	16,650	12,075	4,575	...
Africa	1963	6,135	3,385	2,585	165
	1965	9,140	5,065	3,800	275
	1966	9,505	6,305	2,920	280
	1967	8,000	5,750	2,250	...
	1968	7,920	6,080	1,840	...
	1969	8,950	6,825	2,125	...
Asia[b]	1963	2,140	1,355	660	125
	1965	3,450	2,310	965	175
	1966	2,740	1,870	740	130
	1967	1,200	750	450	...
	1968	1,005	635	370	...
	1969	525	350	175	...
Near East[b] (and South Asia)	1963	3,765	2,455	1,310	0
	1965	3,090	2,125	955	10
	1966	2,995	1,925	1,065	5
	1967	3,825	2,675	1,150	...
	1968	4,845	3,565	1,280	...
	1969	5,200	3,450	1,750	...
Latin America	1963	760	525	235	0
	1965	1,240	935	305	0
	1966	1,470	1,115	355	0
	1967	1,400	1,100	300	...
	1968	1,980	1,500	480	...
	1969	1,975	1,450	525	...

Notes:

[a]Figures are for December of each year.

[b]The method of compiling figures changed in 1967. For the earlier years, Asia includes South Asia, but in 1967 South Asia is listed along with the Near East.

Table B.6. TECHNICAL TRAINEES FROM DEVELOPING COUNTRIES TRAINING IN COMMUNIST COUNTRIES[a]

Country	Year	Total in Communist Countries	U.S.S.R.	Eastern Europe	Communist China
TOTAL	1965	2,180	1,360	785	35
	1966	2,555	1,520	935	100
	1967	2,125	985	1,090	50
	1968	1,660	955	700	5
	1969	2,005	1,205	800	0
Africa	1965	805	330	440	35
	1966	500	100	365	35
	1967	800	375	375	50
	1968	440	220	220	0
	1969	175	50	125	0
Asia[b]	1965	760	520	240	0
	1966	1,040	725	315	60
	1967	75	...	75	...
	1968	35	5	30	0
	1969	20	0	20	0
Near East[b] (and South Asia)	1965	615	510	105	0
	1966	855	610	240	5
	1967	1,225	600	625	...
	1968	1,185	730	450	5
	1969	1,800	1,150	650	0
Latin America	1965	0	0	0	0
	1966	20	5	15	0
	1967	25	10	15	...
	1968	0	0	0	0
	1969	10	5	5	0

Notes:

[a]As of December of each year.

[b]The method of compiling figures changed in 1967. For the earlier years, Asia includes South Asia, but in 1967 South Asia is listed along with the Near East.

Table C.1. BASIC DATA ON CMEA COUNTRIES

Country	Population 1969 (Millions)	Communist Party Membership 1969 (Thousands)	Area (Sq. Kilometers)	Population Density (Persons Per Sq. Kilometer)	National Income 1967 U.S. Dollars (Billions)
Albania	2.07	66.3	28,748	70	.70
Bulgaria	8.43	613.4	110,912	76	8.20
Czechoslovakia	14.42	1,700.0	127,869	113	26.30
East Germany[a]	17.10	1,769.9	108,174	158	28.80
Hungary	10.30	600.0	93,030	111	12.60
Poland	32.56	2,030.1	312,519	104	33.90
Romania	20.01	1,800.0	237,500	84	18.80
U.S.S.R.	240.57	13,500.0	22,402,200	11	384.00

Note:

[a]Including East Berlin.

Table C.2. RELATIVE PER CAPITA OUTPUTS IN CMEA COUNTRIES (Index Numbers GDR = 100)

	Year	Albania	Bul-garia	Czecho-slovakia	Hun-gary	Mon-golia	Poland	Romania	USSR	All Comecon[a]
95 farm products	1959-63	68	117	101	136	..	141	97	..	117[b]
Global output of agriculture	1958	37	81	97	99	..	117	63	93	94
	1962	..	107	87	107	135	131	75	93	96
	1961-65	..	109	89	107	127	130	77	88	93
Sample of 86 industrial products	1958	21	28	90	43	..	79	50	74	73
Global output of industry	1958	15	31	102	48	..	59	38	78	74
	1960	..	33	110	55	..	60	36	..	69[b]
	1960	..	31	102	45	..	59	38	77	73
	1961	..	30	99	45	..	53	38	70	67
	1963	..	44	88	50	15	48	29	65	63
	1965	..	47	80	50	13	50	33	67	75
Net output of industry	1961	..	30	100	36	..	55	48	..	61[b]
Gross capital formation	1955	..	64	143	..	..	100	57	143	89[c]
	1958	..	30	106	51	..	57	32	111	95
	1960	..	80	147	..	..	73	60	133	119[c]
	1963	..	82	111	77	..	76	72	122	111
	1965	..	81	125	..	..	56	69	125	114[c]
Personal consumption	1960	18	47	118	55	..	58	58	92	86
	1963	..	66	92	73	..	71	..	67	..
	1964	..	64	96	75	..	66	55	64	68
Net material product	1958	23	49	97	81	..	76	51	..	77[b]
	1960	18	43	101	55	..	69	45	..	70[b]
	1964	..	56	96	61	..	59	50	75	73
	1965	..	62	85	62	..	62	54	77	93
Gross national product	1960	..	47	100	57	..	54	37	64	64
	1964	..	49	105	73	..	64	49	85	81

Notes:

[a]Excluding Albania and Mongolia.

[b]Excluding U.S.S.R.

[c]Assuming Hungary to be the same level as Poland.

Table C.3. GROWTH OF INDUSTRIAL OUTPUT OF CMEA COUNTRIES (1950 = 1)

Country	All Industry	Fuel and Power	Engineering & Metalworking	Chemicals	Construction Materials
Albania	6.9	14.8	6.7	...	...
Bulgaria	4.9	8.6	10.0	11.0	11.4
Czechoslovakia	3.3	3.4	5.5	5.5	5.1
East Germany	3.3	2.4	4.5	3.4	2.9
Hungary	3.2	3.4	4.2	6.1	3.2
Poland	4.0	4.6	10.8	6.8	4.3
Romania	4.5	6.0	8.3	10.4	5.6
U.S.S.R.	3.6	4.6	5.6	5.2	6.8

Table C.4. GROWTH OF INDUSTRIAL OUTPUT OF CMEA COUNTRIES (1963 = 100)

Country	1948	1963	1958	1960	1965	1966	1967	1968
Albania	14	31	52	82	115	...	...	...
Bulgaria	12	29	53	73	127	142	161	177
Czechoslovakia	31	45	76	87	112	120	129	136
East Germany	19	47	70	85	112	119	127	136
Hungary	24	53	63	78	111	118	125	131
Poland	18	40	65	79	119	128	140	151
Romania	12	33	53	68	129	143	163	182
U.S.S.R.	17	37	63	77	117	127	139	151

Table C.5. INDUSTRIAL OUTPUT IN CMEA

Country	Industrial Output As A Percentage of Net Material Product		
	1958	1964	1967
Bulgaria	41	46	46
Czechoslovakia	62	66	65
East Germany	67	72	65
Hungary	55	64	57
Poland	49	52	50
Romania	43	48	52
U.S.S.R.	50	53	55

Table C.6. OUTPUT OF POWER AND VARIOUS RAW MATERIALS IN CMEA COUNTRIES

Country	Electric Power (Billion KWH)			Coal[a] (Mil. Metric Tons)			Oil (Mil. Metric Tons)			Steel (Million Tons)		
	1950	1962	1968	1950	1962	1968	1950	1962	1968	1950	1962	
Albania	0.02	0.24	0.5[b]	0.1	0.3	0.3[b]	0.1	0.8	1.0	...	...	
Bulgaria	0.8	6.0	15.5	5.6	19.7	28.7	...	0.2	0.5	0.0	0.4	
Czechoslovakia	9.3	28.7	41.4	46.0	96.6	100.8	0.06	0.18	0.2	3.1	7.6	
East Germany	19.5	45.1	63.2	140.1	249.6	243.7	...	...	...	1.0	3.6	
Hungary	3.0	9.1	13.2	13.3	28.6	27.2	0.5	1.6	1.8	1.0	2.3	
Poland	9.4	35.4	55.5	82.8	120.7	155.5	0.16	0.2	0.5	2.5	7.7	
Romania	2.1	10.1	27.8	7.2	8.1	14.8	5.0	11.9	13.3	0.6	2.5	
U.S.S.R.	91.2	369.3	638.7	261.1	493.5	552.2	37.9	186.2	309.2	27.3	76.3	10
TOTAL	135.3	503.9	855.9	556.1	1,017.1	1,127.9	43.7	201.1	326.5	35.5	100.4	15

Notes:

[a]Figures include anthracite, bituminous, lignite and brown coal.

[b]1967 figures.

Table C.7. SELECTED CMEA INDICATORS

Product	Total C.M.E.A. Output (Mil. Tons)			U.S.S.R. Output (Mil. Tons)			U.S.S.R. Percent of Total			Exported By U.S.S.R. to East Europe (Mil. Tons)		
	1962	1967	1968	1962	1967	1968	1962	1967	1968	1962	1967	1968
Petroleum	201.0	305.3	326.5	186.0	288.1	309.2	93	94	95	13.8	22.6	...
Iron ore	74.5[a]	93.9[a]	95.5[a]	71.2	90.3	92.0	95[a]	96[a]	95[a]	18.4	26.0	...
Cast iron	71.2[a]	97.3[a]	100.7[a]	55.3	74.8	78.8	78[a]	77[a]	78[a]	...	...	...
Steel	100.5	135.3	152.0	76.3	102.2	106.5	76	76	70	...	...	...
Coal	1,064.0	1,112.1	1,127.9	517.0	555.5	552.2	49	50	49	12.3	12.3	...
	(Billion KWH)			(Billion KWH)						(Billion KWH)		
Electricity	504.0	788.8	855.2[a]	369.0	587.7	638.7	74	75	75[a]	0.2	1.8	...

Note:

[a]Does not include Albania.

Table C.8. TRADE OF CMEA COUNTRIES (In Millions of Dollars and Percentages of Total Trade)

Country	Year	Total Trade					
		Total Amount	%	Exports Amount	%	Imports Amount	%
Albania	1950	28.5	100	6.5	100	22.0	100
	1955	55.8	100	13.0	100	42.8	100
	1960	129.6	100	48.6	100	81.0	100
	(1964)	158.0	100	59.9	100	98.1	100
Bulgaria	(1952)	329.1	100	170.8	100	158.3	100
	1955	486.1	100	236.2	100	249.9	100
	1960	1,204.1	100	571.5	100	632.6	100
	1965	2,353.5	100	1,175.8	100	1,177.7	100
	1966	2,783.3	100	1,305.0	100	1,478.3	100
	1967	3,030.1	100	1,458.2	100	1,571.9	100
Czechoslovakia	1950	1,418.2	100	778.9	100	639.3	100
	1955	2,228.6	100	1,176.0	100	1,052.6	100
	1960	3,745.1	100	1,929.5	100	1,815.6	100
	1965	5,361.0	100	2,688.5	100	2,672.5	100
	1966	5,481.0	100	2,745.0	100	2,736.0	100
	1967	5,544.2	100	2,864.2	100	2,680.0	100
East Germany	1950	875.7	100	406.0	100	469.7	100
	1955	2,450.9	100	1,278.2	100	1,172.7	100
	1960	4,401.9	100	2,207.4	100	2,194.5	100
	1965	5,879.5	100	3,069.8	100	2,809.7	100
	1966	6,420.1	100	3,205.0	100	3,215.1	100
	1967	6,735.0	100	3,456.1	100	3,278.9	100
Hungary	1950	644.2	100	328.6	100	315.6	100
	1955	1,155.5	100	601.1	100	554.4	100
	1960	1,850.2	100	874.2	100	976.0	100
	1965	3,030.6	100	1,509.8	100	1,520.8	100
	1966	3,159.6	100	1,593.7	100	1,565.9	100
	1967	3,477.2	100	1,701.5	100	1,775.7	100
Poland	1950	1,302.6	100	634.3	100	668.3	100
	1955	1,851.6	100	919.8	100	931.8	100
	1960	2,820.5	100	1,325.5	100	1,495.0	100
	1965	4,568.1	100	2,227.8	100	2,340.3	100
	1966	4,766.0	100	2,272.0	100	2,494.0	100
	1967	5,171.3	100	2,526.5	100	2,644.8	100
Romania	1950	...	100	...	100	...	100
	(1958)	942.1	100	460.3	100	481.8	100
	1960	1,364.8	100	717.0	100	647.8	100
	1965	2,178.7	100	1,101.5	100	1,077.2	100
	1966	2,399.4	100	1,186.2	100	1,213.2	100
	1967	2,941.4	100	1,395.4	100	1,546.0	100
U.S.S.R.	1950	3,253.3	100	1,794.4	100	1,458.9	100
	1955	6,487.7	100	3,426.6	100	3,061.1	100
	1960	11,192.1	100	5,563.3	100	5,628.8	100
	1965	16,219.9	100	8,166.6	100	8,053.3	100
	1966	16,754.3	100	8,841.0	100	7,913.3	100
	1967	18,166.9	100	9,639.2	100	8,527.7	100

Table C.8.   TRADE OF CMEA COUNTRIES (Continued)

Country	Year	Total Amount	%	Exports Amount	%	Imports Amount	%
				Trade With C.M.E.A.			
Albania	1955	46.9	88.9	12.6	96.9	34.3	80.1
	1960	117.0	90.2	45.1	92.8	71.9	88.6
	(1964)	55.6	35.1	28.1	46.9	27.5	27.9
Bulgaria	1955	358.0	73.6	194.7	82.4	163.3	65.3
	1960	969.0	80.5	486.2	85.1	482.8	76.3
	1965	1,716.0	72.9	889.4	75.6	826.6	70.1
	1966	1,900.5	68.2	921.5	70.6	979.0	66.2
	1967	1,938.9	64.0	1,083.8	74.3	855.1	54.4
Czechoslovakia	1955	1,420.3	63.7	735.8	62.6	684.4	65.0
	1960	2,388.6	63.8	1,227.2	63.6	1,161.4	64.0
	1965	3,636.4	67.8	1,800.3	67.7	1,816.1	67.9
	1966	3,501.0	63.8	1,746.3	63.6	1,754.7	64.1
	1967	3,707.0	66.9	1,889.2	66.0	1,817.8	67.8
East Germany	1955	1,570.3	64.1	831.6	65.1	739.8	63.1
	1960	2,975.4	67.6	1,517.2	68.7	1,458.2	66.4
	1965	4,072.4	69.2	2,168.2	70.6	1,904.2	67.7
	1966	4,367.9	68.0	2,202.9	68.7	2,165.0	67.3
	1967	4,667.3	69.3	2,419.0	70.0	2,248.3	68.6
Hungary	1955	619.9	53.6	357.8	59.5	262.1	47.3
	1960	1,160.7	62.7	536.9	61.4	623.8	63.9
	1965	1,966.6	64.8	996.0	65.9	970.6	63.8
	1966	1,982.8	62.7	1,022.5	64.1	960.3	61.3
	1967	2,244.1	64.5	1,107.1	65.1	1,137.0	64.0
Poland	1955	961.7	51.9	467.0	50.8	494.7	53.1
	1960	1,617.5	57.3	748.6	56.5	868.9	58.1
	1965	2,755.1	60.3	1,314.8	59.0	1,440.3	61.5
	1966	2,765.7	58.0	1,267.3	55.7	1,498.4	60.0
	1967	3,184.6	61.6	1,503.1	59.5	1,681.5	63.6
Romania	(1958)	685.4	72.8	324.7	70.5	360.7	74.9
	1960	911.8	66.8	472.0	65.8	439.8	67.9
	1965	1,320.1	60.5	701.1	63.6	619.0	57.4
	1966	1,303.8	54.3	663.4	55.9	640.4	52.7
	1967	1,395.6	47.4	703.9	50.4	691.7	44.7
U.S.S.R.	1950	1,865.1	57.3	999.4	55.6	865.7	59.4
	1955	3,454.9	53.2	1,792.1	52.3	1,662.8	54.3
	1960	5,936.9	53.0	3,117.7	56.0	2,819.2	50.0
	1965	9,412.5	58.0	4,678.0	57.2	4,734.5	58.7
	1966	9,374.4	55.9	4,850.0	54.8	4,524.4	57.2
	1967	10,368.3	57.7	5,218.8	54.1	5,149.5	60.5

Table C.8. TRADE OF CMEA COUNTRIES (Continued)

Country	Year	Total Amount	%	Exports Amount	%	Imports Amount	%
Albania	1955	21.1	37.8	5.4	41.5	15.7	36.6
	1960	69.9	53.2	24.2	49.8	45.7	56.3
	(1964)	0.0	0.0	0.0	0.0	0.0	0.0
Bulgaria	1955	196.1	40.3	107.1	45.3	89.1	35.7
	1960	639.6	53.1	332.3	58.2	307.3	48.6
	1965	1,202.2	51.0	613.4	52.1	588.6	49.9
	1966	1,370.3	49.2	663.6	50.8	706.7	47.8
	1967	1,293.5	42.7	752.2	53.0	521.3	33.2
Czechoslovakia	1955	768.2	34.5	402.8	34.3	365.4	34.7
	1960	1,289.0	34.4	658.6	34.1	630.4	34.7
	1965	1,997.5	36.8	1,022.8	38.0	954.7	35.7
	1966	1,835.0	33.4	920.4	33.5	914.6	33.4
	1967	1,944.9	35.1	979.6	34.2	965.3	36.0
East Germany	1955	937.8	38.3	515.7	40.3	422.1	36.0
	1960	1,882.6	42.8	924.6	41.9	958.0	43.7
	1965	2,515.6	42.7	1,310.6	42.6	1,205.0	42.8
	1966	2,661.0	41.4	1,276.5	39.8	1,384.5	43.0
	1967	2,825.5	42.0	1,407.8	40.7	1,417.7	43.2
Hungary	1955	252.1	21.8	153.0	25.5	99.1	17.9
	1960	559.5	30.2	256.6	29.4	303.0	31.0
	1965	1,079.0	35.6	525.5	34.8	553.5	36.3
	1966	1,044.3	33.0	526.9	33.0	517.4	33.0
	1967	1,205.6	34.7	613.5	36.0	592.1	33.3
Poland	1955	598.2	32.3	284.2	30.9	314.0	33.7
	1960	855.5	30.3	390.2	29.4	465.3	31.1
	1965	1,509.8	33.0	781.4	35.0	728.4	31.1
	1966	1,532.9	32.1	741.2	32.6	791.7	31.7
	1967	1,822.9	35.3	901.8	35.7	921.1	34.8
Romania	(1958)	489.1	51.9	235.3	51.1	253.8	52.7
	1960	547.4	40.1	281.4	39.2	265.9	41.0
	1965	844.6	38.7	438.4	39.8	406.2	37.7
	1966	803.9	33.5	409.8	34.5	394.1	32.4
	1967	829.4	28.2	432.9	31.0	396.5	25.6

Table C.9. PER CAPITA TRADE OF CMEA COUNTRIES AND TRADE AS A PERCENTAGE OF NATIONAL INCOME, 1967

Country	Total Trade As A Percentage Of National Income	Trade With CMEA Countries As A Percentage Of National Income	Trade With U.S.S.R. As A Percentage of National Income	Total Trade Per Capita (U.S.$)	Trade With CMEA Countries Per Capita (U.S.$)	Trade With U.S.S.R. Per Capita (U.S.$)
Bulgaria	37.0	23.6	15.8	362.01	231.64	154.54
Czechoslovakia	21.1	14.1	7.4	386.08	258.14	135.43
East Germany	23.4	16.2	9.8	394.32	270.26	165.42
Hungary	27.6	17.8	9.6	338.90	218.72	117.50
Poland	15.3	9.4	5.4	160.54	98.86	56.59
Romania	15.6	7.4	4.4	149.15	70.77	42.05
U.S.S.R.	4.7	2.7	...	76.39	41.58	...

Table C.10. INTRA-CMEA TRADE (In Percentages of Total Trade)

Country	1950	1955	1960	1963	1964	1965	1966	1967
Albania	100.0	88.9	90.2	35.5	35.1	...	...	...
Bulgaria	83.6	73.6	80.5	79.6	75.0	72.9	68.2	64.0
Czechoslovakia	53.6	63.7	63.8	69.5	68.4	67.8	63.8	66.9
East Germany	72.3	64.1	67.6	74.6	72.2	69.2	68.0	69.3
Hungary	61.4	53.6	62.7	66.3	65.7	64.8	62.7	64.5
Poland	58.4	51.9	57.3	61.1	59.6	60.2	58.0	61.6
Romania	...	...	66.8	64.5	64.9	60.5	54.3	47.4
U.S.S.R.	57.3	53.2	53.0	59.1	59.3	58.0	55.9	57.7

Table C.11. DIRECTION OF CMEA EXPORTS (In Millions of Dollars)

Year	C.M.E.A. Partners	China etc.[a]	Intra-German Trade	E.E.C.	E.F.T.A.	U.S.A.	Under-Developed Areas	World
1948	1,405	150	..[b]	330	600	115	195	3,170[c]
1950	2,535	490	79	235	440	85	231	4,220
1951	3,240	705	35	280	590	70	165	5,380
1952	3,750	860	33	300	550	40	175	6,100
1953	4,340	1,080	70	275	460	37	170	6,850
1954	4,650	1,190	105	350	485	41	260	7,500
1955	4,750	1,190	136	435	625	60	385	7,990
1956	4,830	1,210	154	580	650	65	470	8,590
1957	5,930	1,010	205	635	665	55	570	9,800
1958	6,060	1,220	211	695	620	70	710	10,310
1959	7,380	1,520	230	820	770	75	690	12,230
1960	8,080	1,380	241	930	880	78	830	13,220
1961	9,000	800	219	1,040	970	79	1,390	14,340
1962	10,170	630	210	1,130	940	79	1,560	15,980
1963	11,050	580	242	1,240	1,010	89	1,820	17,220
1964	11,960	560	264	1,330	1,140	105	1,890	18,740
1965	12,460	700	294	1,480	1,290	140	2,090	19,945
1966	12,540	770	307	1,750	1,430	175	2,240	20,910
1967	13,740	810	297	1,950	1,460	180	2,450	22,820

Notes:

[a]Mongolia, North Korea, North Vietnam.

[b]Not available in either U.N. or German statistical abstracts.

[c]Excluding intra-German trade.

Table C.12. CMEA FOREIGN TRADE BY REGION[a]

	1955		1960		1964	
	Billions of U.S. $	Percentage	Billions of U.S. $	Percentage	Billions of U.S. $	Percentage
Imports:						
Total World of which from:	7.31	100.0	12.93	100.0	18.10	100.0
C.M.E.A. states	4.75	65.0	7.72	59.7	11.96	66.0
Western industrialized countries[b]	1.18	16.2	2.52	19.5	3.93	21.7
Developing countries	0.41	5.6	1.18	9.1	1.53	8.5
Other countries[c]	0.97	13.2	1.51	11.7	0.68	3.8
Exports:						
Total World of which from:	8.03	100.0	12.98	100.0	18.38	100.0
C.M.E.A. states	4.75	59.2	7.72	59.5	11.96	65.0
Western industrialized countries[b]	1.51	18.8	2.53	19.5	3.65	19.9
Developing countries	0.39	4.8	0.83	6.4	1.89	10.3
Other countries[c]	1.38	17.2	1.90	14.6	0.88	4.8

Notes:

[a]C.M.E.A. countries, excluding Mongolia.

[b]Excluding trade of West Germany with East Germany.

[c]Rounded off; including China, Mongolia, North Korea, and North Vietnam.

Table C.12. CMEA FOREIGN TRADE BY REGION[a] (Continued)

	1965 Billions of U.S. $	1965 Percentage	1966 Billions of U.S. $	1966 Percentage	1967 Billions of U.S. $	1967 Percentage
Imports:						
Total World	19.04	100.0	19.67	100.0	21.11	100.0
of which from:						
C.M.E.A. states	12.52	65.8	12.54	63.8	13.74	65.1
Western industrialized countries[b]	4.08	21.4	4.67	23.7	5.04	23.9
Developing countries	1.84	9.7	1.90	9.7	1.84	8.7
Other countries[c]	0.60	3.1	0.56	2.8	0.49	2.3
Exports:						
Total World	19.63	100.0	20.91	100.0	22.82	100.0
of which from:						
C.M.E.A. states	12.52	63.7	12.54	60.0	13.74	60.2
Western industrialized countries[b]	4.04	20.6	4.85	23.2	5.23	22.9
Developing countries	2.07	10.5	2.24	10.7	2.45	10.7
Other countries[c]	1.00	5.2	1.28	6.1	1.40	6.2

Notes:

[a] C.M.E.A. countries, excluding Mongolia.

[b] Excluding trade of West Germany with East Germany.

[c] Rounded off; including China, Mongolia, North Korea, and North Vietnam.

Table C.13. FUEL AND RAW MATERIAL IMPORTS FROM USSR, 1966 (In Percentages of Consumption)

Country	Coking Coal	Oil	Iron Ore	Cotton
Bulgaria	82.5	87.5	45.0	65.7
Czechoslovakia	...	97.0	74.6	59.6
East Germany	78.0	94.0	58.7	91.2
Hungary	65.5	79.0	79.5	61.2
Poland	4.1	89.5	70.0	58.6
Romania	32.1	...	54.5	43.4

Table C.14. ENGINEERING GOODS AND RAW MATERIALS IN CMEA TRADE (In Percentage Share)

Country	Engineering Goods in Total Exports to Other C.M.E.A. Countries 1955	Engineering Goods in Total Exports to Other C.M.E.A. Countries 1965	Raw Materials in Total Imports From Other C.M.E.A. Countries 1955	Raw Materials in Total Imports From Other C.M.E.A. Countries 1965
Bulgaria	2.8	29.9	39.9	45.0
Czechoslovakia	51.1	56.3	75.6	59.3
East Germany	53.6	58.6	82.9	78.6
Hungary	37.6	42.8	74.6	59.2
Poland	17.4	48.7	50.8	48.0
Romania	6.1	24.5	50.5	51.5
U.S.S.R.	17.3	18.0	47.7	31.6

Table C.15. USSR CREDITS PROMISED TO EASTERN EUROPE (In Millions of U.S. Dollars)

Country	Year	Credits	Subtotals
Albania	1957	47.5	
	1958	8.7	
	1959	75.0	131.2
Bulgaria	1947	38.5	
	1948	53.0	
	1949	13.2	
	1950	18.6	
	1951	11.2	
	1956	92.5	
	1957	60.0	
	1958	35.0	
	1960	162.5	484.5
Czechoslovakia	1948	33.0	
	1957	13.5	46.5
East Germany	1953	121.2	
	1956	20.0	
	1957	260.0	
	1958	100.0	
	1962	1,200.0	1,701.2
Poland	1947	27.8	
	1948	450.0	
	1950	100.0	
	1956	300.0	
	1957	120.0	997.8
Romania	1947	30.0	
	1954	50.0	
	1956	67.5	147.5
Hungary	1954	25.7	
	1956	25.0	
	1957	260.0	
	1958	35.0	345.9
Grand Total			3,854.4

Note:
    The figures do not include credits for military defense purposes. Dollar values in the source presumably are derived from official rates of exchange.

Table C.16. ANNUAL FOREIGN AID DELIVERIES (DRAWDOWNS) TO CMEA COUNTRIES FROM THE SOVIET UNION (In Millions of Dollars)

Year	Albania	Bulgaria	Czecho-slovakia	East Germany	Hungary	Poland	Romania
1955	1.37	13.86	3.28	...	4.50	88.80	17.77
1956	2.47	12.76	1.94	1.15	2.12	37.84	7.29
1957	2.47	8.39	2.78	1.24	1.22	31.01	3.75
1958	1.80	16.75	4.27	...	1.33	17.48	9.80
1959	5.19	20.56	0.97	3.35	19.52	14.48	23.39
1960	12.81	35.14	0.86	7.11	13.89	12.54	26.11
1961	3.29	47.80	2.53	8.16	12.79	14.30	22.30
1962	...	63.93	7.97	9.85	14.95	23.96	18.26
1963	...	78.73	10.45	11.43	17.85	30.06	35.50
1964	...	93.52	15.61	14.65	18.36	9.08	27.55
1965	...	128.32	4.63	19.41	14.91	19.11	26.41
TOTAL	29.40	519.76	57.62	76.35	121.45	298.64	218.21

Table C.17. Inter-CMEA Loans, as of 1965 (In Millions of Dollars)

Donors	Albania	Bulgaria	Czecho-slovakia	East Germany	Hungary	Poland	Romania	U.S.S.R.
Albania	...	...	...	...	0.05	...	...	...
Bulgaria	11.0	...	...	...	3.00	...	...	...
Czechoslovakia	25.0	40.0	...	...	43.70	213.0	45.5	...
East Germany	15.0	...	...	...	15-28	100-164	28.0	...
Hungary	...	9.0	...	...	...	...	...	...
Poland	...	...	...	...	25.00	...	2.3	78.0
Romania	7.5	...	...	...	15.00	...	...	...
U.S.S.R.	29.4	519.8	57.6	76.4	121.50	298.6	218.2	...

Table C.18. CMEA Organization, 1967

Member States

Council

Executive Committee (Deputy Heads of Governments)

Bureau for Problems of Economic Planning

Secretariat (Moscow)

Permanent Commissions (21), In Order of Formation

1. Agriculture (Sofia)
2. Forestry (Bucharest)
3. Electrical Energy (Moscow)
4. Coal Industry (Warsaw)
5. Mech. Engineering (Prague)
6. Petroleum and Natural Gas Industry (Bucharest)
7. Ferrous Industry (Moscow)
8. Nonferrous Ind. (Budapest)
9. Chemical Industry (E. Berlin)
10. Timber, Cellulose, and Paper Industry (Budapest)
11. Transportation (Warsaw)
12. Building Industry (E. Berlin)
13. Light Industry & Food (Prague)
14. Economic Problems (Moscow)
15. Foreign Trade (Moscow)
16. Peaceful Uses of Atomic Energy (Moscow)
17. Standardization (E. Berlin)
18. Coordination of Scientific & Technical Research (Moscow)
19. Statistics (Moscow)
20. Machine Construction (Moscow)
21. Foreign Exchange and Financial Problems (Moscow)

Specialized Organizations (6)

Admin. for Electric Power System (Prague); Institute for Standardization (Moscow); Freight Bureau (Moscow); Internat'l Bank for Economic Cooperation (Moscow); Railroad Car Pool (Prague); Nuclear Research Institute (Dubna, U.S.S.R.)

Table C.19. Bilateral Treaties and Agreements between the Soviet Union and Other CMEA Countries

Country	1945-1957 Number	1945-1957 Rank	1958-1962 Number	1958-1962 Rank
Albania	37	7.0	19	7
Bulgaria	61	6.0	44	2
Czechoslovakia	64	5.0	35	4
East Germany (1949-1957)	78	3.5	34	5
Hungary	78	3.5	39	3
Poland	81	2.0	61	1
Romania	87	1.0	33	6

Table C.20. TREATIES WITH CMEA COUNTRIES AS A PERCENTAGE OF ALL SOVIET TREATIES, 1958–1962

Country	Number of Treaties With U.S.S.R.	Percentage of All Soviet Treaties	Percentage of Soviet Treaties With C.M.E.A. Countries
Total Soviet bilateral treaties	912	100.00	...
Total Soviet bilateral treaties with C.M.E.A. countries	265	29.06	100.0
Albania	19	2.08	7.17
Bulgaria	44	4.82	16.60
Czechoslovakia	35	3.84	13.21
East Germany	34	3.73	12.83
Hungary	39	4.28	14.72
Poland	61	6.69	23.02
Romania	33	3.62	12.45

Table C.21. WARSAW PACT, ARMED FORCES, 1968–1969

Country	Defense Appropriations 1968 (Mln. Dollars)	Army Personnel	Divisions[a]	Tanks
Albania	$ 76	30,000	2	100
Bulgaria	228	125,000	12(4)	2,000
Czechoslovakia	1,538	175,000	14(5)	2,200
East Germany	1,715	85,000	6(2)	1,800
U.S.S.R.		254,900[b]	20(10)	7,500
Hungary	370	95,000	6(1)	700
U.S.S.R.		55,000	4(2)	1,400
Poland	1,830	185,000	15(5)	2,800
U.S.S.R.		25,000	2(1)	700
Romania	551	150,000	19(2)	1,200
Total		1,209,900	91(32)	21,600
Total U.S.S.R.[c]	$39,780	2,000,000	140(45)	15,750

Country	Security Forces Personnel	Navy Personnel	Naval Craft C[d]	Naval Craft D[e]	Naval Craft S[f]	Air Force Personnel	Combat Aircraft
Albania	12,500	3,000	..		3	5,000	60
Bulgaria	20,000	5,000	..	2	2	22,000	250
Czechoslovakia	40,000[g]	...	..	..	..	50,000	600
East Germany	90,000	16,000	..	4	..	25,000	270
U.S.S.R.	...	(80,000)[h]	(4)	(25)	(75)	...	1,100
Hungary	35,000	...	..	..	..	7,000	140
U.S.S.R.	...	...	..	..	..	...	350
Poland	45,000[g]	19,000	..	3	15	70,000	750
U.S.S.R.	...	...	..	..	..	...	350
Romania	50,000	8,000	..	..	..	15,000	240
		(50,000)[i]	(3)	(20)	(45)		
Total	262,500	180,000	7	56	146	182,000	4,850
Total U.S.S.R.[c]	250,000	465,000	23	106	380	505,000	10,250

Notes:

[a]Armored divisions, included in total, are indicated in parentheses.

[b]Includes 4,900 in Berlin.

[c]Including forces designated to the Warsaw Pact Organization and listed above.

[d]Cruisers.

[e]Destroyers.

[f]Submarines.

[g]Polish security troops were integrated with the regular armed forces and placed under the Defense ministry in July 1965, according to Radio Warsaw, June 30, 1965. The same move took place in Czechoslovakia, effective January 1966, as reported in Allgemeine Schweizerische Militarzeitschrift, CXXXII, No. 2 (February 1966), 93.

[h]Figures in parentheses refer to the Soviet Baltic Sea Fleet, estimated allocation.

[i]Soviet Black Sea Fleet, estimated allocation.

Table C.22. WARSAW PACT MILITARY EXPENDITURES, 1966 (In U.S. Dollars at Current Prices and Exchange Rates)

Country	Gross National Product (In Million $)	Military Expenditures (In Million $)	Percent of GNP
Albania	700	70	10.0
Bulgaria	7,600	210	2.8
Czechoslovakia	23,800	1,400	5.9
East Germany	28,300	1,100	3.9
Hungary	12,200	300	2.5
Poland	33,200	1,750	5.3
Romania	16,600	530	3.2
U.S.S.R.	357,000	47,000	8.0-9.0[b]
TOTAL	478,700	52,290	8.0-9.0[b]

Notes:

[a]These figures do not agree with those taken from United Nations sources and presented in Table C.1, "Basic Data on C.M.E.A. Countries."

[b]The relationship between GNP and military expenditures shown here may not be valid due to use of differentiated conversion rates for particular sectors. If measured in national currency and at factor cost rather than at market prices, for example, Soviet military expenditures would be in the vicinity of 8-9 percent of GNP.

Table D.1. MEMBERSHIP OF COMMUNIST PARTIES

Country/Area	1924	1928	1947	1960	1965	1968
Afghanistan				nil	neg.	400
Albania			5,000	50,000	53,000	66,327
Algeria			25,000	7,500	5,500	< 1,000
Angola				neg.	nil	nil
Antilles					nil	nil
Argentina			30,000	75,000	65,000	60,000
Australia			25,000	5,800	5,000	4,750
Austria			150,000	50,000	35,000	27,500
Bahrain				50	neg.	neg.
Barbados				nil	nil	nil
Belgium			95,000	11,000	11,000	12,500
Berlin, West				< 5,000		6,000
Bolivia				4,000	4,500	6,000
Botswana					nil	nil
Brazil			130,000	50,000	31,000	15,750
Bulgaria			450,000	484,000	528,674	613,393
Burma			4,000	8,000	5,000	n.a.
Burundi				nil	nil	nil
Cambodia				< 1,000	100	100
Cameroon				neg.	nil	nil
Canada			25,000	3,000	3,500	2,500
Central African Rep.				nil	nil	nil
Ceylon				4,000	1,900	2,300
Chad				nil	nil	nil
Chile			50,000	22,500	27,500	45,000
China, Comm. (Mainland)			2,000,000	13,960,000	18,000,000	17,000,000
China, Nat.				neg.	neg.	neg.
Colombia			5,000	> 5,000	13,000	9,000
Comoro Islands						nil
Congo (B)				neg.	nil	nil
Congo (K)				neg.	neg.	neg.
Costa Rica			20,000	300	300	600
Cuba			200,000	27,000	35,000	60,000
Cyprus			4,000	5,000	10,000	13,000
Czechoslovakia	138,996	150,000	1,250,000	>1,500,000	1,676,509	1,700,000
Dahomey				nil	nil	nil
Denmark			60,000	5,000	5,000	6,000
Dominican Rep.			2,000	neg.	n.a.	1,100
Ecuador			2,500	1,000	2,500	1,650
El Salvador				< 1,000	200	200
Ethiopia				neg.	nil	nil

Notes:

neg. = negligible/very small   nil = none
> = less than   n.a. = not available
< = more than

Table D.1. MEMBERSHIP OF COMMUNIST PARTIES (Continued)

Country/Area	1924	1928	1947	1960	1965	1968
Finland			25,000	32,500	40,000	49,000
France	68,187	52,376	1,300,000	250,000	260,000	275,000
French Ter. of Afars & Issas					nil	nil
Gabon				nil	nil	nil
The Gambia					nil	nil
Germany, East	121,394	124,729	1,600,000	1,472,930	1,610,679	1,769,912
Germany, West			350,000	50,000	50,000	7,000
Ghana				neg.	nil	nil
Greece			250,000	20,000	20,000	27,000
Guadeloupe				3,000	1,000	1,300
Guatemala				1,200	1,300	750
Guiana, French				neg.	neg.	neg.
Guinea				neg.	nil	nil
Guinea, Equatorial						nil
Guinea, Portuguese					nil	nil
Guyana				6,000	nil	100
Haiti			500	neg.	n.a.	n.a.
Honduras				400	2,400	300
Hong Kong				n.a.	n.a.	n.a.
Hungary			650,000	437,956	520,000	600,000
Iceland			1,000	1,000	1,000	1,000
Ifni					nil	nil
India			54,000	230,000	135,000	125,000
Indonesia			6,000	1,500,000	2,000,000	5,000
Iran			75,000	1,500	1,500	1,000
Iraq				2,000	15,000	2,000
Ireland				100	100	125
Israel			1,000	< 2,000	2,000	2,000
Italy			2,000,000	1,350,000	1,350,000	1,500,000
Ivory Coast				nil	nil	nil
Jamaica				150	nil	neg.
Japan			60,000	70,000	120,000	250,000
Jordan				200	500	700
Kenya				nil	nil	nil
Korea, North			40,000	1,200,000	1,300,000	1,600,000
Korea, South			10,000	neg.	neg.	neg.
Kuwait				50	neg.	neg.
Laos				100	100	n.a.
Lebanon			15,000		3,000	6,000
Lesotho				· nil	< 100	neg.
Liberia					nil	nil
Libya				neg.	nil	neg.
Luxembourg			5,000	500	500	500
Malagasy Rep.				n.a.	< 100	neg.
Malawi				nil	nil	nil
Malaysia			10,000	5,000	2,000	2,000
Maldive Islands						nil
Mali				nil	nil	nil
Malta						nil
Martinique				2,500	700	700
Mauritania				nil	nil	nil
Mauritius					nil	neg.
Mexico			25,000	5,000	50,000	5,250
Mongolia				36,333	46,000	48,570
Morocco				1,250	1,250	600
Mozambique				neg.	nil	nil
Manibia (South West Africa)					nil	nil
Nepal				3,250	3,500	8,000
The Netherlands			50,000	15,000	12,000	11,500
New Zealand			2,000	< 400	500	400
Nicaragua			2,000	200	250	200
Niger				nil	nil	nil
Nigeria				neg.	> 100	> 1,000
Norway			33,000	4,700	4,500	2,500
Pakistan				4,250	3,000	1,450
Panama			500	neg.	400	250
Paraguay			n.a.	500	5,000	5,000
Peoples Republic of South Yemen					neg.	neg.
Persian Gulf States						neg.
Peru			35,000	6,000	8,500	5,000
Philippines			3,000	1,250	1,200	2,000
Poland			600,000	1,023,577	1,614,237	2,030,065
Portugal			n.a.	2,000	2,000	2,000
Reunion					n.a.	500
Rio Muni					nil	nil
Romania			500,000	720,000	1,240,000	1,800,000
Rwanda				nil	nil	nil
San Marino	Part of Italian C.P.					
Saudi Arabia				neg.	nil	neg.
Senegal				nil	nil	nil
Sierra Leone				nil	nil	nil
Somali Republic				neg.	nil	nil
South Africa			1,500	1,500	800	n.a.
Spain			n.a.	5,000	5,000	5,000
Sudan				300	2,500	7,500
Surinam				nil	nil	nil
Swaziland					nil	nil
Sweden	7,011	15,479	46,000	25,000	20,000	29,000
Switzerland			20,000	6,000	> 6,000	4,000

Notes:
      neg. = negligible/very small   nil = none
         > = less than   n.a. = not available
         < = more than

Table D.1. MEMBERSHIP OF COMMUNIST PARTIES (Continued)

Country/Area	1924	1928	1947	1960	1965	1968
Syria			8,000	1,500	4,000	3,000
Tanzania				nil	nil	nil
Thailand				4,000	n.a.	2,500
Togo				neg.	nil	nil
Trinidad and						
Tobago				75	neg.	nil
Tunisia			20,000	400	1,000	100
Turkey					1,000	1,250
Uganda				nil	nil	nil
U.S.S.R.	446,089	1,210,954	6,000,000	8,366,000	12,000,000	13,500,000
United Arab						
Republic				1,000	1,000	nil
United Kingdom	4,000	9,000	43,500	26,000	34,372	32,532
United States	17,000	12,000	75,000			13,000
Upper Volta				nil	nil	nil
Uruguay			15,000	5,000	10,000	21,000
Venezuela			20,000	40,000	30,000	5,000
Vietnam, North				620,000	570,000	766,000
Vietnam, South				1,800	31,000	n.a.
Yemen				neg.	neg.	neg.
Yugoslavia			150,000	899,310	1,030,041	1,013,500
Zambia				nil	nil	nil
TOTAL	1,222,035	1,707,769	18,634,500	35,000,000	45,000,000	45,055,700

Notes:

```
neg. = negligible/very small        nil = none
  > = less than                     n.a. = not available
  < = more than
```

Table D.2. RANK OF MAJOR COMMUNIST PARTIES, 1968

Country	Membership	Rank
China, Communist	17,000,000	1
U.S.S.R.	13,500,000	2
Poland	2,030,068	3
Romania	1,800,000	4
East Germany	1,769,912	5
Czechoslovakia	1,700,000	6
North Korea	1,600,000	7
Italy	1,500,000	8
Yugoslavia	1,013,500	9
North Vietnam	766,000	10
Bulgaria	613,393	11
Hungary	600,000	12
France	275,000	13
Japan	250,000	14
India	125,000	15
Albania	66,000	16
Cuba	60,000	17.5
Argentina	60,000	17.5
Finland	49,000	19
Mongolia	48,570	20

Table D.3. Communist Party Membership by Region, 1968

Region	Membership	Percentage of World Membership
Ruling-parties	42,500,000	94.2
Western Europe and Canada	1,900,000	4.4
Asia and Oceania	270,000	0.6
Near East and South Asia	193,000	0.4
Latin America	182,000	0.4
Africa	10,700	...
TOTAL of non-ruling parties	2,555,700	5.8
TOTAL of all parties	45,055,700	100.0

CHAPTER IX TABLE SOURCE NOTES

Table A.1 to A.9

Vneshnyaya torgovlya SSSR: Statistichesky sbornik, 1918–1966, Moscow (1967).
Vneshnyaya torgovlya 1955–1959.
Vneshnyaya torgovlya 1959–1963.
Vneshnyaya torgovlya 1965.
Vneshnyaya torgovlya 1966.
Vneshnyaya torgovlya 1967.
Vneshnyaya torgovlya 1968.
"Vneshnyaya torgovlya SSSR za 1969 god," *Vneshnyaya torgovlya,* no. 6 (1970), pp. 53–55.

Table A.8

Population Statistics from: *Itogi vsesoyuznoi perepisi naselenia 1959 goda.* USSR, Moscow (1962), p. 13. E. Z. Volkov, *Dinamika naselenia SSSR za vosemdesyat let,* Moscow (1932), p. 209.
Frank Lorimer, *The Population of the Soviet Union: History and Prospects,* Geneva, League of Nations (1946), p. 135.
Demographic Yearbook, New York, United Nations Statistical Office, for the appropriate years.
Pravda, April 19, 1970, p. 1.

Table B.1

U.S. Department of State, Bureau of Intelligence and Research, *Communist Governments and Developing Nations: Aid and Trade in 1968,* Re-

search Memorandum RSE-65, September 5, 1969, pp. 2–3.
U.S. Department of State, Bureau of Intelligence and Research, *Communist States and Developing Countries: Aid and Trade in 1969, Research Memorandum* RECS-5, July 9, 1970, pp. 2–3.

Table B.2

U.S. Department of State, Bureau of Intelligence and Research, *Communist Governments and Developing Nations: Aid and Trade in 1967,* Research Memorandum RSE-120, August 14, 1968, p. 6.

Table B.3

U.S. Department of State, Bureau of Intelligence and Research, *The Sino-Soviet Economic Offensive Through June 30, 1962,* Research Memorandum RSB-145, September 18, 1962, p. 17.
————, *Communist Governments and Developing Nations: Economic Aid and Trade,* Research Memorandum, RSB-80, July 21, 1967, p. 6.
————, *Communist Governments and Developing Nations: Economic Aid and Trade in 1967,* Research Memorandum RSE-120, August 14, 1968, p. 11.
————, *Communist Governments and Developing Nations: Aid and Trade*

in 1968, Research Memorandum RSE-65, September 5, 1969, p. 10.

———, *Communist States and Developing Countries: Aid and Trade in 1969,* Research Study RECS-5, July 9, 1970, p. 8.

TABLE B.4

U.S. Department of State, Bureau of Intelligence and Research, *Communist Governments and Developing Nations: Economic Aid and Trade in 1967,* Research Memorandum RSE-120, August 14, 1968, p. 11.

———, *Communist Governments and Developing Nations: Economic Aid and Trade in 1968,* Research Memorandum RSE-65, September 5, 1969, p. 10.

———, *Communist States and Developing Countries: Aid and Trade in 1969,* Research Study RECS-5, July 9, 1970, p. 8.

TABLE B.5

U.S. Department of State, Bureau of Intelligence and Research, *The Communist Economic Offensive through 1963,* Research Memorandum RSB-43, June 18, 1964, p. 16.

———, *Communist Governments and Developing Nations: Economic Aid and Trade,* Research Memorandum RSB-80, July 21, 1967, p. 8.

———, *Communist Governments and Developing Nations: Economic Aid and Trade in 1967,* Research Memorandum RSE-120, August 14, 1968, p. 10.

———, *Communist Governments and Developing Nations: Aid and Trade in 1968,* Research Memorandum RSE-65, September 5, 1969, p. 11.

———, *Communist States and Developing Countries: Aid and Trade in 1969,* Research Study REC-5, July 9, 1970, p. 11.

TABLE B.6

U.S. Department of State, Bureau of Intelligence and Research, *Communist Governments and Developing Nations: Economic Aid and Trade,* Research Memorandum RSB-80, July 21, 1967, p. 7.

———, *Communist Governments and Developing Nations: Economic Aid and Trade in 1967,* Research Memo-

randum RSE-120, August 14, 1968, p. 12.

———, *Communist Governments and Developing Nations: Aid and Trade in 1968,* Research Memorandum RSE-65, September 5, 1969, p. 12.

———, *Communist States and Developing Countries: Aid and Trade in 1969,* Research Study RECS-5, July 9, 1970, p. 9.

TABLES C.1 TO C.22

Note: Only figures for the European members of the Council for Mutual Economic Assistance are included. After 1961 Albania did not participate in the meetings of the Council and in late 1967 formally withdrew.

TABLE C.1

Population and Area: *Demographic Yearbook,* New York, United Nations Statistical Office (1969), pp. 120–122.

Communist Party: U.S. Department of State, Bureau of Intelligence and Research, *World Strength of the Communist Party Organizations,* Washington (1969), pp. 1–8.

National Income: United States Arms Control and Disarmament Agency, *World Military Expenditures 1969,* Washington (1969), p. 11.

TABLE C.2

Michael Kaser, *Comecon: Integration Problems of the Planned Economies,* published by Oxford University Press for the Royal Institute of International Affairs, London (1967), pp. 206–207.

TABLE C.3

Michael Kaser, ed., *Economic Development for Eastern Europe,* London and New York, Macmillan and St. Martin's Press (1968), p. 6.

TABLE C.4

Statistical Yearbook 1969, New York, United Nations Statistical Office (1970), pp. 141–154.

TABLE C.5

J. Smilek, *Hospodarske noviny,* Prague, no. 29 (1966), p. 3.

Statistical Yearbook 1968, New York, United Nations Statistical Office (1969), pp. 568–575.
Yearbook of National Accounts Statistics 1968, New York, United Nations Statistical Office (1969), pp. 158, 238, 687.

TABLE C.6

Kaser, ed., *Economic Development for Eastern Europe*, p. 8.
Statistical Yearbook 1969, New York, United Nations Statistical Office (1970), pp. 164–167, 186–187, 338–344.

TABLE C.7

V. I. Zolotarev, *Vneshnyaya torgovlya sotsialisticheskikh stran*, Moscow (1964), pp. 366–367.
Vneshnyaya torgovlya SSSR, Moscow, for the appropriate years.
Statistical Yearbook 1968, New York, United Nations Statistical Office (1969).
Statistical Yearbook 1969, New York, United Nations Statistical Office (1970).

TABLE C.8

Yearbook of International Trade Statistics, New York, United Nations Statistical Office, for the years 1957, 1959, 1962, 1966, and 1967.

TABLE C.9

Calculated from data in Tables C.1 and C.8 above. Official exchange rates used.

TABLE C.10

Soviet figures from Table A.6.
Figures for other countries for 1955, 1960, 1965, 1966, and 1967, from Table C.7.
Figures for other countries for 1950, 1963, and 1964, from Richard F. Staar, ed., *Aspects of Modern Communism*, copyright © 1968 by the University of South Carolina Press, p. 157; reprinted by permission.

TABLE C.11

Kaser, *Comecon:* . . . p. 144.
Yearbook of International Trade Statistics, 1967, New York, United Nations Statistical Office.

TABLE C.12

Neue Zürcher Zeitung, November 20, 1966, Foreign Edition.
International Yearbook of Trade Statistics, 1967, New York, United Nations Statistical Office.

TABLE C.13

Voprosy ekonomiki (Moscow), no. 10, (October 1967).

TABLE C.14

East Europe, XV, no. 11 (1966), p. 28.

TABLE C.15

Lucjan Ciamaga, *Od wspolpracy do integracji*, Warsaw (1965), pp. 39–40.

TABLE C.16

Marshall I. Goldman, *Soviet Foreign Aid*, New York, Praeger (1967), p. 28.

TABLE C.17

Ibid., pp. 28, 54.

TABLE C.18

Nikolai Vasilevich Fadeev, *Sovet Ekonomicheskoi Vzaimopomoshchi*, Moscow (1964), pp. 24–25.
Ciamaga, pp. 76–77.
Alexander Uschakow, "Comecon," *Das Parlament*, January 12, 1966, pp. 50–52, of Supplement.
Krasnaya zvezda, February 26, 1967.
Richard Szawlowski, "The International Organizations of the Comecon Family," *Osteuropa-Recht*, XII, no. 2 (1966), pp. 120–147.

TABLE C.19

Robert M. Slusser and Jan F. Triska, *A Calendar of Soviet Treaties*, Stanford University Press, (1959), p. 462ff.
Jan F. Triska and David Finley, *Soviet Foreign Policy*, New York, Macmillan (1968), p. 423.
R. M. Slusser and G. Ginsburgs, "A Calendar of Soviet Treaties, January–December 1959," *Osteuropa-Recht*, VIII (1962), pp. 137–164.
G. Ginsburgs, "A Calendar of Soviet Treaties, January–December, 1960,"

Osteuropa-Recht, IX (1963), pp. 120–159.

————, "A Calendar of Soviet Treaties, January–December 1961," *Osteuropa-Recht*, X (1964), pp. 116–148.

————, "A Calendar of Soviet Treaties, January–December 1962," *Osteuropa-Recht*, XI (1965), pp. 129–160.

TABLE C.19

See Table C.19.

TABLE C.21

The Institute for Strategic Studies, 1968, from *The Military Balance 1968–1969*, published by The Institute for Strategic Studies, 18 Adam Street, London WCZN 6AL. Figures found in pages 2–4, 6–8.

TABLE C.22

United States Arms Control and Disarmament Agency, *World Military Expenditures 1966–67*, Washington, (December 1968), Research Report 68–52, p. 9, 13.

TABLE D.1

Julius Braunthal, *History of the International*, vol. II: *1914–1943*, New York, Praeger, 1967, p. 319.

Lewis L. Lorwin, *Labor and Internationalism*, New York, Macmillan, 1929, p. 526.

Martin Ebon, *World Communism Today*, New York, Whittlesey House, 1948, p. 491–492.

U.S. Department of State, Bureau of Intelligence and Research, *World Strength of the Communist Party Organizations*, 1960, 1965, and 1969.

TABLE D.2

See Table D.1.

TABLE D.3

See table D.1.